JOSEPH PULITZER

and his 𝔚𝔬𝔯𝔩𝔡

The Rodin bust of Joseph Pulitzer

JOSEPH PULITZER

and his *World*

BY JAMES WYMAN BARRETT, *Last City Editor*

of The World

The Vanguard Press NEW YORK

MANUFACTURED IN THE U.S.A. BY H. WOLFF, NEW YORK

To my devoted Sister

ELIZABETH BARRETT PEEBLES

Contents

Illustrations

Foreword

"Mr. Pulitzer's death occurs at an inopportune moment. . . . Never in our time was there more need for his clarion voice . . . summoning the American people to use their commanding influence in the defense of a weak nation assailed by a lawless aggressor, lusting for territorial plunder.

"May his mantle as a champion of international peace with justice fall on the shoulders of a worthy successor."—WILLIAM T. STEAD

THOSE OF US who have witnessed or studied the final chapter of the Joseph Pulitzer plan must have asked ourselves many times:

What was it all about, and what did it signify?

There is no direct answer, except in the unchangeable rule of the universe that it is man's nature to attempt the impossible.

It is through the failures of men, as well as through their successes, that their hopes and ideals are made perfect. Either way, the compensation is sufficient to encourage others to try again.

Our ancestors dreamed of flying. Later, some hardy souls made the attempt and reaped disaster. But mankind finally learned how to fly.

The solution of the mysterious fate that befell Joseph Pulitzer and his enterprise is to be found, first, in the character of the man himself; and second, in the fallibility of all human endeavor, great or otherwise.

In JP's case, it was not within his nature to be satisfied. Having won success and fortune as a newspaper publisher, at the age of forty-five, he might have relaxed and said, "This is the age when leisure begins." That would have been a good time to try, because physical misfortune had overtaken him in the form of almost total blindness and the breaking down of his nervous system.

In fact, he did make the attempt; but it was of no use. He hated
the idea of giving up when he was known merely as the owner of
a prosperous newspaper. That was not enough. Within him there
was an unquenchable passion which, like the bush observed by
Moses on Mount Horeb, kept on burning but was not itself consumed.

This flaming desire was concerned with public affairs. A journalist, in JP's conception, is a statesman as well as a writer. His
own title, bestowed upon him by the British publisher, Lord Northcliffe, was "the blind statesman-editor who from his yacht in the
Mediterranean could see more than politicians in London or Washington or financiers in Wall Street."

The basis of it was something more profound than persistent
curiosity about people and things. JP, of course, was the most
incorrigible busybody of his day and age. His habit of asking questions about everything under the sun and demanding accurate as
well as immediate answers was an amusing and often annoying
trait, but it was only a mechanism through which an eager, prehensile mind was kept supplied with working material.

He had an objective which he refused to put aside. As long as
he lived, he wanted to inform and to mold public opinion—not
just for the sake of power or profits, but for the sake of reform and
of progress in the direction where he thought America ought to
be heading.

That was the road toward Liberty, Peace, and Justice—a political
trinity which he considered as one goal. Any one of those without
the other two, in JP's mind, was impossible. While hating wars
as much as any man who has ever participated in one, he clearly
saw the inevitability of conflict when Liberty and Justice are threatened. Peace without those, peace without honor, peace with ap-
peasement or peace at any price were utterly abhorrent.

So far as ideals were concerned, he was a man of peace to the
depths of his soul, but he refused to accept it as a soothing syrup
for political wrongs. In everyday life he was a warrior, and not a
happy one. Having been in one continual fight himself from the
time of his first arrival in America as a poor Hungarian immigrant
lad, he foresaw no peace for himself or his newspaper. He kept on

fighting to the end of his own life, and he expected, or at least he fervently hoped, that his chief newspaper, *The World,* would keep on fighting long after he had gone—keep on fighting forever and ever.

"Always fight for progress and reform" . . . "always be drastically independent" . . . "never be afraid to attack wrong" . . . "never be satisfied"—these injunctions which he laid down for the conduct of *The World,* together with his prayer for *The World,* at the laying of the cornerstone, sufficiently prove his recognition of the fact that journalism's fight is constant warfare. That he wanted it to go on forever is just another proof that he had the same impulse as the rest of us: he yearned for perfection. Like Icarus, of whom we hear much lately, we have always wanted to fly to the sun, or like the postdiluvians, build a tower that would reach to the skies.

JP's vision of journalism was, in other respects, entirely realistic and factual. The business of the newspaperman, he believed, was to supply the ammunition with which society can effectively fight its seven deadly enemies: inaccurate information, injustice, special privilege, corruption, public plunder, demagoguery, and inertia. Against these, the journalist's weapons are Facts, Reason, and Moral Courage. One of his favorite sayings was a quotation from Benjamin Constant: "The Press is mistress of intelligence, and intelligence is mistress of the world."

Moreover, he thought, the journalist must not only supply the arms and munitions, but he must himself be in the forefront of the battle, marshaling the facts, drawing the conclusions, and helping to shape the opinions. Journalism's job, in other words, is to lead, lead, lead!

Perpetual warfare, in short. Not a battle to be fought and concluded in one man's lifetime. So it was that after having achieved financial fortune and a national reputation, reaping at the same time physical misfortune, he refused to stay quiet. His was more than a pioneering spirit. Pioneers have a way of blazing the trail through the wilderness and then settling somewhere. JP was not a settler. Having defined his objectives, having proved his point that the domain of the journalist is not only the gathering and distribution of news but the advancement and promotion of the public welfare, he devoted much of his last twenty years on earth to a plan for perpetuating *The World* and a system of journalism in which a newspaper like *The World* could live and move and have its proper function.

The plan which he evolved, out of much suffering, was this:

First, *The World*. Not just a newspaper, but a public institution which should always fight for progress and reform, should never be satisfied with merely printing news, and should always be drastically independent in the public interest.

Second, a school of journalism for the training of newspapermen qualified to carry on the work of a journal such as *The World*. Such a school, he believed, should not only supply the journalist with a profound knowledge of human affairs (especially history and biography) with sufficient technical knowledge, but also with moral courage, and incidentally with good manners.

Third, a system of prizes and scholarships for the encouragement of journalists, and the advancement of American culture on the lines of a wholesome atmosphere, good morals, good manners, good taste. These are the awards which have become popularly (in some instances unpopularly) known as "Pulitzer Prizes."

Most of us, I imagine, will concede that it was a grand project and inherently noble in purpose. Certainly it was drastic in its note of belligerency against the forces of national deterioration and its insistence upon the note of courage. He refused to believe that moral courage cannot be taught. On the contrary, he said, it ought to have a prominent place in the curriculum. If the soldier can be taught and trained to possess physical courage, the mind of the journalist can be trained to moral courage, particularly by example.

The importance of being courageous is demonstrated by the fact that the editor is often tempted to follow the hue and cry instead of sticking to the plain path of fact and reason. By so doing, he risks unpopularity. But JP felt that with moral courage and persistent effort a capable journalist can carry his cause and make it the popular one.

Some parts of the Pulitzer plan survive today, but the keystone is missing. *The World* has vanished, or at least remains only as a sort of ghostly ectoplasm on the front page of another publication. The School of Journalism, which JP devised and endowed for Columbia University, goes forward, though not precisely as he imagined it, and the system of scholarships and prizes remains. The awards are made each year for distinguished work in journalism, and in the fields of the drama, the novel, biography, history, and poetry. The terms of the awards have been modified. The previous insistence upon good morals, good manners, good taste, and the "wholesome atmosphere of American life" as well as the "highest standard of manhood," has been abated, but preference is still given to American material in letters; and, of course, the journalism awards are confined strictly to American newspapers and newspapermen.

Without *The World,* however, the Pulitzer program seems like a solar system without a sun, *Hamlet* without the Prince of Denmark, and Beethoven's opera *Fidelio* without the motif of courage. Or perhaps it is more like the old Pulitzer Building on Park Row at the entrance to Brooklyn Bridge. The building is there, but *The World* has moved away. The once golden dome is encrusted with a greenish rust, the flagpoles on the roof, where the banners of all nations used to fly proudly in the interests of international good will, are bare. The dome is vacant, and on the twelfth floor where the newsrooms of *The World,* and its affiliates, *The Evening World* and *The Sunday World,* used to hum and bustle with ceaseless activity, there is now a law school.

One might think, with some justice, that *The World* is only another example of the relentless march of change and time. JP's town house, the magnificent Renaissance palace on East Seventy-third Street, preserves its noble exterior, but inside, the former drawing rooms and libraries have given way to "modern" one-, two-, and three-room apartments, suitable for light though elegant housekeeping. The famous yacht *Liberty,* upon which JP and his staff used to roam the Atlantic and the Mediterranean in a vain but unrelenting quest for peace and quiet, has now disappeared from the seas. When last reported it was owned by a wealthy Englishwoman, but after the advent of war it undoubtedly went into service. Perhaps it took a gallant part in the rescue at Dunkirk—who knows?

Yes, these may all be just symptoms of the ephemeral quality of all things, which, as Marcus Aurelius says, pass and become as a dream. However, one cannot escape a feeling that the Pulitzer experiment was too short-lived. Other journalistic enterprises have lasted much longer, but *The World* survived not quite twenty years after the Founder died.

Did the hand of the Founder slip? Perhaps so. At any rate he made the Attempt Magnificent. Some of us do not even try. It is something in the realm of the heroic for a man so to inspire a newspaper with his own soul that it can live on for as long as twenty years. It was a great drama while it lasted.

America's debt to Joseph Pulitzer resides in the fact that he not only gave to journalism its most distinctive impulse and its most sensational success, but also provided its most moving tragedy.

That was enough for any man.

1. Joseph Pulitzer

"Wohlauf noch getrunken den funkelnden Wein!
Ade nun, Ihr Lieben, Geschieden musst sein;
Ade nun, Ihr Berge, du vaeterlich Haus!
Es treibt in die Ferne, mich maechtig hinaus!"

—WANDERLIED

THE TALL, scraggy youth with long, thick black hair, large head, and oversized nose who was roaming through Europe in the summer of 1864, looking for permanent escape from home and Budapest, can probably be set down as a case of social and psychological maladjustment. He was about six feet two and a half inches tall, ungainly in appearance, awkward in movement, lacking entirely in the art of human relations. If there were any best-sellers at that time on how to win friends and influence people, the seventeen-year-old Joseph Politzer (as the family in Hungary spelled the name) had not absorbed their contents. In any Dale Carnegie system, young Joseph was a veritable wrong-way-Corrigan. His own technique was to crash into a situation and begin asking questions, without considering the correct approach.

In the matter of social handicaps, nature had given the young JP a flying start. He looked as if he had been created for the express purpose of providing good, rough fun and practical jokes for his fellow men. His height, his head, his nose, and his chin were all out of proportion. The nose overshadowed the chin, giving a false impression of weakness, while at the same time arousing amusement on the part of strangers as well as an inferiority complex on the part of the owner. All through life, JP retained the delusion that he had a weak chin. He compensated, after thirty, by growing a beard of noble dimensions. It covered the chin, but not the complex. As time

3

went on he became excruciatingly sensitive to anything in the nature of bodily exposure. He was worse in that respect than Noah.

There was a sharp contrast also between the youth's face and hands. The upper part of the head was strong and shapely. The eyes, though defective, were bright. The gaze was penetrating. But his hands were delicate. The long slender fingers were those of a musician, a painter, or a sculptor.

Amazingly sensitive, those hands, as well as exquisitely molded—no hands for a soldier or even a printer.

Added to his other incongruities, the lad's complexion was fair and as pink as a woman's. He flushed easily, which made things worse.

But in other respects, JP had the appearance of being older than his years. We might sum it up by saying that the head bespoke nobility, imagination, and courage. The bold aquiline nose—more antique Roman than Semitic—bespoke eagerness and a boldness which the chin contradicted. In moments of animation, there was a fierce, hawklike expression, suggesting large reservoirs of emotion. The tall, rangy body, slightly stooped, suggested a frail physique—an erroneous impression, because the lad was an excellent swimmer and had plenty of endurance. As to fighting ability, his was more of the spirit than of the flesh. The evidence is that he was not at home either with guns, fists, or knives, but somewhere in his early years he learned to ride horses, so well in fact, that in later years he rode in his blindness better than his friends with full vision.

Although this lad came from Budapest, he could not be identified as Hungarian. There was an Asiatic quality about him. The ancestry, I believe, is undetermined. Don C. Seitz, his official biographer, suggests that JP in some previous incarnation (if we can accept such theories) was a "Pathan of the Pamirs," who rode with Attila, the Hun, or in a later embodiment was "one of Pappenheim's Pandours in the Thirty Years' War"—riding always in the van of the battle, just as in his known life he galloped in his mind, always a jump or two ahead of the news; always trying to lead in the never-ending struggle for progress and reform and the liberation of the human spirit. (The reincarnation idea is, of course, merely a flight of fancy on D.C.S.'s part, but it indicates that JP was not averse to being The

Man on Horseback.) Anyway he was a fine horseman, although he probably never imagined that one of his reporters would get to be Chairman of the New York State Racing Commission.

A curious human product—this young JP. His father was part Magyar or Hungarian, part Jewish, the exact ratios uncertain; the mother was German, and evidently a devout Catholic, since Joseph's younger brother, Albert, was educated for the priesthood. (He did not complete the course.) The record of the early home life is distressingly obscure—for various reasons, including JP's own profound aversion to biographical probings. The Politzers, in the Hungarian social scheme of things, fitted in somewhere below the nobility; probably in the upper bourgeoisie. Philip Politzer, the father, was a grain merchant. He established a prosperous business in the town of Mako, about one hundred and thirty-five miles southeast of Budapest, in partnership with one Mathias Reiner. One was probably enough, because the grain enterprise, begun about 1840, was dissolved in 1853, and the Politzers moved to Budapest. Philip had acquired enough to maintain a comfortable home and provide good educations for his sons. They attended private schools and had private tutors. Louis, the oldest boy, and Irma, youngest of the four children, both died in early youth. Albert was four years younger than Joseph.

Joseph was born in Mako on April 10, 1847. One of his pet superstitions in later years, nurtured half in jest, revolved about the number ten. It worked out very strikingly. He was born on April 10. The year, 1847, added up (one plus eight, plus four, plus seven) equals twenty, or twice ten. He arrived in St. Louis, Missouri, on October 10, 1865—the tenth day of the tenth month of a year which, added up, equals twenty or twice ten. He took control of the *St. Louis Dispatch* (later the *Post-Dispatch*) at ten o'clock on December 10, 1878. He acquired possession of *The World* in New York on May 10, 1883 (the year also adds up to twice ten). *The Evening World* began on October 10, 1887. He bought the site of the Pulitzer Building on his forty-first birthday (four plus one equals one-half of ten), April 10, 1888. The cornerstone was laid on October 10, 1889, the twenty-fourth anniversary of his arrival in St. Louis. The building was opened for business on December 10, 1890.

His first "permanent" residence in New York City was No. 10 East Fifty-fifth Street (five and five make ten); and his final city residence was the magnificent mansion at Nos. 7-9-11-13-15 East Seventy-third Street. (Seven plus nine, plus eleven, plus thirteen, plus fifteen, equals fifty-five; and five plus five equals ten. Also, seven plus three equals ten.) JP attached so much importance to the number ten that he always arranged for ceremonies to fall on one of these magical combinations.

But we are getting ahead of the story.

The Politzer family life was disrupted soon after the father's retirement. The father died of heart trouble and the mother (born Louise Berger) married another merchant, Max Blau. Whether this second marriage of Mrs. Politzer produced something like a Hamlet complex in young Joseph we can only surmise. JP's attachment, apparently, was not to the ghost of his father, but to his mother—described as a remarkably beautiful and intelligent woman. In later life he always kept his mother's picture near him and he used to tell—that is, in those rare moods when he felt like telling anything about his youth—how he had to stoop so that his mother could box his ears. The conclusion is that JP and the stepfather did not get along well, and hence it was in the summer of '64 Joseph was looking around for a permanent way out from home ties.

His education seems to have fitted him for nothing in particular and to have developed no special talent except an extraordinary ability to ask questions and drag information out of reluctant or poorly informed sources. Long before JP was a journalist he had formed the "who, what, when, where, and why" habit, and mostly it was "why."

As two of his uncles on his mother's side were officers in the Austrian army, his first move was toward military service.

In those days there was plenty of call to youth of adventurous or warlike disposition. JP's bent lay along lines of adventure, rather than fighting; and his thirst for adventure was later transmuted into the greatest of all adventures—the search for news and information affecting the public interest. But at the moment, the Austrian army looked good as an escape-mechanism. Europe was in a ferment over Bismarck's plan to seize the duchies of Schleswig and

Holstein, with the aid of Austria. From the standpoint of action, the Austrian army looked like a good bet, but not for JP. Only perfect specimens were desired as cannon targets. The young Politzer was rejected. Official reason—"weak eyes—unpromising physique." Joseph had made the mistake of growing too fast for his years.

Angry, disappointed, but not defeated, he went to Paris. Napoleon the Third was organizing a Foreign Legion for the purpose of seizing Mexico and placing Archduke Maximilian on the throne of our southern neighbor, taking advantage of our own preoccupation with the Civil War. It was a glamorous prospect, but JP was not of the stuff from which foreign legionnaires are made. The weak eyes and the ungainly body prevented his enlistment in the Mexican adventure, and Maximilian got along just as badly without him.

We might suspect, at this point, if we did not know better, that there was a streak of the old Irish in JP and that he didn't care whose war it was, so long as he was a participant. The next stop was London. The British army was recruiting for service in India, but the entrance requirements were as rigid as the French. There was no place for the gawky lad from Budapest, even if he had been able to speak English. Rebuffed, and it must be assumed, humiliated, he started back for home, but stopped off in the German port of Hamburg. He tried to get work as a seaman, but was laughed out of the hiring hall.

Providence, which has a way of granting the secret desires of the heart when you least expect it, threw the lad into the path of opportunity. Europe, at that time, was being combed for recruits for the Union army, and there were agents in the principal cities. Under the Civil War draft system, the draftee could hire a substitute or get someone to do the hiring—hence the agents. It was a lively, if unsavory business. The prices for substitutes were up to five hundred dollars a head, and in Europe, the agents kept the whole amount.

Chance, or Fate, whichever you prefer, brought about a meeting between the escape-seeker and the recruit-getter, in the same city of Hamburg. The details were easily arranged. Joseph was booked for passage to America, technically as an immigrant, actually as a recruit, and a raw one too, for the army of the North. We know little about the trip. One story is that JP's never-to-be-suppressed curiosity discovered, on the way over, all about the system, and the potential recruit decided to collect his own bounty. JP seems to have been a natural-born businessman, in spite of his idealism (or perhaps because of it).

[One of the English Rothschilds is quoted as saying that if Joseph Pulitzer had devoted his life to finance, he could have been the richest man in the world. How authentic that remark is, we do not know. In the years when JP had plenty of money he never carried any in his pockets; apparently he never thought about finances except to satisfy himself that his newspapers were prospering and that the proceeds were being spent in the ways that seemed likely to afford the most pleasure or to gain him the greatest relief from pain. Alleyne Ireland, one of his private secretaries, quoted him as saying, "Money's nothing to me: it can do nothing for me; I mean morally—intellectually." Still, for a left-handed and occasional worker in the financial vineyard, JP did not fare badly. He left an estate of about $20,000,000.]

As for this bounty matter, we are left in doubt. Mr. Pulitzer himself seems to have told various tales about it; and here is a truly amazing fact—the great journalist whose consuming passion was accuracy, and whose continual cry was for "facts, facts, facts," was inaccurate about the details of his own life. For example, he used to enjoy relating how he was elected to the Missouri legislature at the age of twenty—when he was neither a citizen nor of legal years. It was a good story, but he was wrong on both counts. Perhaps the past was so intimately bound up with tormenting experiences that he preferred to "take refuge in the natural forgetfulness of a witness," as the late Elihu Root once said in another connection.

At any rate, when his ship docked at Boston, so the story goes, young JP leaped overboard and swam ashore, whence he made his way to New York and handled his own enlistment, presumably for his own profit. September, 1864, found him in City Hall Park, looking over various recruiting stands. There was keen competition at that time in New York, as each city was anxious to fill its draft quota. It seems that the volunteers could choose their city and their regiment. In JP's European mind, regiments were identified with kings, princes, and other famous persons. In Austria, there was the Maria Theresa regiment, named after the great empress. In the

parade of names along City Hall Park, there was one that clicked
—the Lincoln Cavalry! JP knew about Lincoln, and he distinctly preferred horses. He was duly enrolled under the quota of Kingston,
New York.

The Lincoln Cavalry was largely German, having been organized
by Carl Schurz, the famous German-American soldier-editor-states-
man with whom JP was much more closely associated later in St.
Louis. JP could speak little English, but was fluent in German and
French. This was fortunate in one way, disastrous in another. He was
able to speak German to his fellow cavalrymen, but also, unluckily,
able to ask questions.

The new recruit signed up on September 30, 1864, for one year's
enlistment and was detailed to Company L. He did not actually
catch up with the regiment until November of that year, at Pleasant
Valley, Maryland. He gave his age as eighteen, as that was the required minimum—one of the few times JP was ever inaccurate for
public record. Also, he was booked as "Joseph Pouletzes"—which
may have been a typographical error on the part of the recruiting
sergeant. After the war he emerged as Joseph Pulitzer, and the name
stayed that way.

The Lincoln Cavalry had gone through hard fighting in the Army
of the Potomac under Custer and Sheridan, but at the time of JP's
arrival there was comparative quiet in Pleasant Valley. Not, however, for the new recruit. The story is that the Company L captain
took one look and shouted:

"Take that little so-and-so away from here! I won't have him in
my company!"

Why little, and why so-and-so?

We can only infer that Captain Blank, or whoever he was, belonged to the *What Price Glory* or Hard-Boiled Smith type. Scholarly, undernourished, maladjusted boys with large noses had no
appeal for him. The more favored type for a Civil War horseman was
a rough, tough, hard-riding, hard-fighting, hard-drinking, hard-
swearing, tobacco-chewing son of the North (or South) with plenty
of what it takes to go through battle or to absorb the kicks and cuffs
and food of army life.

The captain's opening attack was the signal for a campaign of hazing on the part of the whole company. JP was badgered, teased, tormented, cursed, and buffeted. And all in fun! He was nature's answer to the prayer of the Lincoln Cavalry for comic relief from the tedium of war. We have no exact record, but one can imagine what happened. "The skinny guy with the big nose" was a made-to-order butt for regimental jokes, and it must be admitted that so far as we know, JP didn't make it any easier for himself. He complained about the food, the clothes, the discipline, the horses, and to make matters distinctly worse, he was addicted to the never-to-be-sufficiently-condemned-in-the-army habit of asking questions. It is to be inferred that he seldom if ever received either an accurate, complete, or even a courteous reply. Military "Information Please" sessions are always at the expense of the questioner—unless the present or the coming war is an exception.

Among Mr. Pulitzer's mottoes in later life, for himself and *The World,* were, "Forever unsatisfied," "Never be satisfied with merely printing news," and "Always be drastically independent." Who can say how much of this continual search for accuracy, regardless of consequences, had its foundation in the army where he never got the right answers to anything? It is not reasonable to suppose that a sensitive, eager-spirited boy of seventeen can be kicked around for weeks and months in the hearty spirit of soldier life without deep and permanent effects upon his mind and soul.

In JP's case, the sequences are apparent. He developed a hatred for physical fighting; a loathing for swashbucklers, either military, pugilistic, journalistic—or political. He despised powerful persons who were disposed to kick others; persons who assumed to have rights above others; persons of the petty-officer type, or the petty district-leader politician type who lord it over subordinates.

Above all, he hated with an everlasting hate those who presume to withhold information to which others are entitled. Also, those who by reason of their position, presume to give out false information and hope to get away with it. The real issue between himself and President Theodore Roosevelt, in JP's view, was that the Great Teddy, in the Panama Canal Scandal, tried to falsify the record.

It is not unreasonable to believe, therefore, that the repressions of Joseph Pouletzes, U. S. Cavalryman, furnished some foundation for the later career of Joseph Pulitzer, journalist. Out of his army frustrations, he developed fixed hatreds for all frustrators; and, as companion motives, he also developed passionate devotions to certain ideas which often are marred by ignorance, malice, or stupidity.

Other fixations were added later by the St. Louis chapter, but there is enough material in the army narrative, blurred though it is, to distinguish the process of a soul in the building, a soul that later found powerful expression in the fully developed man and also in his creation, *The World*.

Hence it was, we may infer, that he hated inaccuracy just as passionately as he loved accuracy.

He hated stupidity as heartily as he yearned for perfection—perfect reporting, perfect editing, perfect attention to the business of forming public opinion.

He despised all manner of straw bosses and overlords as profoundly as he sympathized with the underdog. One of his commandments for *The World* was, "Never lack sympathy with the poor." (Meaning, perhaps the poor in spirit, and the poor in pocket, but never the poor in data. Woe to the reporter who turned in half-baked information!)

He was as merciless with editors as he was, generally speaking, considerate of reporters. A favorite saying attributed to him was, "Every reporter is a hope, every editor, a disappointment." (Frank I. Cobb was the notable exception.) *World* men who loved JP said he treated his reporters like sons, and they loved him as a father. This was not universally true, because some *World* men had not the foggiest notion what JP and *The World* were driving at, any more than certain gossip columnists of our own day can appreciate what JP meant when he said:

"Accuracy is to a newspaper what virtue is to a woman."

That might be interpreted in our time to mean that some dispensers of the news have as little regard for accuracy as for the other thing, choosing to consider them as interesting, but non-essential.

With the same fervor as Mr. Pulitzer hated secrecy in government and politics, he had a corresponding devotion for publicity—not publicity in the press-agent or promotional sense, but in the sense of making all affairs of public concern open, aboveboard, and out in the limelight, with frank and full discussion.

Although certainly not lacking in a sense of humor, he loathed personal familiarity—could not bear "joshing" or "spoofing." He would have been utterly out of sympathy with the journalistic pestilence known as wisecracking. You can imagine what he would have said about Mr. Hearst's columnist, Miss Dorothy Kilgallen, who recently suggested a Pulitzer prize for the best wisecrack heard in a so-called "nightclub."

Once he had become the master of his own life (at least so far as physical afflictions would permit) he would not tolerate any kind of practical joking—except one. He liked to interrogate people who thought they knew something, and drive them to the boundaries of their information. His personal Question Bees, conducted in his latter years, mostly among the corps of secretaries after dinner, were masterpieces of inquisition. They were "Truth or Consequence" games with a vengeance, and often the consequences were terrific.

JP knew more about the technique of cross-examination than the late Francis Wellman, the recognized authority on the art. As a private prosecutor of ignorance (or stupidity) he was more deadly than New York's most famous district attorney, the late William Travers Jerome. He knew the weak spots in an opponent's armor better than Charles S. Whitman. JP's victims seldom had a chance, because he was prosecutor, judge, and jury in one person, and if you were found guilty on any one count, the sentence was to go and read up on the subject. In all conversational duels, JP had a natural instinct for the jugular.

But practical jokes against himself were tabu. Whenever he caught any luckless associate telling a funny story about the boss he would say gently:

"Save them until I am dead."

Fate attended to that matter and saved up a whole accumulation of satires to be released after his death. But at the moment, the significant fact is that JP, though endowed with reserve force and endurance, was "not rugged enough for the work," as Herbert

Bayard Swope once remarked about Mary Ross, a *World* staff writer of the early twenties.

It is unlikely that the ill-starred recruit found any adequate release for his emotional and intellectual impulses. More likely, they became dammed up, thereby accumulating a reservoir of passionate intelligence that was to break out one day in a white-hot flame of genius.

In the flood tide of his later power, he accepted with approval the precept of Danton—*"De l'audace, encore de l'audace, toujours de l'audace"*—but his army lot did not stimulate audacity. He saw some hard riding, but not much fighting. He is credited with taking part in skirmishes at Antioch, Liberty Mills, Waynesborough, and Beaverdam Flat. In the last months of the war, the Lincoln Cavalry was divided. As hard-riding Phil Sheridan began his final campaign against Lee, the main body went with Sheridan, but JP's company was detailed to Virginia, where there was little doing.

All this while, the hazing and badgering continued. JP accepted it as part of a life in which his soul found no food. Once, goaded beyond endurance, he lashed out and struck a noncommissioned officer in the face. This was a grave offense. Under the Articles of War, JP ought to have been court-martialed, even though the noncom deserved the blow. What else might have happened—just imagine:

PRESIDING OFFICER: "The court (martial) having duly considered the evidence, finds that the defendant, Private Joseph Pouletzes, otherwise known as Le Foil du Regiment is guilty as charged under Article blank of section so and so. The sentence recommended by the court is that Private Pouletzes be shot at sunrise, but, of course, we shall have to wait until the War Department reviews the case which may take several months. Meanwhile, the defendant will remain in the doghouse."

But it seems that nothing like that really took place. In this instance good luck or perhaps the Angel of the Lord intervened. Among his few but distinctive personal assets, JP possessed ability at chess. In the rare moments of leisure in Pleasant Valley, when he was not being tormented, he played the noble game with a certain Captain Ramsay, unattached to Company L. Captain Ramsay took a liking to the strange lad of the inquiring mind and the few friends.

Hearing of JP's newest difficulty, he interceded with the regimental higher-ups and JP was let off with a reprimand. But there was no immediate relief from the old game of kicking the underdog around.

However, all things pass (as JP failed to remember when he talked of his *World* in terms of eternity) and even the day of torture passed. Some weeks before the end of the war, JP found another friend, a Major Richard J. Hinton. Although not connected with the Lincoln outfit, Major Hinton succeeded in having the problem youth assigned as his orderly. Major Hinton was on special duty of a not too difficult nature, we infer. JP got a breathing spell. Not that the respite made the war any more enjoyable; merely less painful. He rejoined the Lincoln regiment just before or after Appomattox, and rode with the others in the final review of the Grand Army in Washington, May 23, 1865; but the only thing he remembered, as he told Don Seitz many years later, was the man and the horse on either side of him—knee pressed against knee—not another thing.

The story of JP's Civil War service, as handed down by tradition, is pieced together from what he related twenty years or more after the conflict. Some direct research appears to have been done by the late George W. Hosmer, M.D., who was JP's personal physician-secretary-confidential companion for a score of years ending in 1909.

JP himself, as we know, was never a reliable witness on the events of his personal past. But all the narratives appear to agree that so far as "Private Pouletzes" was concerned, Sherman was right—war was hell, not because of the fighting with the enemy but because of the one-man struggle against the Lincoln Cavalry. He seems to have been the only man in the regiment who was in step with his own mental processes.

Little wonder, then, that his private record of the war was only a vague memory of torture which he was eager to forget. Everything else was blurred—even the skirmishes in which he rode and presumably fought. For years afterward he retained the curious delusion that at some time in '64 or '65 he had seen Lincoln; but finally the statement was challenged, and he sat down one afternoon, and date by date, place by place, convinced himself that he could not possibly have seen the Great Emancipator . . . ever!

Thus Complex doth make liars of us all!

The Lincoln Cavalry, minus a few casualties, was mustered out in June, 1865, and the men were shipped back to New York. They remained on Hart's Island in the East River until early July, when each man received his pay and went his own way, some back into civilian life, others to new adventures. The lad from Hungary had nowhere in particular to go, so he returned to the spot most familiar to him in the big city—City Hall Park.

Like many fellow graduates of the Civil War, the young JP found City Hall Park a natural clearing house of useless information for the unemployed. The whole city was swarming with Union Army veterans about whose welfare nobody especially seemed to care. No Veterans' Bureau in those days! And it soon became evident that so far as JP was concerned, jobs were scarce. He would have signed up for a long sea voyage, to get away from it all, but one look at the "hiring hall" on Water Street was enough. He fled back to Park Row. With another "vet" he went to New Bedford, Massachusetts, and tried to ship as able seaman aboard a whaler, but once again he was not the type. He returned to New York.

As summer passed and fall weather set in, his tangible assets were reduced to a small balance from his army pay (thirteen dollars per month); an army overcoat, his uniform, and a few accessories. Even in these reduced circumstances, he was sensitive about his appearance.

Just inside the entrance to French's Hotel, there was a shoe-shining stand, or rather, "a boot-blacking" stand, as these were before the days of grease-polish. Adhering to a habit acquired in boyhood, the young JP, so runs the legend, used to get a shine there every day, even though his funds were shrinking and his army overcoat was rapidly getting into the raggedy-man class. As far as I know, we have only JP's own word for what followed:

One day the head porter took the young G.A.R. graduate aside and suggested that he have the shoes blacked elsewhere.

"Frenchy's" patrons objected to the overcoat!

Did JP shake his fist at the hotel and take a solemn vow never to return until the day when he would buy the whole place for his own newspaper?

There is a legend to that effect. How are we to know? What kind of scholarly research is needed to establish that one Jos. Pulitzer did apply to have his boots blacked at French's Hotel in September, or thereabouts, 1865, and was advised to seek another blackatorium? Can somebody locate the diaries or the private correspondence of the head porter?

"Loafing place" is hardly the right term for the spot where JP did his daily bit at trying to figure things out. Here was the land of the free and the home of the brave which he had done his allotted part to preserve as a nation. Here he was in the greatest city of this great and now free country, without a job, without even the prospect of a job; without social security of any kind; and the people who stayed home and made money while he rode through the Valley of Death in Virginia, to say nothing of absorbing the kicks and cuffs of the Lincoln Cavalry—these people now object to his getting a shine because his coat is ragged. . . .

We must remember, too, that JP was trying to figure all this out in German. He did not begin to think in English until he had lived for some time in the largely German-speaking City of St. Louis.

So far as the overcoat is concerned, he does not have to worry much about it. The overcoat is stolen—that's all we know—by whom, where, when, why, legend sayeth not a word. The uniform looks worse than ever, and the money is about all gone. New York Septembers are mild enough, but October brings the bite, especially if one's club is a park bench.

Why hadn't the young man gone back to Hungary? By this time he must have experienced a complete cure of military ambition, if indeed that ever ailed him, and the accumulation of army pay would have paid the fare. The idea of going home now that the army "adventure" was ended, seems not to have occurred to him; or if it did, he rejected it. Perhaps "Life with Stepfather" could not be endured even for one season. More likely he found that what he mistook for a military impulse was nothing but prehistoric Abramic urge to get him to some place out of his father's home and into a land that he knew not of. Or just possibly it was nothing more than the Wanderlust that seems to be in the blood of every German youth—

"Es treibt in die Ferne, mich maechtig hinaus."

Jobless and well-nigh penniless though he was, it seems not to have entered his mind to go to the nearest Austrian consulate and ask either for immediate help or for transportation back home. Why not? Was it because of love for the United States which he had just helped to keep united? At this stage, we must doubt it. His experiences to date hardly warranted a sentimental attachment, unless we believe that we love those who maltreat us. But evidently something inside him said, "You can't go home again."

Probably the best explanation is that JP like many another lad, didn't know exactly what he wanted to do, and therefore did nothing —not until the prospect of freezing and starving to death forced him into decision. Right after his army discharge he had bought a German-American dictionary. Don't ask us what size or scope because we don't know. It was thumbed to death long ago. We know not whether it was an English-into-German and German-into-English or just a one-way street. But for the time being, it was his only textbook —guide, philosopher, and friend; and it seems to have stimulated the idea that his lack of a foothold in America was due to his inability to speak English.

It is to be noted that when JP did most of his talking and thinking in German, and he also spoke a scholarly French, he seems to have made no use of the Magyar tongue at all—indicating that the German mother was a more powerful molder of youth than the Hungarian-Jewish father. At any rate, the conclusion of the whole matter, as regards the cogitations in City Hall Park, was that he had better get out of New York into some inland, strictly American city *"wo Deutsch nicht gesprochen ist."*

Obviously, he was not thinking in terms of journalism. Even in the sixties, New York was the mecca of newsmen, just as it was in the nineteen hundreds, the nineteen twenties, and to a much lesser extent in the thirties and now the forties. Park Row, at the time JP was looking at it, was the home of the *New York Times,* the *New York World,* the *New York Tribune,* the *New York Herald,* and the *New York Sun.* This was the era when Dana was the *Sun,* and Greeley was the *Tribune* and Bennett the Elder was the *Herald* and Manton Marble was the old *World.*

Here was the great Joseph Pulitzer of the future, less than twenty years away from the day when he was to buy *The World*, looking at America's greatest newspaper opportunity, and yet thinking only of how to get to another environment, and the better assurance of a square meal. If he had any thoughts at all about the journals across the way, they are unrecorded. His immediate concern was to find that all-American city. He inquired among his German-speaking acquaintances. Some of them seized the unparalleled chance to perpetrate one of the greatest practical jokes in history.

They told him the best place in America to learn English was St. Louis, Missouri. They might just as well have said Hoboken, New Jersey, or Milwaukee, Wisconsin (in the later part of that century).

2. St. Louis, Missouri

"If there is anything in my melancholy life's work which I hope and wish may do good, it is that it should give encouragement to thousands of hard-working journalists . . . if there is anything that a hard-working newspaperman really needs, it is encouragement, hope —belief that he may rise from the smallest position to the highest."
—JP.

 T WAS the summer of '68. Hot afternoons have been in St. Louis, and this was one of the hottest. If it were possible to reconstruct the atmosphere of the old "Mound City" of the Midwest, with its buoyant, surging, gay, hearty, and reckless mood in the rebirth of private and public enterprise and the upswing of political corruption in the mad era following the Civil War—this would be a good place to rebuild that merry time. The old French influence of the early explorers and missionaries had just about vanished. Wave after wave of German immigration had made the pioneer city half-German— the rest a mixture in which the frontier American type predominated. St. Louis was neither "northern" nor of the South. It had strong elements of both. One could hardly walk a block without encountering a colonel or two, either from the Union Army, or that of the Confederacy.

Anyway, it was hot. We can just imagine that in those famous German refreshment places, like Tony Faust's, patrons were standing three deep around the bars, the beer flowing like the Mississippi and foaming like Niagara. Blood was thicker than water, and beer was more popular than either. Summer or winter, beer was the accepted antidote for Missouri's climate, ranging in temperature from that of Greenland's icy mountains to Arizona's coral desert. If a full quart stein of Muenchener, Edelweiss, Pilsener, Schuetzenfester, or

19

Oberberchtesgadengegammer, or what had they in those days, failed to produce the proper sense of well-being and adequate response to all conditions of St. Louis, it was merely because the relief-seeker fell into the vulgar error, as Mr. Pickwick remarked, of not taking enough.

On this particular afternoon, there was something doing, in the newspaper sense, in the alley back of the old post office. It might have been a murder, a suicide, an accident, a fire, an encounter between two ex-colonels, a fist fight over the right way to drink beer, or a dispute over a family tree, ending in a retort courteous and a pistol rampant.

Anyhow, it was a good story—this one in St. Louis. The police reporters for all the English-language papers were there—reporters of the *Globe,* the *Dispatch,* the *Democrat,* and the *Post,* "covering the story," no doubt, but in the popular method of letting the police or the coroner gather the facts and then getting the information from these officials later on. (In that way the officers got their names in the papers, and the reporters did not have to work too hard in the hot weather.)

Then somebody said:

"Look, boys!"

The newspaper group is at once all agog. Where? Gawshamighty! Well, I'll be blanketed! I'll be a son of a well-known citizen! What-the-perdition is that? Don't you know? That is—JOEY!

The arrival of the principal character furnishes the rest of the information. The tall, lanky figure that comes dashing around the corner of Olive and Second streets, is upsetting traditions like the nude descending the staircase. His long linen duster is flying behind him like the tail of a kite. He wears a stiff white shirt but no tie or collar. In one hand he carries a thick press pencil; in the other, a wad of copy paper big enough for a full-sized essay on how to improve a school of journalism. As he hurls himself into the midst of the crowd he grabs the first likely-looking bystander.

"I am the reporter of the *Westliche Post!*" he exclaims. "Give me the facts, please!"

What a way to cover news! The man actually wants to work!

Such was the impact of Joseph Pulitzer, reporter for St. Louis's leading German-language daily, already known to newsmen and news sources as "Joey."

"For a beginner," one of the St. Louis reporters remembered years later, "Joey was exasperatingly inquisitive. He questioned everybody in sight. The way in which he went to work to dig out facts proved that he was a born reporter. In fact, he was so industrious that he was a positive annoyance to the other reporters."

"They think," another St. Louis citizen observed at the time, "that because he trundles about with himself a big cobnose, a whopper jaw, and bullfrog eyes, that he has no sense; but he possesses greater ability than all of them put together. . . . Mark me, he is now engaged in the making of a greater man than Editor Danzer, or Editor Preetorius, or even Schurz."

He might have added that the whopper jaw, which Joseph Pulitzer always regarded as a weak feature in his natural makeup, had become even more conspicuous by reason of a tuft of red whiskers just covering the point of the chin—the beginning of what later became a magnificent beard of reddish hue.

"Joseph Pouletzes," late of the Union Army's Lincoln Cavalry, was being metamorphosed into St. Louis's most interesting journalist, but not by easy stages. The German poet could have had him in mind when he wrote, "Where thou art not, there is happiness." Wherever JP went there was turmoil and trouble in which he was either on the giving or the receiving end. Endowed by nature and circumstance with a caricature of a physiognomy, possessed of a thirst and a passion for information that might be impeded or hampered, but never thwarted nor frustrated, he was bound to create a stir. His appearance excited amusement, ridicule, and a strong desire to play practical jokes. The treatment he got in St. Louis was in many respects a repetition of the hazing in the army, but the difference was that in the army he had to take it, whereas in civilian life he could strike back.

He was not long in developing a technique which in time effectually cured the St. Louis reporters of making sport of Joey with the big nose and the whopper jaw. But it is doubtful that he found a way to remove the wounds from his memory. Even if he did finally get them out of immediate consciousness, there is medical evidence that they

remained in his subconscious mind; and certain impressions remained buried in the nervous system, some day to be revived when
the energy reservoirs fell below the safety level.

Meanwhile, we should retrace our steps to fill in some of the gaps
of the narrative. What was it that changed the aimless ex-recruit into
Joey, St. Louis's up-and-coming reporter? Here we enter a no-man's
land of legend, report, and slander, as well as the natural conceal-
ment that always goes with hero-worship. After Joseph Pulitzer became formidable, his enemies dug up or invented all sorts of stories
about his past. A package of such legends is the pamphlet entitled:
"For United States Senator from New York—Joseph Pulitzer," published and distributed anonymously in the early nineteen hundreds.

A few excerpts indicate the tenor of the charges, which are a
model of restraint and elegance:

"Though he now sneers at men of lowly birth," the brochure begins, "Joseph Pulitzer himself began life in America as a roustabout, rising successively to the places of gravedigger (whether First
or Second G. D. is not mentioned), uniformed lackey, and waiter in
a St. Louis saloon."

"Pulitzer," the pamphlet also says, "came to America by way of
steerage on an immigrant vessel. Many a better man came under
equally humble circumstances. He was classed as of Jewish parentage. Since his rise in the world he has denied his Jewish origin, and
let it be said to the credit of the reputable Hebrews of New York,
they have encouraged a belief in the denial. . . . During his first
night in America, Pulitzer slept in a cellar of old French's Hotel.
. . . Finding his way South, he took employment as a roustabout on
one of the river steamboats. At Memphis the boat was quarantined
on account of yellow fever . . . graves were to be dug . . . high
wages were offered. Pulitzer eagerly accepted the offer. He worked
overtime. Victims of the plague could not die fast enough to suit
him. He made money.

"Carrying the hoard which he accumulated as gravedigger to St.
Louis, Pulitzer soon rose to the dignity of a coachman . . . serving
the Brittons of 'Cracker Palace.' He gained repute as THE FIRST
SERVANT IN ST. LOUIS TO WEAR LIVERY, the whites of the city, in
those days, balking at the uniform.

"From coachman he rose to waiter in Tony Faust's restaurant, where he attracted the attention of Carl Schurz, editor of the *Westliche Post,* and Dr. Emil Preetorius, associate editor. . . ."

Lies, lies, all damnable falsehoods, according to the accepted tradition. Most of it never happened, and anyway, it wasn't yellow fever—it was cholera! But in spite of its malice, the pamphlet has one undercurrent of truth. It is no exaggeration to say that in his transition from army to journalism, JP traveled a rough road, impelled chiefly by the most powerful and most primitive human motive, the sheer struggle for existence. The only plan for a career he had between September, 1865, and the time in 1868 when he became *the reporter* for the *Westliche Post* was a plan to keep body and soul together by whatever honest employment he could find.

When he decided to leave New York in search of that, as he thought, strictly English-speaking city, he sold his last cashable asset, a fine silk handkerchief, for seventy-five cents—enough to buy food for a few days, but not much. How he got from New York to St. Louis, nobody knows. JP himself, so far as we can find, never told. The presumption is that he, like many others, "rode the rods," an uninvited guest of the Baltimore and Ohio Railroad.

JP's own recollections, told to associates of a later day, pick up the narrative as of October 10, 1865, when as he said, he reached East St. Louis, Illinois, completely out of money. There was no bridge across the river. Whatever the ferry charge was, he didn't have it. In the gray twilight, through a misty rain, he could see the gas lights of St. Louis across the river. "It looked like the promised land," he said years later, but at the moment it was cold and he felt no temptation to try his art as a swimmer. And there was no chance to turn his ability at chess into transportation.

His one other asset, German, came in more handily.

As the ferryboat edged up to the dock, JP heard deckhands talking in German. (*"Man glaubt es kaum wie gut es klang."*) He called out in German and they answered *"auf Deutsch."* One man came up to the gate. JP's latent reportorial instinct hit on the right technique: first get your man into a conversation. Next came the important question: was there any way for the stranger to get across the river? Answers fell into three possibilities: (A) he might swim, which was unseasonable; (B) he might walk (which suggestion was impious); (C) one of the firemen had quit and they might need a man in his place. Coincidence has done a swell job. Opportunity is seeking the man at the precise moment when man seeks opportunity. They meet, but do not fall in love. Can JP "fire a boiler"? (I never have but)—"I can!" (Response made by advice of counsel—Messrs. Hunger and Cold, attorneys-at-large for all friendless boys.)

(JP, dictating to subconscious mind: Miss Memory, take a note, please. Hold for future release—add precepts for *The World.* "Never lack sympathy with the poor.")

JP, speaking many years later: "The boiler was on the open deck. As I opened the firebox, a blast of fiery air struck me in the face. At the same time a gust of rain and snow struck me in the back. I was roasting in front and freezing in the rear. But I kept on shoveling. I don't remember how many trips we made that night, back and forth across the river, freezing and roasting, but the next morning, I went ashore and walked the streets of St. Louis."

October 11, 1865. The *St. Louis Westliche Post:*
"WANTED: At Benton Barracks; hostler for mules; ex-cavalry-man preferred."

Did JP's eyes deceive him as he scanned the classified ad columns of St. Louis's leading German paper, on this bright morning, following the rough night on the Mississippi? Did someone really prefer ex-cavalrymen? Who would say now that the streets of St. Louis were not more abundantly paved with good fortune than the side-walks of New York? Who said opportunity knocks but once and lightning never strikes twice in the same place? Twice within twenty-four hours luck seemed to have been made to the order of Pulitzer.

Benton Barracks was four miles outside the St. Louis city limits, but JP alternately walked and ran the distance, only to discover on arrival that he had left his army discharge papers with his bundle in St. Louis. He walked and dog-trotted back to the city and out again.

He got the job. He was appointed personal custodian for sixteen mules. But his Lincoln Cavalry training had not included a course on mules. All he knew about them was that they had long ears.

"Never in my life," he used to say, "did I have a more exasperating experience. The man who has never cared for sixteen mules does not know what trouble is." (JP had never been a city editor. He leaped the grades from reporting to owning.)

The job lasted two days, which was a very good record. He quit, not because of the mules, but because of the food. "It was horrible." He went back to the river ferry. This time they needed a man at the gates, though only for a few days. Next, he got a job on a river steamer plying between St. Louis and Memphis. This is where the gravedigger incident comes in. Cholera was raging in Memphis and, between trips up and down the river, "he aided in caring for the dead," as one biographer puts it. Spoken like a true mortician! His job, as it appears from other accounts, was to bury the dead as rapidly as possible, not to care for them. One story is that he organized his own crew of gravediggers, and since the pay was good, he made out very well, until the cholera wave ended.

Tracing the slender thread of the JP narrative—a tale in which legend, imagination, fiction, and slander are combined with an unknown quantity of fact—we find him back in St. Louis, working as a "roustabout" (freight handler) along the levees, loading and unloading the Mississippi steamers. Most of the gang were Negroes. The stevedore boss didn't like the color combination, and so put the white boy to checking. JP learned the business quickly and so well that soon he became a stevedore himself and had his own gang.

The jobs were irregular and the profits meager. To eke out a living, he rented a horse and hack, and carried passengers and baggage to and from the river landings. Failing to get into Big Business through these enterprises, he took a job as a waiter. The stories differ as to his success in this field. One version is that his position was with Tony Faust, the celebrated restaurateur, in whose establishment, it is said, he first met Carl Schurz and Emil Preetorius, owners and editors of the *Westliche Post,* who were so impressed with his intelligence and good manners that they engaged him as a reporter.

Another story is that he hired out as a coachman for Fred Kuhn of Anthony and Kuhn, the distinguished brewers, and embellished the job by wearing full livery—long wine-colored coat, high boots, stovepipe hat, white collar and cuffs, and all the trimmings; and that through the brewers he was graduated into the service of Tony Faust. Still another report, widely accepted, is that his waitership was not with Faust, but in a much cheaper restaurant, lasting exactly one day, the engagement being terminated because of Pulitzer's maladroitness in letting a beefsteak slide off his tray on to a customer's neck.

All sources appear to agree that JP did whatever he could find to do, and sometimes slept on park benches or in hallways when he could not pay the landlady. Whenever he was a few dollars ahead of the game, he invested in board and keep against the rainy days and the lean times. He learned to live on apples and like them so well that all through life he had to have not one but many apples a day, sometimes importing them out of season from as far away as South Africa.

Whenever jobs ran out, he searched the want ad columns of the *Westliche Post*. He answered one for "laborers on a Louisiana sugar plantation." Forty other men applied for the same work. The "agent" collected five dollars a head, took them fifty miles down the river, and left them stranded. They walked all the way back to St. Louis, vowing to kill the swindler. They stormed the place, but the agent had vanished. A crowd collected. The reporter for the *Westliche Post* interviewed the victimized Pulitzer, and heard such a factual account, in such excellent German, that he invited JP to write his own story. It appeared next day in the *Westliche Post,* word for word. Thus was born the career of Joseph Pulitzer, journalist.

At least, there emerged at this point the burning desire to write, and the equally inflammatory thrill of seeing one's own copy in print. The article carried a big headline, big for those days. If it had also been signed "By Joseph Pulitzer" glory would have been complete. But newspapers in those days usually did not carry by-lines and nobody had even imagined a day when two columnists would sign the same story!

But there is yet a gap between the consummation and the wish. Not quite three years elapse before the young Politzer, late of Hungary, late Pouletzes of the Union Army, is able to rush out on the streets of St. Louis to proclaim himself: "Pulitzer of the *West-liche Post!*"

Ten years after that, he was able to sign himself as editor-publisher-proprietor of the *Post-Dispatch*—a poor thing (at that time) but his own! Fifteen years later (i.e., after the first newspaper job) he might truthfully say: "*The World,* it is I."

At the turn of the century, he would have had to qualify the statement. He and *The World* were becoming two in one and yet distinct—the creator coexisting with his creation—of it, but yet not *in* it. Quite unlike anything else on earth, there is a relationship between a man and his newspaper that defies analysis, once the newspaper comes to have a mind and a soul, a will and a spirit of its own.

The relationship has no counterpart either in husband and wife, master and dog, or father and son. In the Pulitzer instance, when he felt himself nearing the Valley of the Shadow, he said in substance in his will:

"I die, but *The World* lives on."

That was what he thought, or at least what he hoped, and fervently prayed for.

But getting back to St. Louis—Mr. Pulitzer's personal school of journalism was one of hard jobs, odd jobs, grim jobs, combined with a constant fight for education. Experience ran a Dotheboys Hall for him. The unsympathetic Mr. Squeers, who teaches youth the hard way when the regular academies are barred, showed JP no favors at all. Everything he learned and earned he had to fight for.

Outside of working hours, the scene of his *Kampf* became the St. Louis Mercantile Library. Many a morning he was waiting on the steps when Assistant Librarian Udo Brachvogel opened the doors and at closing time they literally had to push him out. On jobless days, he omitted lunch and ate apples from his pockets. The apples appeased his hunger for food but all the books he could obtain could not satisfy the thirst for information. If he did not, like Bacon, take all knowledge for his province, he was eager to take on the whole library.

Brachvogel became his Doctor Eliot and his Anthony Fiala. Guiding and advising JP in an otherwise uncharted realm, he also became a lifelong friend. JP's preferences were quickly discernible. Aside from wanting to master English, he hungered and thirsted after history and politics. Like St. John in the Apocalypse, he would take a little book, or a big one, and eat it up.

The wages he earned—whether as coachman, waiter, handyman, roustabout, or disposer of the dead, what matter?—were invested mostly with the landlady, giving that much free time for the library. He filed his first papers for citizenship, and made a connection with a group of lawyers in the Jones and Sibley building at Broadway and Market Street. They gave him reading space and he earned a few dollars at serving papers and running other errands. Patrons of the drugstore soon knew him well by sight. They used to say: "There goes Shakespeare!"

A prominent physician who frequented the store got him a job as Warden on Arsenal Island during the cholera epidemic which hit St. Louis in 1866. The victims were buried on this island. Although JP's title and work was that of "Health Officer," this episode undoubtedly strengthened the "charge" made by enemies in later years that he was nothing but a gravedigger. (Other biographers record a great liking on his part for Shakespeare's plays, especially *Hamlet,* but whether the graveyard scene had a special fascination we are not informed.)

After the plague was over, his lawyer friends obtained for him the work of recording the land rights of the "Atlantic and Pacific Railroad." He had to file copies of the charter in twelve different counties, mostly wild and sparsely inhabited. He made the trip on horseback with a Negro guide. Caught in a flood, both horses and the Negro were drowned, but JP managed to swim the river with his saddlebags and records. Years later, he found some amusement in telling the story—one of the few he cared to relate about his pre-*World* experiences.

He recalled that when he came up out of the river, a farmer who had been watching his struggles, with truly detached interest, put him up for the night.

As JP related it, using one of his rare attempts at dialect, the scene went something like this:

FARMER (Handing JP a tumbler three-quarters full of whiskey):
Hereyah! Drink this. It'll warm yer up!

JP: Thank you. I do not drink.

FARMER: Yer mean ter sit thar'n tell me yer don't drink?

(Long pause for the registration of amazement. Farmer produces
food and they eat.)

FARMER (Producing mammoth plug of "Star XXX"): Take er
chaw er terbaccer!

JP: Thank you. I do not chew.

(Several minutes elapse.)

FARMER (In measured accents): Yer mean ter tell me yer don't
chaw?

(Several more moments elapse. Moments stretch into minutes,
minutes into hours. Off-the-record discussion during this intermission covers the proposed railroad which is destined to become the
St. Louis and San Francisco Railroad, starting from the Gem of the
Mississippi but never reaching the Golden Gate; the crops; the recent
war; the birth of a nation and whether some Mr. Winchell of the
period prognosticated it correctly; carpetbagging, and the impeachment of Mr. Johnson; how fine it is that this war has ended all wars
and there will never be any more; technical difficulties involved in
turning muskets into shares of Plows, Inc., and exchanging swords
for pruning hooks in the ratio of sixteen to one. . . .

(Pre-bedtime dumb show follows. Farmer takes down corncob
pipe from wall, fills it with Ready-Rubbed-Chew-Honey-Dip-Twist,
produces old-fashioned matches measuring six inches from stern to
bowsprit, offers the combination to the guest. JP shakes his head,
regretfully. Farmer shakes his head, Margaretfulleresquely as if to
say one must accept the universe, including them that dwell therein.
Both sides shake heads. Another half hour elapses in silence, then:)

FARMER: Young feller, yer seem to be right smart and able fer
a ferriner, but let me tell you something, Bud: you'll never be a success in St. Louis until [accent picks up here] yer learns ter drink and
chaw and smoke.

JP used to tell this story, with dialect and all, to new secretaries in
order to test their endurance, manners, and tact. He knew it bored
them, and wanted to ascertain whether they could register the proper

amount of ennui without transgressing against the code of a gentleman. The slightly modernized version given above is as good as any,
because the others do not agree on any two points except that there
was a railroad and there was a flood.

Whatever the true facts about this adventure in the wilderness, it
seems to have given JP prestige among the lawyers in the Jones and
Sibley building. Messrs. William Patrick and Charles Philip Johnson, leaders of the St. Louis bar, arranged for the young man to have
desk room and the use of their library to fit himself to be one of
their profession. At about the same time he qualified for citizenship,
receiving his certificate in March, 1867. Nobody seems to have
raised the point that he was then not quite twenty years of age.

Young Mr. Pulitzer was beginning to get a foothold, albeit a
narrow one. Mysterious Fate intervened here and threw JP into the
path of a rare genius who was to have probably the largest single
influence in the molding of his mind, his ideals and his character.
By sheer chance, he found a warm friend in Thomas Davidson, a
notable though eccentric scholar, then teaching Greek and Latin in
the St. Louis High School. Although he was but seven years older
than JP, he seemed to the hungry-minded lad to possess all knowledge; and indeed, some of Davidson's contemporaries rated him
"easily one of the twelve most learned men in the world." To JP, he
was a one-man university. He, at any rate, was the first man, and I
daresay the last, who knew all the answers to the Pulitzer question-
naires.

Davidson had been born in Scotland but was never stingy with
information. Graduated from Aberdeen University with highest
honors in Greek, and with other laurels, he could not or would not
conform to pedagogic customs. He wanted to teach—not to promote
methods. After futile efforts as a schoolmaster in Scotland and England, he sought opportunity in America, failed in Boston, and somehow drifted to St. Louis.

His knowledge was amazing. He could speak, write and think in
practically all languages, ancient or modern. He knew all sciences
except the biological. He knew all philosophies, but eschewed the
German. . . . "Since the world began," he wrote, "there never was

such a piece of huge, solemn humbug. . . . The land of beer never did produce but one great thinker and that was Leibnitz."

Being at heart an intellectual knight-errant, he was too direct, too personal, too deeply interested in pupils to win academic success. He came in time to be like Socrates, having many scholars, but no school. But for seven glorious years in St. Louis he pursued his heart's desire, which was to mold and inspire a young man of genius. His mind furnished the bellows and the flame at which the Pulitzer weapons were forged. He and JP arranged to share lodgings.

The association seems to have been idyllic. Professor Davidson had a one-boy class to which he could lecture by the hour, and JP had a living, talking encyclopedia, abundantly able and willing to respond to all questions with facts, facts, facts, without stint or limit. At nights, on Saturdays, and on Sundays, JP would stretch out on his bed or the Professor's bed, alternately asking questions and listening rapturously as knowledge poured forth from the prodigious Davidson mind into the savagely prehensile and retentive memory of Pulitzer. No other man was ever so satisfactory to JP. Later associates found it hard to believe that the individual ever existed who could survive a question-and-answer session with Joseph Pulitzer. Davidson set the pace and the pattern. Never afterward did JP have any tolerance for men with feeble or inaccurate memories. Alleyne Ireland, one of the private secretaries in JP's last year, made a frightful blunder by saying, in a dinner conversation, that he had a friend who thought that printing was one of mankind's greatest blessings because it recorded the things that other generations had had to commit to memory. Mr. Pulitzer was aroused.

"Your wise friend," he cried, "was a damned fool! What becomes of all your reading, all your observation, your experience, your study, your investigations, if you have no memory?"

Every man has a Garden of Eden chapter in his life, I suppose, and we can readily believe that the memory of the Great Question Asker of the Gay Nineties and the early nineteen hundreds went back yearningly to those dear dead days beyond recall when Davidson was the Britannica, when it was Pulitzer and not the respondent who ran out of steam . . . Pulitzer who finally cried quits for the night, turned over happily murmuring, "Good night, Professor," and dropped off to dream about a Grand Parade of Knowledge, with Davidson riding on a white horse, carrying the Mercantile Library in one hand and in the other a banner with a strange device, the legend reading, "Accuracy, accuracy, accuracy." (Terseness came along later.) In the Grand Parade, Davidson was followed by Homer, Herodotus, Sophocles, Plato, Aristotle, Demosthenes, Cicero, Virgil; Thales, St. Thomas Aquinas, Hypatia, Bruno, Galileo, Descartes, Spinoza, Hobbes (Capital HOBBES in honor of Davidson), Gibbon bearing all the volumes of *The Decline and Fall;* Dante, Shakespeare; Washington crossing the Delaware; Jefferson drafting the first draft of the Declaration of Independence; Webster answering Calhoun; the binomial theorem; the nebular hypothesis wearing a crown of comet's hair; Eliza crossing the ice; Patrick Henry: "Give me Liberty. . . . I mean, give me accuracy, or give me Davidson"; Franklin extracting information from the tail of a kite; Robert Fulton, carrying the First of the Hudson River Day Line boats; Martin Luther: "Here I stand"; Napoleon, betrayed by the inaccuracy of a subordinate at Waterloo; Nelson: "England expects every man to know his history!"; Farragut: "Damn the inaccuracies . . . full steam ahead on the sea of knowledge!"; Disraeli organizing the roustabouts along the Suez Canal. . . . Kant with his Critique of Pure Reason, carrying a St. Louis High School Pennant reading, "Vote for Davidson!"; De Tocqueville carrying one volume of *Democracy in America* under each arm; Pulitzer translating the Articles of War into blows of one syllable—waking with a start and reassured to find the English dictionary safe under his pillow, and Davidson not far away. . . .

Ah, Paradise!

The fact that JP dressed and undressed complacently in the presence of his learned friend was proof enough of the serenity of his life with Davidson. His mind was completely at peace, as happy as a sheep in green pastures. No other man ever won from him so warm a token of regard. The mere thought of being even without a collar in the presence of other men was enough to throw JP into a paroxysm of annoyance.

But Davidson was different. To have him in the other bed was as natural to JP as having the dictionary under his pillow.

In the chess room of the Mercantile Library, Pulitzer first met Carl Schurz and Emil Preetorius. While watching the great editors —at least St. Louis regarded them as great editors—JP gratuitously remarked that one of them had made a poor play.

Surprised, but not angry, they told JP that if he could do better, he should take the place and finish the game. Unabashed, youth played and won. The older men smiled at the result and afterward played with him frequently. On such chances do important events of life sometimes depend! If Pulitzer had minded his own business Schurz and Preetorius might never have given him his first job as newspaper reporter.

"Much has been said about Mr. Pulitzer's marvelous news sense," wrote Frank I. Cobb, nearly half a century later. "There was nothing weird or miraculous about it. It was born of an insatiable thirst for information and a restless curiosity about everything of human interest."

St. Louis newspapermen who worked with "Joey" when he went on the staff of the *Westliche Post* in 1868 as a cub reporter may have discerned nothing miraculous about the young man's news sense, but they certainly believed that there was something mighty weird about it.

From the beginning he had an eccentric conception of a reporter's duty. He liked to work, and work he did, often from ten in the morning until two the next morning, running down hot tips and writing fresh, clean copy. He responded to a news flash like a fireman to an alarm. On the faintest scent of a story, he dashed madly about the streets of St. Louis, a pad of paper under his arm and his long linen duster flying in the wind. "I'm the reporter from the *Westliche Post*. Give me the facts!" was his breathless demand.

William Fayel, an American contemporary of his reportorial days in St. Louis, many years afterward recalled his arrival at the scene of an accident.

"I remember his appearance distinctly," he wrote, "because he apparently had dashed out of the office upon receiving the first intimation of the story without stopping to put on his collar. In one hand he held a pad of paper, and in the other a pencil. He did not wait for inquiries but announced that he was the reporter from the *Westliche Post* and then he began to ask questions of everybody in sight. I remember to have remarked to my companions that for a beginner he was exasperatingly inquisitive. The manner in which he went to work to dig out the facts, however, showed that he was a born reporter.

"He was so industrious, indeed, that he became a positive annoyance to others who felt less inclined to work and, inasmuch as it was considered quite fitting and proper in those days to guy the reporters of the German papers, the English-language reporters did not hesitate to undertake to curb his eagerness for news. Thus, on more than one occasion when Joey was covering the coroner's office, the other reporters would trick him into dashing out on a false alarm. But JP never relaxed; and soon the city editors of the English papers discovered that the *Westliche Post* often contained news which the others had missed."

At length, Major Gilson, city editor of the *Democrat*, posted an order on his bulletin board, directing the staff to give less time to harassing German reporters and more time to competing with them. The English-speaking group learned to appreciate JP's extraordinary capacity for news gathering.

However, they also had plenty of fun. Joseph Keppler, famous cartoonist, who had just established *Puck*, the humor magazine which later was to move to New York and create a national reputation, never tired of teasing the young reporter. When other prospects failed as subjects for cartoons, Keppler would say:

"Joey, there's only one thing to do. I'll go back to the office and draw your nose."

JP soon demonstrated that it was hazardous for the other boys to send him on fool's errands. Whenever he found he had run two or three miles for a story that did not exist, he asked questions in the neighborhood and often dug up a story that his tormentors knew nothing about.

These accomplishments not only pleased Schurz and Preetorius but forced the other reporters to take him seriously. Within a short time he was recognized as one of the most aggressive reporters in

Thomas Davidson

the city. He was also making a definite impression upon public officials and civic leaders.

Early in 1869, JP was assigned to cover the Missouri Legislature in Jefferson City. He had been reading about government; now, for the first time, he was to come face to face with practical politics.

The *Westliche Post* was Republican, yet the young correspondent thought he had the right to attend a Democratic caucus. On one occasion, when Pulitzer suspected that reporters of Democratic papers were in the caucus room, he pushed the guard aside and threw himself against the door. The hinges gave way. Pulitzer strolled calmly to the reporters' table and sat down. His suspicions were correct. The Democratic papers were fully represented. The committee at first considered ejecting him, but finally permitted him to remain. The *Westliche Post* was not "beaten."

The young journalist soon learned that something was rotten in Jefferson City. Certain Missouri statesmen, JP found, were less concerned about the law than about the profits, less careful of the public welfare than of the prospects for plunder.

The bribery, lobbying, and graft that came under the new correspondent's observation in his first few months at Jefferson City were a profound shock. His semi-editorial dispatches from the State capital abounded with sharp criticisms and insistent demands for reform.

In the latter part of 1869, a vacancy occurred in Missouri's House of Representatives through the resignation of the gentleman from the Fifth District, St. Louis. A special election was called for December 21. As the Fifth District had been, for twenty-five years, as solidly Democratic as the state of Georgia, the Republicans expected merely to go through the motions of naming an opposition candidate.

When the Republican convention meets to choose their lamb for the slaughter, JP is covering the proceedings for the *Westliche Post*. During a lull, the newspaper boys go out for a breath of air.

There is a huddle on the platform. A delegate whispers, "Let's give the nomination to Joey!"

The convention shakes with laughter. Yah! Yah! The suggestion is carried. JP returns to the press table. As nearly as one can reproduce it after some seventy years, here is approximately what follows:

A DELEGATE: Mr. Chairman, I desire to place in nomination for the high honor of Representative from this district, the name of a man . . . [Applause] . . . a man who . . . [More applause] . . . a man who is . . .[Loud cheers] . . . the foremost patron of the Mercantile Library . . . [Applause] . . . possessed of a nose for news . . . [Laughter. JP looks up] a friend of the apple growers . . . a great chess player . . . a man who will lead our party to victory if anybody can, because he is always far out in front . . . [Applause and cheers] . . . the greatest question asker since Cicero. . . . Gentlemen, I give you the name of this man—Joey Pulitzer!

Cheers, loud applause, and continued waving of steins. A committee is appointed to bring the candidate to the platform. The convention is in an uproar.

JP: "Gentlemen, I thank you for the honor. No doubt, you expect me to refuse it. My first inclination is to do so. [Cries of "No! No!"] But on second thought, it is evident that the Republican Party needs me . . . St. Louis needs me . . . I accept the nomination! I promise you a sweeping victory!"

The next day, St. Louis rocks with merriment. The papers are full of the story about Joey the reporter's being named for the legislature. A few days later, the tune changes, after JP has made his first campaign speech. For the first time in twenty years, a Republican candidate in the Fifth District goes on the stump. The Pulitzer speeches are delivered in German and in English, and seem to register with the people both ways. His meetings are well attended.

Who paid the bills? There is an apocryphal story that "Ed" Butler, the Democratic boss, secretly supported the Pulitzer ticket—probably a canard. Whoever did, the fact remains that JP, running on his promise to clean up the courthouse ring and fight municipal corruption, went over—tremendously.

On Election Day, the *Missouri Democrat* (paradoxically, a Republican paper) had this to say:

"Mr. Pulitzer is neither an old resident, a great man, nor a rich man, but he is a young man of thorough honesty whose business it has been, as local editor, to understand the workings of our city government; and he has a fine education and natural ability."

When the returns came in that night, the Fifth District had undergone a revolution. Pulitzer was elected.

The Republican delegates realized their mistake after he had taken his oath of office.

The new Representative found it neither difficult nor incongruous to continue as legislative correspondent for the *Westliche Post.* Journalism and politics were so closely wedded in JP's philosophy that he thought it quite natural not only to report news but to create news. He did both.

He also had the notion that campaign promises were meant to be kept. He lost no time in introducing his bill to abolish the County Court. He soon realized that he had stirred up a hornet's nest. The County Court not only appointed tax assessors, and all county officials, but controlled the funds for public institutions and awarded contracts for buildings. Common report had it that the big prizes went to friends of the Court. Under these circumstances, the learned judges failed to sympathize with Representative Pulitzer's bill. They sought political advice.

Presently appeared in the legislative halls at Jefferson City, the tall, powerful, thick-necked, pugnacious Captain Edward Augustine —in public life, Supervisor of Registration for St. Louis County; privately, a contractor who had just been awarded the million-dollar job of building a new asylum for the insane. Captain Augustine put thumbs down on the Pulitzer bill.

Alarmed by the arrival of St. Louis's most effective lobbyist, JP proceeded to expose and denounce the captain, not only in the *Westliche Post,* but in the House.

On the night of January 27, 1870, JP strolled into Schmidt's Hotel, the popular rendezvous of the capital, and found Augustine with a number of legislators, newspapermen, and political hangers-on. Augustine was raging.

JP, never bashful: "What is the subject under discussion?"

One of the reporters said, "You are, Joey."

AUGUSTINE: Yes, I was just saying, that what you wrote about me is a lie and you are a liar!

JP: You should be more careful of your language, Captain.

AUGUSTINE: All right, I will. You are a damned liar!

Joey is no match for the 250-pound politician. He turns and walks quickly out of the hotel, coming into collision with Wallace Gruelle, correspondent of the *St. Louis Dispatch,* the paper that JP bought later on.

GRUELLE (who has already heard about the conversation inside) : What's the matter, Joey, why don't you knock the man down?

JP rushes to his own lodgings, returning presently in great excitement, again running into Gruelle and another correspondent.

"If you want a good story," Joey says, "come on back with me," but they continue to the telegraph office.

Augustine is still haranguing the group in the lobby.

JP: Do you wish to apologize?

AUGUSTINE: No, I don't, you puppy! I called you a damned liar and that is what you are!

Out comes JP's weapon from inside his breast pocket, a big army pistol. Augustine charges down upon him, deflecting the aim as JP fires twice. One bullet pierces Augustine's right leg and the other rips through the floor. Augustine pulls his own gun, hitting with the butt, and JP drops.

January 28, 1870. Gruelle in the *St. Louis Dispatch.* "Pulitzer is more blamed than he ought to be. . . . I had a great notion to shoot him for aiming at Augustine's breast and hitting him only in the leg. Bad marksmanship is to be deprecated on all occasions, and when a member of the press—and a legislator to boot —essays to burn gunpowder I want him to go the whole hog. . . . I am going to put Pulitzer under a severe course of training . . . and at the end of that time I will bet he can snuff a candle at ten steps. If he can't, I now and here pledge you my word of honor that I will shoot him myself."

JP was fined five dollars in police court for disturbing the peace. Some of the Representatives demanded a legislative inquiry.

REPRESENTATIVE LEEPER: Mr. Speaker, this resolution ought not to pass. If we start probing into the private conduct of members, where will it lead? If a gentleman happens to kiss a pretty girl,

[Applause.] should the House investigate? I say, let the law take its course!

The resolution was tabled by a vote of 58 to 42. (This made one hundred, or ten times ten, which was JP's lucky number.)

Captain Augustine was not satisfied. He hounded the District Attorney until JP was indicted, pleaded guilty to assault, and was fined one hundred dollars, plus four hundred dollars court costs, which was not so lucky. Friends advanced the money for the fine and were paid back in full, some time afterward.

Augustine's friends kept up the clamor until one of the professional lobbyists threatened to tell all. "If that boy goes to prison," he said, "he won't go alone." After that, further prosecution was dropped.

This shooting was an incident typical of that period. It did put JP in rather a ludicrous light, but, strange to say, it aroused public sentiment for his pet reform. The Pulitzer bill was passed, and the County Court, with its unsavory aroma of corruption, was abolished. Captain Augustine's million-dollar contract was canceled.

JP's early association with the Republican Party was a natural result of his connection with the *Westliche Post,* which had supported Grant for President in 1868. By the end of Grant's first administration, there was widespread dissatisfaction because of carpetbagging, the Whiskey Ring, the railway land-grabs, and the general failure to bring about unity with the South.

The discontent first took form in Missouri. Schurz and others organized the Liberal Republican Party, elected a governor, and spread the reform movement to other parts of the country. JP became secretary of the organization in Missouri.

The liberal movement received encouragement from Republican papers, including the *Chicago Tribune,* the *New York Tribune,* the *Springfield Republican,* the *Cincinnati Commercial,* and of course the *Westliche Post.* Congress also kept the issue of Administration iniquity alive. Throughout the sessions of 1871 and 1872 Grant was roundly assailed by Schurz, who had become a Senator, also by Charles Sumner of Massachusetts, Levi P. Morton, and Roscoe Conkling of New York. Democrats smiled.

The Missouri Liberals issued a call for all good men to come to the aid of the new party and meet in convention in Cincinnati on May 1. The response was tremendous. Delegations appeared from nearly every state and territory. The "Queen City" was jammed as never before. Delegates had to stay in private homes.

Leading candidates at first were Charles Francis Adams of Massachusetts and Governor B. Gratz Brown of Missouri. After many ballots, the choice veered to Horace Greeley. The ticket adopted was Greeley for president, Brown for vice-president. They accepted. One month later the regular Republicans met in Philadelphia and renominated Grant. The Democrats held their convention in Baltimore, July 9, and in spite of opposition from the *New York Times,* not only nominated Greeley and Brown to head the Democratic ticket, but endorsed the Liberal Republican platform.

The choice of Greeley was a bad mistake. As it turned out, Brown would have been the stronger man. Editors rarely make successful candidates, especially on reform issues, but the Liberals felt it necessary to conciliate Eastern sentiment, strongly influenced by Greeley. The editor also had a following out West, having sponsored the successful Union Colony at Greeley, Colorado, and popularized the slogan, "Go West, young man."

JP, however, threw himself into the campaign with great ardor, denouncing the Grant administration in German and in English as the shame of the country and the enemy of free government. He stumped the whole state of Missouri, making at least sixty speeches, mostly in German, at the same time continuing as political correspondent of the *Westliche Post* and keeping one eye on his other job as Police Commissioner of St. Louis, to which post he had been appointed by Governor Brown at a salary of $1,000.

Greeley lost. The great editorial brain seems to have been in a complete fog all through the campaign, with only occasional gleams of inspiration. Soon after Grant was firmly settled for another four years in the White House, Greeley died—brokenhearted. JP himself was grievously disappointed and made up his mind that there was no hope for the Republican Party. He turned toward the Democrats.

In the meantime, as Police Commissioner, he had crusaded

against gambling but with only temporary results. Gambling is a hardy perennial.

Schurz and Preetorius felt that the Greeley campaign had hurt the *Westliche Post*. They offered JP a share in the ownership—on very liberal terms, he thought; the details were never disclosed. Although only twenty-five years old, the new part-owner immediately put the stamp of his genius on the newspaper. Editorials became crisp and dynamic, the news reports terse and sparkling, though somewhat editorial. The paper crackled with life. JP continued to rage against gambling, but he was much more effective in his demands for a new State constitution and a new charter for St. Louis.

The *Westliche Post* might have become a German version of *The World;* who knows? The other owners, however, became frightened, and offered to buy out the Pulitzer interest for thirty thousand dollars. JP accepted with alacrity.

The thirty thousand dollars was more money than he had ever dreamed of. It looked like the Bank of St. Louis. Anyhow, he had ways of spending it. He went abroad and visited his family in Hungary. (No details here.) He practiced no economies. He traveled in comfort. When he returned to St. Louis, it was in one of the new-style Pullman cars, and not on the rods.

Back again in the city of his adoption, he seized an opportunity to purchase a decrepit German newspaper, the St. Louis *Staats-Zeitung*—buying it for a song, he said later, but he never told for how much. The next day he sold it for twenty thousand dollars to the St. Louis *Globe*, which badly needed the Associated Press franchise.

For the first, and the last, time in his life, Mr. Joseph Pulitzer of St. Louis was now on a sabbatical, and it must be admitted that the former immigrant boy made up for the seven lean years of toil and hardship. He engaged fashionable quarters. He bought a fine saddle horse, and rode every day with two colonels, to the admiration of ladies. He consulted a good tailor; he let his beard grow long and had it impressively trimmed . . .

The apple diet is forgotten. He drinks champagne instead of beer.

At the Sunday night musicales of the Balmer family, to which German opera stars are invited, JP is the life of the party.

In the midst of this gay social whirl JP seems to have temporarily forgotten both politics and journalism, while waltzing in the smiles of lovely maidens. He thought about practicing law; but this was the time of the Lotos.

The young man certainly might have been snapped up into matrimony, and have become just another prominent citizen of St. Louis. The awakening came with the Missouri Constitutional Convention of 1875. As a delegate, he entered heartily into the debates, warmly recommending revisions in the state's basic law every ten years, and also a greater measure of home rule for St. Louis. But this was only a brisk interlude. After the convention, he went off to Europe and did not return until the spring of '76.

That was the year the Democrats nominated Samuel J. Tilden of New York for president and the Republicans, turning down Grant's third-term ambitions, put up Rutherford B. Hayes of Ohio. Schurz and his group, back once more in the G.O.P., announced a speaking tour on behalf of Hayes. JP immediately challenged his old chief to debate the issues, but in vain; Schurz, well knowing the deadly accuracy of the Pulitzer shafts, had no appetite for a hand-to-hand tussle with his former editor.

JP went on the hustings through the Middle West and made such a good impression that he was invited to New York by the Young Men's Democratic Club to speak for Tilden, Hendricks, and Reform at a huge mass meeting in Cooper Union. The next day the New York *World,* then edited by Manton Marble, had this to say:

"Mr. Pulitzer on being introduced, was loudly applauded. He said he would make it a point to answer the arguments of Schurz who now supports Hayes in face of the fact that two years ago he opposed the same man as a candidate for Congress. . . . This position of Schurz the speaker characterized as one of the most remarkable freaks on the part of any politician during the present campaign. [Applause.]

" 'If you believe as I do,' said the speaker, 'in the preservation of one country, one government, and one people with one future, you

will cast your votes on the side where there is peace and patriotism.
. . . [Cheers.]

" 'If you, as intelligent American citizens, denounce the intrigues
and villainies of demagogues, who would array one section of the
country against another; the black man against the white; the Prot-
estants against the Catholics; the Germans against the Irish, you
will vote for Tilden and Hendricks.' "

Cheers, cheers, cheers, and cheers. Hendricks was the vice-presi-
dential candidate, but what about Reform? Did he forget to mention
it? The point is not important. More stirring issues lie ahead. Tilden
wins the election, but Hayes wins the Presidency. Tilden's vote in
the Electoral College was 185; Hayes's 184; Tilden's popular
plurality was about 1,000,000. The trouble was that South Carolina,
Florida, and Louisiana, disputing the Negro vote, filed two sets of
returns, one favoring Tilden, the other, Hayes.

Although the Republican National Committee and Hayes himself had already conceded Tilden the winner, the dispute in the
Southern states threatened to cause violence all over the country.
The G.O.P. cried, "Fraud!" Congress appointed a commission to
decide the election. Eight Republicans on the commission outvoted
the seven Democrats on all points, but it took all winter to end the
controversy. JP remained in Washington, reporting the proceedings
for the New York *Sun*.

Tilden accepted the result gracefully, but JP always contended
that the Democrats were robbed, and most historians agree with him.
He was so upset about it that he went abroad again to ease the bitterness of defeat.

When he returned, it was to engage in much more interesting
adventures.

If there is anything in the theory of astrology, we should conclude
that in the year 1878 there were important "confluences of planets"
in the JP horoscope. The stars in their courses appeared to be shed-
ding beneficent rays on the course of the turbulent young man just
entering his thirties. The Hungarian immigrant, who ten years
before was distinctly a man of no importance, had now definitely
"arrived." Though he had come to his present estate through the

roustabout route, taking fortune's knocks as well as her smiles with a truly remarkable capacity to absorb punishment, the earlier hardships were apparently now swallowed up in affluence and influence. He could go places and do things. Life was at the flood tide. The awkwardness, angularity, excitability, and lack of poise which had characterized the unreconstructed cavalryman of the Civil War and the hungering man of all work in St. Louis had given way to a personality distinguished for impressiveness and downright charm.

"Mr. Pulitzer of St. Louis" was no longer a nobody. Although without any strong professional identity after breaking with the *Westliche Post,* he was widely known and respected, not only for his ability as a writer but more for his force, his clarity, and his uncompromising integrity as a political reformer.

And JP looked the part. His tall figure had filled out, his posture had been corrected; horseback riding, dancing, good living and proper tailoring had done the rest. On the intellectual side, his now complete mastery of the English language; his ability to reason rapidly and aggressively with plenty of facts to back his arguments; his incisive, idiomatic style; his fine voice; his dynamic delivery, and his passionate consecration to a cause—all combined to make of Joseph Pulitzer a commanding figure. His presence was beginning to take on some of the majesty that overshadowed the tragic quality of his last twenty years. The early sufferings—in the army and in St. Louis—were now securely locked up in the deep cellars of the subconscious; the later ones were not yet on his horizon. But there was a warning of trouble ahead; the excitement and hard work of 1876 during the Hayes-Tilden campaign had produced a disturbing cough, accompanied by some discharge of blood.

So far as we know, JP, like most men in his generation, never considered the importance of regular medical checkup. Whenever his mind was completely occupied with an undertaking, which was most of the time, he forgot about his body until fatigue or hunger would no longer be denied. Then he would eat or sleep, get it over with, and rush back to the job. All physical danger signals were habitually disregarded—like an engineer running beyond red lights —until it was too late to avert disaster.

His third trip to Europe, however, seemed to restore the full bloom of health. The cough disappeared.

His immediate concern was to sink his teeth into something in the way of occupation that would satisfy an ever-hungry spirit. Before going abroad he had suggested to Dana the idea of a German edition of the *Sun*, but Dana's publisher turned it down. The special correspondence in Washington was only a temporary outlet, even though his articles were signed and he had the further privilege, rare for the *Sun*, of contributing editorials under his name to Dana's own page. Little did Dana imagine that he was laying the foundation for a career, a newspaper, and even a building that would one day overtop the *Sun*.

Upon JP's return from Europe, his plan was to practice law in Washington. He was admitted to the bar of the District of Columbia, but his clientele appears to have been negligible. The profession failed to fan the fires of his soul; he was rendered still more allergic to law by the fact that the big fees were for lobbying in the corridors of Congress, and not for arguments and briefs in court.

The magnetism of Washington for JP was not in the law. Something much more elemental was taking place in the young man's career at this point. Nature, who is no respecter of professions or of soul's ambitions, was whispering:

"Now's the time to fall in love!"

Not because potatoes were cheaper, or the bank account was fatter —the fifty thousand dollars was going fast—but because the man was ripe, the lady was alluring, and deep was calling unto deep.

Pulitzer's most pressing business in Washington, it soon appeared, was the problem of how to captivate a certain lass with a delicate air who had been occupying the best room in his House of Imaginations ever since the Tilden contest—not a room on the main floor, perhaps, with politics and a newspaper that he had in mind to buy some day, but a very special chamber from which she could by no means be ousted. She was somehow associated with the idea of a new life, "not so aimless, purposeless, and loveless," as he once wrote her, but a life founded on a home, with love, ambition, and occupation the cornerstones, and she the inseparable companion.

Fulfillment was not easy. Kate Davis, though not in the first bloom of womanhood, was in no hurry to be caught. How old was she, anyway? According to newspaper accounts published after her death, she might have been older than JP himself. The *New York Herald Tribune* said she was born in 1853, which would make her twenty-five at the time of the marriage and seventy-two when she died; but according to the same article in the same newspaper, she passed away at the age of seventy-eight (if you can figure that out) : and the *New York Times* stated that she was "more than eighty years old" at her death (July 29, 1927), which would have made her over thirty-one at their marriage.

At any rate, Miss Davis took her time about getting married. Although rated by Washington social arbiters as grade A, top flight, upper crust, and highly desirable, she had somehow eluded matchmakers, and she was certainly not going to be swept off her feet by the impetuous young man from Missouri. Mr. Pulitzer, who, though not a "nobody," would probably not have been classed as suited to the "Southern aristocracy," which included Miss Davis and which then, as now, "figured prominently" in the social life of the capital. Kate was the daughter of William Worthington Davis of Georgetown, D. C., the swank Washington suburb; her mother, Catherine Louise Worthington, belonged to the Worthingtons of Maryland, and her father was related to Jefferson Davis, President of the Confederacy.

The mother and the father of Kate Davis were cousins, but whether first, second, or third cousins is not clear; intermarriage among the bluebloods of the South was not uncommon.

Miss Davis first met the fiery young man from Missouri while JP was covering the hearings in the Hayes-Tilden contest. They were introduced by a St. Louis representative. JP seems to have reacted at once. The lady was persistently in his thoughts during the European trip; she was a challenge. The fact that she was out of his reach, according to Washington standards, only made the flame burn brighter.

"What is a difficulty?" JP used to cry in his later talks with *World* editors. "Something to be overcome!"

The aloofness of the Davis belle was indeed something to be overcome; JP seems to have applied himself to the task with all the charm at his command, and we can well believe that the courtship was ardent as well as graceful. But there was a serious handicap. JP was continually distracted by his Othello status—the lack of absorbing occupation. He kept hearing about opportunities to buy newspapers either in St. Louis or New York, and he was anxious to get started before his money ran out. And so, just when the romance appeared to be warming up, he would be distracted by a business prospect—important for him; not so pressing in the eyes of the lady.

Although Kate Davis had not formally accepted her eccentric suitor, she naturally resented this schizophrenic attention. It is not exactly flattering to be wooed by a man who has something else on his mind. The romance was beginning to cool; and one day when JP, getting wind of a possible newspaper purchase, dashed off to St. Louis, she dispatched a letter after him which must have been a masterpiece of maidenly reserve and womanly decision. In substance, Kate Davis suggested to her knight-errant that he make up his mind either to concentrate on the matrimonial matter or stay away altogether.

He returned almost immediately, after sending what he called "my first love letter." He was apologetic and self-reproachful, offering in extenuation only his desire to find a new life, with her in the place of honor. But even here his latent horror of self-revelation broke out. Don't, he implored her, show the letters to anybody. He could not bear that.

His prompt return to Washington appeared to clinch the engagement. But he was off again the same night, this time to New York, in search of a partnership with his St. Louis friend, the cartoonist Joseph Keppler, who used to draw "Joey's nose"; who had now established his former German magazine, *Puck,* in New York, and in English. The Pulitzer timetable was noteworthy, especially for pre-airplane days: Sunday and Monday, business in St. Louis; Monday night, leave for Washington; Wednesday, straighten out the romance; Wednesday night, leave Washington for New York; Thursday and Friday, negotiations in New York; Sunday, back to Washington.

Nothing came of the negotiations in St. Louis or in New York.

Mr. Pulitzer decided to drop everything else and concentrate on matrimony.

They were married on June 19, 1878, in the Protestant Episcopal Church of the Epiphany, Washington, by the Rev. J. H. Chew—the same church in which the bride's parents had been married. If they did not live happily ever afterward, it was because of outward misfortune and not for lack of complete mutual adoration.

During the honeymoon in Europe, JP contributed several articles to the *Sun*, remarkably prophetic of things to come, including the inevitability of another war between France and Germany. England, he found, was unhappy, because of the burden of British aristocracy; great wealth and great poverty existed side by side; but Germany was worse, afflicted with what JP called "over-government."

"It was bad enough if it affected only the pockets of the people," he wrote, "but it becomes worse by affecting their manhood and freedom."

The happy couple returned to the States none too soon. The small fortune had dwindled to a mere five thousand dollars. During the honeymoon, perhaps under the advice of Mrs. Pulitzer, JP had decided to return to St. Louis and once more take up the law; but back among his old friends, his closest advisors told him frankly that he was cut out for newspaper work and would never be a successful lawyer.

Among the newspaper flotsam and jetsam of the Midwest, the *St. Louis Dispatch* had drifted up on the tide of failure and bankruptcy, wearing the strangest disguise that opportunity has ever presented in journalism. Housed in a one-time three-story dwelling at 111 North Broadway, this paper (born of a political fight among the owners of the *St. Louis Democrat*) had waged a losing struggle for existence for fifteen years, and by the end of 1878 was as nearly dead and buried as a newspaper can be, short of total extinction: the type was worn out, the press was broken down, even the elevator was out of commission, and creditors were howling for their money.

The only distinction possessed by the *Dispatch* was its reputation for hospitality. Tramp printers then roaming the West were sure of getting a night's bed, or a few days' work, by applying to the

Dispatch. They used to sleep on the forms or on the floor or wherever fancy dictated. The *Dispatch*'s one tangible asset was its Associated Press franchise, but even this had been pledged as collateral for a $30,000 loan. A blanket mortgage on the whole enterprise was held by President Taussig of the St. Louis Bridge and Railway Association.

So it was that the Sheriff of St. Louis County stood on the steps of the new courthouse, on the morning of December 9, 1878, and proclaimed to all and sundry within earshot, know all men by these presents, etc., that he would sell at public auction to the highest bidder one newspaper, to wit, etc., the *St. Louis Dispatch*.

In the discussion preceding the sale, some of the creditors thought the *Dispatch* might be worth as much as $40,000, but the consensus of newspaper opinion was:

"It's not worth a damn!"

The sheriff also made clear that the sale was subject to the $30,000 lien. Did he hear any bidders? Would anybody make an offer?

"Twenty-five hundred dollars!"

The bidder was a certain Samuel Arnold, who appears just once in this narrative. The sheriff did not seem surprised. He employed none of the up-to-date auctioneering mechanisms, not even a hog-call aria. He did not offer to throw in a solid-gold-filled watch-an'-chain, a fountain pen, a set of the *Encyclopedia Britannica,* and a pair of fur-lined mittens. He merely called the bid three times, twenty-five hundred dollars—going, going . . . sold! Not to the American Tobacco Company, but to the gentleman on the top step.

Arnold represented Joseph Pulitzer.

According to the story that went the rounds of the newspaper offices in later years, the sheriff knew about the bid before the sale, and did not encourage competition. According to this account, JP had interviewed Ed Butler, the Democratic boss, who was also the leading blacksmith and had the monopoly for shoeing the horses of the St. Louis streetcar system. There is also an apocryphal report that Butler advanced the purchase price. However, the accepted version is that it was JP's own money that was bid.

Anyway, he got the paper, and took full charge the next day. Aside from getting out the afternoon issue, his first task was to ap-

proach John A. Dillon, proprietor of the *Post*, the only other afternoon paper. The *Post* did not have an A.P. franchise. JP suggested
a merger. Dillon laughed. "Why," he said, "there's a mortgage
against the A.P. franchise." Pulitzer would see about that. He went
personally before the directors of the Associated Press, holding a
special meeting in Cincinnati, and argued that the franchise, being
an intangible privilege, could not legally be pledged as loan collateral. He won, thereby establishing a precedent which holds good
to this day.

Two days later, Dillon agreed to the merger. The combined paper
became the *St. Louis Post-Dispatch*. Dillon was to share in the profits,
but the running expenses were up to Pulitzer. He had $2,700, and
calculated that he could run the paper for about seventeen weeks.
Before the money was exhausted, the enterprise had begun to pay,
but once it ran so close to the edge that JP took out three hundred
dollars and put it aside as an emergency fund against the expected
arrival of his first heir.

The first issue of the *St. Louis Post-Dispatch* consisted of four
pages, seven columns to the page. More than half of page one was
taken by advertising. Burrell, Comstock, and Company announced
in bold type: "Christmas is coming. Our Shaw Patent Easy and
Reclining Chair is the Most Appropriate Present for a Holiday
Gift." Vandervoort and Barney desired the public to know that they
were "Continuing to Make Daily Additions to their Immense Variety of Useful, Sensible, and Intrinsically Valuable Articles, Specially
Appropriate for Holiday Presents."

The three columns reserved for first-page news were divided almost equally between "local" and "telegraph" items. None of them
could be classed as "hot."

On the editorial page, Mr. Pulitzer set forth the new policies of
the paper as follows:

"The *Post and Dispatch* [the name was changed a few days later
to *Post-Dispatch*] will serve no party but the people; will be no
organ of 'Republicanism,' but the organ of truth; will follow no
caucuses but its own convictions; will not support the 'Administration' but criticize it; will oppose all frauds and shams wherever and
whatever they are; will advocate principles and ideas rather than

Joseph Pulitzer, owner of the St. Louis Post-Dispatch

prejudices and partisanship. These ideas and principles are precisely the same as those upon which our government was originally founded and to which we owe our country's marvelous growth and development. They are the same that made a Republic possible and without which a real Republic is impossible. They are the idea of a true, genuine, real Democracy. They are the principles of true local self-government. They are the doctrines of hard money, home rule, and revenue reform."

St. Louis was unfamiliar with a paper like that. This new formula immediately attracted a large following. Wild rumors about the source of Pulitzer's backing floated over the city. One correspondent thought that he had discovered the fountain. He wrote to the new editor about it:

"It is common rumor on the streets that the gamblers have bought your silence and they have been running in full blast for the last two weeks undisturbed."

The *Post-Dispatch* made prompt reply:

"If they have bought our silence they have not paid the cash and we have no notes or other evidences of indebtedness to them. The existence of such a rumor, if, indeed, it exists, is merely another illustration of the advantages of looking for the news in the newspaper and not trusting to the idle gossip of the streets."

In the ensuing weeks and months, JP worked at his desk from early morning until midnight or later, interesting himself in every detail of the paper. Frequently he did not pause even for meals. He thought up crusades and news features that the public could not overlook. He exposed wealthy tax dodgers, boldly printing the names and the amount of personal taxes. He contrasted these payments with those of the poorer citizens. He offended the rich tax dodgers, but the poor flocked to his side, and the common people heard him gladly.

He poured out editorial fire upon gamblers, crooked politicians, and fraud in public contracts. He assailed the streetcar companies and the gas trust which but recently had come into existence. He urged the people to understand that the *Post-Dispatch* was their paper and their champion.

Public response was immediate and emphatic. Within three

months he had accumulated a group of wealthy enemies, but the circulation of the *Post-Dispatch* was increasing daily. New advertising was pouring in. Before the seventeen weeks were over he was adding to his cash reserves. Within three years, the *Post-Dispatch* was earning eighty-five thousand dollars a year.

The pace was too strenuous for Dillon. Within a year he retired and left the struggle to his dynamic associate. There was not much in the *Post-Dispatch* that did not receive Pulitzer's personal attention. He wrote editorials, handled news, and drummed up advertising. He refused to consider human limitations. His eyesight, abused by day and night, was becoming fainter, but he was too busy to care. His nervous system was beginning to crack, but he had no time to notice. His lungs, denied fresh air by indoor toil, were beginning to weaken, but he would not leave his desk. He was making frightful demands upon his vitality, but at the moment success was the only thing that counted.

Not until the *Post-Dispatch* had grown in power and circulation and had begun to press the *Globe-Democrat* did Mr. Pulitzer realize the need of another editor. The *Post-Dispatch* had become too big to be run by one man. JP looked over the St. Louis field, but found no one to meet his requirements. He canvassed the news editors of the nation and finally selected Colonel John A. Cockerill, then managing editor of the *Baltimore Gazette,* for ability, independence, and pugnacity. Cockerill accepted the managing editorship of the *Post-Dispatch,* and came to St. Louis early in 1880.

Cockerill was a two-fisted, fighting man, a hard worker, an excellent judge of news, and a born executive. He settled into the St. Louis field with the same ease as he previously had done in Baltimore, Cincinnati, Columbus, and Washington. He caught the Pulitzer spirit. For nearly three years he co-operated in building the *Post-Dispatch*. Then one day, in a flash of anger, he destroyed his usefulness to the paper.

It was in the political campaign of 1882. JP was away on a visit to New York. Colonel Cockerill was in charge of the editorial page. He was opposing the election of Colonel James O. Broadhead to Congress on the ground that the candidate, who was a lawyer, recently had deserted a client who was suing the gas trust and had gone over to the gas company's side.

Colonel Cockerill's caustic comments upon the episode were appreciated neither by Colonel Broadhead nor his law partners. Colonel A. W. Slayback, one of the partners, took personal umbrage at Cockerill's attacks and sought a quarrel with him. General William T. Sherman, however, brought the two men together at a clubhouse and, after a bibulous evening, they decided to forget their grievances. Unfortunately, this convivial settlement was soon upset. At a political meeting soon afterward, Slayback made a bitter attack on the *Post-Dispatch*. Now Cockerill's anger was aroused. He renewed warfare on Broadhead and printed an article about Slayback, sharply questioning the latter's reputation.

At five o'clock on the afternoon of October 2, 1882, as Cockerill was seated at his desk in conversation with two of his associates, Slayback, accompanied by a friend, suddenly appeared in the office. Slayback was yelling excitedly. Cockerill put his hand in the desk drawer, drew out a revolver, and fired. Slayback slipped to the floor and died.

Occurring in the heat of the campaign, the killing caused an uproar in St. Louis. A mob descended upon the *Post-Dispatch* office, muttering violent threats against him. "Let's burn the building!" they shouted. Police arrived and drove them away.

Colonel Cockerill himself was calm. He surrendered to the police, bail was provided, and he retired to his home. He never faced a jury for the killing. St. Louis authorities concluded that Slayback had entered Cockerill's office with belligerent intent.

But the tragedy was a heavy blow to the *Post-Dispatch*. JP rushed back from New York and gave Cockerill his loyal support as long as he could. Yet it was manifest that the episode had damaged the paper's prestige. Public meetings, addressed by JP's enemies, were held throughout the city. Circulation began to fall off. A crisis was at hand.

JP acted decisively. He told Cockerill that he must go. He then turned to his former partner, John A. Dillon, and asked him to become general manager of the *Post-Dispatch*. Dillon accepted and, after months of discouragement, finally turned the tide of opposition. By the spring of 1883, circulation was climbing, substantial advertisers were renewing their patronage, and the *Post-Dispatch* once again was to be found on respectable doorsteps.

JP had saved the newspaper, but the ordeal had affected his nerves. He was unable to sleep. He coughed, his appetite failed, and he lost weight. Severe headaches gave evidence of over-strained eyes. Forced at last to consult physicians, he was ordered to stop work immediately and take a cruise on the Mediterranean.

The patient demurred, but grudgingly surrendered. In May, accompanied by Mrs. Pulitzer and their four-year-old son, Ralph, he boarded a train for New York, where he planned to stay a few days before sailing. He could not foretell that his steamer would leave without him. He knew only that he was a sick man.

3. New York World

. . . Life brought its contest but . . . also the crown of all contest: no proud one! no jeweled circlet flaming through heaven . . . only some few leaves of wild olive, cool to the tired brow. . . .
—JOHN RUSKIN

THE FIRST *New York World* was launched on July 1, 1860, by Alexander Cummings, owner of the *Philadelphia Bulletin*, as a religious daily. Church notices pre-empted page one. Editorials were chiefly admonitions toward a better life here or hereafter. Advertising came largely from patent medicines; theater and amusements were excluded both as news and as sources of revenue.

The new paper attained popularity among the clergy, who received a special subscription rate of four dollars a year, but it failed to make money. After taking heavy losses, this *World* merged with the *Courier and Inquirer*, and the policy changed, but not the title. It was still the *World*.

During the Civil War, the paper was the principal mouthpiece of the so-called Copperheads opposed to Lincoln. Manton Marble, one of the ablest journalists of the period, became part owner and chief editor. Marble might have piloted the *World* safely through the war troubles, if the paper had not fallen for a famous hoax concocted by a former city editor of the *Times* in collusion with some Wall Street manipulators.

On the morning of Wednesday, May 18, 1864, a fake news report, made to look like Associated Press copy, was delivered to the New York newspaper offices, announcing a proclamation by Lincoln, calling for a new draft of four hundred thousand men and appointing a day of prayer for Union victory. Most of the *World*'s editors had gone home when the copy arrived, and the man in charge rushed the story into print. In a few minutes the false news was being bellowed all over the city. The *Journal of Commerce* also carried the report, but the *Times* and the *Tribune* were cautious and detected the fraud. The *Herald* printed a few copies with the proclamation, but was able to recall most of them.

The *World* immediately issued a special edition retracting the story and offering five hundred dollars' reward for the arrest of the forger; but within a few hours, Federal soldiers marched into the *World* building, arrested Marble, ordered the staff out, and shut the offices. The *World* and the *Journal of Commerce* editors were held in custody a few hours until released by Secretary of War Stanton, but the plants remained under military guard.

On the following Saturday, the perpetrator of the hoax was caught. His confession cleared the *World*. Marble resumed publication and printed a bitter protest in an open letter to Lincoln. The President paid no attention and the incident was closed. After the war, Marble became sole owner of the *World* and ran a dignified, conservative paper, not seeking mass circulation, and not getting it—nor much advertising either.

In 1876, Marble offered to sell the paper to William Henry Hurlbert, his associate editor. Hurlbert didn't have the money, but his friend, Thomas A. Scott, president of the Pennsylvania Railroad, bought the paper and put Hurlbert in charge. The new editor was a scholarly, slow-going thinker who loved to polish his sentences. He had occasional fits of rage which caused the *Herald* to nominate him "The Reverend Mephistopheles."

Under Scott's ownership, the *World* managed to retain some circulation and prestige, mostly among hard-shell Democrats. It was acceptable to residents of Fifth Avenue, Gramercy Park, Washington Square, and found favor in Wall Street. But it was a sick newspaper, suffering from chronic loss of circulation and hardening of the advertising. Scott's own health was just as bad, and a newspaper which showed only red figures was no comfort to an invalid.

Within three years Scott managed to unload. Just how it was done remains a mystery. The sale was not immediately announced, but presently the public became aware that the new owner was Jay Gould, the great financier, variously described in literature of the period as "the Wizard," "the Corsair," "the most hated man in America," and "the skunk of Wall Street."

The story that Gould related afterward was that he ran across Tom Scott in Switzerland. "Scott was broken financially, physically, and mentally," Gould said, "I felt a profound sympathy for him. He asked me as a favor to take his Texas Pacific Railroad off his hands. . . . In concluding the details, Scott appealed to me also to include the *World* in the transaction. I cared nothing about it, but finally yielded . . . It was simply an accidental trade."

Hurlbert told a different story. He said he had approached Gould at Scott's insistence and opened the negotiations.

What seems more probable is that Gould wanted the paper for a short while for a particular purpose. Although the chapters of Erie were long since closed, and Black Friday was only a black memory, Gould still had a fight in his system. He was casting eyes at the New York elevated railroads.

Gould changed the name of the paper to *New York World* and removed the twin hemispheres from the top of the front page. Also, he put up a new building for his project, a three-story affair at numbers 31-32 Park Row, where the original Park Theater used to shine. The *World* moved out of the Potter-Jones Building which it shared with the *Times*.

Hurlbert remained and kept on polishing his editorials. John Gilmer Speed was managing editor and business manager in one person—odd combination. News was very rigidly and very stupidly handled. Page one was about as exciting as Gray's *Elegy in a Country Churchyard*. Column one was devoted to "Five Minutes with the News of the Day," a sort of summary which was neither an intelligent condensation of news nor an index to the paper. Much of the news was carried under static heads such as "News of Brooklyn," "The Talk in Washington," "In the Criminal Courts," "Topics in London," "Our Mexican Letter," and "Items for Investors."

One can only surmise how Gould's *World* would have treated a German air raid on London—possibly as "Topic Number One, or The Descent of Sundry Explosives." But the *World*'s technique was not much worse than that of the old *Times* and the *Tribune*. Bennett's *Herald*, and Dana's *Sun* had more flair, both in news and in editorials. St. Clair McKelway, famous editor of the *Brooklyn Eagle,* who was then Washington correspondent for the *World,* said it was the best written and the least read newspaper of its period. But he was partly wrong. The *World's* only distinction was its editorial page. Its news approach was unbelievably crude.

For example, on May 10, 1883; page one, column five:

BROOKLYN NEWS

ALDERMAN PREPARING FOR AN IMMENSE CELEBRATION OF THE OPENING OF THE BRIDGE

It is the intention of the Brooklyn Common Council to have a big celebration over the opening of the East River Bridge. [No mention of the date of opening—May 24, 1883.] Alderman Dimon, chairman of the committee on arrangements, requests that communications may be sent to him by military, social, religious, benevolent, protective, and other societies and all persons and firms willing to take a part in the celebration.

So much for a bang-up advance story on one of the biggest news events of the year, a truly historic ceremony in which President Arthur, Governor Cleveland, Mayor Edson, and many other high dignitaries and distinguished citizens took part.

Gould was not thinking about the Brooklyn Bridge at all; his attention centered on the Sixth, Ninth, Third, and Second Avenue elevated railroads, then operated under a complicated set-up involving three different companies, the Manhattan Elevated Company and the New York Railway Company. Gould thought the system would be much better off and more profitable under one management—meaning, Gould control. In May, 1881, the *World's* financial editor began printing gloomy predictions about the stock of the Manhattan Elevated, the parent corporation. At the same time, under Gould's inspiration, the State Attorney General started suit to revoke the charter, and minority stockholders brought injunction proceedings, all calculated to break the price of the securities. By the end of summer, Manhattan stock which had been $57 a share, had dropped to $15. Gould, meanwhile, in collusion with Russell Sage, the great philanthropist, and Cyrus W. Field, of transatlantic cable fame, had been quietly buying control. By October the coup was completed. The Big Three now owned the elevated lines, and the *World* was gleefully predicting that the stock would rise, since "Mr. Gould and his associates have control and the Manhattan has been rescued by men who have the brains and the means to make the most of it." It rose.

The *New York Times* then ran a series of articles exposing the deal, winding up with the declaration: "There is no more disgraceful chapter in the history of stock jobbing than that which records the operations of Jay Gould, Russell Sage and Cyrus W. Field in securing control of the system of elevated railways in New York."

Later on, Gould wiped out Field and eliminated Sage. The *World* had served its purpose. By 1883, Gould was looking around for a buyer, or, more accurately, a "sucker"; always thoughtful of his friends, he tried to interest his broker, Washington E. Connor, in a one-third control, but Connor, learning that the *World* was losing $40,000 a year, declined with fervor. Gould had caught a bull by the tail and wanted someone to help him let go. The Czar of Western Union could afford to spend much more than forty thousand dollars a year on his Fifth Avenue flower garden, but the *World* was not a hobby. After the Manhattan deal, the public seemed to like the paper even less. Had Wizard Gould retained control, the *World* might have dried up and vanished. . . .

Things were certainly moving in that direction by May, 1883. The circulation was down to twelve thousand daily. But Gould was always lucky. Word came to the Western Union offices at 195 Broadway that a gentleman from out of town wished to discuss an important matter.

Who is the gentleman and what the hell does he want? It is with regard to the *World*. Ah-a-a-a . . . that's different. Mr. Gould will be pleased. The appointment is made for May 8. Gould, who advises his friends not to have compunction if they expect to succeed in finance, is not going to be bothered by scruples. After his masterly double-crossing of his own associates on Black Friday and the trimming administered to Vanderbilt in Erie; the conquests in Western Union, and Union Pacific—to say nothing of that little flier in Manhattan Elevated—selling the *World* at a padded figure ought to be a pushover. If the gentleman is a sucker Mr. Gould will not be un-reasonable, charging only what the gullibility will bear. Mr. Gould is resolved. The old motto still waves as the door opens and the caller is announced: "MR. JOSEPH PULITZER OF ST. LOUIS."

If anybody kept stenographic minutes of the conversations be-tween Jay Gould and Joseph Pulitzer on that bright May 8 when each was angling to get what he wanted out of the other, the tran-script has not been handed down. How much maneuvering was necessary to reach the final price, $346,000, we do not know; the figure did not include the building, which remains in the Gould estate to this day. The $346,000 was just for plant and equipment; for the name and so-called "good will"; and whatever advertising contracts there were.

Gould always contended that he sold the *World* for just what it cost him, meaning the amount he paid Scott, plus the subsequent losses. No doubt, that was his argument in the talk with JP. But it seems more likely that he sized up his prospect, noted a certain eagerness which JP—never a good poker player—could not repress, and put the price as high as he dared.

We may well doubt that JP argued about the price at all. There was a difference between his point of view and that of the man across the desk. The small-statured, heavily bearded money wizard, whose name originally was Jason Gold, was a master salesman—imagine Jason, Gold, and fleece in one genius! Swarthy, thin, bilious-looking, with slightly effeminate manner, Gould seldom looked with his steely, protruding eyes directly at a victim; but he could talk persuasively, calmly, never demonstratively; never doubtful of his ability to consummate a legitimate swindle.

Actually, the *World* wasn't worth very much. There had been a fire in the Gould building the year after he bought the paper and much of the equipment had been damaged. Circulation and adver-tising were almost at the lowest possible ebb; and as for "good will," it was mostly imagination; all *The World* had was a certain aura of respectability—like many newspapers of our own time.

Furthermore, one readily imagines that Gould thought that the tall, strange-looking, scholarly-mannered visitor from the West must be a bit of an ass; otherwise, why should he buy the sheet at all? A man who would pay over a third of a million dollars for a concern that shows only a net loss of forty thousand dollars a year, must be, to put it politely, eccentric! (A similar line of reasoning was used by the Pulitzer trustees nearly fifty years later when Roy W. Howard agreed to pay $5,000,000 for an enterprise that showed, in its last year, a loss of $1,677,000. And Howard's was not the highest bid.)

In Gould's case, the evidence indicates that the wizard guessed wrong. The tall stranger seems to have known exactly what he was doing: in fact, he probably would have agreed to pay even more for Mr. Gould's white elephant. What? Nearly half a million dollars just for a "local habitation and a name"?

Precisely. All JP wanted was a foothold. Perhaps his uppermost thought was to get a nominally Democratic newspaper which he could make truly Democratic, not in the partisan sense, but fighting the battles of democracy with the weapons of fact and public opinion.

Besides, just as in St. Louis, he did not overlook the fact that the *World* had an Associated Press franchise. And the St. Louis experience, a wonderful school of journalism for the founder of a school, had taught him that even a broken-down paper, like the old *Dispatch,* can be revived and made successful if there is a policy: meaning first, a determination to get the news, get it right and get it ahead of the competition if possible, but get it right; second, to present it tersely, accurately, vividly, and in language that all can understand; third, to lead in the interpretation of significance, thus molding public opinion; fourth, to serve all the people, seek only the general welfare and never belong to parties, groups, classes, sections, or sects, or to any interest except the public interest.

For this opportunity which Gould was dangling—the chance to establish his own kind of newspaper in America's greatest field of journalism, in competition with Dana of the *Sun,* Bennett of the *Herald,* Jones of the *Times,* and Reid of the *Tribune*—JP was ready to pay a high price.

As to what price he had in mind when he entered Gould's office, there is not an inkling. Quite probably, he was not even thinking in terms of money, because his later habit was the other way. Of one thing he seems to have been sure: that it was better to start with something in the way of plant, equipment, a name, and an identity, no matter how miserable, than to start a new enterprise from scratch, with no established outlet. He had already developed the theory, tenaciously held through his life, that any young newspaperman, if he works hard, studies, improves his opportunities, sticks to his principles and convictions, and makes reasonably good use of the brains God gave him, can become editor, publisher, and even a newspaper owner; his argument was that there are always dilapidated and depreciated newspapers to be picked up and re-created, if the right spirit goes into the enterprise. "I like reporters," he used to say. "I want to encourage them."

If Jay Gould was satisfied merely to get back the money he had sunk in the *World,* it must be taken as a symptom of his ripe years—ripe for Wall Street; he had passed his zenith. The financier, at the time of the Pulitzer visit, was forty-seven almost to the day (JP had just passed his thirty-sixth birthday); but Gould was already an old man. His era was vanishing. The wave of corruption, financial and political, which followed the Civil War, had reached its denouement in the break-up of the Tweed Ring and the imprisonment of the Tammany boss. (Gould died at fifty-six—and Tweed had died in prison at the age of fifty-five, five years before the Gould-Pulitzer interview.)

Whatever the motives on either side, payment of the $346,000 was contracted for on a time basis: something down, we don't know how much, the rest secured only by the contract and Joseph Pulitzer's word. One thing about Gould—he knew when and how and whom to trust, if the prospective profits were worth the risk.

This is May 8, and the contracts are to be signed next day in Gould's office; the first payment is also due then. After leaving Gould's office, JP suffers an acute attack of doubt. In a nervous system already fatigued, reaction becomes over-reaction. Whether he suspects that he has been taken for a "buggy ride" by the great fox, we cannot say. In later years he remarked with amusement that any man could capitalize earnings, but Gould was the only one who could make capital out of a twenty per cent annual loss! Gould heard the story and was pleased.

In his hesitant mood, JP makes a wrong decision. On the way back to the Fifth Avenue Hotel where he and Mrs. Pulitzer are staying, in anticipation of the European trip, he stops off to impart the news of his purchase to his younger brother, Albert.

We must catch up with one part of the story here. . . .

Albert had come to the United States, encouraged by JP's pioneering, in 1867. From that time on, we catch only brief glimpses of him. He and JP quarreled in St. Louis, for no better cause, it seems, than Albert's extravagant fondness for American ice cream. JP loved luxury but detested all forms of gluttony. Albert had long ago abandoned his mother's plan for him to follow the priesthood; his tastes and inclinations appear to have been more earthy. In St. Louis he seems to have found no toe-hold, and in 1882, just six months before JP's advent, Albert was in New York starting a newspaper of his own—the *Morning Journal*—on a capital of about twenty-five thousand dollars to which JP contributed some small amount, possibly to keep Albert quiet. The *Morning Journal* was a breezy affair, containing mostly personal items and gossip, written in spicy, conversational style; but it made money from the start. And it sold for one cent!

When Albert and Joseph met that May evening, after JP's interview with Gould, the subject for discussion was:

Resolved, that there is room in New York City for another newspaper owned, operated, and edited by another Pulitzer.

Albert takes the negative with more than vigor. His argument is that the local field is already well supplied with editorial effort, and that two Pulitzers cannot occupy the same space at the same time. The summing up of Albert's case is very likely, in the best Cain-to-Abel manner, in substance:

"You're throwing your money away and making a fool of yourself!"

By the time JP gets back to his hotel, he is ready to throw up the whole venture. In a sudden burst of discouragement, nerves in a jangle, he tells his wife to pack up—they are going to Europe after all. She seems to realize that it is a sick man talking, and not the real JP. The story he told later was that he slept not a wink that night, but that she, with a rare combination of good sense and good humor, was able to talk away his fears.

By the time he reappears in the Gould office next morning, there is no hint of indecision in his manner. Gould is ready, the contracts are on his desk in duplicate, needing only the signatures. As he takes up the gold-tipped goose-feather pen, the great builder and destroyer of fortunes has the contented look which, to an experienced eye, always indicates that a sheep is about to be shorn.

But he pauses; habit is too strong; the temptation to slip something over at the last minute cannot be denied. There is just one little detail, he tells Pulitzer, that he has forgotten to mention: his son George, now nineteen years old—a fine lad, Mr. Pulitzer—holds just a tiny block of this *World* stock; 'twas a little present to George from his doting father, not then in his dotage. Mr. Pulitzer, he assumes, will have no objections to the boy retaining this little interest (something to keep George's mind off the women, perhaps?).

Gould has guessed wrong. JP is boiling inside with indignation but remains outwardly calm. There is no objection, he says, to letting the young Gould retain his stock—on one condition: that the *World* carries a standing notice announcing that although George has this interest, neither he nor the Gould family has any control or influence in the newspaper.

Mr. Gould's features take on the injured look he always wears when his motives are understood. Very well, since Mr. Pulitzer takes that view, let it pass. "I just thought you might like to have the young man associated with you."

The contracts are duly signed. JP walks out on Broadway into a new heaven and a new earth. The European plans are forgotten; forgotten also, the fearful panic of the night before; forgotten the headaches, the nervousness, the insomnia, the cough, the loss of weight and the strained eyes. Joseph Pulitzer owns *The World*!

The first installment of the $346,000 was paid out of the treasury of the *St. Louis Post-Dispatch*. The balance came from the earnings of *The World* itself. Gould could never get over it. The thing that had been for him merely a leak in the pocket, in Pulitzer's hands became a gold mine. Within three years, *The World* was bringing in profits at the rate of over half a million dollars a year.

If any prophet had told JP at this time that some forty-eight years later his heirs would dispose of this very property for five million dollars while it was bringing in about thirteen million dollars a year gross business, he probably would have refused to believe; he was becoming blind in more ways than one. He simply could not imagine how it was possible for his kind of newspaper not to make money.

Thursday, May 10, 1883.

This is one of those number ten combination days that seem to dominate the Pulitzer numeroscope. This is the tenth day of the one-half-tenth month of a year whose digits total twice ten. Whether JP has by this time formulated his pet superstition, we are not aware; but we do know he thinks this day is important. This is the day when he is to take over *The New York World* and make it his *World* for better or for worse, to have and to hold until death do them part; in sickness or in health; mostly in sickness, as it turns out, but today, JP rejoices as a strong man prepared to run a paper.

He is dressed for the occasion in a Prince Albert, one of those long double-breasted coats of black broadcloth trimmed with satin which, with light gray trousers, constituted the correct formal day-time attire for gentlemen until the latter part of the Gay Nineties; completing the outfit are a stiff white shirt with high stiff collar, parted at the throat—rather surprisingly spread, considering his shyness to exposure—and a rich black Ascot tie, fastened with a large pearl stickpin.

The Fifth Avenue Hotel is at Twenty-third Street, since converted into the Fifth Avenue Building, but at that time destined to have high political significance in the days of Republican Boss Tom Platt and Theodore Roosevelt. From that point to City Hall today is less than a ten minute subway ride, but in 1883 one had the choice of horse-drawn "stage" or private cab. We assume that JP took the more elegant mode: estimated trotting time—one-half hour.

What is more pleasant than May in New York when it *is* pleasant —with warm air, balmy sunshine, and fragrance from the parks; even more delightful in the eighties because we know not the aroma of the motor exhaust. JP's route is down Fifth Avenue to Fourteenth Street, thence down Broadway, teeming with cabs, and carriages bearing the contemporaries of the Goulds, the Vanderbilts, the Fisks, the Drews, the Whitneys, the Fishes, and all the other "who's-whos" to their places of business.

Today the weather is not up to par, whatever the market may be. There has been a heavy storm overnight. About three A.M. lightning struck the storage tanks of the Standard Oil Company on the New Jersey shore (about where Black Tom stands today) and a million dollars' worth of petroleum has gone up in flames; six men killed; Standard Oil shares not much affected. The storm has passed, but the metropolitan area is covered with a thin haze, half mist and half smoke from Jersey; the thermometer has gone down to forty-nine, but is now rising.

Busy New York hears reports of the million-dollar fire; everybody is talking about the storm; otherwise, as usual, the metropolis is intensely self-absorbed—every fellow firmly adhering to the conviction that he or she is the real center of the universe. We can hardly imagine that anybody cast more than a quick look of appraisal at the tall man in the hansom, except to note that he has a remarkable beard of reddish hue and an extraordinarily large wide-brimmed hat that gives him a theatrical touch. New York might easily have mistaken him for a concert manager, a player of "heavy" parts, or a theatrical producer; it will require much more time for the city to understand that this big, strange, exotic figure is Pulitzer the journalist; Pulitzer the political busybody; Pulitzer the news-getter, the campaign-wager; Pulitzer the self-appointed friend of the poor and trampler on the toes of the rich; Pulitzer, who is *The World*.

Naturally, there is no committee of welcome to honor the new proprietor of New York's weakest paper; no ticker tape, or torn-up telephone books, or contents of wastebaskets dumped out of the windows along Broadway; no red carpet outspread on the steps of City Hall; no Grover Whalen riding beside the new arrival with cutaway coat, high hat, and orchid in buttonhole; no "battery of cameras" waiting on the steps; no "army of reporters," no microphones, no H. V. Kaltenborns, George Hickses, Bob Trouts or other "ace reporters" of the radio. There is no cavalcade or motorcade back of the Pulitzer cab; no Mrs. Hylan riding with Mrs. Pulitzer listening with amusement to the visitor's comments and replying, "You said a mouthful, Queen!"

Nothing . . . absolutely nothing of the kind.

So far as New York is concerned, Pulitzer comes like water, and like wind he drifts down Broadway. Few people—not more than a few thousand—know that *The World* has changed hands again; that Gould is out and the man from St. Louis is in the driver's seat. *The World* of May 10 makes a dignified announcement that this newspaper "will be issued under Mr. Pulitzer's editorial management on and after tomorrow morning, May 11, 1883"—Signed, William Henry Hurlbert, who also commends Mr. Pulitzer to the confidence and good will of the New York public, not only because of JP's newspaper experience, but also because of "his loyalty to sound Democratic principles." JP [aside]: "Never belong to parties, not even the Democratic Party!"

The foregoing communication has created a stir in the New York area exactly equal to the commotion occasioned by the arrival and departure of a Hoboken ferryboat. The populace is not thinking about *The World* at all. As for JP, he is thinking of nothing else. Having been up since dawn, after a stormy night, without and within, he has read the paper from front to back, and as he journeys downtown, is mapping out changes in policy, style, and news development. He pays little attention to the sights and landmarks along the famous thoroughfare.

Arriving at Nos. 31-32 Park Row, Mr. Pulitzer enters his new domain; he shoots up the narrow staircase two and three steps at a clip in the manner of Joey, the St. Louis reporter. At the second floor, on which is the so-called editorial "sanctum," Messrs. Hurlbert and Speed greet the new owner in the careful manner of newspapermen about to lose their jobs. Assistant editors, copyreaders, and reporters watch the ceremony of welcome with mingled hope and fear; hope that Hurlbert and Speed, whom they like well, will be retained; hope, also, that their own positions, which they like still better, will be preserved; but fear that they are wrong in both respects.

JP has no time for ceremony. Thanking the gentlemen of *l'ancien régime* for their kind attention, he whips off his frock coat, impales it on a hook, strides to the nearest available desk, spreads out his well-marked copy of *The World*, and has gone to work before the staff knows what has happened. Hurlbert and Speed retire hesitantly, expecting the coming of the ax—which, it turns out, is not far off.

JP is all over the place. A one-man revolution shakes out the sedate old Hurlbert tradition. *The New York World* becomes *The World*. The twin hemispheres are put back on page one—a strange vignette which attempts to show an old-fashioned printing press shining—yes, actually throwing rays—on two worlds; old and new, presumably. Mr. Hurlbert's "Five Minutes with the News" goes into the hell-box. JP leads the paper with the big fire in New Jersey.

Lead position at that time is column one, front page. Later JP discovered that the last column on page one catches the reader's eye first; today all papers follow that principle.

The headline for the Jersey story is "THE DEADLY LIGHTNING"; subhead, "Six Lives and One Million Dollars Lost"—not so hot by our present standards, but better than "HAIL RABBIT SERUM," which a conservative metropolitan paper brought forth not long ago to herald a new cure for pneumonia. The lightning story takes most of two front-page columns (the art of "jumping" a story from page one—one of the curses of modern journalism—had not yet been found).

Columns two and three produce two stories that will set New Yorkers talking for many a day. Up in White Plains a condemned slayer is to be hanged on the morrow. He refuses to talk to priests. "I'm not a Catholic. I am a Democrat," he shouts, trying to shake the bars of his cell. Two days before Hurlbert gave this story one stick of type. JP dispatches a staff man to White Plains. The resulting story of Angelo Cornetti's last hours is lively stuff, though we never do find out what he was hanged for.

Next to Cornetti's farewell is a Wall Street story—the kind for which *The World* becomes famous. Other papers insist on treating financial news in terms of money instead of men. JP jolts the old custom, even if he does not permanently kill it. This particular story is that James R. Keene, the California skyrocket, has just sold a painting to his old rival, Gould—a famous masterpiece by Rosa Bonheur, cattle going to a fair. Keene bought it for $24,000 and is letting it go for $16,000. *World* reporters interview John Pondir, "Apollo of Wall Street," the broker who handled the sale; Washington E. Conner (Gould's own Broker); Henry Clews, and everybody else they can reach. Is it true that Keene is insolvent? Wall Street thinks so, but prefers to state that he is just short of ready money. JP's hunch is right. Keene is really "broke," as the subsequent bankruptcy proves.

For good measure, JP puts another execution right beside "KEENE'S GREAT SACRIFICE." The second hanging is in Pittsburgh. Ward McConkey pays the penalty for killing George McGuire in Dead Man Hollow, Pennsylvania. As the black cap goes over his eyes, McConkey shouts, "Good-bye, all ye murderers! Yer hangin' an innocent man!"

The last column of page one—there are only six—is comparatively mild, a report of dynamitings in Haiti in which four hundred persons are said to have been killed. The lack of factual detail probably grates on JP, but he needs the story. He fills out the column with the sad fate of Pauline, a much-wronged servant girl. These things may not sound very radical now, but in 1883 JP's methods were cataclysmic. You can judge how drastic they were by the fact that the *Times* next day ran the Jersey explosion on the back page, left out Cornetti, omitted Pauline, and led the paper with Governor Cleveland's conferences on the Public Offices Bill, known as "The Scrubwoman's Own."

By this time, Hurlbert and Speed are too weak to think. JP has already raided his brother's paper and brought in the *Journal*'s managing editor, E. C. Hancock. Hancock is no help at all except that he insists that Mr. Pulitzer must have an editorial about the new policy. Pausing in the midst of the perils of Pauline and McConkey's farewell, JP dashes off the following:

"The entire *World* newspaper property . . . will, from this day on, be under different management—different in men, measures and methods—different in purpose, policy and principle—different in objects and interests—different in sympathies and convictions—different in head and heart.

"Performance is better than promise. Exuberant assurances are cheap. I make none. I simply refer the public to the new *World* itself. . . .

"There is room in this great and growing city for a journal that is not only cheap but bright, not only bright but large, not only large but truly democratic—dedicated to the cause of the people rather than that of the purse potentates—devoted more to the news of the New than the Old World—that will expose all fraud and sham, fight all public evils and abuses—that will serve and battle for the people with earnest sincerity."

The new editor-owner further indicates the changed policy in another editorial:

"TRUE DEMOCRACY

"An intelligent newspaper must be independent. But it must not be indifferent or neutral in any question involving public interests. . . . It must maintain those broad principles on which universal liberty is based. . . .

"Its rock of faith must be true democracy. Not the democracy of a political machine. . . . But the democracy which guards with jealous care the rights of all alike and perpetuates the free institutions it first established.

"*The World*, under its new management, will maintain such a democratic character. . . ."

JP writes the entire editorial page, at the same time handling news copy and directing the writing of stories. Included among the editorials is a nice good-bye to Hurlbert, which is real news to that gentleman. The article entitled "Mr. Hurlbert's retirement" appreciates the *Brooklyn Eagle*'s tribute and concludes: "Mr. Hurlbert's friends may perhaps console themselves for his loss from active work in journalism by the hope that he may devote his well-earned leisure to some work which shall do more justice than the limitations of daily journalism permit to his matured and accomplished talents."

Hurlbert takes the hint. Hancock follows soon after, and JP wires Cockerill and John B. McGuffin to come on from St. Louis.

Pulitzer orders twenty-two thousand copies of the new *World*, and by noon of May 11 the newsstands are cleaned out. It is not in JP's nature to be completely satisfied (he used to say, "There is always a great deficit between aspiration and action"), but in the early morning of May 11, he must feel some gratification. *The World* is a new paper; every part of it—news, editorials, headlines—bears the stamp of a new spirit and a fresh approach.

If his reward is, for the moment, only the crown of wild olive— the pleasure of a job well done—at least he is not bashful. The next day's *World* carries two columns on page one devoted entirely to what New York thinks about *The World*—the verdict of the public, from the Mayor on down, is that the paper has a powerful kick, and they like it that way.

As a special feature for the Sunday issue, JP sends a reporter to interview Jay Gould. We quote:

"Mr. Gould, what do you think of the new *World*?"
"I like it first rate. I think it will be a great success. All I'm afraid of is that it will be a little too bright and pitch into me . . . it is wonderfully improved in its news and general appearance; but its editorial tone is not to my liking. I'm afraid it might become dangerous."

Many others in Mr. Gould's walk and way of life share his apprehension. For two days *The World* continues to circulate among the Fifth Avenue mansions, in the best clubs, and along Wall Street, in very limited quantity. The readers, habituated to Hurlbert's gentlemanly animadversions, thought the first Pulitzer editorials might be a mistake. But the lead editorial of Sunday, May 13, confirms their worst fears and puts *The World* for a long time on the social index expurgatorius. The lead editorial is headed, "Our Aristocracy," a blast that reverberates from the Battery to Central Park.

Here are the highlights:

"The ambition to ape foreign manners and customs has fostered several phases of aristocracy in New York. . . . It is a caricature of the original. It has about it the odor of codfish and not the mustiness of age.

"There are different phases of New York aristocracy. There is the aristocracy of gaudy establishments and mountebank liveries. Plush breeches, silk stockings, shoulder tags, cockades and coats that look as if they were staring at their visitor with a multitude of large brass eyes as big as a trade dollar.

"Then there is the aristocracy of Central Park. The low Victoria.
. . . The sleigh with more nodding plumes than would deck out
a company of lancers.

"There is the sordid aristocracy of the ambitious matchmakers,
who are ready to sell their daughters for barren titles to worthless
foreign paupers. . . .

"The new *World* believes that such an aristocracy ought to have
no place in the republic—that the word ought to be expunged from
an American vocabulary.

"The *World*'s aristocracy is the aristocracy of labor. The man who
by honest, earnest toil supports his family in respectability, who
. . . fights his way through life courageously . . . is the proudest
aristocrat in the American republic.

"Our aristocracy is the aristocracy of brains and honor. . . . The
genius that invents, the skill that accomplishes . . . makes its pos-
sessor an aristocrat for whom the new *World* will always be ready
to speak.

"Our aristocracy is the aristocracy of virtue. . . . Our aristocracy is the aristocracy of true nobility, which sympathizes with, assists
and benefits its fellow men.

"Money alone makes no aristocrats."

This is too much. For a long time thereafter *The World's* only
readers along Fifth Avenue rank no higher than the upstairs maid
or the butler.

Other newspapers throughout the nation comment favorably; the
press of New York takes little notice, but the *Sun* extends a rather
ambiguous welcome.

"We notice without surprise," editorializes Charles Anderson
Dana, "that the journals of this city have not paid much attention to
Mr. Joseph Pulitzer. . . . There is a natural disposition against
gratuitous advertising, but this need not prevent our welcoming a
clever man . . . especially when he has once been a correspondent
of the *Sun*, which shines for all.

"Mr. Pulitzer possesses a quick and fluent mind with a good share
of originality and brightness; but he has always seemed to us rather
deficient in judgment and in staying power. . . . Anyway, we
tender all sorts of friendly wishes. . . ."

JP is delighted. As for being deficient in judgment and staying power, he replies, he "has always stayed where he pleased . . . and he has never made any moves which were not clearly for the better." And he adds—"If the editor of *The World* has shown deficiency of judgment heretofore, it has been because he has tried not only to imitate, but even to excel the *Sun* in its truthfulness, fearlessness, independence, and vigor."

Thus begin the famous duels between Dana and Pulitzer, to become more bitter as time goes on. Respectful of his own intellectual gifts, Mr. Dana is not eager to recognize the Pulitzer genius. Nor does he appreciate JP's indomitable spirit—not until *The World* has cut deeply into the *Sun's* circulation.

By that time, *The World* and Pulitzer were anathema to Dana. In the mind of the *Sun's* illustrious but embittered editor, JP stood for—"Jew-Pulitzer"!

In the frenzied weeks that follow, JP functions with bewildering versatility. Besides bringing Cockerill from St. Louis to be managing editor, and McGuffin to the business office, he also summons David Sutton from the *Post-Dispatch* to *The World's* city desk. Meanwhile, he handles news and writes editorials; he amazes reporters with new kinds of assignments; bombards copyreaders with directions; keeps one eye on the business office; and pokes his nose into the composing room. He bursts into the office early in the morning and remains until the next day's paper comes out.

James B. Townsend, one editor who survived the holocaust, wrote in later years:

"I hardly knew the office. A cyclone had struck . . . men were hurrying around with excited faces . . . messenger boys coming and going in droves. . . .

"JP seemed to be everywhere . . . now arguing with a reporter; now dashing to the composing room; now suddenly descending on the market editor. . . . He loved argument. . . . He told me once that it is in debate that a man's qualities appear—above all, whether he has moral courage. 'Without that,' he said, 'no man can work for me very long.' "

"In one week's time *The World* had become the bull in the China shop of New York journalism. The public wondered . . . then gasped . . . then condemned or admired, while other newspapers began to attack *The World* and its founder."

Cockerill, McGuffin, and Sutton take over some detail, but none of the responsibility. JP has more time for editorials but never for a moment relaxes his grip on the news. The "editorial council" (forerunner of the pompous proceedings held in the Tower after JP's death) is held daily at eleven A.M.

Quoting William O. Inglis, a reporter of those hectic days, later a star of the revitalized *World,* now with Standard Oil:

"The council was a thunderous proceeding, attended by JP, Cockerill, Sutton, and later William H. Merrill [brilliant editorial writer imported from the *Boston Herald*]. The editors met in Mr. Pulitzer's office, separated from the newsroom only by a thin partition. As the voices of JP and his advisers rose higher and louder, Fred Duneka and Fred Shipman at the city desk furnished the gestures, thus combining the thunder of Demosthenes with the acrobatics of Billy Sunday!"

Sometimes an irate visitor added to the general uproar of *The World's* newsroom. There was no reception room and no doorkeeper; anyone could wander in. One day a Tammany district leader burst in.

"What the hell do you mean," he roared at Dave Sutton, city editor, "by printing all this stuff about me? By God, I'll have the law on you! What's more, for two cents, I'd—"

He was pounding Sutton's desk with his fist when a roly-poly little man with white curls walked out from the "sanctum," seized the big politician by the neck and pants, rushed him across the newsroom, and kicked him downstairs.

"The damn fool was making so much noise that I couldn't write my editorial," the little man apologized. He looked little, but in his youth he had been a wrestler and circus strong man known as "Little Hercules." His name was Douglas Levine. Although seventy, he could still toss the big fellows around!

Merrill was the antithesis of JP—perhaps that was why he was chosen. The new owner needed a balance wheel. Pulitzer was impulsive; Merrill, cautious; JP was quick to wrath; Merrill, slow-tempered; JP's life was irregular; Merrill's, ordered by habit.

One day Merrill wrote an editorial about a bill pending in Washington. As the Senate was to vote on the measure that night, Merrill decided to go home for dinner and return later to make any necessary changes in the copy.

"Why do that?" JP fumed. "Why go all the way uptown and back? Why not stay here till the Senate acts and take dinner later?"

"Because," replied Merrill, "in twenty-five years I have never missed dinner at seven."

"My God!"

"Yes," continued the complacent editor. "I rise at seven o'clock, breakfast at seven-thirty, read the papers until eight-thirty, ride my horse in Central Park until nine, and then take the 'El' downtown. By ten, I am at my desk. I lunch at one; finish my work and go home for dinner. At ten-thirty I am in bed."

"What boredom!" JP commented. "I breakfast when I get up, lunch when I get the chance. If I never get it, I forget it. Sometimes I dine at seven, sometimes at midnight, sometimes not at all; and I never get to bed until four or five o'clock in the morning. Everything depends on the news; the hours make no difference to me."

"Perhaps not now," admonished Merrill, "but sooner or later this will break down your health. No constitution could stand it."

As always, until too late, JP disregarded the warning. Patting Merrill affectionately, he said:

"My dear Old Man!"

HOME FOR LIBERTY

The outlines of Joseph Pulitzer's genius now begin to appear. He was not so much a creator as a re-creator. His was not the rugged frontier type which blazes trails through the forest primeval; he belonged to the Second Wave, the builders who follow the pioneers, picking up and refashioning enterprises abandoned or ruined by hardier men. JP did not build an original situation, but he was wonderfully effective in seizing upon an old situation and breathing new life into what looked like a corpse.

In St. Louis and later in New York, JP took over broken-down papers and made them live. But he was not to be the star performer in his own circus. As a newspaperman, he was a good artisan. He could write a story; edit copy; write heads; make up the paper; carve out a strong editorial; even keep the accounts if necessary. But he discovered that other men could do all these jobs better than himself. As a writer of editorials, his ideas were strong, definite, challenging, but his style was not brilliant; he was too fond of reiteration, even alliteration; his effects were labored. In reading a JP editorial, you can feel the man suffer while he works.

His genius was his ability to inspire other men. He would work shoulder to shoulder with them, sharing the long hours, the hit-and-miss mealtimes; the burden of digging out facts. And he was pitiless toward the finished product, even if he had helped to fashion it.

It was JP's prime distinction in the New York arena that he would seize upon the stories which the competitors neglected, either through laziness or stupidity, or false standards of "dignity."

Thus, in the course of his first day on *The World,* he grabbed for exploitation stories like Cornetti's execution and the sale of Keene's art—stories which the *Times,* the *Tribune,* and the *Sun* were too proud to notice. The *Herald* was not so stiff-necked. Dana may have been JP's early model, but James Gordon Bennett became his pacemaker. Pulitzer judged each day's *World* by the yardstick of how well it compared with the *Herald.* The *Herald* set the standard for completeness of coverage, smartness of treatment, and the getting of "scoops." The *Herald* also had something that Pulitzer envied and strove mightily to develop in his own staff: sophistication and the art of irony.

Irony does not flourish in a soil of intense and deadly effort. *The World* editors, for the most part, until long after JP's death, were about as ironical as Barnum's Bearded Lady. The *Herald,* with its dance of death atmosphere, its eat-drink-and-be-smart attitude, could afford to toy with ideas. Mr. Bennett set no standards of public morality which the staff had to respect. Men of *The World,* on the other hand, were constantly hampered by the thought that *The World* was a torch-bearer which could not afford to indulge in levity. This was a complete misconception of JP's attitude.

The contrast between the Bennett and the Pulitzer philosophies is illustrated in a story about JP's meeting Bennett in Paris. Commodore Bennett, as he liked to be called, had just made a long-term lease on the property on Herald Square where the *Herald* stood for many years and where Minerva and The Bell Ringers now dwell alone.

"Why did you not buy the land outright?" JP asked. "I couldn't sleep if I thought that some day someone else would own the ground on which my building stands."

Bennett replied:

"When the *Herald's* lease expires, I shall not be here to worry about it."

The Herald Building is gone. The Pulitzer estate still owns the World Building and the ground, but neither Bennett's paper nor Pulitzer's *World* has retained its identity. Time and change draw no distinctions between Crusader and Stoic.

But for a span of years there is a difference between JP's *World* and its competitors, not only in the getting of news, the development of news, the interpretation of news, and the formation of public opinion through the bombardment of fact and conclusion, but *The World* is under the constant command to *Lead, lead, lead!*

The essence of the Pulitzer policy, the heart and soul of it, is to discover some public good that can be achieved and then work toward the accomplishment of that goal.

For this, the logical as well as the ideal medium is the crusade or newspaper campaign. JP did not originate this technique, but he made it peculiarly a property of *The World*. Having learned the method in St. Louis, he lost not a day getting it started in the bigger field. Having noted, in Mr. Hurlbert's paper, the very inadequate treatment of the Brooklyn Bridge story, Pulitzer made it *The World's* own story. A week before the bridge opened he was demanding that the five-cent fare for foot passengers be abolished. Vehicles, he thought, should in time also go free. Though this was not an intensive campaign, it bore fruit eventually.

There is a legend that JP originated the movement to provide a pedestal for the Statue of Liberty on Bedloe Island. This is not accurate. Long before *The World* changed hands, there was a committee at work trying to raise the money for the pedestal—in fact, this committee had already collected $100,000 and expected to find

the balance, $150,000. On May 9, 1883, the day when JP signed
The World contract, there was a small item in the paper stating that
the committee "expected shortly that a plan will be devised for opening subscription lists in the newspapers."

This, undoubtedly, was the source of JP's inspiration for the
Statue of Liberty crusade. It was not his in the beginning, but like
so many other causes, he made it *The World's* peculiar property.
The situation was that though the site had been selected on Bedloe
Island, and excavation for the base was about to start, the money
was not coming in rapidly enough to insure completion of the pedestal. Meanwhile, Miss Liberty, the $300,000 friendship gift of the
French people to the people of the United States, was waiting to
be shipped across the Atlantic—all dressed up but with nowhere
to stand.

Four days after taking over *The World,* JP took over the committee's idea of a popular subscription. In an editorial he wrote:

"The statue, the noble gift of our young sister Republic, is ready
for us. And here, in the commercial metropolis of the Western
World, where hundreds of our citizens reckon their wealth by millions, where our merchants and bankers and brokers are spoken of
as 'princes,' we stand haggling and begging and scheming to raise
enough money to procure a pedestal on which to place the Statue
when it arrives in our harbor.

"New York ought to blush. . . . The dash of one millionaire's
pen ought to spare the city further humiliation.

"As the rich citizens of New York have shown so much apathy,
let the poorer classes move. *The World* invites a popular subscription and offers to receive sums of one dollar and upwards. . . ."

Immediate results of the appeal were not gratifying. The next
day's mail brought ten dollars. One contributor wrote: "Your editorial strikes the right spot. Here's two dollars!" Another man wrote
that he earned only $1.50 a day, but would be glad to give one dollar
to "save the nation from disgrace." But there was no rush of giving.

JP, disappointed, was forced to postpone the crusade for a time.
Meanwhile the committee went plodding along.

Two years later the fund was still $100,000 short. Work on the
pedestal had stopped. This time JP was not to be discouraged. On

March 15, 1885, he made a fresh appeal. The money for the statue had come from the French people—from workingmen, tradesmen, shopgirls, and artisans.

"Let us respond in like manner," he pleaded. "Let us not wait for the millionaires to give this money. It is not a gift from the millionaires of France to the millionaires of America, but a gift of the whole people of France to the whole people of America.

"Take this appeal to yourself personally!"

Jeffersonian faith in the people was rewarded; money rolled in; work on the pedestal was resumed. In August *The World* announced that the necessary $100,000 was on hand.

The pedestal was completed in 1886 and in June the *Isère* steamed into New York Harbor with Miss Liberty on board. In October, with thousands attending formal ceremonies at Bedloe Island, the statue was officially accepted in behalf of the American people by President Cleveland.

JP always regarded this victory as the symbol of success for *The World*. He altered the page one vignette of *The World* to include the figure of Liberty, and some years afterward, in memory of his first triumph in the metropolis, also named his steam yacht *Liberty*.

It is a strange commentary upon the public spirit of the time that the patriotic task of raising this fund should have been left to an immigrant who had been hoaxed and ridiculed for years in "Liberty's most favored land."

Of all the millions who visit the Statue of Liberty, how many realize that but for the Hungarian immigrant, Joseph Pulitzer, the Statue might still be in France—rather a perilous place for Liberty just now.

In the interval between the Statue of Liberty campaigns, *The World* fought other crusades, most of them successfully.

One week after JP took the helm, the newspaper announced a ten-point program in ten lines:

1. Tax luxuries.
2. Tax inheritances.
3. Tax large incomes.
4. Tax monopolies.
5. Tax the privileged corporation.

6. A tariff for revenue.

7. Reform the civil service.

8. Punish corrupt officers.

9. Punish vote buying.

10. Punish employers who coerce their employees in elections.

The World recommended this platform "to the politicians in place of long-winded resolutions." Nine out of ten of the objectives were realized. (JP himself gave up the idea of "tariff for revenue only.")

Number ten—again the magic number—helped blaze the trail for the Corrupt Practices Act and the Hatch "Clean Politics" Act.

As to the taxing of monopolies, one is inclined to wonder whether the JP *World* would not have advocated a heavy tax on the licenses of radio broadcasting stations which, under the present system, enjoy the use of the public domain free of charge.

By the middle of May, 1883, *The World's* circulation had risen to 39,000 a day and was moving upward every day. Advertising was beginning to keep pace. But in August, JP wrote: "We feel as if our work was hardly begun."

Meanwhile, *The World* had fastened avidly on the Brooklyn Bridge story. For days before the official opening, the revitalized paper was playing up the advance plans, and two days before the historic May 24, *The World* actually ran a woodcut of the famous Roebling structure. The illustration was a forerunner of the days of newspaper photography in which *The World,* to a large degree, pioneered, until the tabloids came along and took away the initiative in that field.

The elaborate ceremonies attendant upon the opening of the bridge gave the Chief and his new staff their first opportunity for a "big spread." The plans were very nearly ruined at the last minute when the composing room went on strike because McGuffin had cut off the ice water and the soap. Hurried night conferences resulted in settling not only the ice and soap issues, but the wage scale too.

Incidentally, the Brooklyn Bridge opening occasioned a warm controversy in the New York papers. Indignant subscribers complained because May 24 was Queen Victoria's birthday; others maintained, with equal heat, that the date was a religious festival and charged that the whole thing was a Catholic plot and that the five-cent toll for pedestrians was for "Peter's Pence"! There were potential K.K.K. crackpots even in those days!

By the fall of 1883, *The World's* competitors were worried. The *Times* cut its price from four cents to two cents—to meet *The World's* price. The *Herald* dropped from three to two. JP commented merrily: "Brother Bennett, like Brother Jones [of the *Times*], now believes in Western journalism. Owing to the pressure of advertisements, *The World* will enlarge its size to at least eight more columns than the *Herald*."

JP's aptitude for human interest and the crusades were making steady inroads on the competition. He also started prize contests. The other papers began to sneer at "the gift enterprise sheet."

But the real ten-strike was in the illustrations—line cuts, of course, as halftone engraving for newspapers had not yet arrived. Pictures won new readers by the thousands and soon the other papers were using them. Years later JP smiled at the success of the experiment.

"They call me the father of illustrated journalism," he once told a group of newspapermen. "What folly! I never thought of any such thing. I had a small paper which had been dead for years, and I was trying in every way I could think of to build up its circulation. I wanted to put into each issue something that would arouse curiosity and make people want to buy the paper.

"What could I use for bait? A picture, of course. . . . On page one, in a position that would make *The World* stand out as the paper lay folded on the newsstand . . . a picture of someone prominent in the news of the day. There was a talented Russian artist in New York with a real genius for making portraits—Valerian Gribayedoff. I sent for him. Could he, with a photograph for model, draw a portrait so that it could be printed in *The World*?

"He could. Next day and every day thereafter, we showed in the upper right-hand section of our first page the picture of a statesman, a blushing bride, a fugitive absconder, or a murderer on occasion—whoever was most prominent in the day's doings. Circulation grew by the thousands.

"Soon we had to print more pictures, install more apparatus, engage artists to report happenings, produce a daily cartoon featuring important developments or whatever was uppermost in people's minds. The expense doubled—quadrupled—but I never regretted it."

The presumption is that Mr. Gribayedoff never did either, for he prospered as well as *The World*. But "Grib" always had a warm spot in his heart for his less fortunate fellow countrymen. Wandering down Park Row one day with a friend, Alexis Mamreov of the *Times,* he met a hulking fellow, dressed in fur cap, fur coat, and high boots typical of a Russian moujik.

"One of our boys," whispered Grib.

He hailed the stranger: "Vieye Russky?"

"Shure an' I like whiskey," said the big fellow, who happened to be from the Emerald Isle, "and right in here you can find the best Irish whiskey in the whole city."

"Come on," laughed Grib. "It's on me!"

Before the end of 1884, *The World's* circulation had reached 125,000 copies a day—ten times what it had been under Gould!

4. For Progress and Reform

"Whenever in the newspaper profession a man rises up who is original, strong, and bold enough to make his opinions a matter of consequence to the public, there will be personal journalism; and whenever newspapers are conducted only by commonplace individuals whose views are of no interest to the world and of no consequence to anybody there will be nothing but impersonal journalism."
— CHARLES ANDERSON DANA

IF GROVER CLEVELAND had suspected in 1874 that in ten years he was to be the Democratic candidate for President of the United States, he would have been more discreet. As it was, he became infatuated with the statuesque Buffalo widow, Maria Halpin, without dreaming that he was thereby providing one of the paramount issues for 1884.

And if James G. Blaine had known for certain, back in the early seventies, that he would be the Republican choice, he would have been more circumspect in his dealings with railroad officials, and certainly would not have confided in gentlemen who lacked sense enough to destroy embarrassing letters. As it was, the handsome and magnetic orator from the rock-ribbed state of Maine entangled himself with a railroad and thereby furnished another all-important issue for that memorable campaign.

And of course, in those years before 1884, neither of the candidates-to-be had the faintest notion that the man who would play the most powerful single part in the campaign was Joseph Pulitzer of *The World*.

JP appears to have been impressed by Cleveland the first day he edited news for *The World*. The report from Albany on the night of May 10, 1883, seems to bear the Pulitzer trade-mark. Instead of a

83

routine story about the governor "conferring on bills," the Albany
man, evidently under JP instructions, played up the governor himself. "Governor Cleveland," he wrote, "apparently likes work and
exhibits no desire to shirk it. [Man here after JP's own heart.] He
is thoroughly Democratic in his manner and modes. He is always
accessible. . . ."

A month later, JP, scanning the political horizon for a presidential
candidate to drive the "rascal" Republicans out of Washington,
wrote in an editorial entitled, "Another Cleveland."

"It may not be Governor Cleveland, who is doing fairly well in
Albany. But it will be another Cleveland," he predicted. "He need
not be great—he may not have distinguished himself in politics,
but he will sweep the country as effectively as Cleveland did when
he carried New York by 200,000 majority.

"The Democrats will find a national Cleveland, first to the astonishment and next to the gratification of the old leaders, who will
be loud in his praise after the election."

During the next twelve months, *The World* became convinced
that no "other Cleveland" was necessary. Emphatically, Grover
would do. From a slow start, he had emerged as honest, fearless, and
capable—a first-rate executive. Beginning as a lawyer in Buffalo,
plodding but conscientious, Cleveland became Sheriff of Erie
County, then Mayor of Buffalo in 1881. (This was long after the
Halpin romance.) Coming to grips with the Buffalo Common Council on political legislation, he became widely known as the "veto
mayor." The Democratic convention of 1882 nominated him for
governor over the fervent opposition of Tammany, led then by John
Kelly. His Republican opponent, Charles J. Folger, nominated
through the combined influences of President Chester A. Arthur
and Jay Gould, was badly worsted. Cleveland took office on January 1, 1883, and when discovered by Pulitzer was, in Cleveland's
language, "working like the devil and enjoying it."

Yes, JP concluded, Cleveland was indeed the man. The Democratic convention was to meet in Chicago on July 8, 1884. *The
World* set the keynote in a JP editorial of June 17.

"Mr. Cleveland," he wrote, "has displayed a straightforward,
unpretending desire to do his duty without regard to political con-

sequences. . . . His administration has shown honesty, sincerity, and good faith. . . . When a blathering ward politician objects to Cleveland because he is 'more of a Reformer than a Democrat' he furnishes the best argument in favor of Cleveland's nomination and election."

Meanwhile, the Republicans met and chose Blaine. His nomination was made possible by the fact that money was back of him and the fact that people forget. Blaine had tried for the nomination in 1876 and in 1880 and had failed both times because of the railroad scandal. A native of Pennsylvania, Blaine moved to Maine as a young man, and became a newspaper editor; was elected to the State legislature and then to Congress, where his ability quickly marked him for leadership. He was chosen Speaker of the House in 1869 and served five years. When a Democratic upsurge removed him, he left the chair with plaudits from both parties. By 1876, when Grant finally decided not to seek a third term, Blaine was the logical man—until it was whispered in Congress that Blaine, as Speaker, had done certain favors for the Little Rock and Fort Smith Railroad, in return for which he had been given a loan of $64,000, on stock of the railroad as security, stock which Blaine had bought at the market but which became almost worthless.

When the whispering became insistent, Blaine rose in the House to a point of personal privilege. Indignantly, he denied the stories. He denied the $64,000 loan. His relations with the railroad, he declared, were only those of an unfortunate investor. Nevertheless, the House voted to investigate. Star witness at the hearings was James Mulligan, former bookkeeper for Warren Fisher, Jr., the railroad's president.

Mulligan produced letters from Blaine to Fisher and Fisher to Blaine. The congressman was frightened. Obtaining a delay in the hearings, he secretly visited Mulligan in a Washington hotel and asked to see the file. Mulligan yielded, Blaine walked out with the letters and never came back. The House Judiciary Committee, outraged, demanded return of the letters. But Blaine got up on the floor of the House, again pleading privilege, and read the correspondence, but not in order. The embarrassing parts Blaine managed to gloss over sufficiently to quiet the outcry, and the investigation was dropped. However, the gossip kept him out of a presidential nomination for eight years.

The G.O.P. convention of 1884 was described by the independent and critical *Nation* as "a mass meeting of maniacs," but Wall Street was in the saddle and Blaine was Gould's man. After Blaine's nomination, JP was positive that Cleveland must be Blaine's opponent. "Grover Cleveland," declared *The World*, "is available—not assailable."

As the Democratic convention approached, *The World* kept telling its readers why it liked Cleveland. JP made it a crusade. *The World* likes Cleveland, he wrote; he comes from plain common people, has no aristocratic ancestry; owes everything to his own efforts and his own character; "does not speculate in stocks, does not build railroads; never did sit with Blaine as an associate. Cleveland," JP summed up, "is certain to make a good president—not brilliant and magnetic—but repulsive to the rascals who are preying on the government and who must be driven out of Washington."

Samuel Tilden, a Democratic favorite ever since Congress counted him out in the race against Hayes in 1876, eliminated himself. "I submit to the will of God," Tilden announced a month before the Democratic convention; "my public career is forever closed." Three days before the delegates assembled in Chicago, Tilden came out for Cleveland. *The World* was jubilant. On the third day of the convention, in spite of Tammany Boss Kelly and Wall Street, Cleveland won the nomination.

In the campaign that followed, the *Sun* lost its leadership of Democratic opinion. Dana gave lip service only. He had a personal grudge against Cleveland because the governor had failed before to appoint one of Dana's friends to the military staff in Albany. However, Dana could not stomach Blaine. "Cleveland may not be satisfactory as a Democrat," the *Sun* editorialized, "but Blaine is not honest as a man."

Dana's lukewarm support only heightened *The World's* crusade. In millions of people's minds, Cleveland and *The World* represented the Great Cause. *Sun* circulation fell off, while *The World's* went up—up to hitherto undreamed-of figures. The Pulitzer genius for stimulating public opinion was coming into its own.

The *Times,* the *Herald,* and the *Evening Post* fell in with *The World.* Newspapers all over the country took up cudgels for Cleveland. Even rock-ribbed Republican organs bolted the Blaine ticket. Party leaders jumped the traces: President Eliot of Harvard; JP's old friend, Carl Schurz; Charles Francis Adams; George Haven Putnam; over in Brooklyn's historic Plymouth Church, the Rev. Henry Ward Beecher condemned Blaine and prayed for Cleveland.

But the rising young Republican assemblyman, Theodore Roosevelt of New York, who had denounced Blaine in the convention, decided to be regular. He was for Blaine.

For ten days everything is going Cleveland's way, which is also *The World's* way . . . and then the scandal! The *Buffalo Evening Telegraph* comes out with the story of Cleveland and Maria Halpin —also charging that New York's governor had once led a dissolute life in Buffalo.

Cleveland had never denied his former infatuation with the lady. As to the parentage of her child, he had his doubts. Paternity seemed to be a corporation, rather than an individual. But, as the distinguished New York barrister, Cornelius Sullivan, remarked in connection with a different incident: "In all such cases, it is the treasurer of the corporation who pays and pays and pays."

In Maria's case, Cleveland is paying the bills to maintain her son in an orphan asylum and makes no bones about it.

The Buffalo story throws a bombshell into the Democratic ranks. Leaders all over the country telegraphed: "What shall we do? What'll we say?"

Cleveland answers: "Tell the truth."

Dana promptly seizes on the Halpin affair as an excuse to break away from Cleveland. The *Sun* comes out for the third-party candidate, General Benjamin F. Butler, nominee of the Greenback and the Anti-Monopoly minorities. It is a bad mistake. Before the campaign is over, the *Sun's* daily circulation has taken a nose dive from 137,000 down to 85,000.

Republican clergymen who have been supporting Cleveland are assailed by doubts and fears. Beecher demands that Cleveland clear himself. Conservatives from coast to coast are deeply shocked. Cleveland's campaign hangs by a thread.

Pulitzer is not dismayed. He refuses at first to believe the charges.

"Contemptible," he calls them. "Nobody but a dolt would pay any attention . . . no candidate with an ounce of common sense would be stupid enough to notice them . . . nothing but an old political trick."

The real issue of the campaign, JP volleys and thunders, is Blaine, whose corruptions have been exposed and affect his public record. No decent Republican paper, he predicts, will print the Cleveland scandal. He is wrong here. The whole country resounds. The "moral elements" are profoundly shocked. Dana exultingly demands that Cleveland withdraw. . . .

"At last," shouts the *Sun,* "the whole truth seems to be revealed. . . . Mr. Cleveland stands forth as a coarse person, unworthy of confidence and above all, most unworthy of high political preferment. . . . Cleveland should be withdrawn as a candidate by the indignant voice of the deluded and outraged Democracy."

A group of prominent clergymen, organized by the *Independent,* a powerful religious weekly, and headed by the Rev. Kingsley Twining, D.D., undertakes to find out the facts. Dr. James Freeman Clarke, Boston's Unitarian patriarch, also investigates. Clarke goes to Cleveland direct. The candidate cheerfully admits the indiscretions but denies that he railroaded Maria Halpin into an insane asylum or that he led a "dissolute life."

Dr. Clarke, satisfied, publicly defends the candidate. The report of the Twining committee also finds Cleveland a man more sinned against than sinning. *The World* prints the full document two days before it appears in the *Independent.* The headline is, "ENDORSED BY CLERGY." But the report is not that strong.

"There was no seduction, no adultery, no breach of promise, no obligation of marriage," Dr. Twining asserts. "But there was . . . a culpable irregularity of life, living as he was, as a bachelor, for which it was proper and is proper that he should suffer. . . .

"Whether such an offense can, in the course of years, be forgiven, will depend on one's eagerness to cast the first stone. For my part, I can forgive it when it has not been denied and its bitterest fruit has been accepted and all the duties which grew out of it generously discharged."

Plenty of others, however, are eager to cast that stone. The *Independent* repudiates the report, although Twining is a member of its own editorial staff, and the "personal impurity" of Mr. Cleveland moves the *Independent* to declare: "The attempt to force such a candidate upon the people would, in our opinion, disgrace the party which nominated him, and the whole nation, if he should be elected."

The World refuses to be shocked. JP furiously attacks Dana's insinuation that Cleveland, if elected, "would carry his harlots with him to Washington and lodge them near the White House." It is only the *Sun's* "filthy record" and its "cankered imagination" which paints Cleveland "as a sensuous beast and an animal."

"It is true that Gov. Cleveland once had a sporadic association with a middle-aged female," *The World* roars. "Is such an offense unpardonable? . . . If Grover Cleveland had a whole family of illegitimate children . . . he would be more worthy of the Presidential office than Blaine, the beggar at the feet of railroad jobbers, the prostitute in the Speaker's chair, the law-making broker in land grabs, the representative and agent of the corruptionists, monopolists, and enemies of the Republic."

A hot campaign—and dirty! Mr. Cleveland's friends are not overlooking any scandal, either. Some of them have been digging into Mr. Blaine's private life. The "evidence" is transmitted to Cleveland. The Democratic candidate throws the whole package into the ashcan, but the *Indianapolis Sentinel* comes out with a sensational story about Blaine's marriage, suggesting that the G.O.P. candidate's eldest son was born out of wedlock.

Blaine orders his attorneys to sue the Indianapolis paper for libel. JP applauds. He deplores the fact that the campaign has fallen to this low level. *The World* has received scores of letters, many of them from responsible sources, about the Republican standardbearer's private life, "and has destroyed them all."

"We make war," declares *The World,* "on a candidate's public record, not his private relations. There is enough that is open to attack in Mr. Blaine's official life without inquiring into his bachelor or family life." JP invites Blaine to sue *The World* for libel. The candidate does not respond.

Mulligan, meanwhile, has been looking over his old files, and finds more letters from Blaine to Fisher and Fisher to Blaine. One of them is a communication from Blaine, asking Fisher, the railroad official, to sign a letter enclosed by Blaine in which Fisher would exonerate Blaine of any improper conduct in the Little Rock matter. Fisher had refused to subscribe. In another letter, Blaine offers to assist Fisher's friends in establishing a bank in Little Rock. "It will be in my power," the former Speaker wrote, "to cast 'an anchor to windward in your behalf.' "

The new Mulligan discoveries appear in the newspapers of September 15. *The World* prints them "with humiliation."

"This amazing exhibit," JP declares, "is one to bring the blush of shame to every American."

The World calls particular attention to a letter of Fisher's detailing the loans he has made to Blaine without any repayment. Fisher adds: "Of all the parties connected with the Little Rock and Fort Smith Railroad no one has been so fortunate as yourself in obtaining money."

"All other issues sink into insignificance," sums up *The World*, "beside the crying necessity for reform—to see this self-convicted political prostitute presented to the suffrages of a great nation for their highest honor—the place once held by a Washington!"

Even then it is a toss-up as to whether Blaine's venality and political corruption will overshadow Cleveland's illegitimate child. According to the standards of the eighties, bribery does not compare in turpitude with adultery or "free love." Any Gallup poll conducted at that period would show Blaine well ahead in public favor. In spite of JP and *The World*, Blaine's election seems to be "in the bag." But in the closing days of the campaign he blunders into New York to snatch defeat from the jaws of success.

In almost every political campaign there comes a "break" which makes one candidate the certain victor and ruins the other one. In 1916 Hughes lost California by slighting Hiram Johnson. In 1928 Alfred E. Smith turned the tide the wrong way by injecting the

religious issue into his fateful Oklahoma City speech. In 1940 John
L. Lewis came out for Willkie and administered the kiss of death.

In the Cleveland-Blaine campaign, the bad breaks had been about
equally divided, but on October 29, the Republican nominee has the
misfortunes all to himself. In the morning, he attends a rally of
Protestant clergymen in the Fifth Avenue Hotel.

This is where the Rev. Samuel Burchard carves himself a permanent niche in the Hall of Famous Blunders. Delivering the address
of welcome to the candidate, Burchard casts this immortal monkey-
wrench into the Blaine campaign:

"We are Republicans, and we do not propose to leave our party
and identify ourselves with the party whose antecedents have been
. . . RUM, ROMANISM, and REBELLION!"

There is a flurry of applause. Blaine has either been out late the
night before, or has been thinking about the adventures of Grover
and Maria, or his campaign expense account. At any rate, his attention has been wandering. If he has heard, he does not compre-
hend. He lets the Burchard remark go by unrebuked.

Saddest words of pen or tongue: it might have been aborted (the
Burchard *faux pas,* that is)—but it isn't. Not until he reads *The
World* the next day does Blaine awake. But now it is too late. Politically he is dead and buried, and *The World* is conducting the funeral
service. JP rubs it in. How do the Irish supporters of Mr. Blaine
relish this one? he asks. "Mr. Blaine and his friends, in their eagerness to clutch at every chance of making political capital, have not
hesitated to inflame religious prejudices and to drag creeds into
politics. . . . Let the party of 'Rum, Romanism, and Rebellion'
resent the insult at the polls."

"The good Lord," Blaine lamented, "sent me an ass in the shape
of a preacher!"

This is Blaine's Black Wednesday. The evening performance is a
repetition of the morning, in terms of political asininity. Although
warned by friends to stay away, the G.O.P. standard-bearer cannot
refrain from attending a banquet at Delmonico's, given in his honor
by Jay Gould, Russell Sage, and other money kings of New York.
The handsome candidate is enthusiastically cheered as he makes his
way to the seat of distinction. The table, as *The World* reported next

day, is laden with the choicest of foods and rarest of wines. *World* reporters are barred, but the Associated Press is permitted to take down speeches. Blaine expands like the common stock of a Gould corporation.

Happiness reigns for a night, but grief cometh in the morning! *The World* has a story about "Belshazzar's Feast." Not only a news report of the dinner, but a cartoon by Walt McDougall, spread across the front page. The cartoon, entitled "The Royal Feast of Belshazzar Blaine and the Money Kings," shows the Republican candidate surrounded by diamond-studded millionaires feasting on Monopoly Soup, Lobby Pudding, Gould Pie—and at one side, a poor hungry man with wife and child, with hands outstretched to catch the crumbs from the rich man's table.

The McDougall cartoon causes the greatest sensation since Thomas Nast's caricatures of Boss Tweed and the Tammany Tiger. Even today, many regard it as the most effective political cartoon ever published in America. (Rollin Kirby's "Tammany!" cartoon published by *The World* in 1928 was just as striking, but not so vote-getting.)

The World's editorial page of October 30 is nearly all Blaine. JP writes:

"From 'Rum, Romanism, and Rebellion' at the Fifth Avenue Hotel, Mr. Blaine proceeded to the merry banquet of the Millionaires at Delmonico's, where champagne frothed and brandy sparkled in glasses that glittered like jewels. . . .

"The mask is off and Blaineism stands revealed in its true colors.

"Up to the present time we have heard from Blaine and his organs nothing but expressions of affection for the workingman of the country and eulogies upon the Republican Party as their 'protector.' . . .

"Read the list of Blaine's banqueters who are to fill his pockets with money to corrupt the ballot-box. Are they the friends of the workingman? What humbug! Are they in sympathy with labor? Fraud! Are they not mostly railroad kings, Wall Street millionaires, greedy monopolists, lobbyists, speculators and peculators, who have grown wealthy on public grants, legislation, and special privileges? . . .

THE ROYAL FEAST OF BELSHAZZAR BLAINE AND THE MONEY KINGS.

BELSHAZZAR'S FEAST, by Walt McDougall, from THE WORLD, October 30, 1884

"Do the people believe that the Jay Goulds, Sages, Fields, and others who banqueted at Delmonico's last night poured a corruption fund into Blaine's pocket without a consideration? . . .

"Shall Jay Gould rule this country? Shall he own the President?"

Nothing in the political annals of the nation compares with the excitement that prevailed in the last days of the Presidential campaign of 1884. Charges and countercharges are hurled indiscriminately. Street brawls are common all over the country. Thousands of Republicans parade up Broadway from the Battery to Madison Square from noon till long after dark shouting the familiar taunt:

> *"Ma! Ma! Where's my Pa?*
> *Gone to the White House,*
> *Ha! Ha! Ha!"*

The Democrats, not to be outdone by their rivals in this stimulating method of campaigning, form huge torchlight processions and tramp through the streets of New York crying:

> *"Blaine, Blaine, James G. Blaine,*
> *The continental liar from the State of Maine!"*

In this feverish state a nation went to the polls on Tuesday, November 4, 1884, and elected Grover Cleveland President of the United States. The vote was close and the result was in doubt for days while the country trembled in fear of civil strife.

Though misgivings may have assailed others, Joseph Pulitzer, rushing wildly about *The World* office, never doubts the result. Early in the evening it is evident that Cleveland has captured the doubtful states of New Jersey and Connecticut and that he is running well in the pivotal state of New York. Later, when word is flashed that the Pacific Coast is also going Democratic, JP is sure that the fight is won. He has predicted that Cleveland will carry New York by 60,000. He fails to make allowance for Tammany's hostility and a generous campaign fund.

Five editions of *The World* are printed for the morning of Wednesday, November 5, and 148,000 copies of the paper are sold. The last "extra" is published at eight A.M. with VICTORY! in its first column; beneath is the figure of a crowing rooster.

Whitelaw Reid's *New York Tribune* declares with equal assurance that Blaine has triumphed.

Actually, the election is in doubt. The count in New York is excruciatingly close. Cleveland apparently has a small majority, but the later returns from up-state, where the election machinery is Republican, threatens to reverse the advantage.

The fifth edition of *The World* concedes that Cleveland's majority in New York State will be reduced, but puts the Empire State's electoral vote definitely in the Democratic column.

Wednesday. Park Row is jammed. Thousands neglect their work, to stand in front of newspaper bulletin boards. Returns from up-state suddenly halt. The crowds become suspicious. Rumors spread that Jay Gould's Western Union Telegraph Company is holding up the returns.

Someone shouts, "Let's hang Jay Gould!" A crowd starts toward Gould's office at Dey Street and Broadway, singing, "We'll hang Jay Gould from a sour apple tree." Police break up the demonstration.

Next morning, *The World* still claims Cleveland's election, though conceding that his majority will be narrow. JP urges calmness and moderation until the official count is completed.

Eventually the official count proves that Cleveland has carried New York, but by less than 1,200. Cleveland has 219 electoral votes to Blaine's 182, but his popular plurality, in a total vote of more than ten million, is a bare 24,000.

Saturday morning the Associated Press flashes: "CLEVELAND ELECTED!"

This is no news in *The World* office. JP has known it ever since Tuesday night.

(What would he say if told that *The World* in 1916 would concede the election of Hughes before California came in with the vote that gave the victory to *The World's* candidate, Woodrow Wilson?)

But as to Cleveland's victory, JP writes:

"The beauty of this close contest is that it enables every political factor that strove for the election of Cleveland to say, 'We did it!' . . . While claims for the defeat of Mr. Blaine and the preservation of the Republic are coming up from every quarter, *permit us also to say that* The New York World *did it!"*

When *The World* was celebrating its first quarter-century, Cleveland sent a letter recalling the great struggle of 1884, and how brilliantly and sturdily *The World* fought for democracy, in this the first of its great battles in that cause.

"It [*The World*] was here, there, and everywhere, showering deadly blows upon the enemy," Cleveland acknowledged. "The contest was so close that if it had lacked the forceful and potent advocacy of democratic principles at that time by *The New York World* the result might have been reversed."

On high authority, therefore, credit for the first election of Grover Cleveland goes in large measure to the former Mississippi stoker and stevedore. And in making Cleveland president, JP was also making *The World* truly a national newspaper.

On the anniversary occasion, JP acknowledged Cleveland's tribute, but he also pointed out that *The World* was never a strictly Democratic party newspaper. And right after the 1884 election, he made it clear that *The World* was not going to be Cleveland's mouthpiece, either.

"*The World* is chained to no conqueror's chariot," he wrote. "It will gladly and zealously support all that is good in President Cleveland's administration, but it will oppose anything clearly wrong or mistaken.

"*The World* is as great a public trust as the Presidency."

Not until the election of Cleveland was officially settled did *The World* pay much attention to the minor contests. Then it was discovered that in the Ninth Congressional District of New York, the winning candidate for U. S. Representative was—Joseph Pulitzer.

During the campaign, JP had made not a single speech on his own behalf. He had been so absorbed in the Cleveland crusade that nobody thought to inquire, "Why don't you speak for yourself, Joe?" Having accepted a nomination only in the interests of "united Democracy" at the insistence of W. Bourke Cockran of Tammany Hall and William C. Whitney, leader of the independent faction, he could put no heart into the race. He took his seat in

Congress in December and in four months established a record for absence—unable to stay away from his own door. Opposition papers did not fail to play up his neglect of Congressional duties. He resigned in April.

From then on he was in politics up to his ears, but only with *The World*—never as an individual, either candidate or leader. Politically there is no distinction between Joseph Pulitzer and *The World*.

As to why one newspaper succeeds and another fails or merely stands still, we can only say that there is no universally accepted authority on the subject. Every owner, every editor, and every reporter who amounts to anything, has his own ideas and his own methods. Every newspaper shop has its own atmosphere and traditions.

One formula that seems to stand the test of time is to assemble a group of first-class newspaper men and let them fight it out. In the Hearst organization this has worked with a certain amount of success for the past fifty years. In the Hearst service (where I spent nearly three years) one has to fight to achieve something, and also be smart enough to prevent somebody else from undoing or preventing the thing you are trying to accomplish. The idea is to divide your time between doing something for the paper (something that will not only interest or astonish the public but also gain the attention of Mr. Hearst), and disparaging or blocking the efforts of your associates. You have to keep sharp watch on your desk and chair; if you go out to lunch, some other editor is apt to be sitting in your place when you return.

It reminds one of the old game called "Going to Jerusalem," in which there are more players than chairs. The contestants march around the chairs until the signal. The man who doesn't reach a chair fast enough is out of the game.

In *The World* office, after the passing of JP, the tendency was the other way. One was apt to reach a certain position and freeze there, neither advancing nor retreating. As city editor of *The* (morning) *World,* I established the record, holding the job from November, 1922, until the sale of the paper on February 27, 1931.

But in the early days under JP there was constant turmoil. If there was a method in his mad zest to make *The World* a great newspaper, the method was one that he evolved himself and did not learn from textbooks. Perhaps that is why he established the first really important school of journalism.

JP's tendency was to have more men than jobs, and all equally good men or nearly so. There would be two men, sometimes three, assigned to practically the same position; or assigned to supposedly different positions with different titles, but overlapping duties.

Soon after bringing Colonel Cockerill from St. Louis to take charge of the news, JP reached out and enticed Ballard Smith away from the *Herald*. Smith, coming originally from "Marse" Henry Watterson's *Louisville Courier-Journal,* had also served on the *Sun* before linking up with the *Herald*. In addition to being a gentleman and a scholar, he was a good newspaperman, and very important, had excellent social connections. He was a "find" for *The World*. JP appointed him "managing editor," at the same time designating Cockerill as "editor-in-charge." Whatever distinction existed in JP's mind was not apparent to the editors or the staff. However, this was only the beginning of a long series of conflicts and duplications of effort. As nearly as we understand the Pulitzer theory, the idea was to arouse competition, not directed toward the undoing of each other, but competition in doing most for the paper. The struggle between Smith and Cockerill finally ended in Cockerill's getting tired and resigning. But in the meantime, they worked out a *modus vivendi* which was all for the benefit of *The World*. They replaced the old staff and brought in fresh blood. Nellie Bly, who was to make the famous trip around the world in seventy-two days, was the first of some outstanding women reporters. Nellie was a lady but some of her "feature" assignments would make your hair curl. Bill Nye, the famous humorist, was brought in to do Sunday specials. Ward McAllister took over society news.

Cockerill was a great man for ideas, whereas Ballard Smith seems to have been a specialist in putting ideas into execution. Between them, they worked out a series of campaigns and exposés that thrilled and sometimes shocked the metropolitan populace. JP had to guard against over-sensationalism to prevent the real spirit of the crusading editorial page from being overbalanced by too many shocks and thrills on page one. That was one reason why he could never get away from *The World,* even in the latter days of his invalidism.

One of the Cockerill-Smith exploits was to send a woman reporter to the insane asylum on Blackwell's Island for several weeks. They sought to establish that the committing physicians and judges were incompetent and that conditions on the island were appalling. The young lady's reports bore out the theory. Although perfectly sane, she had been passed as crazy. "The police, the judge, the insanity experts, and the hospital physicians were thoroughly hoodwinked," *The World* asserted. "We regret the necessity of misleading these gentlemen even temporarily, but it was in the public service."

On the second anniversary of JP's ownership, *The World* announced its Sunday circulation as 150,054.

"As shown by interviews with news agents and dealers," *The World* declared, "its readers are not confined to any one locality or class. *The World* is sought after by the banker, the broker, the merchant, the mechanic, the artisan, and the wage earner. . . . Its devotion to the interests of the working people and its watchfulness on their behalf are rewarded by tens of thousands of readers."

As if symbolic of the bursting energy of *The World,* the Gould building was no longer big enough to house the business office. Outside space had to be rented. JP was beginning to think of a new building. A further barometer of the paper's popularity was the growth of the "want ads" (29,811 in one month) "reflecting the desires, wants, and needs of the masses."

In two years more, JP was able to announce that the annual profit was $500,000. The debt to Gould had been paid off. JP took notice, but by 1887 he had become almost completely absorbed in a civic battle that was not only to test his capabilities, but bring him right to the door of his own physical tragedy.

During the political excitement of 1884, New York's Board of Aldermen were absorbed in something besides the Blaine-Cleveland battle. This honorable body remained in session most of the hot summer debating the matter of a horse-car street railway for

Broadway. Jacob Sharp, reputed millionaire, owner of the Seventh Avenue Line, was bidding for a new franchise.

New York did not take altogether kindly to the idea of surface cars along Broadway. Most of the merchants were opposed. They thought it would "lower the tone" of the thoroughfare. *The World* was also against it. An editorial by JP called it "vandalism." Property owners united to fight the project.

Jacob Sharp first went up to Albany where the legislature was in session and had a "General Street Railway Act" introduced, empowering the New York Board of Aldermen to grant him a franchise. According to contemporary report, passage of the bill cost Sharp about $400,000, although he never admitted it. In fact, he didn't like to talk about that phase of his enterprise at all.

Returning to his fine residence on West Twenty-third Street, Sharp restudied the law and learned to his dismay that he would also have to persuade the aldermen. He made tactful advances. The answer he got was that the Board was not giving away franchises, but they might consider selling one. Sharp was discouraged. He had half a mind to drop the plan and let the old-fashioned stage coaches have Broadway forever. But his smarter nature prevailed. He asked, what price?

He was told that it was $500,000. He thought again.

"Will they take bonds of my company," he asked, "or do they insist upon cash?"

That was why the aldermen were in session all summer. Of course, they did not discuss the matter openly, but killed time with routine matters, while the leaders made up their minds behind closed doors. By the time the leaves began to fall, the question was settled.

The aldermen had decided to take the cash and let the credit go.

The act granting the franchise was passed but with two dissenting votes and repassed over the veto of Mayor Franklin Edson.

Now there *is* a hubbub! JP suspects fraud. Cockerill and Smith agree. Mayor Edson protests; he declares the rental ridiculous. *World* reporters are assigned to dig, dig, and dig. They can get little evidence. *The World* opposes the franchise on esthetic grounds for the present, while waiting for better ammunition. Property owners engage counsel. They obtain a temporary injunction; but, on May 23, 1885, the Supreme Court vacates the order, and before Joseph H. Choate, representing the property owners, can file an appeal, Sharp's workers are tearing up the paving stones and have begun laying the tracks from Fourteenth Street to City Hall. In the editorial words of JP, "The only grand thoroughfare of the city was torn up to make place for a street railway track which nobody but the jobbers want."

"This Broadway Railroad job," he charges, "was carried through the Board of Aldermen by bribery. It is a piece of vandalism as well as scoundrelism . . . another illustration of the helplessness of the public when unscrupulous capital organizes for plunder."

JP is short of proof, but feels sure of his ground, even though *The World's* reporters are unable to obtain concrete evidence of the crime. By December he has enough to justify *The World's* editorial demand for a legislative investigation. *The World* skirts the edge of libel by putting its charges in the form of questions.

Was any money put into the hands of John Keenan, commonly known as "the Bismarck of the County Democracy"? Was any money paid by Keenan to any member of the Board of Aldermen? If so, what amounts and to whom? Was $52,000 paid to one alderman representing an East Side district? Was $23,000 paid to a certain Republican alderman? Let them question William H. Moloney, the reading clerk, as to his knowledge of money having passed, etc.

Not until April, 1886, does the New York County Grand Jury get around to the matter. They indict all but two members of the Board—Hugh Grant, who was afterward elected Mayor, and John C. O'Connor, lawyer. Both had voted against the franchise. JP's editorial hails it as a "triumph of public opinion." And, he adds, it is gratifying to know that the bribe-givers will also be prosecuted, because their offense is worse than that of the bribe-takers.

Destiny seems to take a strong hand at this point. District Attorney Randolph B. Martine delegates the prosecution of the grafters to a young assistant, De Lancey Nicoll, whose conduct of the case deeply impresses JP. Before the end of summer, the first of the aldermen has been tried, convicted, and sentenced to prison. In October, the grand jury indicts Jacob Sharp. The promoter is arrested in front of his home just as he steps toward his coach. As the coachman, dressed in a bottle-green suit with silver buttons and red stripes, opens the carriage door and Sharp says "Central Park, James," three detectives step up.

"Sorry, Mr. Sharp, but you've been indicted for bribery and you're wanted downtown."

"All right," replies the streetcar magnate. "Jump in, gentlemen. Never mind Central Park, James. Drive to police headquarters!"

Late that evening the same coachman drives a weary and dejected Jacob Sharp back to the mansion on Twenty-third Street—at liberty for the time being on fifty thousand dollar bail.

The trial of Jacob Sharp does not take place until the following May. No fewer than two thousand talesmen are questioned and it takes over four weeks to get a jury. While the burden of the State's case falls chiefly on the shoulders of young Nicoll, another assistant, Colonel John R. Fellows, also plays an important part. "At least I was in the courtroom," Fellows remarked afterward. Nicoll's opening address to the jury lasts five and a half hours. Colonel Fellows cross-examines the defense witnesses, argues points of law, and sums up for the People.

The trial continues for nearly six weeks. Meanwhile Sharp comes and goes every day in his fine coach driven by the coachman in the bottle-green coat. But on June 29, the coach drives away from the Criminal Courts Building without the owner. Jacob Sharp is found guilty. The jury returns the verdict in thirteen minutes. Sharp is sentenced to serve four years in state's prison and to pay a fine of five thousand dollars.

While counsel argues his appeal, Sharp languishes in jail. Late in November, the Court of Appeals grants a new trial and the prisoner is released on bail, but his spirit is broken. Before another trial can be held he becomes gravely ill. On April 5, 1888, newspaper reporters wait outside his residence. A physician emerges.

"How is Mr. Sharp tonight, Doctor?"

"He will never face another jury," the physician replies. "Jacob Sharp is dead."

Immediately after the conviction of Sharp, JP in a *World* editorial calls upon Tammany Hall and the County Democracy, rival factions of the party, to unite on Nicoll for District Attorney. At first the *Herald* and the *Sun* join in the boom. The suggestion meets with little enthusiasm among the district leaders. Young Mr. Nicoll is altogether too much of the crusader type to please the politicians.

Before the city Democratic convention meets, the *Herald* and the *Sun* drop their support of Nicoll. The *Herald* endorses Martine for re-election (although the District Attorney has been slated for a judgeship) and Dana switches to Assistant D. A. Fitzgerald, who, it is reported, refused to prosecute the streetcar franchise boodlers.

Indignantly, JP threatens to bolt the party if the Democrats fail to nominate Nicoll.

"The friends of Jacob Sharp," he writes, "and the Aldermanic boodlers in and out of the penitentiary, the jobbers in politics and the enemies of this municipality generally are shouting that Mr. Martine must be kept in the District Attorney's office. This means that the thieves hope to place a docile friend on the bench and are extremely anxious to prevent Mr. Nicoll from becoming the successor to Mr. Martine."

In a front-page story next morning, *The World* speculates as to the reason for Dana's curious political somersault, one of a long series which has never been adequately explained. The *Sun's* editor does not like *The World* article. The fight is on. The editorial duel of the century gets into full swing, with the following blast from Dana:

"*The World* has taken up the cause of Mr. Nicoll after the fashion of a highwayman with a pistol. . . . *The World* breaks into the affairs of the city as train robbers enter an express car . . . does not plead the cause of Mr. Nicoll, but demands his nomination with coarse threats. . . . We have withdrawn our support from Mr. Nicoll because we distrust *The World* and its motives. . . ."

Dana goes on to imply, not very delicately, that the reason why a St. Louis grand jury failed to indict Colonel Cockerill in the Slayback affair was because Pulitzer had a hold on the Missouri prosecutor; and he insinuates that Pulitzer and Cockerill are now trying to control the District Attorney's office in New York.

"Can the *Sun* espouse this tainted cause?" Dana answers his own question: "We look with horror upon the contingency."

This is a challenge which *The World* cannot possibly ignore. In an editorial, on October 19, JP lets loose. (This is long before he had decided to treat opponents with exquisite politeness.) He shoots epithets recklessly—almost obscenely. The manner of attack reminds us of the Augustine incident in Jefferson City.

"The statements are malicious lies," *The World* declares, "about what might be expected from Charles Ananias Dana. A mendacious blackguard who, not content with four months of virulent lying about a candidate for the Presidency, has insidiously attacked his wife and sister; who has sought to annoy the widow of General Grant, and who has polluted the grave of Henry Ward Beecher to gratify his personal hatred, is capable of any distortion. . . .

"The revival of the St. Louis affair . . . is worthy of an assaulter of women and a mortgaged, broken-down calumniator in the last agonies of humiliation. . . . Two grand juries thoroughly investigated the case of Mr. Cockerill and refused even to return a bill. . . . No influence, direct or otherwise, was ever employed upon the public prosecutor. This is a plain statement of fact which mortgaged Dana, with all his ingenuity as an unmitigated scoundrel and actuated by a hatred which amounts to insanity, cannot controvert.

"It pleases Mr. Charles A. Dana to formulate a wicked lie defending his alliance with thieves. . . . The public will judge this as it has judged his other acts of cowardice, malice, and mendacity, and will punish him as it has for the last four years."

To our modern journalism, this type of Wild West rough-and-tumble encounter between editors may seem like opera bouffe, but in the eighties it was as common as insults between lawyers. The thing that distinguished the Pulitzer-Dana duel was its deadly character. Dana was fighting for his newspaper life and knew it. The tall, Jove-like scholar who had been setting the editorial pace for New York since the Civil War was thrown completely off balance by the young Lochinvar who had come out of the West and was taking the *Sun's* readers and advertising.

The tone for the campaign being thus pitched, Dana proceeds to hit Pulitzer in what he believes is the most vulnerable spot—race and religion. The *Sun* calls Pulitzer a renegade Jew who has denied his breed because he is ashamed of it. This was at least inaccurate. JP's father was only part Jewish and his mother was German-Catholic. In New York, the Pulitzer family, from the first, identified itself with the Protestant Episcopal Church, first at St. George's in Stuyvesant Square, later with St. Thomas's on Fifth avenue. JP was married in an Episcopal church and was buried in the same faith.

JP never discussed his religion. One of his secretaries, Harold Pollard, was of the opinion that Pulitzer shared the views of Disraeli, who said: "All sensible men have the same religion, and sensible men never tell."

It may have been in keeping with the robust journalism of 1887 for Dana to call JP a renegade Jew, but of this particular line of attack, *The World* took little notice.

When Tammany and the County Democracy, the two factions of the party, finally hold their convention, the nominee for District Attorney is neither the choice of *The World* nor of the *Sun*. The Democrats choose Assistant District Attorney John T. Fellows. Dana rushes to join the Fellows bandwagon, while *The World* supports Nicoll, now the candidate of the Republicans and the minority groups. On the same ticket, Martine is nominated for Judge of General Sessions.

The *Sun's* editorial page lashes itself into a fury. "The Democrats of New York," declares Dana, "will not yield one hair's breadth to the insolent demands of that political road agent [JP] . . . The candidate who stands for boss dictation is Nicoll and the boss behind Nicoll is Judas Pulitzer, who exudes the venom of a snake and wields the bludgeon of a bully . . . he has accepted the candidacy of Nicoll from the Republicans with as much thankfulness as in the days when he cringed for a nickel on a barroom floor. . . .

"If this Dick Turpin of journalism were capable of understanding . . . the remorse of the first Judas Iscariot would be as practically illustrated by his successor. But the contemporary Judas has not the sensibility of his prototype. . . . He will simply throw up his hands and exclaim, 'Vy, it was only my poom [boom]. I haf nothing against Meesder Vellows.' "

After finishing one of these literary stink-bombs, Dana wipes the vitriol off his pen and drives to Cooper Union where a mass meeting is rooting for Fellows. Next morning, the *Sun* reports Mr. Dana greeted with tumultuous cheers. But, according to *The World*, Dana was hissed. JP accepts *The World* reporter's version.

"That the dotard Dana should have been hissed by the friends of Fellows," he remarks editorially, "is not strange . . . they know his record as a Republican, a tool of Jim Fisk and Gould, an advocate of Boss Tweed, a betrayer of Hancock, a bolter against Tilden, an insulter of General Grant's widow, and a poltroon in an hour of danger. . . . How humiliating it would be to Ananias, if he had even the sensibility of an armadillo, to know that the men he seeks to serve despise him. Hissed in the home of his supposed friends! Poor, despised, disgraced, old Ananias!"

But while not letting Dana get away with anything really vital, *The World* never permits its readers to lose sight of the paramount issue. Again and again voters are reminded that the election of Nicoll is necessary to continue the prosecution of the "Boodle Aldermen." As *The World* has fought for more than two years to bring the bribe-takers to justice, it strongly suspects a political plot to obstruct justice. Dana, on the other hand, centers his fire mostly on Pulitzer, hoping to reduce the prestige of *The World*. His only reason for dropping Nicoll is to disparage Pulitzer, although he affects to believe that any candidate approved by Pulitzer must be inimical to public interest.

Dana's personal attacks on Pulitzer now become as rank as anything in the history of American journalism. And it must be admitted that JP's language regarding Dana is no model of restraint. Curiously, Dana gives particular notice to a purely collateral controversy—the question of whether Pulitzer is a Jew. Right on the morning of Election Day, the *Sun* reprints a piece from the *Hebrew Standard*.

"This would-be Sahib of the Bohemian race," the *Standard* asserts (meaning Pulitzer), "happens to be of Jewish extraction, which he denies. . . . He is a Jew who does not want to be a Jew. . . .

This unholy ambition to lord it over the people will probably not be laid at the door of the Jews, who have never been anxious to count him as their own. . . ."

Dana adds his own comment:

"The Jews of New York have no reason to be ashamed of Judas Pulitzer, if he has denied his race and religion . . . the shame rests exclusively upon himself. The insuperable obstacle in the way of his social progress is not the fact that he is a Jew, but in certain offensive personal qualities . . . his face is repulsive, not because the physiognomy is Hebraic, but because it is Pulitzeresque . . . cunning, malice, falseness, treachery, dishonesty, greed, and venal self-abasement have stamped their unmistakable traits . . . no art can eradicate them.

"Jewish citizens have the same interest as all other intelligent, self-respecting, and law-abiding people in the defeat of Pulitzer and his young dupe, Nicoll. The Jewish vote will contribute very largely to that effect."

Also cropping out on the Dana editorial page during the last days of the campaign: "Hungry Joe cannot deliver his green goods into the District Attorney's office." And: "I vonder vere I can get some hemb cheab!—Choe Bulitzer."

It seems amazing to us of the "new era" in journalism that an influential newspaper like the *Sun* would attack a competitor on Jewish grounds.

(For this, we should, in fairness thank the part-Jewish pioneer, Joseph Pulitzer, who took all that Dana could dish out in the way of racial inflammation and chose to ignore it. He refused to be diverted from the real issues by slurs against his origin or religion, thus helping to blaze the way for newspaper owners like the late Adolph S. Ochs, founder of the *Chattanooga Times* and rebuilder of the present *New York Times*.)

Election night. Tuesday, November 8, 1887. One of the fiercest and foulest campaigns in all New York history has finally ended. The votes are being counted and the returns are coming in to the newspaper offices. At the *Sun*, Dana has drafted his editorial for Wednesday's paper. The *Sun's* political reporters have canvassed

Tammany leaders and have given assurance that Fellows, the brilliant, easy-going ex-Confederate soldier, is as good as elected. The sixty-eight-year-old Dana waits at his desk like a seasoned watchdog, ready to spring at the throat of the political intruder, Pulitzer, as soon as the signal is given.

In his journalistic bones, Dana feels this is The Night when the death-blow will be struck at "Jew Pulitzer" and New York will be rid of his disturbing presence for good and all.

Over in the *World* Building, 31-32 Park Row, the newsroom surges with excitement. Cockerill is racing from desk to desk, sorting out the Associated Press copy. JP starts an editorial, tears it up, rushes out to hear the latest figures, leaps back to his own desk, keeping up a running fire of instructions to head-writers, rewrite men, make-up men, and tabulators.

Of all the election contests, only one has any real meaning for *The World* staff: is it Nicoll, or is it Fellows? Will *The World* score another victory like the election of Cleveland? Or is it true that New York, this time, is against *The World?*

JP is a very sick man but does not know it. His fair, womanlike complexion is alternately burning as with a fever, or turning deathly white. The strain of the campaign, the poundings of Dana, the bitter anger that cannot be fully released on the editorial page; the incessant demands for facts, the long, long hours—added to twenty years of overwork and neglected health—all are taking a terrific toll of a constitution never too rugged. Something devastating is going on inside his nervous system; his eyesight is breaking. But this is all forgotten in the flame and fury of a never-to-be-forgotten night.

We are spared the details. None of that *World* staff has handed down the complete record. Some time around twelve o'clock, the trend of the returns is too strong to be mistaken: Fellows is winning, Nicoll is beaten. . . . *The World* has lost its fight.

The final figures are: Fellows, 99,798; Nicoll, 77,556.

There is no magic number ten combination in those results. They spell defeat for *The World,* humiliation for Pulitzer, triumph for Dana!

Tammany Hall resounds with jubilation; in the Democratic clubhouses throughout the city the workers are hailing Dana. This is

Dana's night, no mistake. The Great Editor wastes no time. Before the count is finished, his editorial, calculated to write "Finis" to Pulitzer's career in New York, is ready. Dana orders the crowing rooster put on page one, signifying "Democracy Wins"!

On the *Sun's* editorial page, Dana lets fly the works:

"And now, Pulitzer, a word with you!

"You stand before this community in the same startling light that you stood in some years ago in St. Louis when your career of scandal and blackmail culminated in murder. You have reached your apogee of remunerative infamy here without having had to resort to any form of homicide. In fact, your path here has been easier than it was there, and marked by fewer asperities. The main thing, Pulitzer, is that you have arrived. You have got here.

"Now, however congenial to you may be the contempt of mankind, and however you may prize the testimony of general aversion, it cannot be denied that such an attitude on the part of the public has for you its practical disadvantages. We could wish with all our heart, Pulitzer, that St. Louis had possessed a stronger stomach. You might have stayed there, Pulitzer, and then we should have been spared the infliction of your presence here. Today you are a fugitive from the unexecuted justice of that town [untrue] . . . a fugitive from the scorn, the ridicule, and the contumely of its people. However much you enjoyed earning these evidences of their consideration, you suffered too much incidental annoyance in practical matters of life to make it possible to abide there further: and hence your despicable excursion to this metropolis. We wish, Pulitzer, that you had never come.

"But that you are here is indisputable, and that the public has found you out is obvious. In this experimental stage of universal sentiment it is not possible to state definitely what your fate will be. We do not know. We can only see clearly that it will be something unpleasant.

"Perhaps your lot will be like that of the mythical unfortunate of the same race you belong to and deny, that weird creation of medieval legend, a creation, by the way, far more prepossessing than you are— we mean, The Wandering Jew! In that case it may shortly please the inscrutable Providence, which has chastened us with your presence, to give you that stern and dreadful signal—

"Move on, Pulitzer, move on!"

It is one of JP's predominant characteristics (to become still more marked as years march on) to fret, or even go into a fury over some small thing, like a mistake in names, or a wrong address, or bumping his nose into a door. In such instances he might fall to cursing "like a very drab, a scullion"—even splitting words to insert a profanity, like "inde-goddam-pendent" or "stupid piece of re-goddam-porting." But in emergencies and crises, he is calm and cool as a cucumber. After his blindness he would curse when strangers accosted him on the streets of Nice or Monte Carlo, but when an automobile narrowly missed him, he would stand stock still without a word or a tremor!

Although flaming with excitement throughout the 1887 campaign, dishing out as much abuse as he took, he accepted the result with amazing poise. There were no cursings, no rantings. After the "people's verdict" was beyond doubt, he went behind his partition and wrote an editorial of unsurpassable suavity. (Presumably, he had not yet read Dana's philippic in the *Sun*.) He wrote this:

"*The World's* interest . . . has been wholly impersonal, and its judgment upon Col. Fellows' official conduct will be wholly impartial. We desired to secure a District Attorney who would carry on the prosecution of the public enemies in the same determined spirit and with the same ability as have thus far characterized the conduct of the cases against the bribe-takers and the bribe-givers. We knew that Mr. Nicoll would do it. We hope that Mr. Fellows will do it. If he does not, we shall not fail to say so. If he does, we shall be as generous in our praise as we have been frank in our opposition."

Victory of the Spirit!—The battle is over, but the war goes on. In JP's mind there must be some formulation of the "Forever" kind of newspaper, the kind that will always fight even though the pathway of progress and reform is marked out with lost causes and battles waged but never won.

November 8, 1887, after all, is just another day, aromatic with a double portion of hard work and a triple burden of anxiety. The editorial for November 9 is put into type, JP reads his own proofs, and the paper goes to press just the same as on any other day. Somehow, if you can only keep a newspaper going, it manages to come out every morning or afternoon in spite of heartbreaks, mistakes, and severe jolts.

As JP walks from his editorial room, his face is drawn with many a heavy line. Here is a man, dead tired, but blessed with the newspaperman's peace of mind which exceeds most people's understanding. In his belly the defeat is bitter, but in his mouth there is the sweet taste of knowing that *The World* will go forward just the same.

There is no sadder nor more unspoken tragedy than the defeat of a cause or a candidate into which a newspaper has put its utmost effort. There is nothing anybody can say. As JP leaves his office, *The World* staff surrounds him. Everybody feels like the devil. Sometimes an office wise-cracker can think of something to relieve the tension, but not in this case. The Chief has lost his big battle; there are no words to express the sympathy of the men who fought in the ranks.

JP says something approximately adequate to the moment.

"Gentlemen," he pauses as he moves toward the door—"Gentlemen, we have been getting out a fine political paper. From now on I want a fine newspaper every day!"

The next day he formulates his answer to Dana. There will be no moving. *The World's* leading editorial for November 10 is headed: "YES, HERE FOR GOOD!"

The background for the editorial is that *The World's* circulation has been mounting steadily throughout the campaign and has now passed 250,000 a day, while the *Sun's* has been dwindling. Furthermore, right in the heat of the battle, JP launched *The Evening World,* with an initial circulation of 115,000, soon to become, as JP described it, "the prize bantling of the century."

Dana has been striving desperately to turn the Nicoll campaign into a popular uprising against *The World,* but he has failed. The reign of King Dana is ending, as JP salutes the new day in these historic words:

"For nearly three weeks, the *New York Sun,* arrayed upon the side of the worst elements in our politics, after a career of unparalleled treachery, has teemed with the vilest abuse of *The World* and its editor. So far as the virulence of this blackguardism is concerned, it has perhaps never been equaled in American journalism, at least not since Mr. Dana devoted himself for four months to slandering and vilifying Grover Cleveland, the Democratic nominee for President.

"The editor of the *Sun* has been frank enough to say that there was no issue involved in the late local canvass save that of opposing the influence of *The World*. He attempted no defense of tainted candidates; he gave no reason for returning to the service of the Democratic bosses save that he seemed to think that by helping to elect a man whom *The World* opposed on public grounds, he could boast of a triumph and thereby affect the prestige of a newspaper which he long ago ceased to compete with.

"The editor of *The World* accepts the hatred of Mr. Dana as a compliment. He is only one of a vast number of people who have been favored with the creature's malice and have prospered under it. He especially appreciates the agonized heart-cry of Mr. Dana, which appears in yesterday's issue of the *Sun,* in the midst of a literary muck-heap, which could only be found on the editorial page of that paper.

" 'We wish, Pulitzer, that you had never come.'

"Nothing could be truer than this. From his innermost soul the broken and humiliated editor of the *Sun* wishes that the regeneration of *The World* had never taken place. In four years' time he has seen the circulation of his paper dwindle until it has fallen into the third rank; he has seen his dividends vanish; his income swept away. He has seen a mortgage for $175,000 placed upon a property which once yielded monthly dividends of 10 per cent. He has seen himself despised and contemned. With the hatred of a felon on the way to prison or worse, he has sought to hold *The World* and its editor responsible for the damage which he has mainly inflicted upon himself by his total lack of principle and honor. That the discriminating public should prefer *The World* to his vile sheet he has held as a cause for a quarrel with the editor of *The World*—such a quarrel as only the jealous bankrupt can make with the successful rival around the corner.

"Sad, no doubt, Mr. Dana is, that somebody came who could provide the New York public with the newspaper which it wanted. But the man is here, and he will remain. *The World* is stronger and better today than it ever was. It has never advocated a bad cause nor proved recreant to a good one. Its circulation *is three times that of the Sun* and its influence is in proportion. It will continue to war against corruptionists with renewed vigor. It rests upon a solid foundation of Honesty and Public Service and against it the disappointed, malice-cankered, envious sons of darkness cannot prevail."

Brave words and truly prophetic, as regards *The World* for the next forty-three years after this memorable campaign. But as to its owner and editor—not accurate. *The World* is to stay for nearly half a century, but the man will go. Dana's curse is working better than he knows; causes more devastating than the *Sun,* in that very November, are saying, "Move on, Pulitzer, move on!"

Even as JP pens his defiance, blindness and collapse of the nervous system are just around the corner.

But for a few days, he is permitted to enjoy his triumph—not victory for his candidate, but success for his paper. It has emerged more powerful than ever from a blitzkrieg of unequaled violence and rancor. Dana has done his worst and Dana has lost. From now on, the *Sun* shines with diminishing brilliance; even though it keeps up the slogan that "It Shines for All," it cast its luster on fewer and fewer subscribers. Dana is heading westward toward the Great Divide that indiscriminately welcomes newspapers and newspapermen—the noble and the unscrupulous alike; the fighters along with the lazy and the merely ambitious. Ten years after the fury of the Nicoll-Fellows campaign has been swallowed up in history, the *Sun,* following to the letter the instructions of its own editor, carries this brief paragraph:

"Charles A. Dana, editor of the *New York Sun,* died yesterday afternoon at his home in Glen Cove, Long Island."

With all his political experience, Dana should have known, as *The World* had to find out the difficult way, that in New York City, at least, candidates for local office win or lose regardless of newspaper support or editorial opposition. In 1917 John F. Hylan was elected mayor in spite of fierce opposition from *The World,* and from all other New York papers except Hearst's *Journal* and his *American;* in spite also of the devastating disclosures in *The World's* "Who Is John F. Hylan?" series. Notwithstanding the reform wave that followed the Becker case in 1912, John Purroy Mitchel, Fusion candidate and favorite of the newspapers, lasted only one term. Hylan beat the newspapers again in 1921, and Tammany's favorite son, "Jimmy" Walker, opposed by most of the newspapers, served two terms as mayor, finally resigning while under investigation by Governor Franklin D. Roosevelt.

Dynamic and spectacular Thomas E. Dewey, successful prosecutor of rackets and racketeers, is the first "reform" candidate to be elected District Attorney in New York County since Charles S. Whitman, who convicted Becker and sent him to the electric chair. Even in the upsurge of reform and recovery of 1933, on a Fusion ticket headed by the redoubtable Fiorello H. LaGuardia, the anti-Tammany forces, powerfully supported by the press, could not carry the District Attorneyship. They did four years later.

The Nicoll defeat was soon forgotten; the brilliant young prosecutor went into private practice to become one of New York's ablest and highest-priced corporation lawyers. But it is rather curious that none of the published biographies of Dana, and none of the several books about Dana and the *Sun,* makes any mention of the encounter with Joseph Pulitzer. Nor is anything said about "The Wandering Jew" editorials.

Whatever deductions JP made from the Nicoll campaign were soon to be forgotten in the shadow of a much greater catastrophe. In the latter part of that same November, 1887, coming to his office after a sleepless night, he called for proofs of the day's editorials. . . .

He could not read one line of type!

5. Tragedy

"God who took away my eyes
That my soul might see. . . ."

"THE BLIND PLOUGHMAN,"
by RADCLYFFE HALL

OR THE sake of the medical record in JP's case, let us assume:

1. That the Subject was born in Hungary of ancestry unknown but believed to be partly Asiatic, his father being part Jewish, part Magyar, his mother, German; that he was the second of four children; that the oldest, Louis, died in youth, and the youngest, Irma, at the age of fifteen; that the third child, Albert, became insane at about the age of fifty and committed suicide at fifty-eight; and assume

2. That the father of the Subject died when the Subject was adolescent; that the mother, to whom the Subject was greatly devoted, married a second time; that the Subject, at seventeen, was overgrown, undernourished, awkward, possessed of weak eyes (no further information as to the original cause of trouble); delicate complexion, high forehead, prominent nose, and a short chin which the Subject regarded as "weak" and in later life sought to conceal under a beard; and assume

3. That the Subject, being anxious to get away from home, sought military service, but was rejected by the Austrian, the French, and the British armies because of defective eyesight and "unpromising physique"; that upon being accepted for the United States Army (Northern) during the American Civil War, the Subject enlisted in the Lincoln Cavalry; that he was the constant object of ridicule and practical joking on the part of his associates; that his persistent questions were met with evasive or false or humorous answers; that on

115

one occasion when pestered by a petty officer, he struck his tormentor in the face, but was saved from military punishment through the intervention of a superior officer; and assume

4. That upon being mustered out of the army, the Subject sought in vain for employment in New York City and elsewhere; that he was refused the privilege of having his shoes polished in a certain hotel, being informed that its patrons objected to his poor appearance; that his overcoat was stolen; that upon inquiring where there was a city in the United States in which no German was spoken, he was informed by a practical joker that the city was St. Louis, Missouri; and assume

5. That upon arrival in St. Louis, by means of travel unknown, the Subject was forced to engage in the meanest sort of occupations, being variously deckhand on a ferryboat, gravedigger, stevedore, freight handler, coachman, waiter, and man of all work; that the Subject employed all his spare time in a library in search of knowledge and constantly sought to learn the English language, and was addicted to reading in bed; and assume

6. That, upon becoming a reporter on a German newspaper, the Subject was treated to various kinds of teasing and practical joking on the part of English-speaking colleagues; that a certain cartoonist, when lacking in other material, often made caricatures of the Subject, featuring especially his prominent nose; that in spite of ridicule, the Subject attained proficiency in the newspaper art, and was appointed legislative correspondent at the State capital for the said German paper; and assume

7. That upon being nominated for a vacancy in the Missouri House of Representatives, as a practical jest on the part of a Republican minority in a strongly Democratic district, the Subject conducted a vigorous campaign and was elected; that upon taking his seat in the legislature he immediately started a fight against the so-called "county courthouse ring," and denounced a certain lobbyist; and assume

8. That the said lobbyist, a man of powerful build, publicly called the Subject a damned liar and other opprobrious epithets; that the Subject rushed to his lodgings, returning with a four-barreled pistol and fired two shots at the lobbyist, wounding the latter in the

leg, and was struck down by him with the butt of a pistol; that the Subject pleaded guilty to assault and was fined about $400; and assume

9. That the Subject became intensely interested in national and state politics, finally leaving the Republican Party because of its notorious corruption, also, because of political differences, parting company with his German newspaper associates, by disposing of his interests for $30,000; that the Subject bought, for a nominal amount, another German newspaper and immediately sold it for $20,000; that thereafter the Subject enjoyed a brief period of comfort, during which time he fell in love and was married; and assume

10. That upon returning to St. Louis after his honeymoon, the Subject purchased a broken-down newspaper and built it up into a position of prosperity and influence, by arduous work and various editorial crusades designed to benefit the public and to remove special privileges of a wealthy few; that for about five years he worked eighteen, twenty, and often twenty-four hours a day, neglecting the bodily need of rest and recreation; having no regular mealtimes, and abusing his eyesight through editorial labors under open-flame gas lights; and assume

11. That through his unremitting efforts, the St. Louis newspaper was enjoying very large income, circulation, and prestige, until one day an editor shot and killed a prominent citizen of St. Louis in the offices of the newspaper, thereby causing great public indignation and also loss of influence to the newspaper; that as a result, the Subject suffered impairment of his health, the symptoms of which were nervousness, a cough accompanied by some loss of blood, sleeplessness, indigestion, and recurrent attacks of asthma, also some symptoms of diabetes; and assume

12. That the Subject, while bound for Europe with his wife in search of rest and recuperation, seized an opportunity to purchase a newspaper in New York for the sum of $346,000; and immediately plunged into new activities, involving long hours, irregular meals, loss of sleep, eyestrain, and constant nervous tension; the Subject being a perfectionist-idealist, forever unsatisfied either with his own labors or the work of those about him, but able to inspire his associates with the desire and the capacity for greater achievement; at the

same time intolerant of injustice or corruption in public affairs; and assume

13. That the Subject, by reason of his perspicacity, energy, and unremitting study of national politics, his editorial vigor and warm devotion to a chosen cause, was largely responsible for the nomination and election of Grover Cleveland as President of the United States in 1884; that the same talent for arousing public opinion and for stimulating the nobler sort of sentiment in the American people was largely responsible for completing the base for the Statue of Liberty, a gift from the people of France to the people of America, this being accomplished through popular subscriptions to a fund in spite of indifference on the part of the wealthier classes; and assume

14. That the Subject, possessed of a burning hatred of incompetence, dishonesty, special privilege, and government favoritism toward predatory plutocracy as represented by certain groups in what is known as "Wall Street," labored and clamored relentlessly against a system of taxation falling largely on the poorer classes and the housewife and falling lightly upon the rich—in all of which efforts he received approval from the masses of the people and opposition from the wealthy groups and their newspaper mouthpieces, particularly one Charles Anderson Dana, editor of the (New York) *Sun,* a man learned in letters, but in politics eccentric—to put it mildly—a scholarly scamp if there ever was one; and assume

15. That the Subject, being convinced that a certain streetcar franchise for Broadway had been obtained through wholesale bribery to the tune of half a million dollars distributed among the New York Board of Aldermen by one Jacob Sharp, a promoter—the Subject, by means of news articles and editorials, was greatly instrumental in arousing public opinion and bringing about an investigation resulting in the Grand Jury indictment of all but two members of the said Board, indictment, trial, and conviction of the said Jakey Sharp, resulting directly or indirectly in such impairment to the health of the said Sharp that the said Sharp died from the results thereof, thereby causing much recrimination and blame to be hurled at the Subject; and assume

16. That the Subject, appreciative of the great public service rendered by De Lancey Nicoll, Assistant District Attorney, in the said

boodle cases, proposed the nomination of Nicoll for District Attorney, a plan which was accepted by the Republican party in New York City, but rejected by the Democrats (although Nicoll was a Democrat and *The World* was regarded as the Democratic paper); and assume

17. That the aforesaid Charles Anderson Dana, then in his sixty-ninth year and on his way out, journalistically speaking (politically he never amounted to anything)—that the said C.A.D. greatly alarmed over the growth of *The World's* circulation and the decline of the *Sun's* business and erstwhile prestige, infuriated as only an aged and pseudo-scholarly newspaper poseur can become when confronted with an up-and-coming editor-owner (especially one from the West) who habitually attacks the interests and sources from which C.A.D. and the *Sun* have been drawing large and often unexplained increments; and assume

18. That the said C.A.D., although he had previously endorsed Nicoll, proceeded to throw him overboard, and supported the Tammany candidate, at the same time publicly declaring that the one and only reason for the sudden switch (one of a series on Dana's part) was the alleged menace of the Subject and his newspaper; that the *Sun* continually and continuously for several weeks in the campaign attacked and denounced the Subject to the utmost resources of C.A.D.'s imagination and mastery of language (which was something)—applying to the Subject such epithets as

"Hungry Joe"
"Renegade Jew"
"Cringer for nickels in a barroom"
"Wandering Jew"
"Fugitive from unexecuted justice"
"Resorter to homicide"
"Choe Bulitzer."

And concluding, after the campaign had resulted in the defeat of Nicoll, in a torrent of abuse and denunciation, climaxing with the admonition, "Move on, Pulitzer, move on!"

And assume

19. That the Subject, by reason of the constant excitement and arduous work during the campaign, cast aside all thought of eating,

sleeping, rest, recreation, and counter-actions to worry about the outcome of the election; and assume

20. That after absorbing the shock of defeat and the culminating invective of the aforesaid C.A.D., the Subject announced his intention of remaining in New York for good . . .

21. That shortly thereafter, the Subject, upon coming to his office and starting to examine editorials for the next day, found he could see nothing except the sheet of paper . . .

22. That medical examination showed that the Subject's eyesight was seriously impaired (one report says through the rupture of a blood vessel in one eye) and the prognosis indicated that he might never see again . . .

Which proved to be correct . . .

23. And that medical examination further indicated an acute nervous disorder which, according to physicians, could be remedied, if at all, only through prolonged absence from all work and all worry and complete rest, together with change of climate (California preferred) . . .

24. And assume, to make this quasi-hypothetical question no longer than necessary, that the Subject did not recover his eyesight; that it became progressively worse, resulting in almost complete loss of vision, except that in the late afternoon or early evenings he could dimly distinguish faint outlines of objects near by;

25. This nerve condition, although showing intermittent brief improvement, became steadily more acute, making the Subject so extremely sensitive to noise that the clink of a spoon, the sipping of soup, the closing of a door, the cracking of almonds by a guest at dinner, the rattle of a paper—anything in the nature of sniffling, or scratching, or scraping, or any kind of noise whatsoever except such as he could expect and identify and could enjoy, such as the rumble of surf, or the wind, or the galloping of horses—would react upon the Subject like a cannon shot, precipitating a paroxysm of pain and anger, and a certain degree (we must assume) of fright; the symptoms of which were violent cursing, shouting, shaking of the fist, stamping of feet, and culminating usually in weeping or sobbing, followed by long periods of extreme exhaustion, during which periods the Subject was an easy prey to colds, coughs, bronchitis,

asthma, indigestion, inflammation of the lungs, certain indications of diabetes, and weakening of the heart;

26. That the series of nervous attacks and seizures continued for a period of twenty-four years, varied only occasionally with "good spells," during all which time the Subject's mind was continuously active; his curiosity insatiable; his demand for improvement on the part of his papers and their editors and reporters unrelenting; his thirst for knowledge unquenchable—for the latest or most authoritative information on politics, art, science, government, literature, drama, music, education, history . . . even to the extent, at one time, of commanding *The World* to find out if it was really true, as alleged by Guglielmo Ferrero in his *Greatness and Decline of Rome* (1907) that Marc Antony *did not* deliver a funeral oration (famous or otherwise) at Julius Caesar's funeral. . . .

[JP's equilibrium was gravely upset over Ferrero's "discovery"; he wanted to know: Where did Shakespeare get his information? He cabled orders from *The World* staff to interview scholars like Woodrow Wilson, James Ford Rhodes, John Bach McMaster, *et al.*—what did they think about it? Well, *The World's* reporters tried hard, but unfortunately were unable to locate anybody who had attended, or had any first- or second-hand knowledge of, the last rites for Caesar.]

And assume:

27. That the Subject had a multiple-track mind; that while one part or another of his stream of consciousness might be occupied with the reading of Monypenny's *Life of Disraeli,* or the description of a painting a secretary had seen in Munich, or the latest reports about his family, or the further advances in the art of soundproofing such as might be applied to the "town residence" at No. 7-15 East Seventy-second Street, New York; or the summer home, "Chatwold" at Bar Harbor, Maine, or the yacht *Liberty;* or the "cottage" on Jekyl Island, Georgia, or a rented home at Lakewood, New Jersey; or various other homes, villas, hotel suites, steamship accommodations and special trains—the main track of the mind was occupied exclusively with *The World* and what it was doing to promote progress and reform, to combat injustice and corruption, to stimulate public opinion and public welfare; how to prevent *The World* from becom-

ing satisfied with merely printing news, or coming to lack sympathy with the poor, or not marching ahead and always leading in the unfolding of the nation's history; and assume

28.   That a cross section of the Subject's consciousness in what he called the period of "horrible invalidism and absenteeism," might be something like this:

"Take this cable to Cobb order the horses for eleven Ireland is to ride with me so he thinks he has a good memory does he editorial on Cortelyou weak very weak for God's sake how many times must I say *The World* must lead, lead, lead why wait two days before commenting tell Dunningham to remove the almonds entirely point out that Roosevelt denounces malefactors of great wealth while at the same time accepting their campaign contributions praise him for whatever good he does never fail to expose and denounce all acts of jingoism egoism blowing up the war scare Bryan must not be a candidate again reading for tonight is *Vanity Fair* no make it *Mill on the Floss*—but after all, no style like Jane Austen's—Thwaites was dull at dinner last night Ireland must be memorizing those figures on British income taxes Billing's analyses of Sunday papers very shrewd find out who wrote the editorial about Mrs. Rockefeller going to church it wasn't worth more than a paragraph what does Ralph say about his trip next summer who hit a glass with a spoon last night treat Hearst with restraint, almost respect, etc., etc."

And assume

29.   That the inner battle between suffering and editing continued up to the end of the Subject's life; the physique gradually becoming less and less resistant to the after-effects of the nervous attacks, finally ending in a heart attack at the age of sixty-four years, six months, and nineteen days, during which span of life there had never been the slightest diminution of the Subject's mental virility as expressed in curiosity, memory (copper plate), analysis and co-ordination, formulation of statement (although frequently repetitious and alliterative, always forceful and attention-compelling), appreciation, adequacy of reaction (sometimes over-reaction), ability to sift chaff from wheat at lightning speed; and during which time, barring the period of adolescence, the emotional life, barring the disturbances mentioned, was, generally speaking, ade-

quate, normal, wholesome; the ideals noble and not at all egocentric; said ideals being concerned with honesty and efficiency in government and politics; the better education of youth; the establishment of a school and schools of journalism for the purpose of attracting into newspaper work men of superior ability and character . . .
AND CHARACTER . . . the teaching of moral courage; the promotion of international peace; the lessening or removal of political, social, and economic discriminations and all manner of special privilege; the spread of culture and knowledge; the encouragement of American drama, music, art, science, poetry, and other literature (including biographies of distinguished Americans), history of the United States, and fiction, emphatically and especially fiction reflecting "the wholesome character of American life and the highest standards of morals and manners"; and assume

30. That the Subject, in the last ten years of his life, devoted much time, thought, energy, and attention to a plan for perpetuating a newspaper which should always fight for progress and reform, never tolerate injustice or corruption, always fight demagogues of all parties, never belong to any party, always oppose privileged classes and public plunderers, never lack sympathy with the poor, always remain devoted to the public welfare, never be satisfied with merely printing news, always be drastically independent, never be afraid to attack wrong whether by predatory plutocracy or predatory poverty. . . .

31. And in the same plan, the Subject included a system of annual prizes for the encouragement of American drama and other literary types; prizes for high-school students desiring further education; for university or other students manifesting special talent or genius in journalism, music, and art . . . which prizes became known in time as "Pulitzer Prizes"; the system also including annual awards to newspapers and newspapermen for good work in exposing wrong and accomplishing public good; the keynote of the whole system being Sincerity, Nobility, Generosity (which keynote in recent years appears to have been forgotten or overlooked or misplaced, or, in some instances, entirely ignored)—all tending to show

32. That the Subject was a stiff-necked idealist as well as intel-

lectually, politically, and sociologically the most incorrigible busy-body of his day and age.

Assuming that the foregoing is truthful, that it is characterized by Accuracy, Accuracy, and Accuracy, if not Terseness . . .

What is the diagnosis?

From the medical standpoint, after consultation with qualified members of the neurological, psychological, and psychiatric special-ization groups, the best explanation seems to be:

PSYCHO-NEUROSIS, resulting from a mental, emotional, neuro-logical cataclysm, followed by a long period of exhaustion, out of which there developed a fear complex associated with noises.

The theory is that the early hardships and persecutions in JP's life; the abuses, the badgerings, the tormentings, goadings, and teasings inflicted in the Lincoln Cavalry; the frustrations of his natural curiosity and the blocking of his natural emotional outlets; the mistreatment experienced in New York after discharge from the army—i.e., inability to find work after fighting for the country, his exclusion from the shoe-shining department of French's Hotel, the practical joke perpetrated in sending him to St. Louis in search of an all-American city; the extreme difficulty of sustaining life and at the same time pursuing knowledge in a robust environment; the practi-cal jokings of the St. Louis reporters; the abuse inflicted by Captain Augustine (resulting in "over-reaction" with a pistol); followed by the public outcry occasioned by the Cockerill-Slayback affair; fol-lowed later by the savage thrusts of Rapierist Dana, accompanied by the "Hungry Joe" and "Renegade Jew" excoriations. . . .

The theory is that the cumulative series of torments produced a storehouse of emotional conflicts which did not find outlet until after JP unfortunately had so neglected his health that the reservoirs of nervous energy became depleted; the reservoirs fell below the safety level and the complex began to scream and shout. Nature has a way of storing away memories of emotional disturbances. They seem to be forgotten, but they are not. When exhaustion sets in, they return in full force, often accompanied by other devils more deadly than themselves.

The blindness was something else. The progressive deterioration of the retina in one eye, gradually affecting the other, seems to be attributable to downright neglect and abuse of an eyesight never strong. At seventeen Joseph Pulitzer was rejected for military service because of defective vision—which should have been a warning, but turned out to be only an invitation to work, work, work because, as he seemed to sense, the night was coming.

And it finally caught up with him.

Advent of tragedy is not always fully appreciated at the time of its arrival. In JP's case, on that day in the latter part of November, 1887 (the exact date seems to have been forgotten), when he picked up his proofs only to find a dull blur, he did not realize that the Great Turning Point had come; nor did he suspect that when he left *The World* office that day he would not return for a long time and that from then on he was to become practically a stranger to the staff, so far as personal appearances were concerned.

At first he thought the blindness was only from an attack of indigestion. He said nothing about it to Merrill and the others.

"The next morning," he told Alleyne Ireland (near the end of JP's life), "on my way downtown I called in at an oculist's. He examined my eyes and then ordered me to go home and remain in bed in a darkened room for six weeks.

"At the end of that time he examined me again and told me I had ruptured a blood vessel in one of my eyes, ordered me to stop work entirely and take a six-months' rest in California. That was the beginning of the end. . . ."

So he phrased it. But actually it was the end of his beginning. An entirely new Pulitzer and a new *World* were emerging.

In calling JP a "Wandering Jew" Dana was more accurate than he thought. JP was only partly Jewish, but he was to become indeed a wanderer, a constant searcher for the Fountain of Health, which, of course, he never found; never staying for more than a few weeks in any one place; always hoping for some permanent relief, but never finding it; always goaded into new travel; it was the voice of Pain and not of Dana which kept saying, "Move on, Pulitzer, move on."

For twenty-four years (lacking a few weeks) he kept up the amazing travel series—trips, alternating with stops; now a voyage, now a "residence"; sometimes pausing for a few days, or a few weeks, or a few months in one or the other of his several "homes"—New York, Bar Harbor, Lakewood, Jekyl Island, London, Paris, Aix-les-Bains, Cap Martin, Wiesbaden, Baden-Baden, Berlin, and various spots in Switzerland or along the Riviera; at other times crossing the ocean and coming back without even a pause.

As the journeys continued, it became more and more evident that complete restoration of health was out of the question; his eyesight was becoming fainter all the time; and the only hope for his nerves was that if, by some fortunate chance, he could manage to find some rest and quiet, Nature would repair the shattered network. Consequently, the record of JP's travels is mostly a history of a search for escape from noise, coupled with continuous efforts at mental distractions (one could scarcely call them amusements)—something to occupy his mind, or that part of it which was not pre-empted by *The World*.

The chronology of JP's last twenty-four years would seem to contradict any notion that here was a man looking for rest and quiet; the timetable would not appeal to anyone in search of the peaceful way of life; but one must remember that with the Pulitzer travels, all details were arranged by the resourceful and indefatigable major domo, Jabez E. Dunningham (now a leading citizen of Queens Borough, New York City), and a whole corps of secretaries; all JP had to do was to issue his wishes and then follow Dunningham's more specific directions.

Thanks to Dr. George W. Hosmer, who was private secretary, private physician, and confidential companion in one person for twenty years (1889-1909), it is possible to reconstruct the story of JP's travels. Hosmer had a rare combination of talents. Although a graduate of New York's College of Physicians and Surgeons, he never practiced medicine (except on JP when no specialists were available); although admitted to the bar, he never practiced law. Like many another practitioner in both fields, he somehow got into newspaper work and never emerged until it was too late to take up another profession.

Dr. Hosmer was correspondent for the New York *Herald* throughout the Civil War; afterward, he went abroad for the *Herald* and reported the Franco-Prussian conflict. He entered the service of *The World* in 1889, at the age of fifty-nine, and after a brief term on the editorial staff was detailed to the most difficult of all assignments: life with the Founder. Being a fairly good stenographer, a medical man without practice, a lawyer without clients, and an experienced newspaperman made him acceptable. To have been the ideal confidential secretary-companion, he would have had to speak with the tongues of men and of angels and to have been possessed of all knowledge like Davidson of St. Louis, who, in JP's opinion, knew all about everything.

Hosmer's other handicap, in addition to lack of complete knowledge of all things, was his age. He had to conceal the fact that he was seventeen years older than JP, and did it rather cleverly in spite of the efforts of his chief and the other secretaries to trap him; but age will tell in time, and after twenty years of trying to keep up with Joseph Pulitzer, Hosmer's own health gave way. He retired to his home in Summit, New Jersey, still on the Pulitzer payroll but with only optional duties of writing an article for *The World* whenever he felt like it. He wrote occasionally, mostly about the Battle of Gettysburg; also two books, *Politics and People* and *As We Go Marching On*. At the same time he began writing the life of Joseph Pulitzer, and after composing something like 25,000 words, informed the principal victim.

JP nearly fainted.

He immediately threw obstacles in Hosmer's way. First, he wanted a 2,500-word summary of the proposed Life; second, he wanted the narrative confined to the twenty years which Hosmer had actually witnessed. By the time Hosmer had completed the synopsis his powers had faded and he did not finish the Opus Major. The summary, however, which he did leave to posterity, is a valuable year-by-year chronology.

(Hosmer died on June 2, 1914. *The World,* for some reason, did not publish the story until two days later, along with the funeral plans and the information that "carriages will meet the train which leaves Hoboken at 2:30 P.M.")

The Hosmer narrative picks up at the point where JP left New York for California in the early winter of 1888. The much-publi-

cized climate failed to benefit him. This is no reflection on the balm
of America's Gilead. The truth is that even in the eighties, California
was too close to New York to assure complete rest for a perturbed
spirit: JP could not keep his mind off *The World,* nor break the connection with the home office. For one thing, the need of more
Lebensraum for *The World* and its new companions, *The Evening
World* and *The Sunday World,* was importunate. More floor space
was needed right away.

Although "unable to read or write," as he said, JP found a
sincere disappointment in his inability to attend the dinner of the
New York Press Club in honor of its president, Colonel Cockerill.
He sent a letter, dictated in the dark, expressing his keen regret at
not being permitted to add his tribute to the Colonel's "high talents
and charming amiabilities or character."

(This is the first sign that Cockerill is on the way out.)

Absence and distance brought no relief from *World* problems.
The newspaper, which was afterward to go on under its own mo-
mentum (plus JP's original inspiration) for nearly twenty years
after his death, was not yet able to walk by itself, especially without
breathing room. Pulitzer left California in April.

On his way back East, he stopped off in St. Louis—the last of the
only three times he is known to have revisited the Queen of the
Mississippi after 1883. On all three occasions there was a fire in the
hotel where he and Mrs. Pulitzer stayed—not exactly restful experiences for a blind man afflicted with nervousness. Furthermore, he
found that many of his old friends had gone.

Of course, there was the *Post-Dispatch.*

Meanwhile, he had been bombarding Cockerill and the others
with messages about the new building. French's old hotel had come
into the real-estate market during his absence. There will always be
some doubt whether JP bought the property chiefly because it was a
good investment (or seemed like one at the time), or whether he
wanted to help "the whirligig of time complete his revenges" by
acquiring the very site from which he had been barred as a Civil War
veteran. At any rate, the purchase was completed on JP's forty-first
birthday, April 10, 1888. The price was $630,000. [The present

Pulitzer Building (End without World) was assessed for 1941-1942 at $1,800,000.]

At the same time, JP moved his family into the residence at No. 10 East Fifty-fifth Street, and remained in New York City during the Cleveland-Harrison Campaign of 1888. He spent most of that summer in Lenox, Massachusetts.

Unproductive as was the California trip for health, it was lucky in a way for the invalid journalist. He was out of town at the time of the Great Blizzard. Bad enough to be engulfed in a blizzard; worse to be one of the blizzard's witnesses without being able to see it, and having to hear all about it, then and forever afterward.

Transportation was paralyzed throughout the East. Communication lines were down. The metropolitan district was threatened with famine. Publication of newspapers was almost impossible. If all the stories and first-hand experiences published and unpublished about the Blizzard were placed end to end—but why strain? There is no end to them. As regards *The World,* we offer the narrative of Hugh Hastings, reporter, who came in on the last train that day from New Jersey, and years later wrote his experiences for *The World Forum* (one-time house organ of the Pulitzer organization), as follows:

"The ferryboat that brought us across the Hudson was the last to cross for twenty-four hours. The oldest navigator never saw the river lashed by such heavy seas. Waves broke over the deck . . . spray invaded the pilot house, drenching the steersman. For half an hour the wind and terrific waves baffled the attempts to land. When the boat made fast in her slip she remained there. Thus early in the day the downtown streets were absolutely impassable and practically deserted. On coming out of the Astor House, where I engaged a room for the night, I met the late Fred Keith, its manager.

" 'If this condition continues for twenty-four hours,' he observed lugubriously, 'New York will face a famine. We haven't coal enough to last forty-eight hours. Our milk and eggs will run out in twenty-four hours.'

"Full of enthusiasm, I rushed to the office and poured out to the city editor my narrative of the difficulty in reaching New York, the famine menace, the transportation problem by land and sea, and the danger to one of our favorite boys, W. O. Inglis, who, a few days before, had ventured off on a pilot boat to seek 'new sensations.' He got them sure enough.

"The city editor nodded his head gravely. He then suggested that I should proceed to Thirty-first Street and Third Avenue, as the north wall of a theater was threatening to fall.

" 'How about transportation?' I asked. 'Here are four street-cars abandoned in sight of this window. The elevated roads have ceased to run. Cab fare to Fourteenth Street costs $12.50.' [This was 1888—or was it just a bid for an expense account?]

" 'Never mind, then,' said the city editor.

"The late Timmy Gill was detailed to walk over the Brooklyn Bridge. Jonas Whitley was sent to parade around the Battery. . . . But the banner story came from Captain T. C. Summers, who accomplished the almost incredible feat of hoofing it in from Coney Island. . . .

"I was grinding out copy on general principles, with enthusiasm somewhat below par, when upstairs there was a wild scurrying of feet. Boys and messengers clattered downstairs, crying out names of the staff.

" 'Mr. Smith wants you at once!'

"Ballard Smith had weathered the tempest and surged into the office with energy, resourcefulness, and *esprit de corps* as irresistible as it was infectious.

" 'Did you come in from New Jersey this morning?'

"Before I could answer, he shouted,

" 'Put it in six columns—more if you think it worth it! Make side notes as you go along and let me have them just as soon as possible.'

"He sprang at the famine suggestion as a bear at a hive of honey and detailed William E. Simmons to cover it. And a comprehensive exclusive Simmons made of it.

"*The World* outdistanced its rivals in comprehensiveness, accuracy, and estimates of the devastation and destruction, the hardships, and the dangers likely to follow. The whole story was marvelously told—but the headline was confined to one column. In those days space did not seem to be squandered on 'heads.'

"New York would have been absolutely isolated from the rest of the world except for one long-distance telephone wire and the cable. For thirty-six hours the Pennsylvania Railroad's telegraphic system was completely out of commission and it handled its transportation

Col. John A. Cockerill

and official business from the editorial rooms of *The World* over this wire. New York's only method of communication with Boston was by cable to Liverpool and back."

Thus did the Great Blizzard prove that *The World* could function in emergencies without the Founder; not so well did the newspaper acquit itself on politics. JP's absence from the office was keenly felt during the 1888 presidential campaign not only by *The World,* but by the Democratic Party.

If there was any question as to Joseph Pulitzer's influence in the first election of Cleveland, it was answered in the race for a second term. The editorial support for Cleveland was there, but not the fiery zeal. Merrill was good, but not good enough. The difference between JP and Merrill was as marked as the difference between the late Frank I. Cobb (who inherited JP's mantle) and Walter Lippmann in the early twenties. The Merrill and the Lippmann editorials are unimpeachable from the standpoint of clear statement, reasoning, and deduction; but whereas JP and Cobb had the ability to get action on the part of the reader, Lippmann used to say, "Damn it—I can't be sounding bugle calls!"

In the second Cleveland campaign, with JP out of the office and communicating only through the medium of dictation, there were no trumpetings from Merrill, except a few outlined and practically dictated by the Chief himself.

After Cleveland's first victory, the "normalcy" of Republican sentiment, revolving chiefly around the protective tariff, had reasserted itself. The Congress was divided. Cleveland possessed the form but not the substance of power. On the one great issue—the reduction of the tariff and the lifting of internal taxes—he was vocal but not potent. Meanwhile, the tariff continued to pile up a huge Treasury surplus—$140,000,000 for the fiscal year of 1888.

The World kept putting it this way:

"The Democratic policy: Off with the needless taxes on clothing, fuel, shelter, food. Let alone the taxes on whiskey, beer, tobacco.

"The Republican policy: Off with the taxes on whiskey, beer, tobacco, so as to keep the war taxes on clothing, fuel, shelter, food."

Obviously, the JP punch was lacking.

James G. Blaine, now called by *The World* "as dead as a cock in a pit," eliminated himself from the race because of illness, but he made a bargain with the Republican nominee, Benjamin Harrison, by which Blaine spoke for Harrison in return for a promise to make Blaine Secretary of State.

The World's appraisal of Harrison was neither hot nor cold: "He is a thoroughly equipped lawyer, and he has experience as a statesman. Moreover, he has always been a practical civil-service reformer. . . ."

Although the editorial page commended Cleveland, there was divided opinion inside *The World*. Cockerill had turned Republican.

In the country generally, the memory of Republican corruption was fading, just as did the Teapot Dome scandals of the Harding administration. People could not get away from the idea that Republicanism meant prosperity. Do they ever?

The fact that after the Civil War, under successive Republican regimes, there had been the greatest saturnalia of corruption, bribery, special privilege, and predatory plutocracy that the nation has ever seen, did not register strongly enough with the voters to re-elect Cleveland. In spite of the 1884 disclosures about Blaine, he was "probably the most popular man in the United States," as George William Curtis told *The World;* and Blaine was the spokesman for Harrison.

In New York State, David B. Hill, running for re-election on the Democratic ticket, refused to back up Cleveland on tariff reform; Hill traded votes with the Republicans. He carried the state and Cleveland lost it, thereby losing the election. Cleveland had a slim popular plurality in the country—98,000 votes—but lost the electoral vote by 65.

Mostly, *The World* was on the defensive—the difference between supporting a candidate and fighting for him at the expense of nerves and eyesight. In this campaign, Cleveland had his own Burchard. The "break" came when the British Embassy received a trick letter asking advice—how should former British subjects who had become American citizens vote in this election? Ambassador Sir Lionel Sackville-West replied:

"Vote for Cleveland. The Democratic party wants to maintain friendly relations with Great Britain."

There is a terrific uproar. In vain *The World* seeks to stem the tide: "What party isn't in favor of friendly relations with Great Britain? Is the Republican party in favor of war?"

The argument fails to carry. Britain's envoy has committed a fatal blunder and Cleveland is obliged to ask for his recall, but too late.

The World is philosophical in defeat. There are no tearful scenes in the office. Merrill's editorial post-mortem thanks the President for giving his party "an issue worthy of a national campaign . . . a noble contest for a principle."

But a losing one. The Democrats are left to extract what comfort they can from *The World*'s assurance that "taxes will be reduced . . . the surplus will be stopped . . . the tariff will be reformed," and that "President Cleveland and his party can afford to wait for the vindication of their position."

As it turns out, they have to wait only four years, but in 1892, there is a different *World*. By that time, JP has worked out the new technique of absentee editorship. No other *World* man was ever able to do it.

By the end of Cleveland-Harrison campaign No. 1, JP was resolved to take a prolonged leave of absence. He planned a trip around the globe, but first he must consult the best European specialists. There had been no improvement, either in vision or in the nervous condition.

Before starting abroad, he creates a triumvirate. Not one man but a Big Three to administer *The World* with its owner away. It consists of Cockerill, managing editor, George W. Turner, business manager, and JP's own brother-in-law, another colonel, William L. Davis, mining engineer, unfamiliar with the newspaper business. All three have equal power, but Davis was to act as a sort of mediator-without-portfolio, preserving a nice balance between the other two.

Ah, JP! Rome under Antony, Augustus Caesar, and Lepidus had better auspices. When will he ever learn that in a newspaper three heads are no better than one! The answer is—Never! JP's genius is not in organization, but inspiration. Somehow he manages to empty himself into the paper so forcefully, so thoroughly, that the machine will work in spite of the handicaps of bad management.

For the European trip, Dr. James W. McLane, personal physician, accompanies the errant Chief. The first stop is London. "The eminent British specialist," Sir Andrew Clarke, confirms the diagnosis of his American colleagues. The prescription is: complete separation from work and the surroundings of work—rest, rest, rest, and rest.

In Paris, other distinguished physicians are consulted—Charcot, Brown-Sequard, de Wecker, Lamboldt, and Meyer. They agree on one thing—the patient needs a long rest. By all means, a trip around the world, but keep your mind off *The World*.

One thing about JP—he never does a thing halfway. Being now engaged in getting medical opinion, he must have the best of the most. As years go on, he consults more and more physicians. One time, when at Cap Martin, he sent for a German specialist and then refused to admit him. Dunningham had to explain:

"Mr. Pulitzer's regrets, sir, but he is too ill to see a doctor, sir."

JP engages a British secretary—Claude Ponsonby, son of Sir Henry Ponsonby, the first of a long line of capable young men with a taste for travel and capacity to withstand cross-examination. Plans are made for the journey, but first, JP must stop off in Wiesbaden, the famous German watering place (where Hitler's commissioners met with those of conquered France in 1940 to complete the details of occupation). He is to rest there—also to confer with Dr. Hermann Pagenstecher, foremost European oculist.

New York, October 10, 1889

"GOD GRANT THAT THIS STRUCTURE [the new Pulitzer building, No. 59-63 Park Row] MAY BE THE HOME OF A NEWSPAPER FOR-EVER UNSATISFIED WITH MERELY PRINTING NEWS. . . ."

The cablegram from Wiesbaden is part of a ceremony; the man who conceived the building in his mind's eye, including the Golden Dome, has dictated painfully from a sickbed his prayer for *The World,* but one must doubt that the reading of it grips the listeners. The large crowd attending the laying of the cornerstone has much else to think of. This is a grand occasion, even for New York. The program includes addresses by Governor Hill, who failed to give 100 per cent support to *The World's* candidate the previous year; Chauncey M. Depew, the famous after-dinner speaker (who is also, when occasion requires, the voice of the Vanderbilts and their New York Central Railroad, which JP has sharply attacked for poor management); Daniel Dougherty, Philadelphia's "silver-tongued orator" (this was before Bryan). Also present are George W. Childs of the *Philadelphia Public Ledger,* General Charles H. Taylor of the *Boston Globe,* and many, many others, too numerous and too notable to mention, but not forgetting JP's particular friend, William C. Whitney and his young daughter, Dorothy (later Mrs. Willard C. Straight and now Mrs. Leonard Knight Elmhirst, a British citizen) who alone has the privilege of climbing on JP's lap and rumpling his hair.

In the recess beneath the cornerstone are duly and ceremoniously deposited various papers and documents; a photograph of "Joseph Pulitzer and His Family," at that time consisting of Mrs. Pulitzer; Ralph, then aged ten years; Lucille Irma, the favorite, aged nine; Joseph, junior, aged four and one-half years; Edith, aged three; and Constance, aged ten months.

(Herbert, the youngest, was born November 20, 1895, six years after the cornerstone event. A fourth daughter, Katherine Ethel, died in her second year, just before the Cleveland-Blaine campaign started. Lucille Irma, who was most like her father, died in December, 1897. The School of Journalism is dedicated to her memory.)

In addition to the documents and the photograph, there are also deposited gold and silver coins of the period (not in the ratio of 16 to 1) totaling $36.75. The money is still there, but try and get it.

The most active Pulitzer on this occasion is Master Joseph, Jr., who is elected to do the honors for the stone. Junior, according to *The World* reporter's account, is adequate to the occasion:

"A pretty, round-cheeked, rosy-faced lad . . . dressed in the daintiest of sailor suits, with the bluest of little trousers, the whitest of vests and a cunning little blue jacket, with shining brass buttons, and a jaunty cap set on the back of his head . . . curling black hair

clustered in masses about his forehead . . . very manly in his little
suit."

Master Joseph experiences difficulty in ascending the steps to the
platform beside the cornerstone, but, refusing outside aid, he
scrambles up, followed by the Right Reverend David S. Tuttle,
Protestant Episcopal Bishop of Missouri.

BISHOP (patting Joseph, Jr.) : "You are a brave little fellow!"

Thomas Alva Edison, the rising young inventor, overlooked until
now among the brilliant group on the platform, whispers to another distinguished onlooker, "Handsomest lad I ever saw!"

Under subdued coaching, JP, Junior, pulls a small silver trowel
from his bluest of little trousers. The official Masons lower the stone
into the right place and the young JP hits it a smack with his trowel
three times, piping out,

"It is well done! It is well done! It is well done!"

A high Mason also pronounces this cornerstone to be "Well and
truly laid!"

As a matter of fact, there is nothing wrong with the cornerstone.
When the real trouble comes along some years later, it starts in the
Golden Dome and in the business office. At that time, millions of
people wonder what is wrong with *The World,* but few remember
the *closing part* of JP's prayer:

"GOD FORBID THAT THE VAST ARMY FOLLOWING THE STANDARD
OF *The World* SHOULD IN THIS OR IN FUTURE GENERATIONS
EVER FIND IT FAITHLESS TO THOSE IDEAS AND MORAL PRINCIPLES
TO WHICH ALONE IT OWES ITS LIFE *and without which I would
rather have it perish."* (Author's italics.)

JP went to Paris to complete his plans for the long voyage away
from home. The trip started off with fair prospects, but not as the
doctors ordered. JP was not cutting himself off from *The World.*
He cabled full directions as to how mail was to reach him at various
points along the route—Bombay, Singapore, Yokohama. And he
added to Davis, "I want you to cable me fully, whether it costs four
dollars a word or forty, anything of real importance." By mail, he
wanted regular, full, "and, I trust, favorable reports."

Alas, alas! Even the first reports are anything but favorable. Davis
is having an engineer's own time trying to steer between Scylla

Cockerill and Charybdis Turner. The brother-in-law's communications, catching up with him at Mediterranean ports, throw JP into tantrums.

Just as the ship was about to leave Constantinople, he remarked, "How dark it is!"

Dark indeed. To everyone else on the ship it was broad daylight; but for JP, this was the onset of continuous night. The retina of the worst eye had become detached, leaving only faint vision in the better one.

He and Ponsonby left the ship and hurried to find the best physicians in Constantinople. Little enough can be done. Their advice is to return at once to Paris.

At Naples, JP is taken to a hotel and placed in a darkened room. Some sort of artillery practice is going on, with heavy firing from the big guns. To the nerve racked patient, every shot is like the crack of doom.

Ponsonby implores the Italian authorities, and they finally stop the exercises, but for long days, JP must remain quiet until calm enough to endure the journey to St. Moritz, Switzerland—a bad choice, because the patient, exhausted by the ordeal at Naples, immediately catches cold and develops acute bronchitis. Weeks later, Mrs. Pulitzer, accompanied by Dr. Hosmer, joins him in Lucerne, August, 1890.

From Dr. Hosmer's notes:

"He was very ill—in a state so feeble that he could scarcely get around on foot. He passed days on a sofa . . . it was a physical strain for him to cross the room and sit at the table. . . .

"Physical collapse had assumed the form of nervous prostration . . . directly due to his intense efforts in building up *The World*. He had previously compromised his health by his labors on the *St. Louis Post-Dispatch* which he had also raised from the dead.

"He remained in Lucerne several weeks, slowly recuperating . . . went to Paris for a few weeks, thence to Trouville. In the pleasant atmosphere of the seaside, at a place which was very quiet—for the gay world was already gone—he recovered from bronchitis and to some degree from his great physical debility.

"With this small recovery, however, he listened to the telegrams from home which urged him to new activities. . . . His return home [in October, 1890] was due in part to the conviction that *The World* needed him. In steering through the depths and shoals of politics, with Tammany always dominant, evil to the public welfare might be done with a feeble hand on the tiller. . . ."

Other reasons for being homeward bound were: Dr. S. Weir Mitchell, the great Philadelphia neurologist, who was also the author of current best-sellers like *Hugh Wynne, Quaker.* (As often happens, the best medical minds of Europe had recommended the outstanding American specialist); the new Pulitzer Building was about ready for the big opening; Congress was in a turmoil over the McKinley Tariff bill.

In vain *The World,* through Merrill's editorials, argued the folly of protecting infant industries now grown to monopolies. In vain the public anger rose. Blaine, following the policy later adopted by Cordell Hull, sweetened the tariff with reciprocity treaties with "most favored nations." In vain *The World* pointed out the worldwide depression. In vain even Harrison counseled moderation. The Republican party in power seemed determined to dig its own grave.

While JP is on the ocean, the McKinley bill is passed. Harrison signs it, and Blaine smiles. Does he suspect that Harrison is affixing his name to his own political death warrant? And with the election only one month away?

"McKinley and his fellow partisans," *The World* declares, "have completely united the Democratic party."

Following JP's arrival, new life surges into *The World*. The editorial page picks up. The paper starts a fresh crusade for the election of a Democratic Congress and Democratic governors; and the issue is, the tariff—one thousand individuals are protected with special favors while fifty million people pay the bills.

The World's appeal is directed in particular to "The Shopping Woman"—the housewife who pays the high prices which the tariff breeds.

This appeal is effective. New York goes Democratic. *The World* is right. Throughout the nation, the party is reunited. McKinley is beaten in Ohio. Massachusetts elects a promising young Democratic governor, William E. Russell, whose brilliant career is to be cut short by death; Democrats also carry the state tickets in New Jersey, Connecticut, Illinois, Indiana, Michigan, Nebraska, Pennsylvania, and Wisconsin.

The House of Representatives goes Democratic. The popular plurality is 800,000. Speaker Thomas E. Reed, still smarting under *The World's* lashings for his arbitrary changing of the rules to push through the McKinley Bill, is flabbergasted. His comment is: "The Shopping Woman did it!"

Meanwhile, JP has consulted Dr. Mitchell. The diagnosis is bitter news; and the medicine is worse. The prescription is—exile from *The World*. Here are the orders:

Immediate separation from "agitations and excitements" incident to the conduct of *The World*. The separation must be not merely nominal but effective and complete. JP is not to have any contact with newspapers; not even to have them read to him; no reports from the office; no telegrams; no telephone calls; and more specifically:

Take a yacht and cut loose from all contact with news—a voyage of many, many months, entirely away from the former ways of life —all means of communication absolutely cut off.

And don't worry.

We must give JP credit. He does try to carry out Dr. Mitchell's treatment, since that way lies the only hope of even partial recovery. *The World's* European correspondents are instructed to look around for a good yacht—one that can be made soundproof.

Elaborate preparations are started immediately for the comfort of one who is to be not only a man without a country, but an editor without news. Philip Nolan had the easier lot. JP is not even allowed to attend the opening of his new building.

The golden-domed $2,500,000 skyscraper (for so it was at the time) has been shooting upward impressively. *The World's* new home overtops the *Sun*. Dana has been viewing it with concern if not alarm.

One day when the Pulitzer Building became high enough to shut off the *Sun's* outlook on Brooklyn Bridge, Dana remarked to his publisher, "Laffan, this begins to look serious."

Laffan replied, "A mere episode, my dear fellow, a mere episode."

The *Sun* and other old-time newspapers nourished the delusion that *The World* would soon fold up. The *Herald* called it "a gift enterprise" because *The World* gave prizes to help circulation.

Well, Laffan was right in a way. *The World* did vanish, but the "mere episode" lasted forty years.

New York, October 16, 1890
From *The World:*
Announcement:

"Yielding to the advice of his physicians, Mr. Joseph Pulitzer has withdrawn entirely from the editorship of *The World*.

". . . The entire control of *The World* has been vested in an Executive Board of its principal editors who have been long in its service, and have conducted it in the absence of its chief. The change is thus more nominal than otherwise. It involves no change of men, of methods, or principle or policy.

"The World will continue to be guided by the ideas of the man who made it what it is. It will follow the lines marked out by him in dedicating this journal to the public service—to the cause of justice, of good morals and good government."

New York, October 17, 1890
From the *New York Herald:*

"Mr. Joseph Pulitzer the other day resigned his direct control of the *New York World* . . . a great vacuum is made in the present actuality of American journalism.

"As for us of the *Herald,* we droop our colors to him. He has made success upon success against our prejudices; has succeeded all along the line; has roused a spirit of enterprise and personality, which, up to this time, has not been known. . . . We cannot refrain from regretting that he did not encourage us . . . instead of merely astonishing us, frightening us, and we may add—now that it is past —perhaps a little bit disgusting us.

"But, *le Roi est mort, vive le Roi! The New York World* is dead! Long live *The World. Pacet!"*

Bennett's tribute pleases JP; and thereafter, by his orders, there are no more digs at the *Herald*.

The new Pulitzer Building, home of three *Worlds,* Morning, Evening, and Sunday, has its grand opening on December 10, 1890, the twelfth anniversary of JP's taking over the *Post-Dispatch*.

Merrill is master of ceremonies. His address of welcome is answered by three governors: Hill of New York, Beaver of Pennsylvania, and Morgan of Connecticut; also by General Taylor of the *Boston Globe;* Murat Halstead, editor of the *Cincinnati Inquirer;* St. Clair McKelway, editor of the *Brooklyn Eagle,* and the indispensable, golden-voiced orator from Philadelphia, Daniel Dougherty.

The World of that morning carries the brief item that Mr. and Mrs. Pulitzer have already departed for Europe. They sailed the day before.

And thus begins the exile of the man who was banished by the very best medical opinion. . . . Six months later he is back in New York raging at the blunderings and ineptitudes of the Executive Board. Exile be damned! The cure didn't work. There is no way to separate the man from his worries. He chooses invalidism, even if it means death, rather than divorce from his newspaper. Nerves and blindness make it impossible for him to work in the Pulitzer Building, but as for giving up his *World* . . . he can stay away from it, but he can't live without it.

6. New World

"Money lost—something lost;
Bestir thyself—create new wealth;
Honor lost—much lost . . .
Win Fame, and make the world forget.
Courage lost—all is lost!
Better thou hadst not been born!"

—GOETHE

FROM the Memoirs of the late George W. Hosmer, M.D., LL.B.:

December, 1890—"Mr. Pulitzer went to Paris, and remained there only until a sufficiently commodious yacht could be found. He chartered the English steam yacht *Semiramis*—large, staunch, roomy, and comfortable.

1891—"He went to the Riviera and went on board the yacht at Mentone on January 10. Mrs. Pulitzer had determined to accompany Mr. P. on this cruise but soon made the discovery that nature had not intended her for a sailor and she reluctantly withdrew. . . . The company was made up of Charley Fearing; Lionel Earle, nephew of Lord Lytton, and G.W.H. Later additions were—Captain Wiliam Emory, U.S.N., Dr. J. Madison Taylor of Philadelphia, and Mr. John Foord.

Itinerary—"Nice to Barcelona and down the Spanish coast to Gibraltar; eastward along the coast of Africa. Several days at Algiers . . . things unpleasant outside the harbor. He remained at Tunis long enough to visit the place where Carthage had been, to see the queer old stones that have been dug up and at least prove that the famous ancient city really stood at that site.

"To Tripoli and thence across [the Mediterranean] to the Grecian coast and had a chance to see a first-class storm at sea . . . the cap-

142

tain skillfully ran the ship into the Bay of Navarino, which, indeed, was none other than the Windy Pylos of garrulous old Nestor [Hosmer's Odyssey, not Homer's]. This is the scene of a famous battle in which a poor little Turkish fleet was reduced to splinters in 1828. . . . The water is so clear that anchors and cannon can be seen at the bottom.

"The little Greek town beside the bay did have a telegraph office. . . . The telegrams were paid for in drachmas, but the messages were not in contravention of the law of isolation from the life and politics of New York. On the contrary, the rule of separation was adhered to with rigid fidelity.

"All those days on the yacht, conversation was an abundant resource to lighten the steps of time; there were cards also [for the staff, not for JP]—but the grand resource was BOOKS. Walter Scott, though read before, was as good as new; George Eliot told *The Mill on the Floss* and *Felix Holt* to our satisfaction. Even Hall Caine in *The Deemster* and *The Bondsman* was pleasant company; and Thackeray with *Vanity Fair* redeemed even the days when the sea was nasty.

"We made our way to the Piraeus and had a look at Athens, thence for Alexandria, but went into Smyrna on account of bad weather. From Smyrna we steamed away to the Dardanelles . . . and so on from port to port.

"Mr. Pulitzer continued this pursuit of repose for nearly four months and then returned to Nice. He had rigidly adhered to his purpose to keep out of his life all those sources of irritation that had induced his malady . . . but the old enemy, insomnia, was not conquered . . . other evils were mitigated, but not cured.

May—". . . He made a journey from Paris to Rome to see Dr. Mitchell and ponder with him the problem whether anxiety due to long-continued separation from concerns of great importance might not be as bad as any activity in producing cerebral irritation.

June—"Mr. Pulitzer was forced to take a temporary departure from the medical regime and make a journey to New York by unforeseen complications and the ambitions of men on his staff. He sailed on June 3. . . ."

Whatever Dr. Mitchell may have advised on the question of whether worry without *World* was worse than *World* with worry, JP evidently cast the deciding vote. Somehow or other, repercussions of trouble back home had caught up with him. The unfortunate triumvirate of Cockerill, Turner, and Davis was in a turmoil.

Although 1890 had been a banner year for circulation and advertising, Turner and Cockerill could no longer agree on anything, and Davis, though holding the title of vice-president, was powerless. Turner was demanding a controlling voice in *The World*. Result—Cockerill spent most of his time at the Astor House, Turner was usually away on his yacht, and Davis, through family channels, poured out messages of grief. . . .

JP arrives on June 10, cleans up the situation in one week, and is off again to Europe. The weather is excessively hot. Equally torrid, *The World* situation. JP dismisses Turner and orders Cockerill to St. Louis, at the same time summoning his old associate, John A. Dillon, from the *Post-Dispatch*. . . . Cockerill resigns.

In the week of upheaval within *The World* and terrific heat, JP suffers a severe aggravation of the old trouble. Hosmer reports, "There was a partial loss of even the little eyesight that he possessed. He went immediately to Wiesbaden for advice as to his eyes and remained there under treatment all summer, troubled with insomnia and asthma . . . always in the shadow of the fear of absolute loss of sight.

"Many of these days were lightened by literature—reading [aloud] was the main resource to exclude the devil of worry . . . Scott, Trollope, Brontë."

Pulitzer sailed for New York again in October. "This time," says Hosmer, "he remained for six months, not all that time in New York, but kept in daily touch [with *The World*] by telegraph.

"It seemed as if he might be compelled, as he feared, to give up altogether. . . . He wanted to devote a few months to putting things in good shape out of regard to those that were to follow. [This is the first hint of a famous will in the making.]

"He remained in New York until the middle of January [1892], a great part of the time in bed suffering from asthma . . . went to Washington and remained a few weeks. On January 25 he had an obstinate and exceedingly severe access of asthma, with imminent asphyxiation.

"He went to Jekyl Island, Georgia, in February and from there to Lakewood, April 1. . . . During all this time he was in constant communication with his staff in New York and suffered as much from labor and worry as though he had been in New York, but there was mitigation of life in the more genial climate. On April 10 he sailed for Europe. . . ."

The rest of that year included stops in Paris; Wiesbaden (where he took treatments from Dr. Pagenstecher and finished *The Life of George Eliot*); Baden-Baden, where he had a visit from sons Ralph and Joe, and failed to find "a quiet place for sleep"; Paris until January.

Hosmer notes that "Egypt was investigated at this time as a land of possible tranquillity with negative result. . . . On January 2, Mr. Pulitzer went to Monte Carlo and remained there three months."

Meanwhile, he has again been compelled to crack down on the editors of *The World* and put the ship back on its intended course.

The World had been veering badly toward the left.

In the early summer of 1892, the threat of labor war hung over the Carnegie steel plant at Homestead, Pennsylvania. Andrew Carnegie's agreement with the Amalgamated Association of Iron, Steel, and Tin Workers was about to expire. "Gentle Andy" had decided not to renew it. He had his reasons. The Carnegie Company's net earnings for 1891 were only $4,300,000, a low figure.

Less than half of the Homestead workers were enrolled in the union. Carnegie warned:

"The firm cannot run union and non-union. It must be one or the other."

Still, he was reticent about declaring his choice. Perhaps it was because he had only recently offered a new addition to the Ten Commandments: "Thou shalt not take thy neighbor's job!"

Labor leaders thought this a declaration against strikebreakers, and Andy Carnegie became very popular. But not for long. Three months before the Amalgamated contract expired, Carnegie sailed for Skibo, Scotland, leaving the negotiations in the hands of Henry

C. Frick, man of action. Labor was rather fond of Carnegie, but had no use for his associate.

Frick called in the union leaders.

"We do not care whether a man belongs to a union or not," he declared. But he refused to renew the old agreement and offered a greatly reduced wage scale. Leaders argued, but Frick was deaf; he demanded acceptance or rejection by June 24.

In vain, the workers tried to reach Carnegie. Andrew's castle in Scotland was officially "closed"; nobody knew how to reach him, except Frick, who was cabling daily reports. On June 23 the men turned down Frick's offer.

"All right," said Frick. "We'll close the plant on July 1 and reopen July 6 with what labor we can get—no further dealings with the Amalgamated."

Crowds of workers burned Frick in effigy. There was a general rush to join the union. When the lockout started on July 1, the workers seized the plant and drove out officials.

Frick hired three hundred Pinkerton guards and announced that the plant would reopen on schedule.

William H. Merrill, sitting up in the dome of the new Pulitzer Building, wrote his first editorial on the steel crisis for the paper of July 2. JP was in Baden-Baden. He knew nothing of the quarrel except from brief accounts in foreign newspapers. Merrill had to decide *The World's* position for himself. Without hesitation he sprang to the side of the men.

Under the McKinley Tariff, he declared, the people are paying nearly twenty million dollars a year, supposed to protect an infant industry and the American wage earner. And yet, said the editorial, since the passage of the McKinley Bill wages have been reduced. "The only beneficiary of the tariff is the capitalist, Carnegie, who lives in a baronial castle in Scotland, his native land." The article went on to say that Carnegie's company had hired "Hessians"; that the plant of "the foreigner" had been turned into a fort against the American wage earner, the enemy whose attack is feared.

And this, Merrill sums up, "is the kind of amity engendered by the tariff . . . in the most thoroughly protected State in the Union."

Merrill did not know, when he wrote the editorial, that the men

The Pulitzer Building, Park Row, New York

had seized the plant and had barred the owners. But the news, when it did come over the wire, does not seem to have affected *The World's* attitude, either on the editorial page or in the news columns. Ballard Smith, who had become managing editor, dispatched a small army of *World* reporters to Homestead. On July 3, *The World* printed a news story headed, "The Iron King's War."

"As Carnegie's millions have increased from year to year," the article declared, "so have the wages of his employees decreased. The strike at Homestead may be the decisive battle . . . Carnegie's mills have been filled with European laborers . . . every year Carnegie has tried to reduce wages . . . the man of millions acquired through the high tariff on steel is the foe of organized labor."

Homestead, Pennsylvania, July 6, 1892

Frick tries to open the plant. Three hundred "Pinkerton Hessians," as *The World* calls them, are towed up the Monongahela River in two barges, pulled by the tugboat, "Little Bill."

As the barges approach Homestead, the "Pinks" are greeted with bricks, presently with revolver shots. One Pinkerton captain is wounded. The guards fire back and two strikers fall dead.

Infuriated, the workers cry: "Kill the hired thugs!" From behind barricades they keep up a steady gun fire and try to set the barges on fire by means of flaming rafts.

The Pinkertons fight back, but by nightfall are glad to run up a white flag and ask for safe conduct out of the city.

As the Pinkertons march to the railroad station, the mob gets out of hand. Two Pinkertons are beaten to death and many others badly injured. Total casualties for both sides are twelve dead and sixty-five in hospitals.

July 7—*The World* devotes three pages to the reporters' accounts of the battle, illustrated with action drawings. A subhead calls the casualties, "The first fruit of the Ironmaster's resolve to crush his men." Merrill's editorial deplores the conflict, but blames it chiefly on "Pinkertonism." "Is it right," he asks, "that a private detective agency shall maintain a standing army?"

As for Frick's defense—that the owners have a right to employ force to regain their own property—Merrill makes light of it. There

is no justice, he declares, if private force is used before legal resources are exhausted.

July 7—*The World* commends Governor Pattison of Pennsylvania for refusing to call out the militia. Merrill declares:

"It was the Sheriff's business to repress lawlessness . . . military
force should always be a last resort. . . . The use of troops is ob-
noxious . . . is always inexcusable unless forced by absolute necessity."

July 10—Disorder continues at Homestead. Workers are still
holding the plant. Governor Pattison, finally yielding to the Sheriff's
pleading, orders out Pennsylvania's entire National Guard. *The
World,* grudgingly, approves.

"It is probable," Merrill admits, "that the Governor had reason to
fear a more desperate battle. . . . If force must be used to sustain
the beneficiaries of protection in reducing wages and breaking down
labor—better it should be the citizen-soldiery. . . ."

Baden-Baden, July 11.

Joseph Pulitzer is greatly agitated over foreign reports of the
Homestead riots.

"Why," he exclaims, "there are more killed and wounded than
in a Latin-American revolution. I want a summary of *The World's*
editorials and news stories at once!"

When the cables arrive, JP is thrown into a frenzy of rage and
disappointment. What in the name of all that's consequential are
those fellows up in that golden-goddam-dome thinking about? How
often has he told them, "Never be afraid to attack wrong, whether
by capital or labor." Cable Merrill right away: editorials news stories
Homestead grossly sensationalized . . . *World* completely over-
looks greater question public safety law and order.

Later, realizing that Merrill cannot do a Dana without hurting
The World, he wires the substance of tomorrow's leader.

New York, July 11—*The World* today says, editorially:

"Governor Pattison called out the troops at the right time and
in the right way. He waited until it became evident that the civil
army was inadequate.

"There is but one thing for the locked-out men to do. They must submit to the law. . . . They must not make war upon the community.

"On the other hand, there ought to be a concerted effort to secure justice for these men. . . . The case is one for negotiation and arbitration, not one for the arbitrary condemnation of men to a permanent loss of employment."

The ship is back on the narrow course between "predatory plutocracy and predatory poverty." But the snow flies before the Homestead dispute is finally settled. The workers lose. (What would JP say about sit-down strikes?)

August—JP cables:

"Give Ballard Smith a farewell dinner at Delmonico's."

This is Smith's first intimation of good-bye. (In the Hearst organization the method is to present you with a watch or an increase in salary.) B.S. does not need to be kicked on the shins.

The dinner at Delmonico's is an orgy of sentiment, such as only *World* men can enact. The champagne is dry, but the party is wet. JP is the host not present, but never-absent.

The cable from Baden-Baden conveys "grateful memories for loyal services, sorrow for parting . . . [parting is sweet sorrow in this case] . . . confident hopes for a happy career." *The World,* JP adds, will always be a tender Alma Mater to Smith.

After a brief absence, Smith went back on the payroll as London correspondent, but only for a year.

Waverley, Massachusetts, July 31, 1900—Ballard Smith, former managing editor of *The New York World,* died in a sanitarium, after an illness of seven years.

The winter and early spring of 1893, which JP spent in Monte Carlo, enabled him to be out of doors much of the time. "Yet in going to the opera at Nice" (quoting Hosmer here), "he caught cold which kept him in bed two weeks and neutralized the advantages of the climate. Another detriment was the avalanche of reports from New York. No climate has any curative compensation for evils of that character. On May 3 he sailed for New York on the *S.S. Majestic.*"

The ship had been given special soundproofing in the area of the

Pulitzer suite. He arrived on May 10 just in time to attend his own dinner at Delmonico's to celebrate *The World's* tenth anniversary. The Commemoration Edition, Sunday, May 9, was a record-breaker, with 400,000 copies and 100 pages. Sir Edwin Arnold, author of *The Light of the World,* contributed a poem, and the business office contributed the more interesting information that *The World* had spent $17,680,000 in these last ten years.

At the dinner, attended by "principal editors and managers," Merrill sits on JP's right hand; S. S. Carvalho, nominally managing editor of *The Evening World,* but with manifold other duties, on the left; also present are Colonel George U. Harvey, *The World's* new managing editor, later known, chiefly to himself, as "the man who discovered Woodrow Wilson," George Cary Eggleston, editorial writer, and many others.

Harvey and Eggleston propose so many toasts and drink so many healths that their own are in danger. Toward midnight, Harvey rises for about the twenty-fifth time.

"Jellmun—lehuzz dring tooozz—ah-ah-a-a-a- tooo ZZZ Mazhuzz-tee . . . uh KING!"

JP explodes.

"Damn it, Harvey! No kings—NO KINGS!"

By the end of the week, he is off to Europe again, and quite soon afterward Harvey is off *The World.* JP has learned all about Harvey's trying to edit *The World* from uptown clubs. (In later years, with fair success, Swope did it from the race tracks.)

Returning in July, JP spent the summer and early fall at Chatwold, the Livingston villa which he leased near Bar Harbor, Maine—a property which he purchased two years later. He had a fairly tranquil summer, Hosmer notes, "as tranquil as possible with all the worries, agitations, hard problems of business and caprices of subordinates at the other end of the wire."

One of the "caprices" is *The World's* handling of the J. J. Van Alen matter. This is one instance where *The World* and Grover Cleveland parted company. Van Alen, an exquisite gentleman of Newport, Rhode Island, a son-in-law of Mrs. William Astor, had contributed fifty thousand dollars to the 1892 Democratic campaign fund, upon assurances that he would be appointed United States Ambassador to Italy. Cleveland made good the promise.

The World editorially urged the Senate not to confirm Van Alen's appointment. But the opposition was very mild. The substance of Merrill's arguments was, "Van Alen has never held public office, has no training in diplomacy, and, in short, Mr. Van Alen should not go to Rome."

The news editors thought Merrill *et al.* were pulling their punches. The city editor assigned a staff man to Newport to find out all about Van Alen. He came back and wrote a story, which for combination of news fact and editorial opinion has never been surpassed.

Here are some of the highlights:

"Mr. Van Alen believes that America is no fit place for ladies and gentlemen to live in. . . .

"Everybody who knows Van Alen knows that his appointment could not be justified. . . . No secret of the situation was made by Van Alen's friends. At a Newport dinner one of his ardent supporters spoke up thus:

" 'If Van Alen doesn't get that appointment, the Democratic party need expect no aid from gentlemen in future. *He paid for the office like a gentleman.*' . . .

"Van Alen is short and fat. He prides himself on his resemblance to the Prince of Wales [the future King Edward VII]. There is a resemblance. . . .

"America, with the aid of Anglo-mania, has produced in Van Alen a man who looks less like a Prince than the Prince of Wales.

"He wears a single eyeglass with a heavy string attached. He speaks with a weird bastard cockney, which fills Englishmen with wonder. It is the sort of English accent that a man with no talent for imitation might get from hansom-cab drivers and Strand barmaids.

"A prize-fighting gentleman of the Bowery was brought to Newport to train the fat off Van Alen. The fighting gentleman, called One-eyed Connelly, said he had never met a man who seemed less fit to be on the earth than Van Alen.

"Van Alen has all the vanities that an American Ambassador could do without.

"He informs whoever will listen that he keeps English mustard in a mustard pot of English silver and French mustard in a French mustard pot.

"He entertains few convictions except those which refer to clothes, horses, and Scotch whiskey.

"He owns twenty pairs of breeches for hunting, this despite the fact that a Shetland pony could buck him off with a gentle shrug. . . .

"Van Alen, who had lived all his life in England, married Emily Astor, much against the wish of her family. His father-in-law, old William Astor, would not speak to him. His progress has been slow in spite of his wealth. This Ambassadorship for $50,000 is the greatest bargain in his life.

"Mr. Cleveland certainly does not know the character of the man whom he is sending to Rome. He is sending a second-hand Englishman. . . .

"There is nothing in common between Grover Cleveland of Buffalo and J. J. Van Alen of Newport.

"If Abraham Lincoln could meet Van Alen . . . his inclination would be to lift Van Alen up by the coat collar and duck him in a muddy pond as a graceful compliment to the Stars and Stripes. If Mr. Cleveland knew Van Alen his inclination would be the same."

This remarkable "story" created a furor in Washington and Newport. But the President did not lose confidence in his appointee. He wrote to Richard Watson Gilder, editor of the *Century Magazine:*

"I have not the slightest doubt of Mr. Van Alen's entire fitness. His contribution, since it did not induce his appointment, is, it seems to me, irrelevant. I believe this act of mine will fully vindicate itself; but the incident demonstrates how readily prejudicial newspaper chatter is picked up and scattered."

And, in reply to a letter from Oscar S. Straus, the President wrote:

"I am amazed by the course pursued by some good people in dealing with this subject. . . . They have chosen to eagerly act upon the frivolous statements of a most mendacious and mischievous newspaper [the newspaper which had helped to elect Cleveland] . . . I think it would be a cowardly thing in me to disgrace a man because *The New York World* has doomed him to disgrace."

How curious that Straus raised the question of Van Alen's bargain! Some twenty-three years later, Straus himself was under fire.

The Republicans charged that Woodrow Wilson appointed him Minister to Turkey in return for a fifty-thousand-dollar campaign check. As a *World* reporter, I asked Straus about it.

"Certainly, I gave the money," he said, "and I consider it the best bargain of my life, because it enabled me to serve my country."

After I got back to the office, Straus called up and wanted to kill the statement, but Arthur Clarke, then city editor, said, "Nothing doing. If he gave that statement, we'll print it." And we did.

The Senate confirmed Van Alen, but the Newport macaroni declined the honor. Having been "vindicated," he had no further appetite for the job. Cleveland was as angry as a man can be when he is wrong and a newspaper is right. But he had to mark the incident "closed."

The same summer, JP astonished *The World* staff from top to bottom by appointing another "colonel" as "editor-in-chief" without bothering to define his duties. This was "Colonel" Charles H. Jones, another St. Louis alumnus, who had just sold his share in the *Republic* of that city. Jones hailed originally from the South, and was primarily a magazine man. He wore side whiskers and had delicate mannerisms.

Jones was to be a thorn in *The World* for some time. He started by going to Washington and writing against the repeal of the Sherman Silver Act. *The World* editors in New York quietly strangled the stories. Then in 1894 along came the American Railway Union's violent strike against the Pullman Company. President Cleveland called out troops to protect property and a Federal court enjoined the strikers. Eugene V. Debs, later Socialist candidate for President, was arrested and imprisoned.

Jones published a red-hot editorial called "Government by Injunction." It was too much for JP. He suspended the colonel and, after much negotiation, induced him to go back and take over the *Post-Dispatch* with a half interest. Later it cost JP much time and money to recover the property.

The phenomenal growth of *The Sunday World* at this stage was originally the work of Morrill Goddard and later of Arthur Brisbane. In 1894 Goddard did brilliant work as city editor during the campaign which resulted in the election of William L. Strong, Fusion candidate, over Mayor Hugh J. Grant, Tammany nominee for re-election. Grant's one term had convinced JP that Grant's personal honesty was insufficient to offset his affiliation with Tammany. *The World* again jumped party traces and supported the Fusion ticket.

After Strong's victory, JP offered to make Goddard managing editor. Goddard demurred. "I'll do better work at the city desk," he said.

"If you have no more confidence in yourself than that, I will not give you the post," JP retorted.

But Goddard had possibilities not yet fully developed. He was prolific in ideas for "feature stories." He would see in some obscure paragraph the germ of a good human-interest yarn, and bring it to striking development in *The World's* columns. Goddard also had a flair for the new "illustrated journalism." He could think in terms of pictures. Finally JP took him off the city desk and made him Sunday editor.

At that time many good people believed that a Sunday newspaper violated the Sabbath and for a long time Whitelaw Reid refused to publish the *New York Tribune* on Sundays. His course received high approval, but he took a weekly loss equally lofty.

"Old friends went out of their way to congratulate me on setting my face against Sunday publication," Reid once explained. "I told them that my noble stand resulted merely in sending my readers, when Sunday came, over to my competitors. 'By the way,' I would ask, 'what paper do *you* read on Sunday?' Then came stammering and hesitation. I usually found that the very men who were exhorting me to set the noble example were themselves reading some Sunday paper."

Pulitzer never regarded publication of a newspaper as a desecration of the Sabbath, unless the paper was dull, which to JP was an unforgivable sin any day in the week.

With Goddard as Sunday editor revolutionary things began to happen. He prevailed upon the Rev. J. Winthrop Hegeman, prominent Episcopal pastor, to live in a tenement in Hell's Kitchen for six weeks and write his impressions for *The Sunday World*.

"I would rather live in hell than in Hell's Kitchen," was the way the good parson began his story.

Goddard engaged a shopgirl to review the English play *A Shop Girl*. She wrote:

"Can it be possible that such a stupid specimen as Ada Smith could get a situation in any of the London shops?"

Goddard conceived the idea of a Sunday comic supplement. One of his first artists was Richard Felton Outcault, later famous for "Buster Brown" which ran for years in the *New York Herald*. Outcault created "Shantytown," a full-page comic, and followed with "Hogan's Alley," introducing the one-toothed youngster who came to be known as "The Yellow Kid."

Outcault deserted Pulitzer for Hearst and later went to the *Herald*, but always held a deep affection for *The World*.

Goddard's comic supplement and magazine features boosted *The Sunday World's* circulation by leaps and bounds. It soon passed 500,000. JP was delighted.

"Goddard," he said, "if next Sunday's circulation exceeds last Sunday's, you shall receive two weeks' salary instead of one."

Thereafter Goddard's pay envelope was doubled, practically every week. Unlike most newspapermen of his day (or ours), he put the extra amount in the savings bank. By the end of 1895, *The Sunday World's* circulation was 600,000. A year later Goddard left *The World* in the "great exodus" to Hearst, and in time became editor of the *American Weekly* at a salary of $150,000 a year.

But that's another story.

The Pulitzer Timetable—(1893-1896):
  (Recorder, Hosmer)
Oct. 27—Lv. N.Y.C. for Paris. House in Rue Murillo "very unsatisfactory because of noise."
December to April, 1894—French Riviera; "a commodious house with large garden touching the sea."
April to June—Ragatz, Switzerland (Rented villa).
June to January—Bar Harbor (Chatwold).
January to May, 1895—Jekyl Island.
May-June—Moray Lodge, London.

July to November—Chatwold and New York City.
November to January—"Cleveland Cottage," Lakewood, N. J.

PEACE ON EARTH

"And seeing the multitudes, he went up into a mountain: and when he was set, his disciples came unto him: and he opened his mouth, and taught them, saying, . . . 'Blessed are the peace-makers.' . . ."—Matthew 5:1-2, 9.

December, 1895.

The jingoes of America are clamoring for war with Great Britain.

For weeks, President Cleveland has been bombarded with demands for action on the Venezuela boundary dispute. The line drawn by the British explorer Robert Schomburgk in 1840 to divide Venezuela from British Guiana has never been accepted by Venezuela. In April, 1895, Venezuelan authorities arrest two British police officials. Pressure from London compels their release. President Crespo of Venezuela begs for help from Washington.

December 18—President Cleveland, in a special message, asks Congress for a special commission "to determine the true divisional line." If Britain refuses to recognize it, the United States should be ready to fight. Great Britain's attitude, Cleveland declares, is a menace to the peace and safety of the United States and "the integrity of our free institutions."

"In making these recommendations," Cleveland solemnly asserts, "I am fully alive to the responsibility incurred and keenly realize all the consequences that may follow."

December 22—The Senate passes the Hitt resolution, previously adopted by the House, appointing the boundary commission, and not forgetting an appropriation of $100,000 for "expenses." Cleveland signs the measure the same day.

New York Sun: "Any American citizen who hesitates to uphold the President of the United States is either an alien or a traitor. Not an hour should be lost in making ready. . . ." The *Sun* also urges Secretary of State Richard Olney to make allies of France and Russia.

New York Times: "Under the teaching of these bloodless Philis-

The first page of THE WORLD, *Christmas Day, 1895*

tines, these patriots of the ticker [meaning Wall Street men who deprecate "the reign of unreason"] . . . American civilization would degenerate to the level of the Digger Indians who eat dirt all their lives and appear to like it."

New York Tribune: "The [President's] message will not be welcome to the peace-at-any-price cuckoos who have been clamoring that the Monroe Doctrine is a myth."

Prices tumble in Wall Street, ten to twenty-five points. Several firms go to the wall. The President's message is read in public schools. Civil war veterans offer their services. Newspapers throughout the country shriek for war. Britain's warmongers refuse to be out-roared.

From the "Cleveland Cottage" in Lakewood, a blind man sees the folly of a war between the two great English-speaking nations, and also the fallacy of the Monroe Doctrine as applied in this instance. JP dictates the editorial which appears in *The World* on December 22:

"President Cleveland's message to Congress on the Venezuelan matter is a grave blunder. It is a blunder because it is based on a wrong conception, because it is not sustained by international law or usage and because it places the United States in a false position.

"The President . . . assumes that the policy of Great Britain in Venezuela involves a menace to this country. . . . The assumption is absurd. And with it falls the structure of ponderously patriotic rhetoric reared upon it by the President.

"It is a grave blunder to put this government in its attitude of threatening war unless we mean it and are prepared for it and can hopefully appeal to the sympathizers of the civilized world in making it."

On the Sunday before Christmas, *The World's* leading editorial is headed: "PEACE ON EARTH."

Prominent in the background of the editorial is the fact that several notable groups of clergymen from coast to coast have passed resolutions favoring Cleveland's message. *The World* declares:

"What have the two representative Christian nations of the earth been doing? . . . The two nations who make Christmas both a memorial and a mockery . . . have been set by the ears over a remote and unimportant boundary line, and fill the air with threats of war. . . . Even ministers of religion have carried human hero-worship so far as to forget the mission of their Master, and have joined in the clamor for war.

"Before *The Sunday World* again appears we shall have taken down our wreaths; the holly and the mistletoe will have gone . . . but we shall retain our hopes. The white doves, unseen, will be flut-tering somewhere. . . . Rancor and revenge have come and gone but they will not dampen the desire of men for peace on earth."

All during that week, *The World* sent out cables to leaders of opinion in Great Britain—clergymen, statesmen, the Prince of Wales, Lord Salisbury, William E. Gladstone, editors, archbishops, bishops, leaders of Parliament. The cables were signed: "Joseph Pulitzer."

The responses are immediate and unmistakable. England—that is, the people of England—want no war with America. Gladstone cables: "Only common sense is necessary." The Prince of Wales and the Duke of York, with Queen Victoria's approval, thank Pulit-zer for his telegram. They earnestly trust that the present crisis will be arranged in a manner satisfactory to both countries and will be succeeded by the same warm feeling which has existed between them for so many years.

Reaction in the United States after publication of the British messages turns the tide toward peace. Catholic, Protestant, and Jew-ish leaders take up the appeal. Churches hear fervent prayers. By the New Year, jingoism has evaporated. In a few days, *The World* announces:

"Facts proved to the country that it had been a victim of false alarm. Truly, 'Peace hath her victories no less than war.' Benjamin Constant was right: 'The press is mistress of intelligence and intelli-gence is mistress of the world.' " (JP's editorial dictation, without a doubt.)

The White House was not very happy, and Secretary Olney spoke of invoking an old statute passed in 1799, which provided that any citizen who addresses a foreign government may be fined up to five thousand dollars and put in prison for five years.

The World, in sardonic vein, urged Mr. Olney to enforce the "aged, obsolete, moldy, moth-eaten" law more effectively than the administration prosecuted the anti-trust laws. And the editorial added:

"*The World* will not descend into the dungeon and put out its million-candle-power torch of liberty and intelligence without a struggle."

The new arbitration treaty between Great Britain and Venezuela was ratified a year and a half later.

POSTSCRIPT TO PEACE

"*. . . We have received grace and apostleship for obedience to the faith among all nations . . .*

"*Destruction and misery are in their ways; and the way of peace have they not known; there is no fear of God before their eyes.*"

—*Romans 3:16-18.*

June 5, 1896, London, England—Representatives of British peace and arbitration societies assembled today to pay a tribute to an American journalist.

The large delegation which gathered at Moray Lodge, the residence of Mr. Joseph Pulitzer, proprietor of *The New York World,* included Cardinal Vaughan, the Roman Catholic Primate; Sir Lewis Morris, Hon. Rev. Carr Glynn, Sir James Reckitt, Sir Robert Head Cook, editor of the *Daily News* (London) . . . also present was Colonel Henry Watterson, editor of the *Louisville Courier-Journal.*

Organizations represented were the Peace Society, the International Arbitration and Peace Association, the International Arbitration League, the Peace Committee of the Society of Friends, and the Dublin Peace Society.

On behalf of the assemblage, Cardinal Vaughan presented an engrossed memorial to Mr. Pulitzer in recognition of his efforts in behalf of good feeling between the United States and Great Britain. . . .

"We congratulate you," the memorial stated, "on the immense and gratifying success resulting from that beneficent exemplification of the marvelous facilities of modern journalism in the dark days of last December.

"Your prompt intervention evoked from the best, wisest, and most influential persons of the day so united and emphatic a protest that the counsels of moderation and sanity were enabled to exert their rightful sway over the public sentiment."

Cardinal Vaughan said (in part):

"Your efforts were widely appreciated. But your task is far from complete. You, with us, must desire and must work for a permanent memorial. . . ."

As Mr. Pulitzer stepped forward to receive the testimonial, there was much applause.

MR. PULITZER: I am deeply touched, but unfortunately I am an invalid and under doctors' orders. . . . I ask permission for my address to be read by a young American friend—my son.

Mr. Ralph Pulitzer, eldest son of *The World's* owner and editor, read his father's response, which was entitled "THE REIGN OF REASON VS. THE REIGN OF FORCE."

The most striking parts of Mr. Pulitzer's address are these:

"I am deeply sensible of the great compliment of your presence. Yet I feel that you come to do honor to a principle and not to a person. . . .

"I know of no purely moral sentiment that has been advanced in England since the abolition of slavery that appeals so strongly to the mind and heart as this idea of substituting civilized methods of peace and reason for barbarism and needless war. . . .

"True Americanism means arbitration. If the great Republic across the sea stands for anything it stands for the reign of reason as opposed to the reign of force; for argument, peaceful discussion, and lawful adjustment as opposed to passion and war.

"America is proud of the fact that arbitration is an American idea.

"Even our jingoes all were and are for arbitration, and the dark cloud that recently passed over America was only made possible by an unfortunate refusal of arbitration.

"It was a noble idea that stirred the American people, even though that idea was based upon a mistaken conception of fact. The spirit of protest was called out by a natural sympathy with the underdog, as we say—with the weak against the strong—and not by any personal feeling for Venezuela, with which country Americans have hardly anything in common. . . .

"If *The New York World* has been to any degree helpful in this Venezuelan affair, your warm words of appreciation are welcome, and are an encouragement to all members of my profession on both sides of the Atlantic who have fearlessly discharged their duty under great difficulties. For it is not pleasant both to criticize the Government and offend the people in force behind the Government. Where that opinion is subject to impulses, often from an excess of enthusiasm, the responsibility of the press becomes most grave.

"It is a duty to interpret the right, to expose the wrong, to teach the moral, to advocate the true and to oppose the false, constantly and conscientiously, judicially and fearlessly.

"Without sacrificing conscience to the natural desire of plaudits and popularity, it must attack error, whether emanating from the Cabinet or from the people themselves.

"It must do its duty against that false and perverted patriotism called jingoism.

"True patriotism, true Americanism, mean love of and pride in country. But we love our great Republic not because it has 70,000,000 of people, not because of its vast area and exhaustless resources, not even because of its wonderful progress. We love her because her cornerstone is enlightened intelligence, and her foundations are freedom, equality, public morality, national honor, tolerance, *and, above all, justice.*

"Jingoism is not confined to any one country, but is found in England as well as in America; in Germany as well as in France; in Russia as well as in Japan. Jingoism is an appeal to national vanity, national prejudices, or national animosities.

"Every day there rests upon the conscientious press the responsibility of combating these prejudices and of teaching lessons of enlightenment. . . .

"In no case have the United States ever refused arbitration. In no case have they made war, except for independence and self-preservation. Those facts go far toward assuring peace as an outcome of the Venezuela case. . . .

"You may feel assured that the decision of the American Commission, composed of four judges and scholars, will be as fair and judicial as would be the result reached by any four of your own judges. The American Commission, gentlemen, will justify both the moderation and the confidence of the British Government.

"The outcome will be peace; peace with a better understanding, with friendlier good will, with kindlier feeling.

"But I hope and believe that both nations will provide against the recurrence of such a crisis. If you will vigorously carry on your campaign of education you can make it most improbable that any government will refuse to arbitrate such trifling disputes again.

"But as to the future danger, let us trust that there will be either a treaty or a tribunal making it impossible for the two nations to go to war about any issue that does not involve the national independence, the national honor, or the national existence.

"Civilization means that disputes and differences, whether individual or international, shall be settled by reason or by some judicial process, and not by force. Civilization is no more possible without peace than permanent peace is possible without arbitration. *Yet this does not mean peace at any price.*

"There are certain issues that are not arbitrable.

"War against a cruel despotism or slavery Americans regard as not only just, but as inevitable.

"They believe in the French Revolution. They naturally sympathize with the uprising of any people against despotism, whether in Greece or Hungary, or Poland in the past, or in Cuba today [1896].

"I cannot help feeling that you, as Englishmen, share with the Americans at least in some of these sympathies. I have always held it one of England's greatest glories, almost equal to her matchless literature, almost equal to her genius for conquest, colonization, and government in the remotest parts of the globe, unsurpassed since the days of the Romans, that for a century she has been for all Europe the strong place of refuge for political offenders.

"She, with Switzerland, has been practically the only European asylum for liberty-loving revolutionists and political exiles. She has protected all alike, whether anarchist or monarchist, whether rebel or pretender to a throne. And since England has shown this devotion to political freedom, Englishmen will understand a similar spirit in America.

"However we may differ on many questions, we have common sympathies for liberty and humanity, just as much as we have a common language.

"We speak, we read, we think, we feel, we hope, we love, we pray—aye, we dream—in the same language. The twentieth century is dawning. Let us dream that it will realize our ideals and the higher destiny of mankind.

"Let us dream not of hideous war and butchery, of barbarism and darkness, but of enlightenment, progress, and peace. . . ."

The foregoing is regarded as a clear statement of JP's aims as a statesman-editor. He regarded journalism as the hope of civilization and he was decidedly in favor of peace.

Postscript: But Peace, only with Justice. . . . In other words, while negotiation and arbitration are greatly to be desired among civilized nations—there is no peace for the despots, the oppressors and the despoilers of men. . . .

To promote peace on earth, in JP's view, it is sometimes necessary to fight for it.

Lakewood, N. J.

According to Dr. Hosmer's notes: Mr. Pulitzer's reading during this exciting time included Thomas Hardy's *The Woodlanders,* Maarten Maartens's *My Lady Nobody,* Conan Doyle's *The Sign of the Four,* R. L. Stevenson's *Treasure Island,* Voltaire's *Candide* and *Zadig,* W. D. Howells's *Tribulations of a Cheerful Giver,* and Schopenhauer's essay on "Noise."

Excerpt from Schopenhauer (*Essay on "Noise"*) :

"I quote what Thomas Hood says—'For a musical nation they [the Germans] are the noisiest people I have ever met . . . when they hear a noise, it does not affect them much. It does not disturb them in reading or thinking, simply because they do not think.' "

Joseph Pulitzer, as we have seen, was a man of peace. He constantly sought it as a balm for his tortured self, and highly commended it as the standard of decency among nations. He loved it so much that he was always battling for it. . . .

There was no peace for him in Wall Street. Himself one of the richest men of his time, a firm believer in sound American investments, especially railroads, he had no use for purely money-making devices—even though he was not averse to picking up a quick bargain, as in the case of the German paper in St. Louis.

With JP, money never came first.

One night in the early nineties, shortly after *The World* took possession of the new Pulitzer Building, fire broke out in the press-room. Smoke spread rapidly, forcing the editorial and composing room staffs to the street. After the blaze was extinguished, the management discovered that the damage in the pressroom made it impossible to print the morning edition.

In this emergency, the *Staats-Zeitung* offered *The World* facilities for publishing an eight-page paper. *The World* accepted, but a practical question arose: How much of the limited space should be used for advertising? The managing editor and the business manager clashed. They finally agreed to refer the question to JP, who happened to be in New York. One of the three telephones then in the Pulitzer skyscraper was used. JP listened to the managing editor, who pleaded for news. Then he heard the business manager, who urged the claims of advertisers. JP gave swift orders:

"Throw out all advertising. Print eight pages of news. News always comes first."

In the same spirit he instructed his editors never to remember that he was an investor, but always that he was a servant of the news. When *The World* had news stories or editorials concerning Western Union or the Delaware, Lackawanna, and Western, the editors were under strict orders not to consider that Pulitzer held stock in these corporations. He made them take a solemn oath that if, by some strange chance, he should ever instruct them to soft-pedal a story about corporations in which he had a personal stake as a shareholder, they were to disobey the orders.

From the time of his opening attack on "aristocracy," JP was at war with what he called predatory plutocracy—the individuals and groups who exploit corporations or manipulate the stock market for their own benefit, to the detriment of the common stockholder. Speculation was anathema.

The World's war against "the money kings of Wall Street" reached its first crest during the Blaine-Cleveland campaign, culminating in the editorial and the cartoon on "Belshazzar's Feast."

From then on, the feud between *The World* and Morgan and Company continued, with occasional truces and intermissions, right up to the crash of October 29, 1929, when A. A. Schechter—the not-to-be-denied reporter—broke down the tradition. Schechter arrived at the corner of Broad and Wall, where reporters were gathered on the sidewalk outside the Morgan building.

"What are you fellows waiting for?" he asked.

"A statement—we hope," was the reply.

"Rats! Why don't you go in and get hold of somebody?"

Just at that moment, Thomas Lamont, Morgan partner, emerged. His limousine was waiting at the curb. Police guarded the passageway from Morgan steps to the Lamont car.

Schechter blocked the way by standing in front of the car.

"Listen, Mr. Lamont," he said. "Everybody wants to know what is the story back of the market collapse. They have a right to know and it's *The World's* job to inform them. Now we want the straight of it, and I'm going to get it!"

"All right," said Lamont. "Get in the car and ride uptown with me and I'll tell you all I know about it."

The Wall Street press was flabbergasted. . . .

But up to that time, neither Morgan nor his partners would speak to a *World* man, at least not when anybody else was looking. *World* men were not invited to the Morgan "press conferences." Even the late S. S. Fontaine, head of *The World's* Wall Street bureau, was *persona non grata*.

On one occasion, *The World's* bureau was notified, by mistake, that Morgan wanted to see the press. A staff member went over. But when the meeting came to order, the present J. P. Morgan recognized *The World* man.

"I regret," he said, "that this discussion cannot proceed while a representative of *The World* is here."

The World man left, and the paper carried a story about the incident next day.

It is only fair to say that after the great social and economic changes resulting from the Depression, Morgan changed his policy. He surprised the ship newsmen by granting a leisurely interview on one of his returns from Europe, and even posed for photographs, much as he disliked the ordeal.

During the Pecora investigation in Washington (Early New Deal), Mr. Morgan's new attitude toward the pictorial press was imposed upon. Somebody tricked him into posing for photographers with a female midget on his knee. Mr. Morgan's mind was on the investigation and he rather thought the midget was an amiable child. But even after the cruel hoax, he continued to be gracious to newsmen.

Between *The World* and the late J. Pierpont Morgan, founder of the dynasty, there was complete hostility—although, for a time, JP attended Morgan's church, St. George's in Stuyvesant Square, and both were members of the ultra-exclusive Jekyl Island Club. But between JP and other Wall Street financiers, there were very friendly relations. Lewis Latham Clarke was a friend, and William C. Whitney, former Secretary of the Treasury, an intimate friend. They, and others, learned the distinction between Pulitzer the charming, cultivated friend, and JP—*The World*.

Personally, JP had many friends, but not *The World,* except such as chose to be. Morgan J. O'Brien, noted Wall Street lawyer, was for years a riding companion of *The World's* owner. JP had O'Brien in mind as one of the trustees under his will. One day when they were riding together in Central Park, JP mentioned the matter. O'Brien, who was at that time presiding justice of the Appellate Division of the Supreme Court, was ready to accept; he said *The World* was a great paper, except for one fault—it did not stand by its friends. JP said a newspaper should have no friends, and that ended the trustee proposition.

Certainly that attitude was exemplified by *The World's* relations with Grover Cleveland. The final controversy between the two had to do with finance. This was in the holiday season of 1895-96, right after *The World's* feat in preventing war between the United States and Great Britain over the Venezuela affair.

The very day after its "Peace on Earth" Christmas editorial, *The World* cautioned the White House about a forthcoming government loan. "There should be no further costly dickers with a bond syndicate," the editorial declared.

The history back of this was that in February, 1895, the government bought 3,500,000 ounces of gold from a syndicate headed by Morgan and Company at the price of $17.80441 per ounce (today's price is $35 an ounce), paying for the metal with four per cent bonds. The gold, at the mint price, was worth $65,116,244.62. The government paid with bonds to the total face value of $62,315,400. The syndicate, therefore, was paying $104.50 for each $100 in bonds.

The purpose of the loan was to build up the Treasury's gold reserves, which were being steadily drained. Immediately after the contract was signed, the price of bonds on the market went as high as $120, and *The World* charged that enormous profits were being made by the syndicate.

The World overlooked the fact that it was not the syndicate that profited so much as the middlemen, some of whom made 15 per cent.

Under the contract, Congress could have substituted three per cent gold bonds for the four per cent "Morgan bonds," but the Free Silver sentiment in Washington blocked the legislation. Herbert Satterlee, J. Pierpont Morgan's authorized biographer, states as a matter of fact, that the expenses connected with the syndicate were so large that Morgan and his principal associate in the transaction, August Belmont, made nothing at all.

On the face of things, however, it looked as if the syndicate had cleaned up about $12,000,000, and *The World* was not slow to appreciate the opportunity to attack Mr. Cleveland's ideas of government finance. The opportunity grew better as the bond sale failed to check the flow of gold out of the treasury. In August, *The World* sounded another warning: "The government should not again be caught napping . . . should not again allow itself to be cornered . . . should not again sell bonds to a syndicate at 104½ which the people are eager to take at $120 or more."

Long before the end of 1895 it became perfectly apparent that another bond issue would be needed. The drain of gold, through the "endless chain" created by the redemption of currency, was becoming serious. Cleveland was advised not to offer bonds at public subscription. The late John H. Tennant, then Washington correspondent for *The World,* later managing editor of *The Evening World,* received authoritative word that another bond issue was forthcoming and that it would total $100,000,000.

On December 23, while the country was still reverberating with the excitement of Cleveland's message on Venezuela, Morgan went to Washington with Robert Bacon, a partner, and Francis Lynde Stetson, the Morgan attorney—at Cleveland's invitation. Cleveland had begged Congress not to adjourn over the holidays without acting on the gold crisis, but the leaders disregarded the appeal. The Silverites were clamorous.

After reviewing the situation with the President, Morgan decided that the government ought to have $200,000,000 worth of gold, obtainable through a new bond issue. The fact that negotiations were pending became known and served to allay fears in Wall Street, but did not silence the outcry in the newspapers. Morgan passed up his Christmas holidays and organized a new syndicate which included James Stillman, president of the National City Bank; the representative of the Deutsche Bank of Berlin; John A. Stewart of the United States Trust Company; and Harvey Fisk and Sons.

The syndicate agreed to deliver not less than $100,000,000 and not more than $200,000,000 in gold. But before a contract could be concluded with the Treasury, fixing the price of the bonds, *The World* startled the country by calling upon the people to subscribe for the bonds and setting the example by offering to buy $1,000,000 in gold coin. In its editorial of January 3, 1896, *The World* said:

"To you, Mr. Cleveland, *The World* appeals. It asks you to save the country from the mischief, the wrong, and the scandal of the pending bond deal. . . . If it is consummated its memory will be a colossal scandal and you will bear the blame.

"The needless waste of ten to fifteen millions in this transaction is not the only or even the chief objection to it. . . . It involves popular confidence in the integrity of government, that faith of the people in their rulers which is the life-blood of free institutions. . . .

"Trust the people, Mr. Cleveland! You can get all the gold you need in Europe at one per cent or less premium. You can get it in our own country without paying any premium at all. . . .

"So sure are we of this that *The World* now offers to head the list with a subscription of one million dollars on its own account . . . and it will promptly find and furnish the gold with which to pay for the bonds. The whole country will respond with alacrity. Europe will clamor for them. Trust the people, Mr. Cleveland.

"And smash the Ring!"

The World followed up with another appeal to patriotism.

"Better a hundred millions lost, or a thousand millions, than that the people of the Republic shall doubt the integrity of the government and learn to believe that money has taken the place of manhood as the controlling force in the nation."

The people did not respond right away, and Morgan, not hearing anything further from the White House, dissolved the syndicate, but kept his group ready to bid when the loan should be announced. *The World* tried a different method. It sent out 10,370 telegrams to banks and other financial houses throughout the country urging them to support the bond issue, and prepaying the answers. About 5,300 replies came in, enthusiastically endorsing *The World's* plan, incidentally breaking the Western Union record for the number of messages received in a single day. As a result, *The World* announced total pledges of more than $235,000,000.

Cleveland was loath to yield. In a letter to Senator Caffery of Louisiana, the President denied that the government was secretly negotiating with a syndicate. He said the charge was made by a "maliciously mendacious and sensational newspaper," but he said that Mr. Morgan had a right "to put himself in a position to negotiate."

Finally Cleveland and Secretary Carlisle gave in and the bond issue was announced. Public subscriptions were invited. Morgan urged the syndicate members to subscribe. When the pie was opened the bids began to sing; the loan was subscribed nearly six times over. Morgan and a group led with $100,000,000 at 110.6877; other syndicate members came in . . . altogether, there were nearly five thousand bids, including *The World's* for $1,000,000 at 114, which was among those accepted.

But only 781 bidders were accepted, including *The World*. The Morgan group was allotted $33,179,250, but this was later increased to $38,000,000 because some of the less responsible bidders defaulted.

It developed afterward that a number of the bids were without substance. Some people subscribed on a purely speculative basis, others as though they were picking tickets for a lottery. One story is that a young clerk in a brokerage office bid for $3,000,000 without any visible means of redeeming the offer. His bid was accepted, however, and the young man immediately sold his allotment to Russell Sage, making a $50,000 profit, which enabled him to buy a seat on the Stock Exchange.

The World announced:

"The credit of the government is maintained . . . the confidence, the resources, and the patriotism of the people are splendidly maintained . . . it is indeed a famous victory."

There was also a by-product. *The World's* bid was $114, but the price of the bonds almost immediately went higher, and there was a profit of $50,000. JP was concerned. He called a conference of editors and managers at Lakewood. What to do with the "unearned increment"? Brisbane suggested a gift to West Point, but there were legal barriers. Don C. Seitz suggested, "Why not keep it?" The motion was carried.

The calmer light of history and research shows that there were two sides to the bond story. Mr. Morgan seems to be vindicated, so far as motives are concerned. Until *The World* aroused the people, it was considered impossible to float a big bond issue through popular subscription, but we know better now. *The World's* campaign ended for all time the system of government deals with private syndicates.

EXODUS, 1896

In 1895 William Randolph Hearst came east to survey the metropolitan newspaper field. He was only thirty-two years old, but he had made a success of the *San Francisco Examiner*. His father, United States Senator George Hearst, had turned this paper over to young "Willie" with great misgivings; the *Examiner* had been such a heavy financial drain that the Senator said: "I've been planning to give that paper to some political enemy."

After transforming the *Examiner* into a good money-maker, the young Hearst turned to New York.

James Melvin Lee (*History of American Journalism*) wrote: "Hearst broke into New York with all the discreet secrecy of a wooden-legged burglar having a fit on a tin roof."

Hearst bought the *New York Morning Journal* from John R.

McLean, who had acquired it for $1,000,000 from Albert Pulitzer, JP's younger brother. Under Albert, the *Journal* had been a penny paper, but McLean raised the price to two cents. Circulation quickly shrank; McLean was glad to unload to the ambitious young Californian. Hearst cut the price to one cent and looked about for a competent staff; taking note of the swelling circulation of *The Sunday World* under the brilliant Morrill Goddard, Hearst quickly sent for Goddard and made an offer which astonished the young editor.

"But," protested Goddard, "I need my writers and my artists."

"All right," returned Hearst. "Let's take the whole staff." And so it was arranged.

Reliable report says that Goddard was given a spot cash bonus of fifteen thousand dollars, and hastened to five different banks, depositing three thousand dollars in each.

Then came the exodus. Giving only one day's notice, Goddard and the whole staff of *The Sunday World,* down to the newest copy boy, moved over to the *Morning Journal,* then in the Tribune Building. But they did not stay long . . .

> *"They walked right in and turned around*
> *And walked right out again . . ."*

Because JP, learning of the desertion, ordered S. S. Carvalho, *World* business manager, to bring them back. The price was high, but Carvalho succeeded. The next day, Goddard and his associates were all back in the Pulitzer Building. Goddard revisited the five banks and returned the fifteen thousand dollars.

Money was no consideration to Hearst—at least not then; he got in touch with Goddard again and the new offer was irresistible. Once more Goddard gathered his staff and within an hour *The Sunday World* office was as empty as it is today—even the office cat had gone over to Hearst. The cat subsequently lost four out of nine lives, but survived on the *American* under the name of Hypo.

Arthur Brisbane became *The World's* Sunday editor; with ingenuity that matched his predecessor's, Brisbane produced new magazine features and enlarged the Sunday humor section. George B. Luks, then a young artist, continued "Hogan's Alley" with the

Yellow Kid, although Outcault was now drawing the same comic for the *Journal. The World* lost none of its juvenile followers.

At this time Brisbane was frequently in JP's company. It was he who persuaded Pulitzer to get back into the saddle and take morning rides in Central Park.

"I can't ride any more," protested Pulitzer. "I am blind."

"Yes, you can," Brisbane assured him. "Once a cavalryman, always a cavalryman." Brisbane was right. He and JP often rode together amid volleys of questions and answers.

JP was especially indignant over the walkout of the Sunday staff because Hearst had conducted the negotiations from the *San Francisco Examiner's* New York office, which was on the eleventh floor of the Pulitzer Building. He ordered the *Examiner's* lease canceled, declaring: "I won't have my building used for purposes of seduction!"

Hearst moved out and the *Boston Globe's* bureau moved in.

Hearst's one-cent paper soon became popular. In a few weeks the *Journal's* circulation was 150,000 a day, only 35,000 less than *The World's* daily figure. *The Sunday World's* circulation was, of course, much higher.

The Hearst competition did not affect the higher-priced papers like *The World,* the *Tribune,* the *Times,* and the *Herald,* but it made havoc among the one-cent group. JP's most insistent advisers at this time were S. S. Carvalho, who had become assistant vice-president, and John R. Norris, business manager. They strongly urged cutting *The World's* price to one cent. Don C. Seitz, assistant business manager, demurred. JP went away to Jekyl Island, taking Carvalho and Norris along; they got as far as Philadelphia, and then returned, with the announcement that *The World* henceforth was a one-cent paper. An editorial on the subject stated that Mr. Pulitzer preferred power to profits; but there was no important increase in either; the circulation increase was only 88,000 a day, whereas Norris figured that it would go to a million; advertisers failed to respond. The profits went down. The *Journal's* popularity was unimpaired. JP was then persuaded to raise the advertising rates and cut down the number of pages; book reviews were eliminated and Wall Street news cut to half a column. The effect was bad. Hearst now figured that he had the enemy on the run, and began a big promotion campaign.

The World's management became excited. The Hearst and the Pulitzer organizations began spending dollar for dollar. Promotion expenditures rose enormously. Hearst testified years later, in the settlement of his mother's estate, that the fight with Pulitzer had been "very expensive." Estimates run as high as eight million dollars. During the Spanish-American War, the competition for news and circulation became terrific.

This was the era of "Yellow Journalism."

One difference between *The World* and the *Journal* during the fight was that *The World* paid its way out of earnings, whereas Hearst paid out of his own pocket.

Eventually both sides realized the futility of cutthroat tactics and arrived at a design for competition. In time, even the editorial rancor subsided; JP respected Hearst's abilities, though not always commending his policies and principles. He described Hearst as a master in the great art of attracting attention, and, when Hearst was running for governor, as "an able, independent man." After Hearst had organized the Independence League, JP said he was doing a marvelous work; and the instructions to *World* editors were: Treat Hearst with respect; and, if you can possibly control your feeling, without silence, anyhow encourage him.

(Does anybody know of a newspaper war that has been worth while? Roy W. Howard and Fred Bonfils fought almost to the death in Denver, Colorado, in the twenties when Howard bought the *Rocky Mountain News*. Bonfils's *Denver Post*—"the paper with a heart and soul" [and a bankroll]—matched the *News* in giving away premiums for want ads. Both papers gave free gasoline, free groceries, free tickets, and what not, until Merlin Hall Aylesworth, then president of the National Broadcasting Company, brought the gladiators into a peace conference.)

On the night of February 15, 1898, the American battleship *Maine* was blown up in Havana Harbor with a loss of two hundred and sixty-six men. Sylvester Scovel, Havana correspondent of *The World*, flashed a bulletin immediately after the explosion and, by fast work, succeeded in getting a special cable dispatch, with all available details, into the office in time for a fourth edition extra, which was published at five A.M. on the morning of the sixteenth.

Strained diplomatic relations with Spain, growing out of her cruel colonial administration in Cuba, made responsibility for the disaster a grave international issue. *The World* did not wait for the Government to act in this crisis. Within an hour after receiving the first bulletin, night editors of the paper had telegraphed the Key West correspondent to engage expert divers and proceed to Havana to inspect the wreck. The following special cable then was sent to Scovel:

"HAVE SENT DIVERS FROM KEY WEST TO GET ACTUAL TRUTH, WHETHER FAVORABLE OR UNFAVORABLE. FIRST INVESTIGATION BY DIVERS WITH AUTHENTIC RESULTS WORTH ONE THOUSAND DOLLARS. EXPENSES EXTRA. TOMORROW ALONE.

"THE WORLD."

In the same edition that carried news of the disaster *The World* announced it was sending a special tug, with submarine divers, to Havana to find out what had caused the explosion. Unfortunately, when the tug reached Havana Harbor the Spanish authorities firmly declined to allow the divers to inspect the *Maine's* sunken hulk. Sylvester Scovel pleaded with them that *The World's* investigation might dissipate ugly suspicions of Spain that were spreading over America, but they remained impervious to his arguments. *The World's* correspondent in Madrid was equally unsuccessful in obtaining permission to examine the *Maine,* and so *The World's* enterprise came to naught. The next morning *The World* made the following announcement:

"Special cable dispatches from *The World's* own correspondents in Havana and Madrid are to the effect that Spain will not allow the crew of five expert divers employed by *The World* to examine the hull of the wrecked battleship. These men, headed by the *Maine's* chief engineer, Howell, were at the wreck at seven o'clock yesterday morning ready to go to work. They were prevented by the Spanish officials. And now it is proposed that only 'official divers' shall make the investigation, and divers employed by the United States shall be watched by divers employed by Spain. Meanwhile the cause of the disaster remains a mystery. If Spain had not halted the work of *The World* the true cause of the disaster would be known before this."

Spain and the United States drifted toward war. In the midst of the rising hysteria an extraordinary thing happened in *The World* office.

Ernest O. Chamberlain had been transferred from the managing editorship of *The World* to the same position on *The Evening World*.

Chamberlain was one of the best newspapermen of his time. He worked day and night, often spending eighteen or twenty hours at his desk, not pausing for meals, but sending to the little restaurant in the Dome for milk and crackers. He ate while skimming through proofs or scanning papers. He lived for nothing but work.

One night, late in February, 1898, when an impatient country was goading Congress into action against Spain, Chamberlain sat alone at his desk in *The Evening World*. The last edition had gone to press. Editors and reporters had left for the day.

Suddenly, according to Albert Payson Terhune in his autobiography, *To the Best of My Recollection,* Chamberlain jumped up from his chair. He dashed up the stairway to the composing room.

"War!" he cried. "War! We must get out an extra!"

He ran down the stairway again to his desk, snatched up an office directory, and checked off the names and addresses of reporters and editors. He dispatched telegrams ordering them to return to the office at once. When they arrived Chamberlain was calm and collected.

"The war has begun, boys," he said. "We must get out an extra!"

He sat down and wrote the headline himself. It consisted of a single word: W A R ! He sent it to the composing room where it was set in type that spread across the form. Editors looked about for dispatches from Washington, for bulletins from the Associated Press, for cables from Madrid. They found nothing. Nor could Chamberlain help them. He had only one word: "War!" and he had sent that to press.

In a short time Chamberlain's "extra" was on the street. A boy hurried copies of it to *The Morning World*. The editors looked in astonishment, rushed across to the *Evening* rooms.

Chamberlain was mumbling, "War! War! War!"

Shortly afterward he was removed to his home in a cab and boys were dispatched to recall the few copies of his "extra." A very few days later pneumonia developed. When war actually was declared, Ernest Chamberlain was dead.

Covering the Spanish-American War was an expensive undertaking for *The World* and other New York newspapers. Public excitement was out of all proportion to the importance of the conflict, and reportorial machinery and mechanical equipment of the times were strained to meet the enormous demand for fresh news. Most of the papers, including *The World,* lost much of their accustomed poise in the mad struggle to be first on the street with bulletins from the front.

In these feverish days newspapers turned for the first time to large streamer headlines. They were used upon the slightest provocation and often upon none at all. Evening papers issued "extras" with bewildering frequency. Hearst's *Journal,* which had become an evening paper under the managing editorship of Arthur Brisbane, sometimes issued as many as forty editions a day and *The Evening World* under Foster Coates, who replaced the unlucky Chamberlain as managing editor, printed nearly as many. To add to the general confusion, first editions often were called the ninth, second editions the fourteenth, and so on. As a result of this ingenious enumeration, the one hundred and seventh edition at six P.M. was not entirely uncommon.

With all this breakneck rivalry, only one real "beat" was scored during the war. That was *The World's* exclusive bulletin on Dewey's sweeping victory at Manila, which appeared in late editions of *The World* on the morning of May 7, 1898, six days after the battle was fought. About one o'clock on that morning *The World* office received the following cable from E. W. Harden, *The World's* special correspondent on board the gunboat *McCulloch*:

"HONGKONG, MAY 7, 1898

"WORLD, NEW YORK.

"JUST ARRIVED FROM MANILA. MCCULLOCH. ENTIRE SPANISH FLEET DESTROYED. ELEVEN SHIPS. SPANISH LOSS THREE HUNDRED KILLED, FOUR HUNDRED WOUNDED. OUR LOSS NONE KILLED, SIX SLIGHTLY WOUNDED. SHIPS UNINJURED. BULLETIN.

"HARDEN."

The flash was followed a few hours later by a graphic description of the Battle of Manila Bay, running to about eight hundred words and cabled from Hongkong at a cost of $1.80 a word. Two million copies of *The World* might have been sold that morning if mechanical facilities could have met the test. It was a clean "beat" not only upon the other newspapers of the country, but upon Commodore George Dewey, the hero of Manila. The President and the Secretary of the Navy received their first news of the victory in telegrams from the editor of *The World*.

Twelve hours later Dewey's brief official report began to filter into Washington. In the meantime *The World's* bulletin had been flashed all over the earth. Indeed, *Anglo-American* cable officials estimated that the message, credited always to *The World,* was read within half a day by 500,000,000 people in the Eastern and Western Hemispheres.

The next morning, the White House issued this announcement:

"The New York World apparently had the only information to be had on the subject and it would be wise for the Navy Department to depend upon it for its information.

"WILLIAM McKINLEY."

The World's Greatest Circulation Record
The **World** 1,011,068
1,011,068
Per Week-Day April Average
GAIN in One Year · 338,748 "*Circulation Books Open to All.*" "*Circulation Books Open to All.*" GAIN in Three Years · 461,205

VOL. XXXVIII. NO. 13,401 NEW YORK, MONDAY, MAY 2, 1898. PRICE

DEWEY SMASHES SPAIN'S FLEET

VICE-ADMIRAL MONTOJO. ## Great Naval Battle Between Asiatic Squadron and Spanish Warships Off Manila. COMMODORE DEWEY.

THREE OF THE BEST SPANISH VESSELS WIPED OUT OF EXISTENCE.

The Damage Done to the American Boats Engaged Only Nominal----Hundreds of the Enemy Slain in the Encounter.

The Defeated Commander of the Spanish Fleet. Who Won the First Great Victory for the New American Navy.

LISBON, Portugal, May 1, 11 P. M.----The Spanish fleet was completely defeated off Cavite, Philippine Islands, according to trustworthy advices received here.

WASHINGTON, May 1, Midnight.----President McKinley expresses entire satisfaction over the reported battle between Commodore Dewey's squadron and the Spanish fleet. He accepts the news as true, but believes it is worse for the Spanish than they will admit. There has been no official confirmation of the news. Nothing official is expected for forty-eight hours

THE THREE SPANISH CRUISERS COMPLETELY DESTROYED.

CASTILLA.

DON JUAN de AUSTRIA.

FLYING SQUADRON STRENGTHENED.

SPANISH FLAG SHIP "REINA MARIA CRISTINA"

MADRID OFFICIAL REPORT ADMITS DISASTROUS DEFEAT
(Despatch Scrutinized by Spanish Government and Passed by the Censor.)

MADRID, May 1, 8 P. M.----The following is the text of the official despatch from the Governor-General of the Philippine Islands to the Minister of War, Lieut.-Gen. Correa, regarding the engagement off Manila:

"Last night, April 30, the batteries at the entrance to the fort announced the arrival of the enemy's squadron, forcing a passage under the obscurity of the night.

"At daybreak the enemy took up positions, opening with a strong fire against Fort Cavite and the arsenal.

"Our fleet engaged the enemy in a brilliant combat, protected

(Continued on Second Page.)

LONDON'S EARLY MISINFORMATION.

LONDON, May 1.----The Exchange Telegraph Company sent out this afternoon a despatch saying tha' it was rumored in Washington that Commodore Dewey had defeated the Spanish fleet, that the Spaniards lost 3,000 men and that Commodore Dewey lost two ships and 300 men.

SCENE OF THE FIRST GREAT BATTLE OF OUR NEW NAVY.

CHINA SEA.

South China Sea, off the Philippine Islands, showing Manila Bay and Subig Bay, where Commodore Dewey, commanding the United States' Asiatic Squadron, won on Sunday, May 1, 1898, a signal victory over Admiral Montojo, known as Spain's "fighting Admiral," in command of a numerous fleet of Spanish war vessels.

How THE WORLD *trumpeted news of Dewey's victory*

7. Turn of the Century

"The work of the world is never done. In the struggle between good and evil there is on this earth no final victory. . . . Nothing is indestructible if it is not cherished, kept in good repair and vigilantly defended. . . . The institutions of a nation live on only if the people continue to understand them."—WALTER LIPPMANN

THE WORLD of January 1, 1901, was the only one that reflected none of the Pulitzer ideas. Indeed, it was the strangest-looking *World* ever published except *The World's* very last issue on February 27, 1931.

Alfred Harmsworth, editor of the *London Daily Mail,* had been invited by Mr. Pulitzer to conduct the paper for one day.

Harmsworth, who later became Lord Northcliffe, was in sole charge. The entire staff was at his disposal; he could do as he pleased with news, editorials, pictures, and make-up. Harmsworth turned out a twenty-four page tabloid, eighteen inches long and nine inches wide. He led the paper with the story of the arrival of the Twentieth Century and the noisy demonstration on Broadway. On the editorial page Harmsworth announced: "Today's *World* will come as a surprise to its readers. Let me explain at once that it is merely a twentieth-century suggestion on my part . . . closely resembling the newspaper of the future." [It must be admitted that today's tabloids are far more interesting than *The World* that came out on the first day of the new century.]

The World office presented an unusual spectacle that New Year's Eve. In deference to Harmsworth, editors and reporters appeared in evening dress—all except Pomeroy Burton, city editor. He called dressing up silly. Three years later Lord Northcliffe persuaded Burton to work for the *London Daily Mail;* he became a British citizen and was knighted.

Promptly at midnight, William H. Merrill, dean of *The World's* editorial writers, rose with a glass of champagne in his hand and addressed the staff:

"Once in a century we can afford to let duty wait for a moment upon pleasure," he said. "It is surely a pleasure to engage tonight in what may prove to be an epoch-marking international episode in the history of journalism. If our blanket sheets shall in time become napkin sheets, the change will date from this experiment we are making tonight.

"From a brief conversation with our absent chief I gathered that he does not altogether accept that idea of our great and—shall I not say it?—our Easy Boss pro tem. But he admires and likes him immensely and recognizes in him a master craftsman. Gentlemen, on behalf of Mr. Pulitzer, and of the staff of *The World,* I ask you to join in drinking the health and continued good fortune of Mr. Harmsworth."

Harmsworth responded by thanking everybody for the co-operation.

"I don't suppose," he said, "that anywhere in the world there is another newspaper staff that could have entered so heartily and ably into plans imparted almost without warning. . . .

"I don't suppose any great newspaper proprietor in the world except Mr. Pulitzer would entrust his entire plant for one day to the discretion of a young man who has no other recommendation than some little success three thousand miles away. I regret that Mr. Pulitzer is not with us tonight."

Harmsworth asked the judgment of *World* readers on "this scheme of a portable, time-saving, abridged newspaper." The response was mostly unfavorable.

"The best thing about Mr. Harmsworth's experiment," one subscriber commented, "is that Mr. Pulitzer limited it to one day. It would not last over thirty days."

Another criticism was: "Americans do not want to take their roast beef in 'essence' nor their drinks in capsules."

When Northcliffe enticed Pomeroy Burton away from *The*

World, JP accepted the loss with equanimity; but when the British publisher snatched up Alfred Butes, confidential secretary on whom JP heavily depended, *The World's* owner cabled to Northcliffe:

"I always knew you were a hard man, but I didn't think you would steal a dog from a blind man."

The School of Journalism at Columbia University seems to have overlooked something which the founder considered very important—the art of eating soup. But according to Pulitzer standards the final test of a newspaperman was—"How does the man eat soup?"

If a candidate for editorial position on *The World* guzzled, smacked his lips, or tried to mix soup with air, using the mouth as a carburetor—he was lost. To escape JP's displeasure, every *World* man must be able truthfully to say:

"I eat soup but I do not inhale it."

Even the great Frank I. Cobb had to pass the soup test, although he was not aware of it at the time. . . .

It was in the spring of 1904.

William H. Merrill, who had been dean of *The World's* editorial writers ever since JP took hold, was getting old in more ways than one; he was past sixty; his hair had turned to silver, and his sideburns turned to gray. The staff had begun calling him "Pop"—which is always a bad sign.

Yes, Merrill was beginning to slow up. No matter how hard he tried, he was no longer Bill the Zipper; Merrill knew it, Pulitzer knew it, and Merrill knew that JP knew—which made him write worse; he was always looking to JP for guidance, even from afar off.

Much displeased, the blind man wrote bitter letters!

Editors, he said, either have opinions which they are afraid to express, or they have no opinions; either way, they do not do their duty. JP was tired of being not only a scarecrow, but a scapegoat for Merrill; nor did he hesitate to mention Merrill's age and declining vigor; and since "Pop" seemed to miss the point of the letters and kept doggedly hanging on, JP began looking around for Merrill's successor.

Barring this weakness at the top, *The World's* editorial staff in those days was capable and well balanced: John Langdon Heaton understood municipal and state government; Horatio Seymour was a master of American history and politics; Albert B. Kingsbury had a sense of humor, coupled with understanding of social problems; Samuel E. Moffett (Mark Twain's nephew) specialized in foreign policies; L. R. E. Paulin, foreign affairs and Washington; E. W. Osborn, books and drama. Ernest Howard was the late night man for emergency editorials. The staff subsequently was augmented by Ralph Pulitzer, who possessed a sense of irony and became the lad with the delicate touch. Ralph was then in his twenties.

Yet none of these was chosen to succeed Merrill. JP had confidence in Heaton, whom he afterward chose to be a life member of the Advisory Board at Columbia; but Heaton was forty-five and JP wanted a younger man.

What he really wanted was another Joseph Pulitzer.

About this time, a bright, well-informed, and charming young reporter named Samuel M. Williams was detached to act as newspaper secretary to the Chief.

In Bar Harbor one day at lunch, Williams having passed the soup test, JP lamented his inability to find the right editor.

"Really," Williams replied, "there are lots of able editorial writers in this country. They would not all meet your—ah—exacting specifications, but they could be trained."

"If you think so, Williams, suppose you go find one for me."

Brashly, Williams answered: "All right, I will."

"When are you starting on this hunt for the ideal editor?"

"At four o'clock this very afternoon." (It was then two P.M.)

"My God!"

"Don't let anybody know your mission," JP instructed. "Don't tell anyone who looks like a prospect; above all, don't make any commitments."

Williams packed his bag. Here is his own account of the great editor-hunt:

"My plan was to find the man through his own writings. I knew pretty well what JP wanted—his young men had to know history, biography, have keen perception, and a concise, direct, simple, forceful style. In editorials, he especially wanted clarity, brevity, and a punch in the last paragraph.

"As I journeyed from city to city, I read the editorials in the local papers. The prevailing style was ponderous. I read yards and yards of the stuff. Finally, I discovered some editorials in the *Detroit Free Press* which seemed to meet Pulitzer specifications. I bought back numbers, read and reread the articles, picking out those I thought were by the same man.

"I looked up an old friend, Lou Bert, who knew everybody in Detroit, and asked about this writer.

" 'That's Frank Cobb,' said Bert, 'a mighty fine, able chap. He's coming to my house to dinner tonight—join us.'

"At the table, Cobb proved himself a brilliant conversationalist, an omnivorous reader, a shrewd observer, a forceful talker, and a keen analyzer of men and affairs. He had vitality of brain and body, yet was so simple in manner, so modest, so lovable, that I knew immediately I had found the Ideal Editor; but I must get the information necessary to answer the thousand questions JP would fire at me.

"We smoked and talked until a late hour. Cautiously, I questioned Cobb about his tastes, his studies, his reading, his opinions of men and politics and his ambitions. He answered freely, not suspecting my motive."

Past midnight, Mr. Williams took his leave and went directly to the nearest telegraph office.

"JOSEPH PULITZER, BAR HARBOR, ME.

"THINK I HAVE FOUND EDITOR. FRANK COBB, DETROIT FREE PRESS. KNOWS AMERICAN HISTORY AND BIOGRAPHY. HAS A PASSION FOR POLITICS. ONLY HANDICAP IS HE OVER-ADMIRES THEODORE ROOSE-VELT. WRITES WITH PUNCH IN LAST PARAGRAPH AND KEEPS EDI-TORIALS WITHIN A COLUMN."

Williams added a brief biography of Cobb—Martin, Michigan, high school principal; reporter for *Grand Rapids Herald, Grand Rapids Eagle, Detroit Evening News,* and *Detroit Free Press*; and mailed some of Cobb's recent editorials.

Next day Williams received the following wire:

"WHAT HAS COBB READ IN AMERICAN HISTORY, RHODES, MCMAS-TER, TREVELYAN, PARKMAN? WHAT WORKS ON THE CONSTITU-TION AND CONSTITUTIONAL LAW? HAS HE READ BUCKLE'S HISTORY

OF CIVILIZATION? WHERE DID HE STAND DURING BRYAN FREE SIL-
VER CAMPAIGNS? WHAT ABOUT THE STATE OF HIS HEALTH? HOW
TALL IS HE? IS HIS VOICE HARSH OR AGREEABLE? MY EARS ARE VERY
SENSITIVE. TAKE HIM TO DINNER AND NOTE HIS TABLE MANNERS.
IS HIS DISPOSITION CHEERFUL? SOUND OUT HIS AMBITIONS;
WHETHER SATISFIED, OR LOOKING TO A LARGER FIELD. BE VERY
CAREFUL TO GIVE NO INTIMATION I AM INTERESTED. DESCRIBE
MINUTELY HIS APPEARANCE, COLOR OF EYES, SHAPE OF FOREHEAD,
MANNERISMS, HOW HE DRESSES. SEARCH HIS BRAIN FOR EVERY-
THING THERE IS IN IT. JP"

"I took luncheon with Cobb," Williams related. "I probed him
inside and out, but the operation was easy and successful. Cobb was
joyously candid and innocently revealed himself on every one of JP's
points.

"He had read all the books on JP's list. He was against Bryan
and free silver. Although admiring Theodore Roosevelt, he had
attacked the Great Teddy editorially. As to personal appearance,
cheerfulness, tone of voice, and table manners—highly commendable! He ate soup without a gurgle."

The luncheon-audition being satisfactory, the only remaining difficulty was Cobb's ambition.

"I am well situated here and fairly well satisfied," he said. "I
doubt that I could have the same freedom of expression and opinion
on a New York paper. Yet I realize that New York is the newspaperman's goal."

Still JP was not satisfied. He wanted to open Cobb's head and
poke into every brain cell. He sought to ascertain Cobb's innermost
thought, as well as his views on many, many public problems. There
was another inquest, lasting two hours, followed by another report
to JP, with more editorials from the *Free Press*.

Williams was then ordered back to Bar Harbor for cross-examination, after arranging to correspond with Cobb. The Detroit editor
was not at all eager to visit JP in Maine, and several months elapsed
before he accepted an invitation to the Pulitzer cottage on Jekyl
Island.

"Cobb will do," JP announced. "He knows American history
better than anyone I have ever found. He has that damnable Roose-

velt obsession and he must learn to be brief. But in time, we can make a real editor of him."

So, in the spring of 1904, Frank Irving Cobb, age thirty-four, tall, broad, muscular, clear-eyed, smooth-faced, and buoyant, walked into *The World* office and reported to Merrill.

The newcomer quickly distinguished himself, not only by his writings, but by his way of asking for information. He would end each inquiry with a sort of grunt which sounded like *uhn* but was really a question mark.

A year later Merrill, slightly bewildered, went back to end his days on the *Boston Herald*. And Frank Cobb, after sharing responsibility for a time with Heaton, became chief editorial writer.

Seymour became editorial supervisor, having the final word on all copy from the Dome before it went to press. This responsibility lasted until Seymour's death in 1920—except for one unhappy year when he was editor of the *St. Louis Post-Dispatch*.

Cobb's relation to JP became almost like son to father, but not without a tortuous breaking-in process. The Pulitzer technique, after ascertaining that a *World* man had great potentialities, was to goad the man to the limit of resistance. JP had no use for a man who refused to stand up and fight. Always making allowances for the fact that a boss is usually treated with respect, JP liked to drive his editors and managers to the point where they would shout back. He was merciless toward Cobb in this respect.

While the young Detroit editor was getting his bearings in the Golden Dome, which was always a difficult process, JP kept bombarding him with criticisms, taking the Cobb editorials and dissecting them, sentence by sentence, word by word, pointing out inaccuracies if he could find them, inconsistencies, and deficiencies in clear thinking.

During his first year on *The World,* Cobb felt uneasy and somewhat homesick for Detroit; the latchstring at the *Free Press* was always out for him—in fact, the owners were urging him to come back. This, together with the doubt that he would ever be able to satisfy JP, almost persuaded Cobb to abandon the New York venture. And when JP finally pushed him beyond the limit of endurance, he resigned.

JP received the news calmly at his winter home on Jekyl Island. "Too bad," he said. "Really too bad. . . . I rather liked that young fellow. . . ." He thought it over for a few minutes, and then sudden rage seized him.

"No, damn it!" he shouted. "He shan't resign! Tell that young puppy I won't let him resign!"

On his return to New York, he sent for Cobb, and was as nice as pie. Cobb must understand, JP explained, that the owner of *The World* is never satisfied; *World* men ought also to remember that JP is blind and nearly always in pain. He was genuinely sorry about hurting Cobb's feelings, but the steel hand remained underneath the kid glove . . . he would tolerate no imperfections in writing, no matter whose feelings were hurt.

Cobb resigned several times after that, but nobody took it seriously. Resignations of that kind were filed away in the collection with JP's own announcements that he was resigning as chief editor. After the first half-dozen of these JP good-byes, the editors pleasantly ignored them; they felt the Chief was getting to be in Adelina Patti's class.

JP regarded fights with editors as part of the day's work. The bursts of anger were quickly forgotten, followed usually by some gesture of reward and conciliation. *World* editors and managers came to realize that the time to be worried about their positions was when JP arranged testimonial dinners in their honor.

But some of the fights were classic. One night, about the time of the Panama Canal excitement, JP was aboard his yacht *Liberty*, cruising off the Jersey coast. Cobb had come aboard during the afternoon. After dinner they had a late session, discussing local, state, and national politics. They disagreed.

JP raised his voice in anger. Cobb raised his. JP summoned the skipper.

"Put into Atlantic Highlands," he ordered, "and throw this man off the yacht."

"But, sir," said the skipper, "it's late at night and Mr. Cobb would have a lot of trouble getting back to New York from Atlantic Highlands."

"I don't care how much trouble he has getting back to New York. The more trouble he has the better I'll be pleased."

So the yacht put in at Atlantic Highlands and Cobb was "thrown off." He had to wait hours for transportation to the city. A few days later he received a brief note from Pulitzer. "What would you think of a trip to Japan during July and August at my expense?" it read.

JP had a deep affection for his editors, reporters, and secretaries. If editors often received messages of complaint, it is equally true that they received verbal pats on the back. Presents of fur coats and expensive hats were not infrequent. Silk hats were favorite gifts for good work. Once he told Don Seitz to order one, but Seitz demurred. "After much thought," he wrote, "I cannot bring myself to order a silk hat, for it is difficult for me to wear one gracefully. I will, however, order a crush—for the opera."

When the eleventh edition of the *Encyclopedia Britannica* was issued, JP bought a hundred sets which he ordered sent with his compliments to deserving members of his staff. Sometimes, in appreciation of special accomplishments, he sent to editors and reporters checks the size of which often astonished recipients.

Similarly, when the whim pleased him, he gave costly presents to members of his secretarial staff. Once when Mr. Pulitzer and his entourage were at his villa at Cap Martin, Mr. Pollard asked for a brief leave of absence.

"What do you want it for?" asked Mr. Pulitzer.

"I want to spend a few days in Paris," replied Pollard.

Pulitzer objected. He pointed to many reasons why Pollard should not leave him at that time. He always thought it downright inconsiderate for any of his secretaries to leave him at any time. Only by insistence did Pollard finally win his consent.

The next morning Pollard packed his bags and prepared to leave. The major domo, Jabez E. Dunningham, handed him an envelope. Inside was a bank draft of substantial amount, and a note: "Mr. Pulitzer begs that Mr. Pollard will practice no mean economies while in Paris."

MR. HYDE COMES HOME

By the beginning of the twentieth century, the Gilded Age of economic plunder and rococo Society was dying out. The financial and industrial giants who dominated the seventies, the eighties, and the nineties were giving way to a new generation which had inherited the expensive tastes acquired by their forefathers, but not their ruthless aggressiveness. Well-educated sons of pioneering builders and promoters were coming into the management of vast interests, but with ears more sensitive to symptoms of public disapproval. The shift from the Era of Exploitation to a new regime of social conscience was being accomplished—smoothly, in some instances; with dust and heat and uproar in others. However gentle or rough the process, the result was the same. The "public be damned" attitude, attributed to Commodore Vanderbilt, was changing to the "public be pleased" motto, first adopted by the big utilities.

John D. Rockefeller, Jr., was succeeding the original John D. at the head of an industrial and philanthropic empire. J. P. Morgan was succeeding J. Pierpont Morgan; and at the head of the $500,000,000 Equitable Life Assurance Society, James Hazen Hyde was preparing to take over the powers created by his father, Henry Baldwin Hyde. And in the other two of the "Big Three" life insurance companies, sons were being groomed to step into fathers' shoes —and would have succeeded, but for a cataclysm that shook the life insurance world clear down to bed-rock.

In life insurance, the change from the old order to the new was attended by the lightning of public exposure, the thunder of popular indignation, the earthquake of legislative investigation, and widespread wreckage of personal reputations. The thing that preceded the Future in this case was a tidal wave that not only swamped Wall Street but sent a flood of scandal and outraged public opinion all the way up to Albany, with important repercussions in Washington.

In this metamorphic transition, *The World* played a distinguished role. Luckily, it was well equipped for the task. JP was abroad during the most frenzied period of the life insurance uproar, but the staff was well organized and rarin' to go. In fact, *The World* went farther in its daring attack on vested interests than its owner had ever expected; he was inclined at first to disapprove, but subsequent events demonstrated that *The World* was justified and JP, for once, too cautious.

By the early winter of 1905, there were distinct rumblings of trouble in life insurance. Insiders knew that the big financiers who dominated the great companies were making millions, not only out of the business itself, but out of collateral speculation in securities, using the treasuries of their companies as a back-stop. Still, there was nothing the public could do about it. The insurance companies were heavy advertisers; the policy holders and small stockholders were unorganized. The directors of insurance companies were pillars of society. Their families helped to make up the so-called "Four Hundred" that shone with almost sacred allure in the Golden Horseshoe of the Metropolitan Opera; at the resplendent Horse Shows in old Madison Square Garden; the races, and the never-ending cycle of balls and banquets at Sherry's, Delmonico's and the old Waldorf.

To attack life insurance was like throwing a bomb into Trinity Church at the head of Wall Street just before the close of the market at a time when the Sons of the Revolution and the Knickerbocker Greys were marching down Broadway to welcome the King of England. Yet *The World* made the attack.

Up to the time when *The World* first touched off the fuse, practically everybody in Wall Street who amounted to anything knew that the interests back of the Big Three were getting away with enormous quantities of boodle and plunder, but comparatively few knew the real facts. By the expenditure of millions, the companies, working in sympathetic co-operation, effectively strangled remedial legislation and all attempts at investigation, not only in Albany but in the other state capitals, and in Washington. At the same time, the Big Three—Equitable, Mutual, and New York Life—were contributing heavily to the Republican campaign funds of 1896, 1900, and 1904, to kill the "menace" of Bryanism.

Here was the picture of the Big Three at the end of 1904:

New York Life: Outstanding policies—924,712, representing $1,928,609,308 of insurance; assets, $390,660,260. Dominant figure—John A. McCall, president; salary $100,000. Up-and-coming figure—John C. McCall, son of the president, and secretary of the corporation. Outstanding figure—George W. Perkins, son of a high official; chairman of the finance committee, as well as a vice-president, while at the same time a partner in J. P. Morgan and Company.

Mutual Life Insurance Company: supposed to be truly mutual, but policyholders, at that time, did not vote. Outstanding policies—659,544, representing $1,547,611,660. Assets, $442,701,327. Dominant figure—Richard A. McCurdy, president; salary, $150,-000. Next most influential—Robert H. McCurdy, son of the president. In about twenty years, the younger McCurdy, in addition to salary in various posts, cleaned up nearly $2,000,000 in commissions and renewals on policies.

Equitable Life Assurance Society: Capital only $100,000, but assets about $500,000,000. Outstanding policies, 564,594, representing $1,495,542,842 of insurance. President, James W. Alexander; salary $130,000; first vice-president, James Hazen Hyde, salary $100,000, with $27,000 additional from banks controlled by Equitable.

In its directorate, Equitable had the cream of the cream, although it was admitted that most of the thirty-five directors or "trustees" were appointed because of their prestige and were neither asked nor expected to do anything serious. Of the more active directors whose names gave sparkle and austerity to Equitable were James J. Hill, George J. Gould, Cornelius N. Bliss, Colonel John Jacob Astor, Chauncey M. Depew (who also received a salary of twenty thousand dollars for some unspecified legal work); Henry Clay Frick, E. H. Harriman, Levi P. Morton, Alfred G. Vanderbilt, A. J. Cassatt, Alvin W. Krech, Jacob H. Schiff, and Melville E. Ingalls. Elihu Root was counsel.

Equitable unquestionably had the most impressive front, but the most curious inside structure. Founded in 1859 by Henry Baldwin Hyde, with a group of young insurance men, it grew and spread throughout the United States and in Europe, with tremendous impetus. The elder Hyde wrecked his health building up the company, but he reaped a fortune. When he died in 1899 he left an estate of several millions to his only son and heir, James Hazen Hyde, then only twenty-three years old. Alexander, vice-president since the early days of the company, succeeded as president. Henry B. Hyde left his 502 shares of Equitable stock, representing 51 per cent control, to the son in trust, to be possessed by him at the age of thirty, but in the meantime, the young Hyde had the right to vote the stock. Alexander was one of the trustees.

Everybody recognized that James Hazen Hyde was the potential boss of Equitable. The directors, keenly aware of the fact, made haste to establish important relationships, appointing young Hyde a director in their own corporations and banks as well as pushing him to the top of Equitable as fast as his years permitted. None felt the situation more keenly than Alexander. Outwardly friendly to the heir-apparent, he secretly nourished the hope of shoving him out of the company at a favorable opportunity. It was not long in coming.

James Hazen Hyde was only twenty-one and still a Harvard undergraduate when first appointed a director of Equitable by his father. Four months after getting his B.A. (cum laude, with double honors in French and honors in German), he was elected second vice-president; six months later, first vice-president at the comfortable salary of $25,000, which by 1903 had been quadrupled.

In the journalism of the period, the young Hyde was described as a dilettante. This was inaccurate. He had serious purposes. He planned to take over his father's responsibilities and make a definite career in life insurance. Also, he hoped to establish a more socialized management, admitting stockholders and policyholders as participants. During his vacations, he had traveled extensively in Europe, helping to promote the company's foreign business, and had acquired an intense interest in French culture.

The World chronicled the impression that Mr. Hyde aspired to be "more French than any living Frenchman." More precisely, he spent both time and money in promoting French learning in America and a better understanding of America in France. At Harvard, he founded and became the first president of Le Cercle Français de l'Université Harvard, for which and other francophile activities he was made a Chevalier of the Legion of Honor, later a Commander, and was finally awarded the Grand Cross. As a Harvard senior, he established a fund of $30,000 to bring French men of letters each

year to Harvard and other institutions. These purposeful enterprises,
together with the honors in languages, dispose of the idea that Hyde
was a "wealthy idler."

Undeniably, he was picturesque. Six feet, two and a half inches
tall and lean as a greyhound, he was an expert fencer and a fine
horseman, either in the saddle or driving a coach and four. He
established new records in coaching by driving from New York to
Philadelphia and back using relays of seventeen teams; and by using
fifty horses, drove a French-built coach from New York to Lakewood, New Jersey, in seven and one-half hours (eighty miles), giving the press a bountiful dinner at Lakewood and sending them
home on a special train.

Emerging from Harvard, he plunged into New York life with
élan, gusto, and an eye for the spectacular that astonished even that
lavish era. "I had money, like many other young men of my time,"
Hyde said in a recent reminiscence, "and I enjoyed spending it. But
I always used it for a purpose."

He grew a Vandyke beard and had it barbered every day. He
drove to his office, whenever weather permitted, in a "T-wagon"
with a fine pair of trotters in front and a couple of high-hatted coach-
men backstage. He helped to organize the first Metropolitan Opera,
with Conried as director and an option on Caruso as a principal
asset. He gave elaborate dinners and entertainments. Notable in all
respects was his dinner in honor of the French Ambassador, Jules
Cambon. Equitable paid for that.

Most sensational of all, for publicity, was a French costume ball
which he gave at Sherry's early in 1905, in honor of his debutante
niece, Miss Anna Ripley. Newspaper accounts said it cost $100,000,
but Mr. Hyde said the actual bill was about $20,000. Sherry's was
decorated to look something like the gardens of the palace at Versailles in the time of Louis XVI. The guests wore period costumes,
while the host appeared in the dress uniform of his favorite hunt
club.

What else happened at this famous party? Reports differ. In the
midst of the gaiety, the doors opened and a group of flunkeys in
period outfits brought in a sedan chair, bearing the famous French
actress, Mme. Réjane—a sensational entrance! According to some

accounts, Mme. Réjane got up on the center table and gave her interpretation of the can-can. This was thirty years before Tin Pan Alley had produced the song:

> *"We're havin' a heat wave*
> *A tropical heat wave . . .*
> *The temp'rature's risin'*
> *Which isn't surprisin'*
> *'Cause she certainly can can-can."*

. . . but the naughty dance was known even then (though not with high approbation). To this day, Mr. Hyde insists that nothing of the kind took place—that Mme. Réjane merely recited a poem intended to promote better relations between France and America. Other guests agreed that although the poem might cause a discreet smile it was not abrasive.

"Mme. Réjane," said one authority, "was too old and too fat to can-can. Besides, she was not a dancer."

However, the papers next day sizzled with stories about the ball. The can-can version was widely accepted. Denunciations poured forth from pulpit and press. Business leaders professed to be shocked that a vice-president of Equitable would engineer such a scandalous affair. None did a better job of holding up hands in holy horror than James W. Alexander. Confidentially, he was delighted. Now, he said, is the time to get rid of Hyde.

Many of those who attended the French ball declared that the clamor was all due to spiteful old cats who failed to receive an invitation. But Alexander was not one of those.

The World had an exceptionally good staff of editors and reporters to handle the Scandals of 1905. The personnel included:

Caleb M. Van Hamm, managing editor; quiet, efficient, practical; never removed his hat in the office; always seemed about to take a walk, and finally he did.

Robert Hunt Lyman, night editor; scholarly; as to accuracy, deadly —almost infallible; friendly; ambidextrous; Yale graduate; previous newspaper service on *Springfield* (Mass.) *Republican* and *New*

York Herald; during the Spanish-American War he was secretary to JP—after which any task was easy.

William A. Thayer, night city editor; short, very stocky; alert but never excited; affectionately esteemed; always signed himself "wat," but it was good on expense orders.

Robert Adamson, staff reporter; later secretary to Mayor Gaynor and still later Fire Commissioner under Mayor Mitchel.

Samuel G. Blythe, chief of *The World's* Washington Bureau, and its political commentator; fond of throwing penguinislandesque darts at T.R.; never betrayed a confidence; never suppressed *news;* never manufactured gossip.

Winfield R. Sheehan, then engaged in exposing police protection to vice and gambling; subsequently became secretary to Police Commissioner Waldo; after that became a Hollywood potentate; married Jeritza, the opera singer.

Gus C. Roeder, criminal courts reporter; top-notch investigator; used to sit on bench with judges, believing this a good way to get news; a newer way is to get it from East Fifty-second Street.

Jacob Dreyfuss, a real old-time reporter; slight cast in one eye but saw news clearly; fond of diamonds; favorite slogan—"Don't make a damn fool out of *The World*." (Others attended to that, later on.)

Isaac D. White, greatest of all newspaper investigators; later in charge of *The World's* Bureau of Accuracy and Fair Play; identified the would-be assassin of Russell Sage.

Edward Ziegler, music reporter-critic; now vice-president of the Metropolitan Opera Company; was succeeded on *The World* by:

Reginald De Koven, American composer; ate peanuts by the peck; wrote the famous light opera, *Robin Hood,* including the great love song, "Oh, Promise Me."

Louis V. De Foe, in charge of drama news and criticisms; used to work day and night under now obsolete impression that critics must actually cover news.

Louis R. Southworth, ship news reporter, known as "skipper"; most illegible writer since Horace Greeley, but got all the news.

Louis Seibold, star political reporter; at home wherever politics was hottest, whether in Washington, Albany, New York, Chicago, or Cody, Wyoming.

And a masterly reporter heretofore unmentioned—*The World's* Number One Warrior on the news fronts, David Ferguson!

No specialist, this Mr. Ferguson; just a fine general practitioner, as the doctors would say; but in *World* language, "a first-class, first-string man" (vanishing species); enormously effective, whether at City Hall, State Capitol, Bellevue Hospital, Wall Street, Appellate Division, political conventions, weddings, shipwrecks, or anywhere; on any kind of assignment, Ferguson knew where to seek for the news and how to extract it.

And yet, to the general public, he was practically unknown. In *The World,* no article ever appeared signed "By David Ferguson." In this day of columnists and by-line reporters, it seems incredible. Yet he was well known, sometimes painfully known, to the big men of business, finance, industry, and politics. He had a way of ferreting out the facts they might be trying to conceal. So they acquired the habit of telling him the truth, because they discovered that he was not easily misled.

In the early days of 1905, Ferguson started looking into life insurance. Making the rounds in Wall Street, he heard rumblings of trouble in Equitable. After several days of careful checking and rechecking, Ferguson, on February 12, put out a story that roused the entire country. He told of the break between Alexander and Hyde; of Alexander's charges alleging "misconduct, incompetence, and misuse of funds"—mentioning also the Cambon dinner and the French costume ball.

Wall Street was galvanized. To think that any newspaper would dare to attack the sanctum sanctorum of high finance! Equitable officially denied the story. Directors threatened to sue *The World.*

Ferguson smiled and followed up his exposé with the full text of a round-robin signed by Alexander and some twenty-five other Equitable officials in which all threatened to resign if Hyde continued as vice-president.

Mild-mannered Ferguson kept on digging, putting out one good exclusive story every day. *The World* backed up the campaign with ringing editorials by Cobb and William McMurtrie Speer. There was plenty going on. For the first time in Equitable's history, the dummy directors were called into action. Secret meetings were frequent, and heated.

The limelight fell most unfavorably upon Hyde, but *The World* regarded him rather as a victim of a system than the promoter of it. The campaign against Hyde, skillfully engineered by Alexander, was based on something more than the eccentricities of the young man's dazzling social flights. Powerful interests wanted to get rid of Hyde because he stood in the way of a very important project conceived in the fertile imagination of George W. Perkins.

At the age of fifteen, the resourceful and engaging Perkins had started his career in New York Life as a clerk in his father's office in Pittsburgh at thirty dollars a month. "Your advancement," said the father, "will depend upon your ability to improve, especially in spelling and penmanship." He advanced rapidly in spelling. Arriving at the dual, but highly strategic, position of finance committee chairman and at the same time partner in J. P. Morgan & Company, Perkins took for his province the syndicate system. Not satisfied with engineering the transfer of industrial securities from the banking house into life insurance treasuries, he proposed a gigantic life insurance merger to include not only the Big Three, but Metropolitan and Prudential as well. The total assets of the projected super-colossus would have exceeded two billions of dollars.

Other companies were understood to be willing, but in the Equitable, Hyde opposed it. While accepting the old syndicate system as part of his inherited activities, and profiting by it, he was against any extension of it. At the same time he made known his desire to admit the policyholders into the management.

Since Hyde, in the final analysis, represented control of Equitable, the only remedy was to eliminate him, pleasantly, if possible. Before the scandal burst, several approaches were made to induce Hyde to sell out. President Hegeman of Metropolitan and Dryden of Prudential added their persuasions. Hyde was offered as high as ten million dollars. He rejected it.

Another move, more subtle and ingenious, was to suggest the appointment of Hyde as Ambassador to France. This he would have accepted. But the White House was not receptive. President Theodore Roosevelt considered Hyde too young for the Paris post, but was willing to name him as Minister to Argentina or Belgium. These he declined to accept.

After *The World* started the exposé, more offers came to Hyde. Henry Clay Frick, the Pittsburgh steel man, who was an Equitable director, offered $5,000,000 for the 502 shares or half the amount for half the shares; George W. Young, identified with Mutual, offered $7,000,000. Others offered various amounts, but none less than $1,000,000.

In view of the fact that the shares, by law, were limited to 7 per cent return on par value of $100 per share, the collateral possibilities in the way of syndicate participation and speculation may be imagined. Nominally, a purchaser of the Hyde stock could expect no greater return than $3,500 a year, yet Hyde had already made over $60,000 in syndicate profits, aside from salary.

Since Hyde stood firm, and answered the Alexander charges with counter-charges, the big brains behind Equitable became very busy. Frick was summoned from Pittsburgh. He had been appointed a director in 1901, as a graceful compliment, and had regarded it as an honor. But after one committee meeting, he was amazed, shocked, and chagrined to find himself associated with such reckless management. The hard-boiled industrialist, who successfully resisted the Amalgamated in the Homestead riots, who had survived attempted assassination by the anarchist Alexander Berkman, was a puritan in corporate control. Any faint suspicion of irregularity or loose auditing was in Frick's eyes a deadly sin. The Equitable picture nauseated him, and he said so. Under such righteous prodding from one whose only weakness was the collecting of respectably fat ladies by old masters, the directors appointed him chairman of a special committee to investigate the Alexander-Hyde charges. The other members were E. H. Harriman, Cornelius N. Bliss, Melville E. Ingalls, and Brayton Ives.

Hyde was called first. He was both calm and candid. Admitting some of the charges right at the outset, he disproved others. The Cambon dinner, he admitted, was charged up to advertising, but the French ball was a private affair. He admitted his participation in the syndicate; admitted charging up his traveling expenses abroad, claiming this to be a legitimate business item, but denied that the house he maintained at No. 18 Rue Adolphe Yvon, and the hire of the servants there had been billed to Equitable. He tendered his check in repayment of the Cambon dinner and the syndicate profits.

"Of course, gentlemen," Hyde said, "you realize that I was not alone in these matters. The president knew all about them."

The committee became well aware of that, after calling Alexander on the carpet. Other witnesses confirmed the stories of loose book-keeping and unauthorized expenses. Some of the committee were in favor of a soft-pedal report, but Frick was adamant. Doubly angry because he had indirectly countenanced the irregularities, he practically wrote the report himself while the others nodded assent.

As laid before the entire board, the Frick report called for the dismissal of Hyde and Alexander for neglect of duties and irregular conduct, for a drastic reorganization, for a new management in which policyholders should participate, and restitution of profits by all who had participated in the syndicates. The report was unanimous.

Getting advance word of the report, Alexander and Hyde reconciled their differences and mustered a majority among the "dummy directors" to defeat the Frick program. For the record, Hyde moved the adoption of the report, but the final vote was 24 to 15 against it. Frick, Harriman, and Bliss resigned immediately.

Editorially, *The World* said:

"Rejection of the Frick report was not surprising. A grand jury could hardly be expected to indict itself. The fact remains, nevertheless, that the committee pleaded guilty on behalf of Equitable to the charges of corruption."

The big powers moved again in favor of a settlement behind closed doors. Thomas Fortune Ryan offered to buy out the Hyde interest for $2,500,000. Hyde countered by offering to sell to the company itself—the stock to be kept in trust. This was found to be legally impossible. The Ryan offer was renewed. Harriman objected. He "doubted the sincerity of Mr. Ryan's intentions." Finally Ryan bought it, subject to restrictions. He put the stock in a trusteeship that included Grover Cleveland, George Westinghouse, and Morgan J. O'Brien, former Presiding Justice of the Appellate Division. Ryan insisted that he was interested only in preventing a financial collapse. *The World* regarded the arrangement with suspicion. Wall Street conservatives were also dissatisfied, because, at a later date, J. Pierpont Morgan bought out the Ryan holdings at cost plus interest, the total price being $3,000,000.

The World, meanwhile, clamored for a legislative investigation into the entire life insurance business. Small stockholders and policyholders backed up the demand. But Governor Higgins was reluctant and evasive. Unwillingly, he requested a report from State Insurance Superintendent Francis Hendricks. This official questioned witnesses privately, and informed the governor that a much more exhaustive inquiry would be needed to determine how much the stockholders and policyholders had lost. Hendricks and the governor refused to make public the testimony, although newspapers were calling for it.

The record was locked securely in Hendricks's private safe. Higgins insisted that he had not seen it. New York's District Attorney William Travers Jerome professed to be unable to get a copy. But on July 11 *The World* published ten full pages of the testimony, and the revelations amazed the whole country.

"Very strange," Jerome remarked, "that a newspaper is able to obtain this testimony, while the District Attorney, aided by the Governor, is unable to obtain a copy."

Hendricks was angry and embarrassed. He did not know how *The World* got the testimony—that was a fact. All three copies of the report were found in his safe; but if he had looked during the week end, he would have discovered one copy missing. It was in *The World* office.

Seibold, the political expert, was in Albany that week covering a special session of the legislature. He is the only man alive today who knows the whole story.

"Every newspaperman in Albany was after that report," Seibold related recently. "The *Herald* was offering five thousand dollars for a copy. I had a good friend in the Insurance Department, but he must be nameless forever. 'It's a tough job,' he said, 'but I'll try to help you.' He told me to go to New York for the week end and wait for word. On Saturday afternoon he telephoned me to meet him for dinner at the Central Park Casino. Under a solemn pledge that I would return the document before six o'clock Monday morning, he turned over to me the record of the testimony—about 600,000 words.

"I worked with a corps of stenographers at the office all through Saturday night, Sunday, and Sunday night, with no pause for sleep and little to eat. At a quarter to six Monday morning I returned the copy to my friend and he took it back to Albany.

"All it cost me was the price of the dinner in Central Park—less than fifteen dollars."

"Did you receive special recognition from *The World?*"

"Yes. JP fired me. The old man was abroad when the Equitable story broke and he did not have the right perspective. He thought *The World* was overzealous and might destroy public confidence in life insurance. Actually we restored it. After Ryan bought out Hyde he induced George B. McClellan Harvey to see JP in Europe, and Colonel Harvey's dulcet voice persuaded the Chief that *The World* was wrong.

"Returning from Europe, JP dictated an editorial, stating his conviction that the misdeeds of a few scamps did not reflect upon the integrity of the big companies. He arrived on the very day when *The World* published the Hendricks report, and sent his editorial to the office. Cobb refused to print it as an editorial. He ran it in the paper a few days later as a letter in the 'People's Forum' and signed it 'P.J.' instead of 'JP.'

"The old man suspended Cobb for three weeks, but nobody paid any attention to the order. JP summoned Van Hamm to the house and forced him to tell where we got the Hendricks testimony. 'Fire the man immediately,' he said (meaning me); 'I won't stand for such things.' I heard nothing about it until the next Friday, when I returned from Albany. Van Hamm and I met by appointment at the old Hotel Belmont.

" 'Louis,' he said, 'you don't know it, but JP fired you last Tuesday. He wants to see you at his home tomorrow morning.'

"At the East Seventy-third Street house, next day, JP said:

" 'My God, Seibold, you made a lot of trouble for me. I spend four days on shipboard writing an editorial and you go and do something that makes me look foolish. You deserve to be punished, Seibold; and, Great God! you shall be punished. Go down to the office and report to Bradford Merrill.'

"When I arrived at the office, Merrill handed me a check for $1,000 and a note from JP in appreciation of my work on the Hendricks beat. 'Only,' he added as a postscript, 'don't use the money to start a rival newspaper.' "

Cobb went right ahead with his campaign for a legislative investigation. On the last day of the special session, Governor Higgins bowed to the popular wish and requested a joint committee of inquiry. It was headed by Senator Armstrong, Republican. The G.O.P. members were of high standing, but the Democrats were machine politicians.

Charles Evans Hughes was named counsel to the committee. He had already conducted successfully a gas investigation. The Armstrong committee hearings lasted from September 6 to December 30. Hughes's examination of reluctant witnesses was masterly. Patient, persistent, infallibly polite, he unwound the tangled affairs of Equitable and its friendly rivals, revealing the enormous expenditures for political manipulation, the operations of the syndicates, and the lavish use of stockholder and policyholder money for high salaries and magnificent surroundings.

Alexander refused to testify and left the country, broken in mind and spirit, finally dying in seclusion. Hyde was a voluble witness and appeared anxious to co-operate, although his personal counsel, Samuel Untermyer, stayed close to his elbow. Harriman was pleasantly evasive. Other reputations went to smash. President McCall of New York Life, under a merciless questioning by Hughes, tried to prove there was nothing wrong about using company money to help the Republican party or influence legislation. But he left the witness stand crushed and humiliated, and soon resigned. President McCurdy of Mutual, also questioned by Hughes, defended his $50,000 office furnishings as "adding dignity to life insurance." He saw nothing wrong about enjoying a $150,000 salary while dividends to policyholders dropped from $110 down to $7. After the investigation, McCurdy was a physical wreck. He went abroad and died.

But in the wake of personal tragedies came a better day for the public. The Armstrong Bills, resulting from the investigation, brought the abolition of lobbying, political contributions, and other forms of fixing. As *The World's* closing editorial on this campaign said:

"The signing of the last of the Armstrong Bills by Governor Higgins crowns with complete victory *The World's* long struggle against life insurance corruption."

The investigation also put Mr. Hughes on the road to fame and distinguished political service. Elected governor in 1906, with enthusiastic support from *The World,* he was re-elected in 1908. JP wrote during the first term: "I am simply crazy about Hughes." He resigned near the end of the second term to become an Associate Justice of the United States Supreme Court. The rest of the story is familiar. Defeated by Woodrow Wilson for president in 1916, Mr. Hughes retired to private practice until he was made Secretary of State in the Harding Administration. He resigned under Coolidge in 1925, and in 1928 was appointed a Justice of the Permanent Court for International Justice at The Hague. In 1930, President Hoover appointed him Chief Justice of the United States Supreme Court. He retired in June, 1941.

All through the Armstrong investigation, David Ferguson, *The World* reporter who never got a by-line, was at Hughes's elbow; and, said *The World* when Ferguson died in 1919, "it is not too much to say that David Ferguson had an important part in launching Mr. Hughes on his eminent career."

In his first race for the New York governorship, Hughes defeated Hearst, the Democratic nominee. The publisher described his opponent as "an animated human feather duster," referring to the most distinguished set of whiskers in American political history.

Hughes paid no attention to personalities, but he had a quiet sense of humor. On one of his campaign stops, he ordered lobster for supper after a hard day of speaking. The waiter brought a lobster with one claw missing.

"What's this?" demanded the candidate.

"Well, you see, sir," the waiter explained, "these lobsters come

in a barrel alive and they get to fighting in the barrel and sometimes
lose a claw."

"Very well," said the future Chief Justice. "Take this lobster
back and go pick me out a winner."

As the insurance campaign drew to a close, Ferguson had a
chance to relax and talk to the other reporters.

"What are you going to do next, Dave?" one of them asked.

"Get acquainted with my family," he replied with a grin. "I
haven't had a day off in nearly two years, and my son thinks I am
the rent collector."

James Hazen Hyde went to France after the Armstrong investigation and remained there for thirty-five years. As he had no other
occupation in New York than life insurance, he felt that his best
opportunity for a life work lay in the promotion of the arts and
sciences in France, and helping to better Franco-American relations.
He bought a big house at Versailles, once owned by Madame Pom-
padour, and thereby acquired the designation, "The American Pom-
padour." During the First World War he turned over his homes
to the Red Cross for hospital purposes. He also worked for the Red
Cross Committee on Public Information. In 1938 he was elected
an Associate in the French Academy of Moral and Political Sciences,
taking the chair vacated by the death of Thomas G. Masaryk, first
president of Czechoslovakia. He endowed a chair in the Sorbonne
for an American professorship exchange with Harvard. He took a
charming French lady as his second wife.

Although he visited other European capitals, and appears at various times in Ambassador Dodd's diary during the tense years of
1933-1938, Mr. Hyde did not return to America until after the
German occupation of Paris in 1940. He found a change more vast
than the one that confronted Rip Van Winkle. The residential Fifth
Avenue with its millionaire palaces on which he used to drive his
horses was a thoroughfare of offices and stores. The elegant dining
places had moved, or vanished entirely. The Frick residence was an
art museum. The Cornelius Vanderbilt mansion had been sold and
was to be demolished to be replaced by a business structure. Social
customs have completely changed. Dining or supping at home is

almost a forgotten custom. People eat where they can dance and smoke and gossip and be photographed.

And, of course, *The World* also has vanished, and there are no more David Fergusons to upset financial applecarts.

During the Russo-Japanese War, *The World* was greatly concerned over the whereabouts of the Russian fleet. For more reasons than one, Admiral Rojestvensky, after delaying at Madagascar, suddenly put the Russian naval forces out to sea. Days and weeks passed. Nothing was heard of it. Nobody, in the United States at least, had any really authoritative idea as to where the fleet could be—as this was before the days of newspaper military experts.

Naval strategists of all nations pored over maps and shook their heads. At first, they thought Rojestvensky might be heading direct for the coast of Japan to make a bold assault on Admiral Heihachiro Togo's defending fleet. But as time passed, the theory was abandoned. Naval authorities didn't like it anyway—it was too simple.

Mysteries of any kind had a great appeal for Joseph Pulitzer. The Russian fleet mystery was no different from the others. JP wanted to know where Rojestvensky's fleet was and he wanted someone to find out. Right away, too.

One morning, in 1905, L. R. E. Paulin, *World* editorial writer, sat at his desk in the dome of the Pulitzer Building. A copy boy entered and laid a paper on Paulin's desk.

"WORLD, NEW YORK.

"TELL PAULIN EVERY DAY TO HAVE EDITORIAL LOCATING RO-JESTVENSKY'S FLEET. J.P."

Why Paulin was chosen for this assignment, he never understood.

"I thought the old man had lost his mind," he said recently. "The only thing I knew about naval affairs was what I learned on the Staten Island ferryboat. I had been a cattle rancher in Colorado, but that gave me no insight into the maneuvers of an Asiatic fleet.

"But there was a job to be done and I had to do it. Every day I studied maps intently. Every day I put out an editorial, surmising that Rojestvensky might be here, there, or somewhere. I had one assurance—as long as Rojestvensky remained in hiding nobody could contradict me.

"Luckily, in one of my daily guesses, I placed the Russian fleet near the Straits of Singapore.

"Suddenly, after three painful weeks, the Japanese Admiralty announced that Rojestvensky's fleet had been sighted. Guess where? In the Straits of Singapore! I relayed the news to JP and breathed a sigh of relief—'I hope the old man is satisfied now.'

"But in a very few hours, another message came from JP—

" 'HAVE PAULIN SAY FOR ME THAT TOGO WILL WIPE THE RUSSIANS OFF THE SEA WHEN WHERE HE CHOOSES TO MEET THEM.'

"I was dumbfounded. I talked to Frank Cobb, John Heaton, and the other editorial writers. We thought the old man must be upset. We tried to dissuade him by telegraph, but his only answer was:

" 'FOLLOW DIRECTIONS.'

"So, I wrote the editorial; Rojestvensky's fleet was plunging into the China Sea to its doom! How foolish and wicked of the Czar, to insist upon this Russian sacrifice! That was the tenor.

"Events proved that JP was right and we in *The World* office were wrong. Just as the Chief predicted, Togo did fall upon Rojestvensky and he did wipe the Russians off the sea."

About this time, *The World* went into a dull period. It failed to produce the lively news features which had come to be recognized as "*World* stories." JP was perturbed and called Don Seitz, then business manager, down to Lakewood.

SEITZ: Possibly a shake-up would benefit the staff.

JP: No, not now; the trouble is, that nobody on the staff gets drunk any more. Bradford Merrill never gets drunk; Van Hamm [managing editor] never gets drunk; Pomeroy Burton [city editor] never gets drunk; and you never get drunk. When I was in the office, someone always got drunk and we got out a paper. Go back to New York, and find a reporter who gets drunk. When you find him, hire him for life.

On his return to the city, Seitz hunted along Park Row and came face to face with a man who once had been a physician but had drifted into journalism—one of the most brilliant news writers in New York. He seemed a bit unsteady, and down at the heel.

SEITZ: What are you doing, Doc?

DOC (glum): Nothing.

SEITZ: I thought you were on the *American.*

DOC: Same old thing. I was let out—can't leave the hard stuff alone.

SEITZ (beaming): You're just the man!

In a few minutes Doc was added to *The World's* pay roll.

The World immediately picked up and became lively again— sometimes a little too lively. On one extra-bibulous occasion, the Doctor thought he saw a blue dog on the glass door of the managing editor's office. Doc struck at the image and cut a vein in his wrist.

The Doctor was one of the most honorable men on Park Row. Having learned that he had been hired because he got drunk, he felt morally bound not to disappoint his employer.

But the blue dog worried him. The next time he saw the strange ugly form on Van Hamm's glass door, he knew better than to attack with bare fists. Standing about twenty feet away, he seized an office chair and hurled it with such accuracy that the chair crashed through the panel, showering glass over Van Hamm's desk.

The next day the Doctor apologized. "All the fault of that damned blue dog," he said.

The Doctor was also valuable as a rewrite man. One day, in fun, the city editor handed him a copy of the new Manhattan directory. "Give us a couple of paragraphs," the editor said.

Doc studied the huge volume as though it were a new History of Civilization. At the end of one hour, he handed in the story—he had been counting the number of Cohens, as compared with the Smiths, and found one side three names ahead. He wrote:

"The Cohens win by a nose!"

At one of the annual staff dinners, Doc made a speech. Holding up a copy of *The World,* he exclaimed:

"The managing editor owes me an explanation. What does *The World* mean by saying that a man is 'lit-up'? Early Christian martyrs were sometimes lit-up, great scientists of later ages were lit-up. But that was centuries ago. *The World* has become a foreign-language newspaper! As a patriotic American, I refuse to work for the damn sheet . . . To hell with the job! I resign!"

The Doctor then sat down and soon fell into a deep slumber.

His name was Esdaile P. Cohen.

JP'S LAST VISIT

It was the summer of 1908. The temperature was hovering about ninety-five and meteorologists were comparing records. "Not since 1873," they reported, "has there been more heat and less rain."

Carrie Nation, the old lady with the hatchet, had been ejected from the White House when she tried to remonstrate with President Theodore Roosevelt because of his young daughter Alice—"She smokes cigarettes and she can't deny it."

William Howard Taft, fat and amiable, had been nominated for President by the Republicans, and William Jennings Bryan, once more by the Democrats.

The Rev. D. C. Hughes, father of the recent Chief Justice of the United States, was calling on the police to stop Gertrude Hoffman's Salome dance at Hammerstein's in New York—"utterly indecent and demoralizing," the clergyman asserted.

Muncie, Indiana—Isabel Turner, actress, was put in jail for wearing in public a "sheath" gown—the latest craze. The technical charge was "interfering with traffic."

London—*Punch* was lampooning the wife of the Prime Minister for receiving Maude Allen, American dancer, as "an equal at social functions."

New York—Charles M. Schwab, steel magnate, tells the ship news reporters this country will snap out of the 1907 depression. "I am an optimist," he says, "a bull on the United States."

Sunday morning, July 26, 1908.

The clock in the cupola of City Hall pointed to eleven.

The newly expanded Pulitzer Building was quiet—the usual Sabbath mood. In the business office, perspiring clerks fixed up classified ads and prepared soon to leave for a half-holiday. In the marble corridor, the shining new elevators rested snugly in their pits. Only the freight elevators were in use for the editorial and composing rooms.

On the twelfth floor—a mortuary stillness, broken only by an old-fashioned electric fan. Not a single reporter was at his typewriter; not a single telegrapher at his key.

Arthur C. Clarke, day city editor, had been poring over the morning papers, glancing through early reports of the New York City News Association and examining the "futures"—clippings and memoranda concerning the day's events. Clarke, quiet and methodical, mapped out his assignments.

Near the city desk, which was on a platform, two young copy boys took care of telephone calls, filed the morning newspapers, distributed mail and attended to other chores (for which they were paid four dollars a week), not failing to study the Sunday comics when the boss wasn't looking.

One of the youngsters was Alexander L. Schlosser, who later became assistant city editor. It is to him we are indebted for a copperplate memory of this day.

George Carteret, telegraph news editor, had not yet begun to function. His roll-top desk, not far from Clarke's, was unopened. Morning papers and a basket of notes from the night desk lay neglected.

Carteret could not easily have concealed himself—conclusion: he had not arrived—Carteret was late! Only a cynic would suggest that tardiness might be associated with convivialities of the night before.

Suddenly the sound of heavy footsteps. The huge form of Carteret appears. His face is flushed. Striding up to the dais, he calls out:

"Arthur, Joseph Pulitzer is in the reception room!"

Clarke smiles. Only twice since 1887 has Pulitzer been in *The World* office, and never in the newsroom.

"Arthur," Carteret says, "I'm not kidding you. Joseph Pulitzer is outside. I saw him when I got off the elevator. He's resting on the couch. Seitz, Lyman, Arthur Billing, and a swarm of secretaries are with him. In one minute the whole crowd will be in here!"

Clarke continues to smile.

"Great Caesar!" ejaculates Carteret, grabbing the morning papers and flinging open his desk. "The Old Man hasn't been here in twenty-one years—twenty-one years, mind you! Now he comes on a morning when I'm late and haven't even read a line of the paper. What rotten luck!"

The tread of feet in the corridor . . . a confused buzz . . . one voice is heard clearly above the others:

"I'll go to Van Hamm's office, if you say so, but I won't go any damned roundabout way."

Carteret is not mistaken. This is Joseph Pulitzer in the flesh.

He wears a dark business suit. Despite intense heat, his vest is buttoned snugly. The eyes are hidden by dark glasses. The bushy hair, now graying at the temples, is ruffled, but the reddish beard is newly trimmed.

There is only one way to get to the managing editor's office and that is through the city room, passing the city desk. JP still insists: "I won't go any roundabout way."

Mr. Pulitzer narrowly escapes hitting his head against a telephone booth. One of the secretaries pushes him gently aside and absorbs the smack.

"Clumsy!" is JP's only comment.

The party reaches Van Hamm's office. JP sits in the managing editor's chair. Van Hamm, after a long night's work, is asleep at home in Montclair, New Jersey.

JP asks:

"How many windows are in this room?" A short pause.

"Three," explains Seitz.

"Where is Lyman's room?"

Billing and Lyman escort the Chief to the office next to Van Hamm's.

"How far is this room from the copy desk?"

"About fifty feet."

"That's damned foolish!" cries JP. "Whose idea was it to put Lyman's room so far from the copy desk? Idiotic! Why not put it over in City Hall Park? The night editor must be near the copy desk. No nonsense about it. Swear you will change it!"

Architectural limitations are tactfully explained, but JP is not impressed. He insists, "I want Lyman's room next to the copy desk!" They solemnly swear the wish will be fulfilled. It never was.

Clarke and Carteret hear all that is being said inside.

"Maybe the old man is friendly," whispers Carteret.

Clarke (aside). "Maybe not."

"Who are on the news desks today?" JP asks abruptly.

"Mr. Clarke is on the city desk and Mr. Carteret on the telegraph desk," Lyman answers.

"Oh! Mr. Carteret!" JP exclaims. "I want to meet Mr. Carteret. Beg him to come in here at once. It will be SUCH a pleasure."

Clarke and Carteret exchanges glances—a merry twinkle in Clarke's eye, but Carteret is filled with dismay.

"Great Caesar!" he mutters; perspiration stands out on his imposing dome.

"Ah, Mr. Carteret," says Mr. Pulitzer in his gentlest tone. "I have wanted to meet you for a long time. I have been watching your work. You show promise."

"Thank you, Mr. Pulitzer. How do you do?"

"Are you a married man, Mr. Carteret?"

"Yes, sir, I am."

"Where do you live?"

"In Brooklyn."

"Why Brooklyn? Anything wrong with Manhattan? Why do all you fellows live out of the city? Seitz, why do you live in Flatbush? Why does Van Hamm live in Montclair? Manhattan is where things happen! Nothing ever happens in Flatbush or New Jersey.

"How old are you, Mr. Carteret?"

"Thirty-five."

"Only thirty-five! Fortunate man! Seitz and Lyman tell me you're a great big fellow, Mr. Carteret."

"Yes, I am, Mr. Pulitzer."

"How tall?"

"Six feet."

"How much do you weigh?"

"Two hundred and fifty pounds."

"My God! Better train down. Do you mind, Mr. Carteret, if I place my hands on your head and face?"

"Not at all, Mr. Pulitzer."

On the arm of Billing, JP moves across the room and stands back of Carteret. Long, sensitive fingers move gently over the young telegraph editor's head, feeling the smooth, handsome face . . . lingering over the chin.

"My God!" ejaculates JP. "You have a big head, Mr. Carteret!"

[Laughter in the city room. Copy Boy Schlosser whispers: "He certainly has a big head this morning."]

Carteret is embarrassed.

"You are right, Mr. Pulitzer. I guess I have a big head."

"You can't deny it. Now tell me, Mr. Carteret, what is in that big head for tomorrow's paper?"

"Well," replies the troubled editor, "ah—well—ah—the day is young yet. I haven't made out my schedule. But I'll be following developments in the Hazel Drew murder at Utica; I have a man covering Bryan at Lincoln, Nebraska, and another covering Taft at Hot Springs, Virginia, and I'll . . ."

"Well, well," JP interrupts, "go on, go on! Those are just routine assignments. What else have you in that big head?"

Gloomy silence.

CARTERET: "Well, you see, Mr. Pulitzer, I er—er—er—"

"Wait a minute," snaps JP, suspecting the truth. "Tell me, Mr. Carteret, what did you have in *The World* this morning that the other papers did not have?"

A nasty question. There are many subjects upon which Carteret is better informed.

"I'm sorry, Mr. Pulitzer, but—er—er—I can't answer that question now."

"Why not?"

"Well, you must remember, Mr. Pulitzer, that I haven't had time to read all the papers yet."

"What? Why not? What time is it?"

"Half-past eleven," one of the group volunteers, trying to stem the rising tide of wrath.

"My God! Only half-past eleven! And you haven't read the morning papers! Great God! What kind of editors are running this paper?"

"I regret it, Mr. Pulitzer, but you see—well, the fact is I was a little late this morning."

"A little late! What time do you get up in the morning? When I was on Park Row I had all the papers read before eight o'clock."

"That's nothing," interposes Arthur Billing in a commendable effort to divert attention. "I used to have them all read before five o'clock in the morning."

"Yes," retorts JP, "but you read them on the way home from some all-night party. You did not know that the papers you were reading were twenty-four hours old!"

Billing laughs—a hollow laugh—the others laugh, hollow laughs, too. Carteret does not laugh.

PULITZER: "Mr. Carteret, you have spoiled my morning!"

"I am very sorry." (Carteret fails to mention that JP also has spoiled his morning.)

"I beg you," solemnly enjoins JP, "go back to your desk and get at the morning papers. You will find them interesting. Some day soon I shall invite you to Bar Harbor. I want to talk to you some more."

"I'll be glad to come." There is little enthusiasm in Carteret's tone.

"And for God's sake, when you come, please be prepared. I swear I shall ask you many questions. You must not mind that. It will be for your own good. Now, swear you will read the papers early every morning."

"I swear, Mr. Pulitzer."

"Good-bye, Mr. Carteret. It was a pleasure to meet you."

"Good-bye, Mr. Pulitzer, and thank you."

Carteret emerged, mopping his brow. His stiff white collar is wilted.

At the city desk, on the way out of the newsrooms, JP pauses.

"I want to say a word to Arthur Clarke."

"How are you, Mr. Pulitzer?" (Shaking hands.)

"My boy, I am glad to meet you again. Are you in good health? You were ill a few years ago. You went out West, I think."

"Yes, I did, Mr. Pulitzer, but I'm all right now."

"That is good. Now tell me, my boy, what are you preparing for tomorrow morning's paper?"

The question does not upset Arthur Clarke. He recites the stories on which developments are expected—also some of the latest bulletins. It is a good summary—but not for JP.

"There isn't a good, bright Monday morning feature on the whole schedule," he complains.

The blind man reaches for Clarke's head.

"What have you in there, Mr. Clarke? That is where your Monday morning feature should be. You must cudgel your brain all week for it."

Clarke swears he will cudgel his brain. Mr. Pulitzer seems pleased.

"I know you will have a good paper tomorrow, Mr. Clarke."

In a few minutes he is out in the corridor—never again to enter *The World's* editorial rooms . . . or even the Pulitzer Building.

8. *United States Against Pulitzer*

"It is idle to say that the known character of Mr. Pulitzer and his newspaper are such that statements in that paper will be believed by nobody; unfortunately thousands of persons are ill-informed in this respect. . . ."—THEODORE ROOSEVELT

"In this chapter of national dishonor . . . it would appear that the President took for his motto, Asperge fortiter, aliquid adhaerebit—*Throw mud vigorously, some of it will stick."*

—LEANDER T. CHAMBERLAIN

IN THE MATTER OF UNITED STATES AGAINST JOSEPH PULITZER *et al.,* and . . . THE MATTER OF UNITED STATES AGAINST THE PRESS PUBLISHING COMPANY

(Publishers of *The World*) and CALEB M. VAN HAMM
(managing editor)
STATE OF NEW YORK   *June 23, 1910*
COUNTY OF NEW YORK

A Sworn Statement:
I, Henry Noble Hall . . . staff correspondent of *The* (New York) *World,* residing at No. 220 West Twenty-first Street, in the City of New York, in the United States of America, do hereby make oath and declare as follows:

That in the year 1908, on the fifteenth day of December, one Theodore Roosevelt, then President of the United States, in a message to The Congress . . . did make grave charges against *The World* and its editor and proprietor, Mr. Joseph Pulitzer, in connection with a series of articles published in *The World* respecting the Panama Canal purchase and the Panama revolution. . . .

That *The World* and Mr. Joseph Pulitzer, in order to establish the truth . . . did instruct me to inquire into this matter and to report on the same. . . .

(Signed)   HENRY NOBLE HALL.

215

WASHINGTON, D. C., *Feb. 9, 1912*
THE CONGRESS OF THE UNITED STATES
(Sixty-second Congress, Second session)
HOUSE OF REPRESENTATIVES
THE COMMITTEE ON FOREIGN AFFAIRS.

CHAIRMAN, Hon. William Sulzer [future governor of New York until removed through impeachment instigated by Tammany]; other members, Hon. John Nance Garner, Texas [future Vice-President of the United States, for two terms, but not the third]; James M. Curley [future governor of Massachusetts]. . . .

MR. SULZER: Gentlemen, we will take up Mr. Rainey's resolution relating to Panama . . . "whereas a former President of the United States has declared that he 'took' Panama from the Republic of Colombia without consulting Congress, etc." . . . Mr. Rainey will proceed. . . .

MR. RAINEY: . . . *The New York World* has placed before me the evidence collected for its defense in the criminal libel suit instituted by the United States Government. . . . I now present Mr. Henry Noble Hall of *The World* staff. . . .

Henry Noble Hall testified before the Committee on February 9, 12, 15, 16, and 20 (two to four hours each day), speaking chiefly from memory, except as his narrative was supplemented by exhibits . . .

And unfolding to the astonished Americas . . .

THE STORY OF PANAMA
The Order of Historical Events
(1) *1846-1848*

The United States makes a treaty with New Granada, South America (afterward known as the Republic of Colombia)—a treaty of "peace, amity, navigation, and commerce"; the southern neighbor grants the United States privileges of railroad and canal transportation across the Isthmus of Panama, while the United States guarantees Colombia's territorial ownership of the isthmus. Both sides pledge . . . "a firm, perfect, and inviolable peace and sincere friendship."

(2) 1876-1894

An Isthmian Canal Commission recommends a route across Nicaragua. Warner Miller of New York and others collect and spend about $4,500,000 but give up the project.

Ferdinand de Lesseps, builder of the Suez Canal, rehabilitates an old project for a canal across Panama; a company is formed—La Compagnie Universelle Canal Interoceanique de Panama; they raise about $240,000,000 and spend it all, mostly in Paris, including about $100,000,000 for political activities—lobbying, bribery, fixing, etc.

De Lesseps also interests a Wall Street group. The first Panama Canal Syndicate is formed, including Seligman Brothers; Drexel, Morgan, and Co., and Winslow, Lanier, and Co. Richard W. Thompson, Secretary of the Navy, resigns to become chairman of the syndicate at $25,000 a year.

The syndicate tries to interest American investors, but in vain. Very different is the response in France. Working people, dazzled by the success of Suez, rush to put up their life savings.

Thompson, afflicted by conscience because of the nonsuccess of the American drive, cuts his own salary in half, innocently unaware that the banking houses in the syndicate are each getting $50,000 a year.

Nor does he know that when the affairs of the De Lesseps enterprise are liquidated, there will be an entry on the books: "Paid to the American financial group: $2,200,000."

One thing the American syndicate does accomplish is to sell the stock of the old Panama Railroad Company (built in 1852 under the treaty with Colombia) to the De Lesseps Panama Canal Company. (When the deal started, the railroad stock was quoted at $140-150 per share; the syndicate sold it to the Canal Company for $291 a share.)

Offices of the American syndicate are next to those of a rising young law firm—Messrs. Sullivan and Cromwell. Algernon Sidney Sullivan, the senior partner, is a fellow Indiana-townsman of Thompson's, and introduces his partner, William Nelson Cromwell.

(Incidentally, it wasn't Thompson whom the syndicate really wanted as chairman. Their first choice was Ulysses S. Grant, but the former President had experienced more than enough of Wall Street during his two terms in the White House and joyously declined the honor.)

Meanwhile, construction on the Isthmus lags; machinery rusts and workmen die of fever in swamps and jungles. The De Lesseps enterprise goes into receivership and the Great Builder dies, a broken man. Now a new group is formed—La Compagnie Nouvelle du Canal de Panama, with $65,000,000 capital. The new group takes over the remaining assets of the old Panama Canal Company, including the Panama Railroad; it agrees to raise $100,000,000 to complete the Canal, and to divide the profits on the basis of sixty per cent for the old company and forty per cent for the new. These figures become important later on.

(3) *1896-1901*

Mr. Cromwell also becomes important. His acquaintance with Thompson connects him with the Panama Railroad as counsel. By strange "coincidence," Elihu Root's law firm discovers that the Panama Railroad, a New York corporation, is owned by "foreign interests" and asks the State's Attorney General to act. Result—the railroad company becomes more "Americanized" and Cromwell becomes a director as well as counsel. After the new Canal company is well started in 1896, Sullivan and Cromwell are made counsel. Cromwell does the heavy thinking and the effective acting. Stated reason for Cromwell's appointment: "intimate relations . . . with men of influence and power in all circles . . . men in political life, in the financial world, or on the Press."

Cromwell has a hard task. The McKinley administration, from the White House down, favors a Nicaraguan Canal, not the Panama plan. The voyage of the battleship *Oregon* arouses public opinion.

The *Oregon* has made the trip around South America, through the Straits of Magellan, just in time to take part in the Battle of Santiago de Cuba in the Spanish-American War, July, 1898.

The Nicaraguan Canal bill passes the Senate, 48 to 6, but Cromwell balks it in the House. Cromwell's own report: "I was able to convince several important members, particularly the Speaker [Reed]; the Chairman of the Ways and Means Committee [Uncle

Joe Cannon]; and the Chairman of the Committee on Rivers and Harbors, Mr. Burton."

Meanwhile, the Nicaraguan route has been endorsed by both major parties. The Republicans include a strong plank for Nicaragua in the 1896 national platform, and so do the Democrats, among their planks inspired by Bryan's Cross of Gold and Crown of Thorns.

Four years later a startling transformation takes place. In May, 1900, Senator Mark Hanna again urges the Nicaragua plan, and sharply attacks the lobbying of William Nelson Cromwell. "It was a bitter arraignment . . . one of the severest ever heard in the Senate." But, in June, 1900, the Republican National Convention goes lukewarm on canal routes. They recommend merely "an isthmian canal."

What has happened? One thing is that Cromwell has contributed $60,000 to the Republican campaign fund to help re-elect McKinley. Hence the change.

From now on, Mark Hanna becomes the outstanding advocate of Panama. The Senate Committee on Interoceanic Canals favors Cromwell's enterprise. Hanna, in a burning address, using as Exhibits A to Z various maps, charts, and statistics, convinces a majority that Nicaragua is dangerous, afflicted with earthquakes, volcanoes, mosquitoes, pestilences, etc. Hanna's exhibits are prepared by William Nelson Cromwell. So is Hanna's speech.

Cromwell, in the meantime, has been organizing an American syndicate with a fund of $5,000,000. The Panama Canal Company of America is incorporated in New Jersey by Cromwell and Francis Lynde Stetson, attorney for J. P. Morgan and Company. Authorized capital—$30,000,000; purpose—to buy up the securities and assets of the French company and complete the canal, which, Cromwell says, is two-fifths finished. Needed—$100,000,000. *The World* announces that the new group includes many "rich men," mentioning Morgan and Company, J. Edward Simmons, Kuhn, Loeb, and Company, Edmund C. Converse, Warren Van Norden, August Belmont, Levi P. Morton, John W. Seligman, Charles R. Flint, J. R. de La Mar, and Vernon H. Brown. Washington is deeply impressed. A *World* dispatch says, "The new Panama Canal company is credited with having the strongest financial backing in the world."

(4) *1901-1902*

Cromwell runs into trouble on his own account. The French promoter, Baron Eugene Oppenheim, has been busy trying to block Sullivan and Cromwell, and succeeds in having them ousted as counsel. There is a seven-month intermission before Cromwell is firmly back in the saddle again. Oppenheim and Cromwell come to terms. Meanwhile, Cromwell has been defending Panama on every front.

The year 1901 is big with news. McKinley is assassinated! Vice-President Theodore Roosevelt becomes Chief Executive. T.R. is a Panama champion. The Hay-Pauncefote Treaty is completed, giving Uncle Sam a clear field in Panama, so far as John Bull is concerned. In 1902 the Isthmian Canal Commission, having undergone certain changes in personnel, ideas, political contacts, etc., takes a new, quick look at the Canal problem and unhesitatingly finds for Panama. Added reason—the French company offers to sell out lock, stock, and barrel, for $40,000,000.

The Big Stick (recommended by T.R. as the proper accessory to soft speaking) is now in evidence—from the White House to Capitol Hill. (T.R. means The Rough-rider.) Monsieur Bo, head of the French company, warns Cromwell not to have recourse to "dangerous or illicit proceedings, notably in gifts or promises." This is for the sake of the record.

When the Hepburn Bill, authorizing a canal in Nicaragua, comes from the House to the Senate, the Cromwell-Roosevelt combination is in full power. Senator Spooner offers a "substitute" bill (substituting Panama for Nicaragua). But the die-hards in the House attach a time clause—a proviso that if the Panama plan is not started "within a reasonable time" Nicaragua will again be favored. The bill authorizes purchase of the French project for $40,000,000. Hanna pushes the bill through Congress and T.R. signs it in June, 1902.

Colombia now feels the pressure from all sides. The wily Cromwell stirs up the government in Bogotá to send a negotiator with power to sign a treaty and do it before the "reasonable time" expires. Minister Concha comes to Washington, but profoundly dislikes the job. Bogotá wants $10,000,000 in cash and a continuance of the $250,000 yearly payments which Colombia has been getting from the Panama Railroad. United States Secretary of State John Hay, under constant prodding from T.R., offers $10,000,000 and $100,000 a year—"take it or leave it."

Concha writes home in bitterness: "This uncle of ours [meaning Sam] . . . can settle it all with a single crunch of his jaws. . . . The desire to make themselves appear as the nation most respectful of the rights of others, forces these gentlemen [Hay *et al.*] to toy a little with their prey before devouring it. . . . The outbursts in the press . . . emanating from Mr. Hay himself or from Mr. Cromwell, who is a rat and is very active in fomenting this and other fusses, have not given them the results they hoped for. . . . My presence here is not only useless—it is improper."

Statement by Sullivan and Cromwell: "Minister Concha informed us he would not obey his instructions . . . he considers them unpatriotic . . . he intended to resign rather than continue the negotiation . . . Minister Concha became so violent in his opposition that on November 22, 1902, he broke off all negotiations . . . without even taking leave of the State Department and left shortly afterward for Bogotá. . . . Mr. Herran remained in charge."

The Sullivan and Cromwell statement is part of Cromwell's brief submitted to the French arbitrators in support of his claim of $800,000 "for services rendered." Cromwell's brief was *The World's* Exhibit A in the evidence produced by H. N. Hall.

December 2, 1902—Congress convenes. . . . A message from the White House, on "the state of the Nation":

"We continue in a state of unbounded PROSPERITY [the capitals are ours] . . . by unwise legislation it would have been easy to destroy it. There will undoubtedly be periods of depression." . . . (History's footnote: "And How!") "The wave will recede but the tide will advance.

"This nation is seated on a continent flanked by two great oceans . . . such a nation so placed will surely wrest success from fortune. . . . The Congress has wisely provided that we shall build an Isthmian canal, *if possible at Panama.* The Attorney General reports that we can undoubtedly acquire good title . . . negotiations are now pending with Colombia. . . ."

(5) *1903 (Panama's Year)*

The Big Stick is now applied to Dr. Thomas Herran, Colombia's chargé d'affaires who has been left holding the bag by Concha.

January 22. Hay to Herran: "The reasonable time has now expired. . . . The annual rental is increased to $250,000. . . . I am not authorized to discuss or consider any other change. . . . With sentiments of high consideration, etc. . . ."

"BOGOTÁ, COLOMBIA
"JANUARY 24, 1903
"COLOMBIAN MINISTER
"WASHINGTON
"DO NOT SIGN CANAL TREATY. YOU WILL RECEIVE INSTRUCTIONS IN LETTER TODAY.
"MARROQUIN." [President]

"WASHINGTON, D. C.
"JANUARY 22, 1903
"FOREIGN AFFAIRS,
"BOGOTÁ
"TREATY SIGNED TODAY ACCEPTING ULTIMATUM TEN MILLIONS AND TWO HUNDRED AND FIFTY THOUSAND DOLLARS ANNUITY.
"HERRAN."

Statement by Henry Noble Hall, *World* reporter: "The message from Bogotá was not sent until after the treaty was signed. It did not reach Washington until January 25. In the meantime, Cromwell had led Chargé d'Affaires Herran around to Secretary Hay's own home to sign the treaty. . . ."

The so-called Hay-Herran Treaty is highly satisfactory to the Theodore Roosevelt administration but not to the people of Colombia. Under its terms Colombia yields a strip of land, three miles wide, on either side of the Canal. But Colombia is barred from any part of the $40,000,000 promised to the clients of William Nelson Cromwell—that is, the stockholders in the new Panama Canal Company.

In Bogotá, the treaty is greeted with rage. Feeling runs high against the United States and against Herran. The Colombian Congress plans to reject the treaty. One Bogotá statesman declares:

"The insult which Herran has cast upon Colombia will never be wiped out. The gallows would be small punishment. . . ."

This violent reaction is a serious threat to Cromwell's interests. If Colombia fails to ratify the treaty, the United States, under the Spooner Act, will have to abandon Panama and proceed with Nicaragua. Cromwell's clients, having no stake in Nicaragua, stand to lose $40,000,000. Cromwell is not the man to accept any such prospect—he boards a train for Washington.

June 14, 1903. From *The World:*

"*Washington*—President Roosevelt is determined to have the Panama Canal. He has no intention of beginning negotiations for the Nicaragua route. . . .

"The State of Panama will secede if the Colombian Congress fails to ratify the Canal treaty. . . .

"The citizens of Panama propose after seceding to make a treaty with the United States, giving absolute sovereignty over the Canal Zone.

"In return, the President . . . would promptly recognize the new government . . . and at once appoint a minister to negotiate and sign a canal treaty. . . . The President has been in consultation with leading Senators and has received unanimous encouragement. . . .

"William Nelson Cromwell, general counsel of the Panama Canal Company, had a long conference with the President today. . . ."

How did this amazingly accurate forecast find its way into *The World* four and a half months before the Panama Revolution took place? Who was the clairvoyant?

Statement by Mr. Hall:

"On leaving the White House, Cromwell sent his press agent, Richard L. Farnham, formerly of *The World,* over to *The World's* Washington Bureau. Farnham assured *The World* correspondent that there would be an uprising on the Isthmus: that it would probably take place on Election Day, November 3: and that five or six citizens of Panama would soon arrive in Washington to consult with

Secretary Hay and other State Department officials concerning the proposed uprising."

[The writer of the article referred to by Hall was Samuel G. Blythe, for many years head of *The World's* Washington Bureau.]

The Panama Revolution began at 5:49 P.M. on Tuesday, November 3. The Colombian Congress had adjourned without acting on the Hay-Herran Treaty. The revolutionists—all on Cromwell's payroll—arrested the governor of the Department of Panama, a few Colombian generals, and the commander of the gunboat *Bogotá.*

The paymaster of the *Bogotá,* an innocent youth, resenting the detention of his commander, fired six shells on the City of Panama. "One Chinaman was killed, lying in his bed. The only other casualty was one jackass, mortally wounded in the slaughterhouse." (Official report.)

Colombia had four hundred troops at Colon and could easily have subdued the insurgents but for intervention by the United States.

The day before the revolt, by T.R.'s own direction, instructions were sent to the commanders of the warships *Nashville* and *Boston,* which "just happened" to be within striking distance of the revolution:

"SECRET AND CONFIDENTIAL. MAINTAIN FREE AND UNINTER-RUPTED TRANSIT. . . . GOVERNMENT FORCE REPORTED AP-PROACHING COLON IN VESSELS. PREVENT THEIR LANDING, IF, IN YOUR JUDGMENT, THIS WOULD PRECIPITATE A CONFLICT."

Commander John Hubbard of the *Nashville* reported to the Secretary of the Navy in Washington on November 4:

"PROVISIONAL GOVERNMENT WAS ESTABLISHED AT PANAMA TUESDAY EVENING; NO ORGANIZED OPPOSITION. . . . I HAVE PRO-HIBITED TRANSPORT OF TROOPS NOW HERE ACROSS THE ISTHMUS."

American warships and marines prevented Colombia from moving troops. Colombia was compelled to give up the Department of Panama. The next week the Republic of Panama was recognized by the State Department in Washington; within a month the new republic sold the Canal Zone to the United States for $10,000,000 and the $40,000,000 of William Nelson Cromwell's mysterious clients no longer was in jeopardy.

From *The World:*

"Mr. Cromwell is in his early fifties, but his long curly hair and handsome moustache have been white for years. His wealth of snowy hair, topped with high silk hat, gives him a theatrical look, but there is nothing theatrical about his methods. He can dig deeper and do big things more quietly than almost anyone downtown. . . .

"His eyes are brilliant light blue, clear as a baby's and as innocent-looking as a girl's. His complexion would not shame a maiden. He can smile as sweetly as a society belle and at the same time deal a blow to a business foe that ties the opponent in a hopeless tangle."

Representative Henry T. Rainey, at a later date, put Cromwell into the *Congressional Record* as "the most dangerous man this country has produced since the days of Aaron Burr."

With all his charm, Cromwell rarely cared to discuss the Panama business and would never disclose the identity of his clients. Even when a Senate committee sought information about the Panama secrets in 1906, Cromwell evaded most of the questions by pleading the privilege of confidence between attorney and client.

"You seem to be suffering from professional lockjaw," said Senator Morgan, chairman of the committee. Cromwell replied:

"I do not mean to be impolite."

Panama's protected revolution fails to excite America. Notwithstanding the importance of the Panama Canal to our national defenses, the people and the press pay remarkably mild attention. *The World* publishes not a single editorial about Panama—not until much later in these proceedings. 1903 is the year of Chicago's Iroquois Theatre fire (500 lives lost); Enrico Caruso makes his debut at the Met.; "Sweet Adeline" is adopted by National Scrap-Iron Quartets, Inc. (Incapacitated); Bill Bailey refuses to come home, even for concessions in rent and cooking; sentimentalists are singing "Dear Old Girl"; concert artists become slightly nutty about Amy Woodford-Finden's "Indian Love Lyrics," words by Laurence Hope ("Pale Hands I Love," et cetera); Babes make debut in toyland; baritones prefer "Mother O' Mine," and church soloists eagerly snap up "Open the Gates of the Temple" . . . but few are much concerned about Panama. Public interest in Panama might never have been revived if Cromwell himself had not become strangely agitated during the Taft-Bryan campaign.

October 2, 1908. The city editor of *The World* received a "hot tip." Cromwell had complained to District Attorney William Travers Jerome that an attempt was being made to blackmail him in connection with the Panama Canal. Jerome declined to discuss the matter. Cromwell was equally uncommunicative; *The World's* reporter returned empty-handed, and the assignment was marked zero.

Late that night Jonas Whitley, another Cromwell press representative—member of *The World* staff back in the blizzard days—called at *The World* and conferred with managing editor Van Hamm. Whitley understood that *The World* was about to print an inaccurate story about Cromwell and he wanted to set *The World* straight. Whitley admitted that Cromwell had appealed to Jerome against certain persons who were trying to blackmail him.

"These persons," Whitley said, "are pretending that Charles P. Taft [brother of the Republican candidate for President] and Douglas Robinson, brother-in-law of President Theodore Roosevelt, were members of a syndicate interested in the sale of the Panama Canal and are threatening to exploit the story for political purposes unless Cromwell buys them off."

Van Hamm had heard nothing about the story. Leaving Whitley in his office, the sagacious managing editor walked out to the night city desk and learned about the unfruitful efforts of the afternoon. Returning to his office, Van Hamm said:

"The story is just being written, Jonas. In the meantime, suppose you tell me your side of this affair."

Fifteen minutes later, while Whitley went out for a walk, Van Hamm summoned a stenographer and dictated in substance as follows:

"District Attorney Jerome is investigating a matter placed before him by W. J. Curtis of the firm of Sullivan and Cromwell. . . . Mr. Curtis represented that men whom he named were endeavoring to obtain money from Mr. Cromwell. . . . Mr. Curtis told Mr. Jerome that it had been represented to Mr. Cromwell that the Democratic National Committee was considering the advisability of making public a statement that Mr. Cromwell, in connection with M. Bunau-Varilla, a French speculator, had formed a syndicate at the time when it was quite evident that the United States would take over the rights of the French bondholders in the De Lesseps Canal and that this syndicate included, among others, Charles P. Taft, brother of William H. Taft, and Douglas Robinson, brother-in-law of President Roosevelt. . . . That the syndicate had gone into the French market and purchased for about $3,500,000 the stocks and bonds of the De Lesseps Company and of the newer concern . . . because of a full knowledge of the intention of the U. S. Government to acquire the French property for about $40,000,000 and thus were enabled to reap a rich profit. The story fixed the profit of the syndicate at $36,500,000, this amount being divided among the Government favorites in the world of politics and finance.

"Mr. Cromwell feared an attempt was being made to blackmail him; that a certain man had represented that the Democratic National Committee would make public this scandalous statement but that his personal influence would stop any publication; whereupon Mr. Cromwell, who is the close friend and adviser of Mr. Taft, concluded that it was an attempt to hold him up.

"Mr. Cromwell's agent last night said that the $40,000,000 appropriated by the United States to take over the holdings of the old French companies, was sent to France through the firm of J. P. Morgan and Co.; that the entire amount was paid into the French courts. . . .

"Mr. Cromwell's agent said most emphatically that there had been no syndicate of any kind at any time . . . that the acquisition of the bonds by the U. S. Government was through regular channels and not through any intermediate holding company. . . ."

On Whitley's return to the office, Van Hamm handed him the statement. Were there any corrections, Van Hamm wanted to know. Whitley carefully read the article; crossed out the name Charles P. Taft and substituted Henry W. Taft; paused for a moment, and then eliminated Henry W. Taft and restored Charles P. Taft.

"The story as it now stands," Whitley said, "is accurate."

One hour later (early morning of October 3) *The World* was out on the streets with the Cromwell story on page one.

Later editions of that morning carried a statement by Mr. Cromwell.

"Neither I nor anyone allied with me," declared Cromwell, "either directly or indirectly, at any time or at any place in America or abroad, ever bought, sold, dealt in, or ever made a penny of profit out of any stocks, bonds, or other securities of either the Old Panama Company or ever received for the same a single dollar of the forty million paid by the United States. . . ."

"Of course," he added, "this does not refer to Sullivan and Cromwell counsel fees."

The next day *The World* carried other denials. Charles P. Taft and his brother, Henry W. Taft, said: "None of us had any part in the Panama Canal sale."

Douglas Robinson refused to see reporters.

During the next few weeks *The World* printed five or six articles on the Panama Canal. The articles were widely quoted by Democratic newspapers, but were totally ignored by President Roosevelt and Republican leaders. They refused to regard the Panama Canal as a campaign issue.

It was not *The World*, but the *Indianapolis News*, which first started the hue and cry about Panama. On November 2, the day before election, the Indiana paper, which was ordinarily Republican, carried an editorial packed with dynamite. It read in part:

"The campaign is over and the people will have to vote tomorrow without any official knowledge concerning the Panama Canal deal. . . . There is no doubt that the Government paid $40,000,000 for the property.

"But who got the money?

"The Administration and Mr. Taft do not think it right that the people should know. The President's brother-in-law is involved in the scandal, but he has nothing to say. The candidate's brother [Taft] has been charged with being a member of the syndicate. He has, it is true, denied it. But he refuses to appeal to the evidence. For weeks this scandal has been before the people. The records are in Washington and they are public records. But the people are not to see them—till after election, if then."

The editorial apparently was effective, because the Republicans lost the Hoosier State ticket, although Taft carried Indiana's electoral vote. After election, William Dudley Foulke, son of Indiana, and a friend of T.R.'s, wrote to the White House, enclosing the *News* editorial and asking: "What are the facts?"

"The White House, December 1, 1908
"My dear Mr. Foulke:

"I have received your letter of the 29th enclosing quotations from the *Indianapolis News,* edited by Mr. Delavan Smith. As Mr. Smith certainly knew that all the statements he made were false. . . . But inasmuch as you evidently earnestly desire some answer to be made and you say that some reputable people appear to believe the falsehoods of the *News* and Mr. Smith . . . I will answer them. . . .

"The *News* says that there is no doubt that the Government paid $40,000,000 for the property and continues—'but who got the money?' . . . Really, this is so ludicrous as to make one feel a little impatient. . . . The fact has been officially published again and again that the *Government paid $40,000,000 direct to the French Government.*

"The United States Government has not the slightest knowledge as to the particular individuals among whom the French Government distributed the sum. This was the business of the French Government. The mere supposition that any American received from the French Government a 'rake-off' is too absurd to be discussed. It is an abominable falsehood, and it is a slander, not against the American Government, but against the French Government.

"The *News* continues, saying that 'The President's brother-in-law is involved in the scandal but he has nothing to say.' The President's brother-in-law was involved in no scandal.

"The scandal affects no one but Mr. Smith and his conduct has been not merely scandalous but infamous. Mr. Robinson has not the slightest connection of any kind, sort, or description at any time or under any circumstances with the Panama matter. Neither did Mr. Charles Taft.

"So far as I know there was no syndicate: there certainly was no syndicate in the United States that to my knowledge had any dealings with the Government directly or indirectly. . . . Mr. Delavan

Smith is a conspicuous offender against the laws of honesty and truth-fulness, but he does not stand alone. . . .

"Very truly yours,

"THEODORE ROOSEVELT."

Tuesday, December 8. An editorial in *The World:*

"PANAMA CANAL SCANDAL—LET CONGRESS INVESTIGATE!

"In view of President Roosevelt's deliberate misstatements of fact in his scandalous personal attack upon Delavan Smith, editor of the *Indianapolis News, The World* calls upon the Congress of the United States to make immediately a full and impartial investi-gation of the entire Panama Canal scandal. . . .

"To the best of *The World's* knowledge and belief, each and all of the statements made by Mr. Roosevelt are untrue, and Mr. Roose-velt must have known they were untrue when he made them.

"WHO GOT THE MONEY?

". . . Only one man knows. . . . And that man is William Nei-son Cromwell. The two men who were most in Mr. Cromwell's con-fidence are Theodore Roosevelt and Elihu Root, Secretary of State.* It was they who aided Mr. Cromwell in consummating the Panama revolution, arranged the purchase of the Panama Canal, made the agreement to pay $40,000,000 with an additional $10,000,000 for a manufactured Panama republic, every penny of which sums was paid by check on the United States Treasury—not to the French Government, as Mr. Roosevelt says, but to J. P. Morgan and Co.

"Mr. Roosevelt says, 'the Government paid this $40,000,000 di-rect to the French Government.'

"Mr. Cromwell testified before the Morgan Committee that the United States paid the money to J. P. Morgan and Co.

"Mr. Roosevelt says, 'the French Government distributed the sum.'

"Mr. Cromwell testifies as to how he distributed it.

"Mr. Roosevelt talks of 'getting the receipt of the liquidator ap-pointed by the French Government to receive the same.'

"Mr. Cromwell testified: 'Of the $40,000,000 thus paid by the United States Government, $25,000,000 was paid to the liquidator

* This was not strictly accurate. Elihu Root was not Secretary of State at the time of the revolution. *J. W. B.*

of the old Panama Canal Company under and in pursuance of an agreement entered into between the liquidator and the new company. . . . Of the balance of $15,000,000 paid to the New Panama Canal Company, $12,000,000 have already been distributed among its stockholders and the remainder is now being held awaiting final distribution and payment.' . . .

"And yet Mr. Roosevelt says that the 'United States Government has not the slightest knowledge' as to the distribution of the $40,-000,000 and that 'this was the business of the French Government.'

"As to Mr. Roosevelt's statement that 'there was no syndicate,' he could have read the 'syndicate subscription agreement' on page 1150, Vol. II, of the testimony before the Committee on Interoceanic Canals—if he had cared for the truth.

"Why did the United States pay $40,000,000 for a bankrupt property whose control could undoubtedly have been bought in the open market for less than $4,000,000?

"Who were the New Panama Canal Company?

"Who bought up the obligations of the old Panama Canal Company for a few cents on the dollar?

"Among whom was divided the $15,000,000 paid to the New Panama Canal Company?

"Whether Douglas Robinson, Mr. Roosevelt's brother-in-law, or any of Mr. Taft's brothers associated himself with Mr. Cromwell in Panama exploitation or shared in these profits is incidental to the main issue of letting in the light.

"Whether they did or did not, whether all the profits went into William Nelson Cromwell's hands or whatever became of them, the fact that Theodore Roosevelt, as President of the United States, issues a public statement about such an important matter full of flagrant untruths, reeking with misstatements, challenging line by line the testimony of his associate, Cromwell, and the official record, makes it imperative that full publicity come at once through the authority and by the action of Congress."

Notes by G. W. Hosmer, M.D.:

JP's new yacht *Liberty* was launched on December 5, 1907, and put into commission in the early weeks of 1908. It was one of the largest private yachts ever built, costing about $1,500,000 to construct and $200,000 a year to operate. From the time JP took possession, the yacht was never out of commission; no matter where he was, the *Liberty,* fully manned, fully equipped, was ready to steam at a moment's notice.

[The *Liberty* was built by Ramage and Ferguson, Ltd., at Leith, Scotland (designed by G. L. Watson and Sons of Glasgow), on very special lines, the chief objective being the convenience of the blind owner and the elimination of noise. The yacht had two decks and an extra shade deck. She measured 268 feet overall; 250 feet at the water line; beam, 35 feet; depth, 17 feet, 10 inches; draft, 16 feet; gross tonnage, 1607, net, 268; maximum speed, 15 knots; cruising speed, 12 knots. Crew, sixty men in all.]

During the early weeks of 1908, JP made his headquarters at Nice, being joined by Mrs. Pulitzer in February. He made several trial spins on the *Liberty* and in June crossed the Atlantic in the new yacht, landing at his own dock at Bar Harbor.

In July the *Liberty* cruised down to New York and JP spent several days on the yacht in and around the harbor, taking advantage of the nearness to New York to interview editors and business heads of *The World.* He visited Ralph Pulitzer's home at Manhasset, Long Island, for a few days.

In August the *Liberty* steamed from New London for Plymouth. The voyage was stormy. Hosmer's chronicle says: "August 29, reached Plymouth and left the same night; August 30, arrived Cowes, England, taking aboard James M. Touhy, head of *The World's* London Bureau; August 31, Ostend—Into port and out again—bad night; September 1—Ran into Maas waterway; great gale outside; September 4—Ran to Amsterdam and thence traveled to Wiesbaden where he remained one month; October 6—boarded *Liberty* at Amsterdam and sailed for Southampton; October 10—Southampton to Cherbourg, picked up Herbert Pulitzer and Miss Keelan [Herbert's governess]; thence to Madeira and sailed for New York, October 18 . . ."

The *Liberty* arrived at Charleston, South Carolina. On December 7, 1908, the day of the Roosevelt-to-Foulke publication, Seitz and Ralph Pulitzer boarded the yacht bringing the local papers. JP listened intently.

"When Delavan Smith says he got his information out of a New York paper," asked JP, "what does he mean?"

"He means *The World.*"

"I knew it! If there is any trouble, *The World* is sure to be in the middle of it."

A few days later, arriving at his home on East Seventy-third Street, New York, JP sent for Van Hamm. With infallible instinct he went straight to *The World's* weakest point. . . .

"What proof have you that Douglas Robinson and Charles P. Taft are involved in this matter?"

"None at all."

"My God! No proof? You print such stories without proof?"

Van Hamm tried to explain that Robinson and Taft had only Cromwell to thank for injecting their names into the case. It was Cromwell alone who first mentioned them in his complaint to the District Attorney.

"All right," said JP, dissatisfied, but philosophical. "Just remember—Roosevelt is likely to make trouble. You and Lyman and Cobb and Speer will not be his targets. He will try to make trouble for me. . . . If he does, I will fight him to the finish!"

One week after *The World* demanded a Congressional investigation, Theodore Roosevelt sent a special message to Congress, which said, in part:

". . . These stories need no investigation whatever. They consist simply of a string of infamous libels. They are in part libels upon individuals—upon Mr. Taft and Mr. Robinson, for instance, but they are in fact a libel upon the United States Government.

"The real offender is Mr. Joseph Pulitzer, editor and proprietor of *The World.* The great injury done is in blackening the good name of the American people.

"It should not be left to a private citizen to sue Mr. Pulitzer for libel. He should be prosecuted for libel by the Governmental authorities.

"It is a high national duty to bring to justice this vilifier of the American people, this man who wantonly and wickedly seeks to blacken the character of reputable private citizens and to convict the

Government of his own country in the eyes of the civilized world of wrong-doing of the basest and foulest kind. . . .

"The Attorney General has under consideration the form in which the proceedings against Mr. Pulitzer shall be brought. . . ."

Less than three years later, Mr. Roosevelt stood before an audience at the University of California:

"I am interested in the Panama Canal," he declared, "because I started it. If I had followed traditional, conservative methods, I would have submitted a dignified state paper of probably two hundred pages to Congress and the debate would have been going on yet: but I took the Canal Zone and let Congress debate, and while the debate goes on, the Canal does also."

If Theodore Roosevelt, in the Special Message of December 15, 1908, expected to intimidate Joseph Pulitzer and *The World,* he was disillusioned. JP was ill. He did not want strife; he needed peace. But the President's words called for action. Up to this time, JP had taken no direct part in any of the Panama articles, a fact which he believed was fully understood at the White House. But now—for *The World's* answer—the editorial, though written by Cobb, was, in spirit and essence, the work of the blind editor.

December 16, 1908. From *The World:*

"Mr. Roosevelt is mistaken. He cannot muzzle *The World.*

"While no amount of billingsgate on his part can alter our determination to treat him with judicial impartiality and scrupulous fairness, we repeat what we have already said—that the Congress of the United States should make a thorough investigation of the whole Panama transaction, that the full truth may be known to the American people.

"It is a most extraordinary circumstance that Mr. Roosevelt himself did not demand such an inquiry. All his protestations of outraged virtue, all his torrents of imprecation and denunciation, end with the amazing assertion that 'there is nothing whatever, in which this Government is interested, to investigate about this transaction.'

"*The World* fully appreciates the compliment paid to it by Mr. Roosevelt in making it the subject of a special message to the Congress of the United States. In the whole history of American Government no other President has ever paid such a tribute to the power and influence of a fearless, independent newspaper.

"*The World* likewise appreciates the importance and significance of the President's statement when he declares to Congress that the proprietor of *The World* should be 'prosecuted for libel by the Governmental authorities,' and that 'the Attorney General had under consideration the form under which the proceedings against Mr. Pulitzer shall be brought.'

"This is the first time a President ever asserted the doctrine of lese-majesty, or proposed, in the absence of specific legislation, the criminal prosecution by the Government of citizens who criticized the conduct of the Government or the conduct of individuals who may have had business dealings with the Government. Neither the King of Great Britain nor the German Emperor would venture to arrogate such power to himself. Yet Mr. Roosevelt proposes to use all the power of the greatest government on earth to cripple the freedom of the press on the pretext that the Government itself has been libeled—and he is the Government.

"We are aware that for many years Mr. Roosevelt has been savagely displeased with the editorial conduct of *The World*. It is true that we have criticized him sharply and frankly whenever we believed the public interest required, just as we have heartily commended and supported him whenever we believed the public interest would thereby be advanced. Mr. Roosevelt's attack on *The World* can be explained only on the theory that he believes he can muzzle the paper, and our recent impeachment of his veracity seems to have been the last straw that broke his autocratic back.

"Mr. Roosevelt's lamentable habit of inaccurate statement makes it impossible to accept either his judgments or his conclusions. In his message he does not state correctly even so simple a matter as the pretended causes of his grievance.

"He says, for example, that *The World* asserted that there was 'corruption by or on behalf of the Government of the United States.' No such charge was made by this newspaper.

"He says it was asserted that there were 'Improper dealings of some kind between agents of the Government and outside persons.' No such charge was made.

"He says that 'among those persons who, it was alleged, made "huge profits" were Mr. Charles P. Taft, a brother of Mr. William

H. Taft, then candidate for the Presidency, and Mr. Douglas Robinson, my brother-in-law.' No such charge was made.

"If *The World* has libeled anybody we hope it will be punished, but we do not intend to be intimidated by Mr. Roosevelt's threats, or by Mr. Roosevelt's denunciation, or by Mr. Roosevelt's power.

"Mr. Roosevelt's seething indignation about *The World's* 'libel upon the United States Government' is an exquisite indictment indeed, coming as it does from a President who less than a week ago officially insinuated in his message that the Congress of the United States was composed of scoundrels who amended an appropriation bill because 'Congressmen did not themselves wish to be investigated by Secret Service Men.'

"No other living man ever so grossly libeled the United States as does the President who besmirches Congress, bulldozes judges, assails the integrity of courts, slanders private citizens, and who has shown himself the most reckless, unscrupulous demagogue whom the American people ever trusted with great power and authority.

"We say this not in anger but in sincere sorrow. *The World* has immeasurably more respect for the office of President of the United States than Theodore Roosevelt has ever shown during the years in which he has maintained a reign of terror and vilified the honor and honesty of both public officials and private citizens who opposed his policies or thwarted him in his purposes.

"So far as *The World* is concerned, its proprietor may go to jail, if Mr. Roosevelt succeeds, as he threatens; but even in jail *The World* will not cease to be a fearless champion of free speech, a free press and a free people.

"It cannot be muzzled!"

T.R. was happy to see the Pulitzer prosecution well started before the Roosevelt administration went out of office. Archie Butt, one of T.R.'s many biographers, wrote: "That is his one weakness; he cannot brook criticism."

Major Butt, who was President Theodore Roosevelt's personal aide, wrote in his volume (*Letters of Archie Butt*) also of a White House luncheon in January, 1909, when the Great Hunter was preparing to go to Africa. George R. Sheldon, treasurer of the National Republican Committee, was present, along with Mr. and Mrs. Douglas Robinson. "They discussed the Panama Libel Suit and both the President and Mr. Robinson think they will put Old Pulitzer in prison. . . ."

About the same time, the Associated Press was begging T.R. to permit their correspondent to accompany him to Africa. "The Yellow Press will be sure to follow," they argued. "And if a lion should happen to do his duty, the A.P. could not afford to be beaten." Teddy still refused.

Knowing the Rough Rider complex for vengeance, JP fully expected Government action. During the very cold winter of 1908-1909, he remained mostly aboard the *Liberty,* darting in and out of New York, with occasional conferences in the town house. He was extremely nervous; worried continually about the defense; considered former Governor Black as defense counsel (Black had nominated T.R. in the Republican convention of 1904) but dropped the matter; he even inquired about Federal prisons.

Impatient at the suspense, he sailed aboard the *Liberty* for the West Indies but got only as far as Havana.

February 17, 1909. Washington—A District of Columbia Grand Jury indicted Joseph Pulitzer, Caleb M. Van Hamm, Robert Hunt Lyman [night editor], and the Press Publishing Company on charges of criminally libeling Theodore Roosevelt, J. Pierpont Morgan, Charles P. Taft, Douglas Robinson, Elihu Root, and William Nelson Cromwell. Indictments were also returned against Delavan Smith and Charles R. Williams of the *Indianapolis News.* Bench warrants were issued for the individual defendants and a summons for the Press Publishing Company.

The *Liberty* steamed back to Charleston.

The indictments were brought under an old statute based on English laws of 1662. But the legal problem was, how to bring the defendants into the District of Columbia for trial.

Long before the libel case came to trial, Theodore Roosevelt passed from the Washington scene and Taft succeeded to the White House. Cromwell had fully expected to be made Attorney General in the new administration, but the Panama aroma was too pungent; the post went to George W. Wickersham.

Prosecution in the District of Columbia was frustrated when the government attempted to extradite the gentlemen from Indiana.

United States Attorney Joseph H. Keating resigned rather than proceed against Delavan Smith and Charles R. Williams of the *Indianapolis News.* Keating said: "I am not in accord with the government . . . in its . . . strained construction of the law. To drag these defendants from their homes to the seat of government while there is good and sufficient jurisdiction in the State courts . . . is very dangerous, striking at the very foundation of our form of government."

Federal Judge Albert B. Anderson of Indianapolis dismissed the writ, remarking that he, too, would like to know—"Who Got the Money?" Judge Anderson said:

"If the history of liberty means anything—if constitutional guarantees are worth anything—these proceedings must fail."

A year later, Theodore Roosevelt, speaking at the Indianapolis Columbia Club, called Judge Anderson "a jackass and a crook." Anderson always considered the remark a compliment.

In the face of the Anderson decision, the government made no attempt to bring *The World's* owner and editors into the District of Columbia. Instead, under T.R.'s guidance, Henry L. Stimson, then United States Attorney for the Southern District of New York, put the complaint before a Federal Grand Jury.

Frank I. Cobb, *The World's* chief editorial writer, is called as a witness, and is questioned by Deputy United States Attorney General Stuart McNamara, who is collaborating with Stimson.

Q. Do you know Joseph Pulitzer?

A. I do.

Q. Did you see him after the President's message of December 15?

A. I did.

Q. What did he say to you about the message?

A. It was a surprise to him. He has been out of the country for several months, and returned to find himself assailed by the President as a vilifier and libeler of the American people. Naturally he wanted to know what it was all about. . . . I told him what the paper had printed, and said I thought the message was a political bluff on Mr. Roosevelt's part. . . .

Q. What did Mr. Pulitzer think of it?

A. He agreed with me—that it was an attempt to muzzle the paper.

Q. Do you recall anything else that he said in that conversation?

A. Not very definitely. I remember he said, speaking as a reader of *The World,* that he had no very high opinion of an editorial I wrote about the President's message.

Q. What did he have to do with subsequent editorials, or what did you have to do with them?

A. I must decline to answer that question.

Q. You plead privilege?

A. I do . . . not knowing the end or purpose of these proceedings. . . .

Q. Do you think it would incriminate you to tell what Mr. Pulitzer said to you about the President's message?

A. I do not. I have told all I remember.

A GRAND JUROR: What do you mean by muzzling the paper?

COBB: I mean—gagging it. Perhaps I can illustrate. . . . At the time of this message, Mr. Roosevelt was also in a controversy with the House of Representatives. He had accused the House of amending the Secret Service Appropriation Bill on the ground that Congressmen themselves did not wish to be investigated; he said the amendment was in the interest of criminals. There was a very bitter controversy . . . the decision as to whether Congress could maintain its prerogatives and dignity depended largely upon public opinion.

Now if *The World* had been intimidated by this libel suit and had shown the white feather, lesser newspapers could hardly be expected to have the courage to criticize the President . . . knowing that he would start libel actions against them too. If we had cringed on this matter, I should say that Mr. Roosevelt then had muzzled, or intimidated, or gagged us. . . .

Q. By muzzling you mean—preventing the paper from printing anything it sees fit to print?

A. I mean, preventing the paper from printing that which it is its duty as a great newspaper to publish.

Q. You believe that a newspaper should print anything it sees fit, without regard to anything?

A. I do not. I believe newspapers should be held strictly accountable to just libel laws, justly administered by courts of admitted jurisdiction.

ANOTHER GRAND JUROR: *The World* printed on the front page the other day an article under a big headline which I regarded as libelous, and later published a correction in small type in one corner of the paper—do you think that was right?

COBB: I do not know anything about the circumstances; but if the article was libelous, I hope the man will get a judgment against the paper.

MCNAMARA: When you go to see Mr. Pulitzer, what do you talk about?

COBB: Mostly about politics, in which he is very deeply interested. But chiefly we discuss the policy of *The World. Mr. Pulitzer conducts a school of journalism in regard to me. He often says he expects that I shall be able to carry on the principles of* The World *for the next twenty years.*

MCNAMARA: When you receive instructions from Mr. Pulitzer do you carry them out?

COBB: Not necessarily. It depends upon the nature of the suggestion and the circumstances.

MCNAMARA: You would feel free to disregard something Mr. Pulitzer told you to do?

COBB: I would.

A GRAND JUROR: You look upon Mr. Pulitzer as your employer, do you not?

COBB: I do not. The first time I ever saw Mr. Pulitzer he told me I must never assume that any such relations existed between us.

JUROR: If Mr. Pulitzer wished to discharge you, however—he could do so?

COBB: I infer that if Mr. Pulitzer wanted me discharged, he would find some way to get rid of me.

JUROR: You regard Mr. Pulitzer as the Big Man of *The World?*

COBB: I regard Mr. Pulitzer as the Big Man of all American newspapers.

(JP's prophetic soul was only partly accurate. Cobb did carry on the principles of *The World* after JP's death, but only for about twelve years. Did Joseph Pulitzer, in saying "twenty years" perhaps foresee the death of his own newspaper? JP died October 29, 1911. *The World* died February 27, 1931.)

March 4, 1909. President William Howard Taft is inaugurated. The Press Publishing Company, owner of *The World,* and its managing editor, Caleb M. Van Hamm, are indicted.

The Federal grand jury has acted—under a bizarre piece of legislation dating back to the Alien and Sedition Laws of 1789. One of these oppressive acts had been revived in 1825, and in 1898, during the Spanish-American conflict, a war-mad Congress had revamped it as an anti-Fifth Column measure—although, of course, the Fifth Column was never heard of until a much later Spanish war.

The statute under which *The World* is accused is entitled "An Act to Protect the Harbor Defense from Malicious Injury, and for Other Purposes." The indictment charges that *The World,* containing a "malicious, libelous, and untruthful article," had been circulated in the Government Reservation at West Point and in the Post Office Building, New York City. The charge is that twenty-nine copies of *The World,* containing the Cromwell statement about Taft and Robinson, were delivered to the U. S. Military Academy at West Point, and another copy delivered to the Federal Building.

(This single copy to the Federal Building was delivered at the Post Office as required by the Postal Acts for inspection as to any unmailable matter. The twenty-nine copies to West Point presumably were bona fide subscriptions, approvable today by the Audit Bureau of Circulation.

(The government seeks to construe this offense as criminal libel, the allegation being that *The World's* purpose was "to stir up disorder among the people.")

In this move, Pulitzer is not indicted. Van Hamm is the only individual defendant.

(As there were at that time no fewer than 2,809 U. S. Government reservations like West Point and the Post Office Building, and as the government insisted that any copy of *The World* containing the article complained of, entering any one of these guarded precincts, thereby constituted a separate offense under the statute, the sky appeared to be the limit so far as prosecution possibilities were concerned.)

It is a trait of JP's to complain of annoyances but never of his fate. In the Roosevelt libel case, he is annoyed. Part of his irritation is due to his personal conviction that *The World* had overstepped the bounds—first, in printing the Cromwell article, second, in the fierce response to T.R.'s attack on Delavan Smith. The weak point in *The World's* defense is its publication of charges against Charles P. Taft and Douglas Robinson, linking them with the Panama Canal syndicate.

The World's answer on that point insistently is, "We didn't make the insinuation—Cromwell made it." Which is no defense at all; libel is libel, no matter who makes the charge, unless it is made in open court under oath and as a matter of public record. The fact that Cromwell started the story about Taft and Robinson does not excuse *The World*—the responsibility for uttering the libel, that is, for publishing it, rests exclusively with *The World,* its editors, managers, owners, and publishers, reporters, too, if they had anything to do with it, and it appears that they did not.

Of course, a libel against Charles P. Taft and Douglas Robinson is not a libel against the United States of America; nor was it libelous or slanderous for *The World* to say that the only men who could answer the question—Who Got the Money?—were Theodore Roosevelt, William Nelson Cromwell, and Elihu Root. (As already pointed out, the statement was probably incorrect as regards Root.)

Was any evidence ever adduced to indicate that Charles P. Taft and Douglas Robinson participated, profitably or otherwise, in the operations of Mr. Cromwell and his American syndicate?

The answer is given by Henry Noble Hall, in his testimony before the House Committee on Foreign Affairs, in the hearings on the Rainey Resolution:

Mr. Hall: Investigation has shown that Mr. [Charles P.] Taft had absolutely nothing whatever to do, directly or indirectly, with the sale of the New Panama Canal Company to the United States.

Mr. Cooper (member of the committee): Douglas Robinson,

brother-in-law of ex-President Roosevelt—he was also absolutely innocent?

MR. HALL: I have no proof to substantiate the charge that Douglas Robinson was connected with the revolution in any way, shape, or form.

MR. COOPER: Then his name ought to be stricken out the same as Mr. Taft's.

At the outset of the Rainey Hearings, there was this passage:

A MEMBER (To Representative Rainey): Do you believe the French company got all that money?

MR. RAINEY: I don't want to discuss that.

MR. COOPER: Do you think that ['Theodore] Roosevelt and John Hay got most of it? Is that your position?

MR. RAINEY: On the contrary, I am convinced that they did not. On behalf of these gentlemen, I deny that.

MR. COOPER: I am glad to hear that.

The World, in short, found not a scintilla of evidence against Taft or Robinson. That was the heel of Achilles. If Robinson and Taft had sued *The World* for libel, and if such a case had ever gone to trial by jury in a state court, the results might have been different. The indications are that JP was painfully aware of this weakness.

However, the fight is on, and JP is not a man to back water. *The World* tells the government to go ahead and do its worst. JP deluges Cobb with memoranda. With all T.R.'s powers and his talks about "malefactors of great wealth," the blind editor points out, the Administration has not sent one of them to jail, but now the power of Washington is directed against the only Democratic newspaper in New York City. *The World,* in other words, is being persecuted for lese-majesty (JP's figure) after the fashion of Germany where "hundreds of editors are always being locked up." (He little dreams how true that is to become.) *The World* editorials overflow with sarcasm . . . never letting the public forget that the great question still is— Who Got the Money?

Meanwhile, *The World* is not neglecting its legal defenses. De Lancey Nicoll is chief counsel. Paradoxically, this is not to JP's liking. Twenty years before the Panama prosecution, he would have welcomed Nicoll's presence in the case—the fighting young Assistant District Attorney who prosecuted the boodlers of 1884—but not now. Nicoll has become a Wall Street lawyer. He is appointed to defend *The World* by John M. Bowers, who, for some unexplained reason, JP has designated as a trustee for *The World* during the Pulitzer absences.

However, Nicoll is in the case now, and there is nothing to do about it. And it must be admitted that this ex-prosecutor puts up a hard, brilliant, and successful fight, equal in quality if not in fierceness to JP's fight on Nicoll's behalf in the elections of 1887. But the heavy work, the pick and shovel work—one might say dirty work (without implying any improper methods) but just grimly toil—falls upon *The World* staff.

While the distinguished law firm of Nicoll, Annable, Lindsay, and Fuller is marshaling *The World's* legal points, *World* reporters are digging for evidence. Earl Harding, Gus Roeder, and others are dispatched to Panama, to Colon, to Bogotá. L.R.E. Paulin, who is on vacation in France, is assigned to dig up the archives of the Panama Canal Company—vain quest; the records are buried in the vaults of the Crédit Lyonnais, one of the big private banks that backed the French Panama enterprise, and no amount of argument can gain access to them. French law, French red tape—and the determination of French financial and governmental powers not to permit the inner secrets of Panama ever to become known—stand irremovably in the way.

The United States Government promises co-operation. President Taft apparently has no liking for this Panama case, but does not wish to offend T.R. (not yet). Wickersham has succeeded Philander C. Knox as Attorney General, and Henry A. Wise replaces Stimson as United States Attorney in the Southern District of New York. Elihu Root succeeds John Hay in the State Department. The Administration, outwardly at least, puts no stumbling blocks in the way of fact-finding.

Wise and McNamara join with John D. Lindsay of *The World's* legal battery in a fruitless "rogatory commission" to Paris. The State Department requests the American Embassy in Paris to use its good offices. Alas, the French position is that it is that it cannot be done.

Not in France. The files of the Panama Canal Company, old, new, and indifferent, are sealed up tighter than Ninny's tomb. The American gentlemen, if they wish, may invite the witnesses whom they wish to question to the American Embassy, but attendance is not compulsory. Lindsay says what is the use. He knows a runaround from a football game.

Mind you, the contract between the United States and the New Panama Canal Company, in consideration of $40,000,000, specified that the French were to turn over the "archives," with the rest of the property; but all they surrendered were the engineering data— not a line of correspondence, not a stock book, not a ledger, a cash book, a journal, or a loose-leaf notebook.

Under the French law, the records of a corporation which has gone out of business—as Panama Canal had, to the tune of forty millions can't be wrong—are sealed up in an official repository for twenty years, after which they are destroyed. In this case, the final cremation was no doubt carefully carried out.

The World's interests in Paris were officially represented by the law firm of Coudert Brothers, with offices in Paris and in New York. Besides retaining such eminent counsel (in addition to Nicoll's firm), *The World* had to pay the government's expenses as well as its own in connection with the "Letters Rogatory" expeditions to Paris, to Bogotá, Colon, and Panama City. No doubt it was a tidy sum, but it was only a part of *The World's* total bill. The investigations in Central and South America ran into big money, but Hall testified in the Rainey hearings that in all his laborious and painstaking prying of information out of reluctant informants in Panama and Bogotá, he paid not one cent of "persuasion money"—entertainment was another matter.

So far as concerns the distribution of the forty millions, *The World's* investigators, chiefly Harding and Hall, obtained only general indications, but no specific evidence as to individual beneficiaries. They did, however, prove beyond any reasonable doubt that Cromwell fomented and paid for the Panama "revolution" with hearty co-operation from Washington, all the way up to the White House.

A lucky stroke was executed by *The World* in this direction when it obtained a copy of Cromwell's brief. This was a long statement, of about one hundred closely printed pages, setting forth in much detail all that Sullivan and Cromwell had done since the very beginning of the Panama enterprise. The New York law firm wanted $800,000 for these remarkable services, ranging all the way from lobbying to campaign contributions. But the French interests objected. Arbitrators were appointed to settle the claim, and to this body the Sullivan and Cromwell brief was submitted. How much of the $800,000 Cromwell and associates received is another French mystery.

How does *The World* obtain Cromwell's brief? That is a newspaper secret, in the preservation of which *World* men are as clever as the French. All we know now is that Cromwell dictates the long statement in English, and when it is completed, he sends it to another lawyer to be translated into perfect legal French. The French translation is sent to a printer, and one copy of it turns up mysteriously in *The World* office (report has it) on the desk of William McMurtrie Speer. Curiously enough, it was Speer who in October, 1908, gave *The World's* city editor, then George Carteret, the tip about Cromwell's visit to the District Attorney.

The Cromwell brief makes its first public appearance in February, 1912, when Henry Noble Hall produced it in the Rainey hearings of the House Foreign Affairs Committee. Representative John Nance Garner of Texas seemed skeptical . . .

Mr. GARNER: Who is the authority for this translation?

Mr. HALL: I translated it myself, sir. . . . I was brought up and educated in France.

Hall clinches the discussion by producing an original French version of the Cromwell MS.

This is all very well as to the Panama Revolution, but not illuminating as to who got the money. By the time the case comes to trial in the District Court of the Southern District of New York, there is divided opinion as to the best procedure. Nicoll thinks *The World* has enough evidence to convince a jury. On the other hand, there is the more important issue: *Free Speech* and *Freedom of the Press*.

The World refuses to concede the existence of a Federal libel law

—a law which would place all newspapers at the mercy of the party in power.

JP casts the deciding vote. *The World* chooses to contest the government's jurisdiction, which is a quick way of getting the matter settled. JP is as anxious to get his paper out of the clutches of lawyers as he is to have it out of the courts.

The trial is called for January 25, 1910. Oyez, oyez, etc. . . . The case of the People of the United States against the Press Publishing Company. The jury is chosen. Nicoll fires the opening shot:

"The Court has no jurisdiction . . . there is no statute of the United States authorizing this prosecution. . . . The Act of 1898 does not apply . . . and if it does it is unconstitutional. . . . The offense, if any, was committed in the State of New York and is prosecutable here . . . and anyway, the defendant is a corporation and is therefore incapable of committing the 'sedition' charged in the indictment."

Congress, Nicoll further argues, never intended the law of 1898, enacted to protect national defenses, to cover libel against an individual; and as for libel against the government . . . utterly absurd!

United States Attorney Henry A. Wise does his duty; he argues that the statute can be construed as a Federal libel law . . . that newspapers are subject to prosecution in Federal courts as well as State courts. He even contends that the President can prosecute a newspaper in any one of the 2,809 instances where the paper circulated on government property, getting convictions, if evidence warranted, in each and every state in the Union.

By the court. United States District Judge Charles M. Hough:

". . . The crime of libel might be considered to impair the authority and interfere with the efficiency of the Government of the United States, but so far as I know, this thought has not found expression in any national statute now in force.

"Therefore . . . the crime charged in the indictment is to be regarded as an offense against the United States *only if it is an offense against the law of New York*. . . .

"The construction of this act by the prosecution is opposed to the spirit and tenor of legislation for many years on the subject of

national territorial jurisdiction. It is a novelty and the burden of up-
holding a novelty is upon him who alleges it. . . . This very interesting question can lawfully be presented to the Supreme Court.
. . . It is therefore ordered that a judgment of this Court be entered
quashing the indictment . . . because . . . the indictment is not
authorized by the statutes upon which it rests."

MR. WISE: I ask that a juror be withdrawn so that no question of
jeopardy [meaning double jeopardy] may enter into the case.

THE COURT: Motion granted. . . .

New York, January 26, 1916. Editorial in *The World:*

"If there exists in Washington the shadow of a suspicion that a
Federal libel law can be created by construction or interpretation—if
there still remains the likelihood that another Roosevelt will prostitute his powers . . . in order to prosecute newspapers that have
offended him—if there be the ghost of a belief that the Federal
Government has co-ordinate power with State governments in the
prosecution of alleged libel, and that every American newspaper is
at the mercy of the President—then the sooner there is a final decision of the Supreme Court of the United States, the better."

The World is deluged with congratulations. Newspapers of opposite political opinion join in the chorus. But *The World* is not
content. JP wants a complete and final showdown on this vital issue,
the right of the President to prosecute the Press, from the highest
court in the land. Cobb keeps up the demand for an appeal.

Finally, under *The World's* goading, the government files its
petition for a writ of error. The argument is heard on October 24,
1910, by the Supreme Court in Washington, but the decision does
not come down until January 3, 1911 (which is pretty fast action).
The opinion is unanimous, written by Chief Justice White.

By the court (in substance):

Two propositions are clearly established. First, that adequate
means were afforded for punishing the alleged libel in the State
courts without resorting to the courts of the United States. Second—
resort could not be had to the courts of the United States without dis-
regarding the law of New York State and frustrating the plain purpose of that law, which was that there should be but a single prosecution and conviction.

The lower court was right in quashing the indictment. No other conclusion was possible . . . without giving to the statute a meaning directly conflicting with the construction placed upon it by the Supreme Court.

New York, January 4, 1911. Editorial in *The World:*

"The unanimous decision handed down by the United States Supreme Court . . . is the most sweeping victory won for freedom of speech and of the press in this country since the American people destroyed the Federalist party more than a century ago for enacting the infamous Sedition law. . . . The Supreme Court upholds every contention advanced by *The World* since the outset of this prosecution.

"The decision is so sweeping that no other President will be tempted to follow in the footsteps of Theodore Roosevelt, no matter how greedy he may be for power, no matter how resentful of opposition. . . ."

There is only one other legal river to cross: the fantastic indictment against Joseph Pulitzer *et al.* in the District of Columbia. This is dismissed on March 31, 1911, *by request of the Department of Justice.*

Joseph Pulitzer has fought and won his last great battle.

The last of his own lifetime, that is; his newspaper, *The World,* won several victories after JP's death . . . but lost in the greatest of all battles—the struggle for existence.

Concluding now "The Story of Panama" . . . the hearings on the Rainey Resolution:

HENRY NOBLE HALL: I wish to thank you, Mr. Chairman and all the members of the committee, for the very kind and courteous attention you have given to my statement. I have not spoken here as the advocate of Colombia, nor as the prosecutor of Mr. Roosevelt. . . . I sincerely hope that you will find some way of settling a difference with Colombia; which ought to be settled, because the United States is losing in South American trade today very nearly as much as it is spending on the Panama Canal . . . but there are other and higher reasons why this controversy ought to be settled. I firmly believe that "righteousness alone exalteth a nation" and that with

nations even more than with individuals, honesty is the best policy.
. . . Truth, justice, honor, demand that Colombia's claims be satisfied. . . .

The committee thereupon proceeded to the consideration of other
business.

Under the persuasion of Woodrow Wilson, in the next administration, Congress awarded Colombia $25,000,000. But that is an-
other story.

As to *The World's* question—Who Got the Money?—the following information is from the files of *The World's* investigation:

The United States Treasury Department issued a warrant for
$40,000,000 in favor of J. P. Morgan and Co., fiscal agents for the
new Panama Canal Company. Morgan and Company, as agents, endorsed the check to themselves as bankers, and exchanged it at the
Sub-Treasury in Wall Street for eleven separate checks drawn on
New York banks. In the record, $25,000,000 went to France and
$15,000,000 remained in the United States—which was retained
and distributed by the Cromwell syndicate. Actually, according to
World investigators, about $15,000,000 went to France and the rest
remained here.

Anyway, as one *World* investigator stated, Charles R. Flint and
Baron Eugene Oppenheim always felt that they did not receive their
just share.

All the rest—as *The World* said, "only Cromwell knows," and up
to now Cromwell has refused to talk.

If he ever does . . .

FOOTNOTES TO PANAMA

The conclusion of the whole matter, as one reviews this episode in
American journalism, is:

First: The World, along with all other newspapers, was negligent
in failing to expose the operations of the Cromwell syndicate in
June, 1903, when Samuel G. Blythe made his remarkable forecast,
inspired by Cromwell.

Second: The World was negligent in failing to expose the character of the Panama Revolution at the time when it happened. This is true of the entire press.

Third: The World was guilty of poor editorship when it published the Cromwell story about his visit to the District Attorney's office.

Reasons for this conclusion:

(*A*) The story was unconfirmed by Jerome's office, or by any other official source. An attempt was made by an inexperienced reporter to see Jerome earlier in the day, to confirm a tip from Speer (which was also apparently inspired from Cromwell's office); but there is nothing to show that *The World* tried to interview Jerome after Whitley had spilled the story in *The World* office. All that Van Hamm did was to get a statement from Cromwell, which was gilding the lily, to say the least, since he already had Cromwell's story from the promoter's own press agent.

(*B*) Apparently, no attempt was made to interview Douglas Robinson and Charles P. Taft, or Henry Taft either, before publication of the Cromwell-inspired story. The rules of Accuracy and Fair Play were recognized rather in the breach than in the observance here; the Tafts issued denials the next day; Robinson refused to talk, but at least he should have been given an opportunity the night before.

(*C*) Lacking confirmation either from Jerome or from the principal victims (Taft and Robinson), Van Hamm could have waited —in fact, I think, *should* have waited—until he had a complete story, even at the risk of losing his exclusive "beat" or "scoop." It is better to be accurate than to be sorry. The other papers probably could not have caught up with the story anyway, unless Jerome gave it out.

(*D*) Van Hamm was altogether too eager to print the Cromwell story. He apparently thought he was very clever in trying to make Jonas Whitley think that *The World* already had the story on the night of October 2, 1908, when Whitley came to *The World*; but, from this distance, it looks as if Cromwell's office planted the tip on *The World* in the first place, and then came around later to make sure that the story got into the paper. Cromwell's object in sending his associate, Curtis, to the District Attorney's office, was (I think, unquestionably) to create a quasi-official basis for the story that Cromwell obviously wanted *The World* to print. The story as it appeared in *The World* next day was libelous on the face of it— as against Taft and Robinson. *The World's* only justification was, "Cromwell told this to the District Attorney"—which is insufficient, especially as the District Attorney did neither give out the story in the first place, nor confirm it; and Cromwell's fantastic charge of blackmail soon vanished into thin air.

These delinquencies on the part of Van Hamm and the others in charge of *The World* that night appear all the clearer in the light of *The World's* failure to get one shred of evidence involving either Robinson or Taft. If either of these gentlemen, or both, had chosen to sue *The World* in the New York State courts, the record, as it now stands, is that *The World* did not have a leg to stand on. The widespread dragnet for evidence failed to bring in a good defense against Taft and Robinson. This is why JP immediately asked, when he learned of the case, for the evidence involving Taft and Robinson, and was properly shocked to find that *The World* had none.

Of course, one is always entitled to ask: Why did not Robinson and Taft sue for damages on their private account? The answer probably is that the ferocious T.R. took charge of the situation and gave orders for all hands.

Fourth: The World rendered heroic public service in demanding a Congressional investigation of the Panama affair. This, as Cobb forcefully pointed out, is an issue entirely apart from the libel against Robinson and Taft. The syndicate operation called to high heaven for a thorough probing, and so did the teapot revolution in Panama. *The World* was on strong ground here, although it had no facts to go on, except Cromwell statements.

Fifth: The World rightfully and forcefully challenged T.R.'s attempted usurpation of power over the press. JP and Nicoll rendered a distinct service to the cause of free press and free speech when they decided to fight T.R. on the ground of jurisdiction and not with evidence. A jury trial would have been more sensational and perhaps more damaging to Administration prestige, but the fight on the question of law was a fatal blow to T.R.'s power drive against the newspapers. If the Rough Rider tactics employed against *The World* and the *Indianapolis News* had been successful, as Cobb pointed out, some other President would have been tempted to go even further.

The question of who got the money remains to plague future historians and biographers; as to that—

> *"Why, that I cannot tell," said he,*
> *"But 'twas a famous fight!"*

Incidentally, Robinson contributed one of the funny stories of the Panama libel case. After *The World* story came out, a reporter for the *Sun* (at least he said he was a reporter for the *Sun*) tried to interview Robinson.

T.R.'s brother-in-law at that time wore sideburns and also spoke with a Scotch accent. When the *Sun* man came to the house, Robinson opened the door himself and the reporter thought he was the butler. Proceeding on this basis, the reporter tried to pry information out of Robinson against Robinson.

"But," said T.R.'s in-law, "if I told you any secrets, I would lose my job."

"That's all right," said the *Sun* man; "the *Sun* will get you another job and give you a cash present besides."

When Robinson told the story at the White House, T.R. roared with laughter. "Douglas," he said, "you are such an incorrigible liar that I'm not sure I was wise in bringing this libel suit in your name."

9. Liebestod . . . . Exit Softly

"The rest is silence. . . ."
"Now cracks a noble heart. Good-night . . .
And flights of angels sing thee to thy rest!
Why does the drum come hither?"—HAMLET

FROM the records of the Surrogate's court:

July 30, 1881. In the name of God, Amen.
I, ALBERT PULITZER, of the City, County, and State of New York, being of sound mind, memory, and understanding, do hereby make, publish, and declare this as and for my Last Will and Testament in the manner following, that is to say:

Item First. I hereby give and bequeath unto my brother, Joseph Pulitzer of St. Louis, Missouri, my gold Waltham watch and chain, my gold cuff-buttons, and my turquoise shirt studs, three in number, with my kindest wishes and blessings, invoking his kindly interest in the education and welfare of my son. . . .

And so, in this legalistic manner of sixty years ago, began the story of the Pulitzer wills—a mystery which has never been solved unto this day.

Joseph Pulitzer and his brother, Albert, four years the younger, were pioneers in the journalism of the late nineteenth and twentieth centuries. Those of us who have been brought up, so to speak, in the Joseph Pulitzer tradition, have always minimized Albert's influence, but a fresh examination of the records indicates that we were wrong. Albert is important. He came to New York from St. Louis while Joseph was still struggling with the *Post-Dispatch*. Albert started his metropolitan career on the *Staats-Zeitung,* changed quickly to Dana's *Sun,* and then to the *Herald.* As a special writer for the Bennett paper, Albert won an international reputation. His interviews with prominent statesmen and other notables of the day were reprinted by the European papers. Within a very few years after coming to New York, Albert was able to organize a corporation, with himself as principal stockholder, and found the *New York Morning Journal*. The new paper was a great success. It was cheap, it was bright, it was urbane, cosmopolitan, and delightfully sophisticated. Albert made a lot of money, and was not at all pleased when his older brother came crashing into the field.

For years, the brothers did not speak. Whether Albert ever changed his will on that account, we cannot say. The only will that ever came to light is the one quoted above—the one leaving his watch, chain, cuff-buttons, and shirt studs to Joseph and bespeaking his kindly interest in the education of his son Walter.

In spite of the family estrangement, Albert continued to prosper; the *Morning Journal* set the pattern for the new school of gossip and personality writers who believe that persons are more important than events, and that the most interesting news sources are the cafés, Wall Street, Park Avenue, Broadway, and Hollywood. Joseph was the pioneer in the other school, which stresses politics before people and believes that accuracy is more important than rumors and that public welfare comes ahead of personalities and purely private matters. (Not that JP had any objection to either a good human interest story or a bit of scandal now and then.)

About 1876, Albert married a high-born British lady, Miss Fanny Bannard. There is a bit of confusion here. Certain newspaper accounts and other biographies, recording the wedding of Albert, state that the son Walter was born two years later, but in his own will, dated July 30, 1881, Albert speaks of his son Walter as being seven years old, and as residing temporarily with his mother at Whitestone, Long Island. Apparently the marriage did not prosper as well as Albert's other affairs, because in the same will he disposed of his wife by giving her the house at Whitestone and all the furniture, and one thousand dollars in cash. The rest of the estate was put in trust for Walter until he should become twenty-five years old, with an extra allowance of one thousand dollars a year for educational purposes between the ages of sixteen and twenty-one.

Albert's New York connections, even in 1881, before the *Journal* was started, were first class. As executors of his will he named Algernon Sidney Sullivan, of Sullivan and Cromwell, and Jesse Seligman. And as a special bequest he gave to John R. Dos Passos of New York "my painted white silk mouchoir, and my two scarf pins, one of gold, the other set with rubies and emeralds, as a token of my kindest regards."

This will of Albert Pulitzer's cropped up in the Surrogate's Court of New York County on December 2, 1909, two months after Albert's death in Vienna. It is the only will of his of which we have any knowledge. As to whether JP ever got the watch and the various articles of personal jewelry, there is no report; nor is there anything to indicate that the Joseph Pulitzer side of the family paid any attention to Albert's request for interest in Walter's education.

The evidence is to the contrary. Two years after Albert's will was filed, the Last Will and Testament of Joseph Pulitzer, very bulky, and supplemented by four codicils of no mean length, was offered and admitted to probate in the same court. But nowhere in the entire document, taking will and codicils together, is there a single mention of either Albert or Walter; there are elaborate provisions for a School of Journalism to educate young men for newspaper work, but no provision for Walter, who by 1911 was a journalist himself.

In *The World* office, during the fifteen years I was with the organization, Walter Pulitzer was not exactly the Forgotten Man but the Man-to-Be-Forgotten. There were strict orders that under no circumstances was he to be identified as related to or connected with the Joseph Pulitzer family in any way, shape, or manner. Several warnings to that effect from the Bureau of Accuracy and Fair Play were inserted in the Walter Pulitzer envelope in the Biographical Department. (This bureau was a unique *World* institution; it investigated complaints from persons who felt that *The World* had treated them unjustly and, in general, rode hard over the news department.) The impression in the office was that Walter was a sort of pretender. Certainly there was no idea that he was JP's nephew.

What was the story? We never found out. Such is tradition in a place where it should have least weight.

Walter Pulitzer never pressed his claim for recognition. After several years of writing for the *Smart Set* type of magazines around town, he suffered a nervous breakdown and had to give up work entirely for three years. During that time he amused himself by the study of chess and became an expert. Upon his return to health he wrote a novelette entitled *That Duel at the Chateau Marsanac,* which was the story of a battle at chess for a lady's hand. After that he wrote *A Cynic's Meditations,* consisting of not too bad epigrams and "affectionately inscribed to my father, Albert Pulitzer." One of his epigrams was, "No family can lay claim to an established respectability that doesn't own at least one black sheep." His next book was *My Auto Book,* a collection of quips about motorcars, which were at that time still something to make jokes about. One of Walter Pulitzer's cracks was this:

"Why did she run away with the coachman?"

"Because her father couldn't spare the chauffeur."

Publication in 1912 of the *Meditations of a Mean Man,* completed the Walter Pulitzer cycle of epigrams. One of the 1912 vintage was this:

"A girl's heart is like an umbrella. Sooner or later some fellow is going to steal it."

By that time, Walter was being acclaimed in the press at home and abroad, although there were no favorable notices in *The World.* Here are some of the tributes:

John Kendrick Bangs (famous American humorist, now forgotten) : "Many of his epigrams are delicious." (Not the ones I saw.)

Alan Dale (New York *American*) : "This is the sort of humor that appeals to me."

London *Academy:* "Some of Mr. Pulitzer's epigrams reach a very high level of gnomic philosophy."

London *Sketch:* "Mr. Pulitzer certainly stands head and shoulders above other American writers of epigrams."

Paris *American:* "He is the American La Rochefoucauld."

Town Topics (New York) : "Few authors have practiced the special art of making epigrams as successfully as Walter Pulitzer."

From which one might infer that Walter was one of the fathers of the modern wisecrack—the parent being a corporation rather than an individual.

Other epigrams from Walter's fountain should be given judicial notice:

"No satirist is a hero to his own epigram."

"One touch of merriment makes the whole world grin."

"No man can serve two chauffeurs."

"A widow and her weeds are soon parted."

Walter Pulitzer seems to have done very well as an individual author, but when he attempted the role of publisher, he was not successful. He started a magazine called *Satire* which quickly collapsed. Undismayed, he organized the Pulitzer Magazine Company in 1913 with a supposed capital of $300,000 and quickly dived into bankruptcy, after which he never again emerged upon the literary horizon.

The silent feud between the Joseph Pulitzer family and the Albert-Walter Pulitzer branch may possibly be explained partly on the ground of jealousy. Albert seemed to have the talent of writing, editing, publishing, and making money without any of the emotional storms that marked the path of Joseph Pulitzer. Walter seems to have been both prolific and for a time successful; whereas Ralph Pulitzer, JP's oldest son, and for a time the rising star of the family, produced only two books of known record. In 1910, Ralph's first book, *New York Society on Parade* (Harper and Brothers), caused a mild sensation among the so-called Four Hundred, chiefly because it emanated from the first Pulitzer to marry into Society. Ralph's first wife was Frederica Vanderbilt Webb. Some of his frontal attacks on what was then Fifth Avenue Society were these:

"Society is held together by the centripetal force of clowns on the one hand and complete acquisitiveness on the other."

"Instead of having an aristocracy whose caste is beyond question and whose mutual hospitalities constitute Society, New York has an aristocracy whose membership is largely arbitrary and whose existence vitally depends upon those activities which are known as social functions."

At a social function, Ralph wrote, "The mistress of the house welcomes them [the guests] with that indelible smile which hostesses share exclusively with coiffeurs' models and the early Christian martyrs."

The former Pulitzer home, No. 11 East 73rd Street, New York

Ralph's other book was *Over the Western Front in an Aeroplane*, published in 1916, while Mr. Wilson was keeping us out of the First World War.

But most of Ralph's work was anonymous, appearing in editorials of the lighter sort in *The World*. JP, as previously noted, commended the "delicate touch" of his then chief heir.

Whatever the true history and explanation of the internal battles of the Pulitzer clan, they are purely collateral issues in the history of JP and *The World*. It happened that Albert's will was recorded two years before JP's death. If JP was affected by the honorable mention, the gift of jewelry, and the solicitude for Walter, he gave no indication of it in the amendments to his own will. His attention was plentifully occupied with the problem of perpetuating his newspaper, providing security for his family, and establishing a system of education for journalists of the future.

Anyway, it was too late to do anything about the education of Walter Pulitzer. By the time Albert's will was filed in Surrogate's Court, Walter was well over thirty years of age.

Joseph Pulitzer began the making and recasting and amending of wills back in 1892, and kept it up almost to the moment of his death. The will which was finally produced after his death is dated April 16, 1904, but obviously it is only one of a series, because it "hereby cancels" all previous wills and codicils thereto. Along with the 1904 will there were four codicils, dated respectively March 23, 1909; January 17, 1910; May 11, 1910; and July 12, 1911. However, JP regarded these merely as stopgaps. In the summer of 1911 (his last on earth) he had ordered the entire structure to be recast, and had a draft of the proposed new and all-embracing will in his possession for final study aboard the yacht *Liberty* shortly before his death. Some indication of its importance may be gathered from the writings of former associates. Lieutenant-Colonel Norman Graham Thwaites in his reminiscences (*Velvet and Vinegar*) says that even the new will was all wrong; that numerous mistakes were being rectified while Pulitzer was on the last cruise; that "the new and unexecuted will contained provisions drastically different from those of the older testament."

James Barnes, who was a temporary secretary-companion, left this record (in *From Then Till Now*) in connection with JP's death: "There is not the slightest doubt that he contemplated making some further changes in his will. As it happened, no changes were made, and there is no occasion to mention the things he discussed with me."

It is not strange that JP, who was "never satisfied with merely printing news"—never satisfied with any situation, in fact—should have been forever dissatisfied with his will. But more than mere intellectual unrest was responsible for the many changes. The making of wills and the adding of codicils were linked with his recurrent contemplations of death. Whenever he had a strong foreboding, as he frequently did, that the Grim Reaper was just around the corner, he started tinkering with his will.

Hosmer chronicles that back in 1892, when Pulitzer had a premonition of early death, he first brought out his plan for the School of Journalism. This was just after he had returned from a long trip abroad, and when, after vainly trying to follow doctors' orders, he had cast prescriptions to the winds and thrown himself unrestrainedly into the victorious campaign for Cleveland. In October of that year, he broached his plan for the education of journalists to Seth Low, then President of Columbia University. The response was not enthusiastic. Low presented the memorandum to the Columbia trustees, but it could scarcely be called a good sales talk. What they said was mostly off the record; if they did not despise the idea of teaching journalists under Pulitzer-*World* auspices, they certainly rejected it. Some called it "visionary." If it was indeed a vision, JP wrote later (in the *North American Review* of September, 1904), it was one which he had long cherished, pondered deeply, and followed persistently.

At any rate, it was a vision which refused to go away. The death-warning stopped, for a while, but the Forecast of Journalism remained. Though rebuffed, JP would not be discouraged. If a school for journalists had been a mere philanthropy on his part, he might have been dismayed by the stuffy attitude at Columbia. The plan could wait, but evidently a recasting of the program was needed. It seemed that the first step toward establishing a new school was the education of the university itself, which only time could accomplish.

JP put the plan back into the laboratory of his mind to acquire maturity while he sifted and tested all of the objections raised against it, "without prejudice," he wrote, "anxious only to find the truth." From this workshop ten years later, in connection with another Thanatopsis, the plan emerged in firmer outline and stronger detail. Beginning in 1902 he reopened negotiations with Columbia, working as usual through intermediaries, including Francis Lynde Stetson, lawyer for the Morgan interests. William L. Merrill, who was still "chief editor" at *The World,* acted as JP's eyes, ears, and mouthpiece, right up to the final agreement when the blind Planner, always seeing things in the dark, suspected Merrill of being too subservient to Columbia and angrily supplanted him.

On the second approach, the auspices were much more favorable. Seth Low had passed from the academic scene, leaving the magnificent Library with the golden Statue of Alma Mater to commemorate his services on Morningside Heights. The successor to the presidency was the redoubtable Nicholas Murray Butler.

It is reasonable to suppose that JP's persistence on behalf of his plan was linked in his mind with his own death—that he was thinking of the time when other newspapermen would be saying, "Just what was it that Old Pulitzer was aiming at?" How could they understand unless there were a permanent reminder? To put it briefly, he was looking toward a profession of journalism which had some foundations; whose builder and maker was Democracy; whose cornerstone was moral courage; whose four sides were accuracy, independence, justice, and fair play; whose mural decorations were good morals, good taste, good manners, and the wholesome aspects of American life; and whose banners at the top were public service, progress, reform, and persistent sympathy for the underdog.

Obviously, the foundation for such a profession begins with the education of journalists themselves. Without inculcation of the ideals which he constantly harped upon, he saw no point at all in any structure of journalism, and as for his own *World,* he would rather have it perish than to pull down those banners. In which respect, his wish was at least partially fulfilled.

President Butler had some misgivings about the Pulitzer Plan; he worried a little about public reaction. He may have had the idea that

Joseph Pulitzer and his *World* were associated with "yellow journalism." If so, he was agreeably disappointed. When the plan was finally published, the response was favorable from coast to coast, from press, pulpit, and platform.

Not so favorable were some of the opinions from JP's associates of *The World*. Don C. Seitz, business manager, was against it. JP first showed him the plan in the winter of 1903, on the way to Jekyl Island. Seitz rode with him on the train as far as Washington. As the train left Jersey City, Hosmer handed Seitz a long memorandum of the Columbia project. Before Seitz had finished reading the syllabus, JP came along, feeling his way down the Pullman corridor.

JP: You don't think much of it!

SEITZ: I do not.

JP: What else can I do? I want to do something. [This is Seitz's version. It doesn't sound like JP.]

SEITZ: Why not endow *The World* . . . make it fool-proof?

JP: I am doing something for it. I'm giving it a new building. [This was the annex completed in 1908.]

If he ever seriously considered the suggestion of endowing *The World,* there is no record of it. His notions of journalism were all to the contrary. It seems never to have occurred to him that a paper like *The World* would ever fail to pay its way; at least he thought there was only a remote chance of financial failure; and for that contingency he threw in the provision that the trustees might sell stock of the Pulitzer Publishing Company, sacrificing the *Post-Dispatch,* if necessary, to keep *The World* going.

Quite probably he felt that an endowment for *The World* would take the edge off the enterprise and lead to the same kind of relaxed reporting and editing that we see in certain publications of today which feel too sure of their circulation and advertising to worry about getting out the best paper possible.

The first agreement with Columbia was signed on JP's fifty-sixth birthday, April 10, 1903. One year later, a new will was executed, confirming the endowments, but also stressing the restrictions on the gift. Under the agreement, Columbia received $500,000 for the building; another half million to put the school into operation, and was to receive another million by JP's will, but only on condition that the School had been going successfully for at least three years and was still flourishing; and also on the condition that the system of prizes and scholarships had been adopted.

"If the plan for awarding the prizes . . . shall not have been agreed upon by Columbia University and myself in my lifetime," so reads the will, "then I direct that such prizes shall be awarded and paid in accordance with a plan to be agreed upon by my executors and the University. Such plan must, before its adoption, be approved by the Advisory Board [of the School of Journalism].

"And," he added in the will, *"it must make provision for the following prizes and scholarships* which shall be awarded or paid annually or otherwise as designated.

"First. Annually, for the best and most suggestive paper on the future development and improvement of the School of Journalism, or for any one idea that will promise great improvement in the operation of the school. $1,000.

"Second. Annually, for the most disinterested and meritorious public service rendered by any American newspaper during the year . . . a gold medal costing $500.

"Third. Annually, for the best history of the services rendered to the public by the American press during the preceding year. $1,000.

"Fourth. Five annual traveling scholarships of $1,500 each.

"Fifth. Annually, for the best editorial article written during the year, the test of excellence being clearness of style, moral purpose, sound reasoning, and power to influence public opinion in the right direction. $500.

"Sixth. Annually, for the best example of a reporter's work during the year, the test being strict accuracy, terseness, and the accomplishment of some public good, commanding public attention and respect. $1,000.

"Seventh. Annually, for the American novel published during the year which shall best present *the wholesome atmosphere of American life and the highest standard of American manners and manhood.* $1,000. (Author's italics.)

"Eighth. Annually, for the original American play performed in New York which shall best represent the educational value and power of the stage *in raising the standard of good morals, good taste, and good manners.* $1,000. (Author's italics.)

"Ninth. Annually, for the best book of the year upon the history of the United States. $2,000.

"Tenth. Annually, for the best American biography teaching patriotic and unselfish services to the people, illustrated by an eminent example, excluding as too obvious the names of George Washington and Abraham Lincoln. $1,000.

"The plan shall further provide that if in any one year, no book or play *written for the prize offered* shall be of sufficient excellence in the opinion of the [Advisory] Board, or if in any other subject of competition all the competitors shall fall below the standard of excellence fixed by the Board, then in that case the amount of each prize or prizes may be withheld in each year; *and it is my intention* in such case that the amount of the prize or prizes not awarded shall be carried to the income of the succeeding year or years and added to the sums offered in future competition for like purposes; provided, however, that in no event shall the postponed accumulation exceed $10,000 for any one subject, and that the Advisory Board shall have power in its discretion to suspend, or to change any subject or subjects, substituting however others in their places if in the judgment of the board such suspension, changes, or substitutions shall be conducive to the public good or rendered advisable by public necessities or by reason of change of time." (Author's italics.)

The agreement provided that the second million dollars was to be divided equally between the School of Journalism and the trust fund for the prizes and scholarships—"one half of the income of this second million shall be applied to prizes or scholarships for the encouragement of *public service, public morals,* American literature, and the advancement of education." (Author's italics.)

The arrangement seems clear enough: the endowment of the School of Journalism was not to be completed unless there was a plan for prizes and scholarships; and Pulitzer's definitely stated wish was that these scholarships and prizes ought to emphasize public service, the improvement of morals and manners and all those other things that in his opinion went to make up a better American life.

After the signing of the final agreement with Columbia (there were three in all) Pulitzer apparently felt so secure about the plan in his own mind that he made no further changes in it, except to provide certain additional temporary income for Columbia out of the newspaper trust.

But with the other provisions of the will, it was very different, especially with the clauses relating to the newspaper and to the family. These he changed again and again and was about to make still other changes when death intervened.

By the dawn of spring in 1909, JP's afflictions of mind and body had apparently reached a crisis. Although we have no exact medical report, there are strong evidences that mental deterioration had begun to set in, along with progressive diminution of the life-force itself. Like Alfred de Musset, he might have cried, *"J'ai perdu ma force et ma vie!"* He seemed to spend his days and much of the nights in tempests of emotion, mercifully relieved by periods of calm, pellucid thinking and uncannily shrewd analyzing of men and affairs.

Throughout the preceding winter, most of which he had spent aboard the new yacht *Liberty,* he had been in continual torment: beset by anxiety over the outcome of the Panama prosecution; humiliated by chagrin and disappointment over *The World's* maladroit handling of the Cromwell charges; genuinely worried over the possibility of having to go to jail or prison, without adequate preparation; much disturbed by evidences of instability in his family; annoyed by the continual internal friction on *The World* staff—all these conditions combined to produce a state of profound distrust of almost everybody within range, and an extremely pitiable condition of nervous agitation.

And through all these upsets, running like a musical accompaniment or the chanting of a Greek chorus, there was the insistent overtone of impending death. For the first time, he spoke openly about it. "We shall not have many more quarrels," he would say to men from the office, "I am not going to live much longer. I've had warnings. From now on you will have to get along more and more without me and see less and less of me. I am not longer able to think or to plan."

Perhaps it was the same foreboding that induced him to adopt the "Liebestod" from *Tristan and Isolde* as the last music to be played to him every night by his secretary-pianist, Friedrich Mann. Like Isolde in her death song, he seemed to be yearning for complete absorption into the Infinite . . . the *Weltgeist,* as the Wagner libretto puts it.

But chiefly he expressed a yearning for companionship. Since the time when he and Professor Davidson shared lodgings and pot luck in St. Louis he had never found a perfect friend. Hosmer was acceptable, as long as he lasted, even though his age was a handicap. But now, at the beginning of 1909, Hosmer had left him—retired to his home in Summit, New Jersey, full of some eighty years, and worn out by the superhuman task of trying to be doctor, legal advisor, secretary, reader, confidential listener, and provider of entertaining conversation for a man whose mind was like a suction pump. Hosmer's departure created not one but several vacancies. To replace Hosmer, JP had *The World's* bureaus in London, Paris, Washington busy combing their territory for eligible men; at the same time, *The World* office and various kind friends undertook to find someone who would be at least in one or more respects a substitute for the kindly old Nestor. James M. Touhy, head of *The World's* London office, searched among the British upper classes, even inserting judicious "wanted" notices in the agony columns of the London *Times.*

Out of thousands of applicants and suggested candidates, not one measured up to the full requirements. There was James Barnes of New York and Lenox, Massachusetts, a noted writer of naval histories and biographies of famous commanders. Mr. Barnes was about forty-three, and he was an excellent sailor. Recommended by Fred Duneka of *Harper's,* a former *World* staff man, as a possible "yachting companion," Barnes took his regents' examination at the hands of the retiring Hosmer.

Barnes thought Hosmer's cross-examination rather amusing. "You might have thought," he remarked long afterward, "that I was a candidate for a degree."

JP's personal staff, with Hosmer gone, consisted of Harold Stanley Pollard; Randall Davies (who was a solicitor-at-law as well as an author); Friedrich Mann, the German secretary-reader-pianist; Norman Graham Thwaites (now a lieutenant-colonel in the British

Army); the yacht's physician, successor to Hosmer in that one respect, Dr. O. E. Wrench, who was also a literary man and author of *The Grammar of Music* and *The Grammar of Life* (Davies also wrote *A History of English Art* and *The History of Chelsea*). Thwaites, Davies, and Wrench were English university men; Pollard was a Harvard graduate; out of the entire group, Thwaites and Pollard were the only ones with newspaper experience.

Barnes joined the ship's company, on an experimental basis, in the fall of 1908, just as JP was beginning the strange winter's cruise that ranged all the way from the ice-bound rocks of Montauk Point, Long Island, to the sunny waters of the Caribbean and the Gulf of Mexico. Barnes was a bit of a problem. He started off by demanding more salary than the others, although the existing wage scale might be termed princely. The point was not argued. He was also inclined to flout the unwritten laws of the *Liberty,* such as not smoking in JP's presence unless invited.

(JP's butler always passed around fine Havana cigars after dinner but the secretaries usually saved theirs until later. JP smoked one cigar after each meal, and, according to reliable witnesses, they were cheap, black, and terrible; probably a survival of St. Louis days. Cigarettes he would not tolerate. "For God's sake," he would cry, "smoke my cigars, not those insufferable things!" Both on the yacht and in his various residences, the secretaries' quarters were always well stocked with cigars and drinks—to be used in extreme moderation.)

The seemingly erratic wanderings of the *Liberty* during the 1908-1909 winter season coincided with the period of greatest tension in the Panama controversy. JP was not dodging arrest, nor was he afraid to suffer imprisonment for the sake of free press and free speech. What he did fear was sudden seizure by the government's agents and being thrown into some out-of-the-way place of detention before he had an opportunity to arrange for bail or start habeas corpus proceedings. Consequently the *Liberty* kept just far enough offshore to escape observation and made quick dashes into New York and other harbors only long enough to get messages from the office.

The winter was unusually rough and cold. JP, always a good sailor, seemed rather to enjoy the pitchings and tossings of the

Liberty as a relief from emotional torment. Frequently the Chief and Barnes would be the only men at table, the others being too seasick to appear. Even the *Liberty's* captain, A. E. Caws, a native Isle o' Wightsman and splendid seaman, was knocked out. Captain Caws caught a cold from exposure, slipped rapidly into pneumonia and died in a New York hospital. Captain Hiram Dixon, able mariner from Brooklyn, succeeded as the master.

JP was hopeful that with Theodore Roosevelt out of Washington, the defense in the Panama case could be safely left in the hands of *World* counsel; he doubted that Taft had much appetite for controversy at the outset of his administration. T.R. seems to have had the same suspicion; because the second batch of indictments, the ones in New York, were handed up on the very day that Roosevelt went out of office and Taft came in.

This move cleared the judicial stage for a court battle, and JP felt that his presence was no longer needed, especially when his whole being was clamoring for escape. He gave the orders to clear for Europe as quickly as possible. Barnes was shooed off to New York with the intimation that the yacht would pick him up later, somewhere on Long Island, but it was not until several weeks afterward that he received an invitation to join JP at Southampton, England, not Long Island.

Considerable mystery attended the departure of the *Liberty*. The yacht put in at Hampton Roads on March 14, and Pollard was put ashore to telephone some last-minute suggestions to *The World*. The casual nature of the suggestions may be judged by the fact that the tolls were $104.

Next morning, the *Liberty* was riding in not too gentle weather off the Carolina capes. JP summoned the skipper.

"Which way are we heading?"

"Due east, sir."

"If we kept straight ahead where would we land?"

Dixon figured and said, "Lisbon, sir."

"Very well," JP ordered. "Due east, then, to Lisbon."

Captain Dixon did not relish the sudden decision, but followed orders. It seemed like a bad choice. The Atlantic was cold and extremely stormy, and the *Liberty* seemed to be heading directly into a gale. The yacht rolled and pitched, but there was never any danger. The *Liberty* was as safe as the biggest ocean liner then afloat.

Dixon set his course and set his teeth, expecting to weather through, but the *Liberty* had not gone many miles eastward before there was a change in the orders. JP wanted him to skirt the tip of Long Island, go into the Sound and anchor off Greenwich, Connecticut. Dixon had yet to learn that in JP's philosophy, the purpose of owning a yacht is to do as one pleases; whereas the captain was old-fashioned enough to think that navigation should take one to a destination.

Dixon's mystification was increased by later instructions from Dunningham, JP's confidential valet. Under no circumstances, the whole company was told, was anyone to speak about the unexpected detour to Greenwich. And so the legend went down into history that JP had ordered the yacht due east to Lisbon. There was a reason for the mystery. JP had been secretly arranging for a codicil to his will, the first of the series.

Between the date of the will, April 16, 1904, and the execution of the codicil, JP had undergone radical changes of ideas and plans concerning his estate. This time it was not the School of Journalism project which bothered him, but the trusteeship of the estate and the distribution of the income from the newspapers, *The World* and the *Post-Dispatch*. In the original document, he had set up a trust consisting of the entire stock of the Press Publishing Company, which controlled *The World,* and most of the stock of the Pulitzer Publishing Company, owner of the St. Louis paper.

The newspaper trust, set up in Articles Seven and Eight of the will, is one of the most remarkable creations that ever came into a court. There were to be five trustees, namely, Ralph Pulitzer; Joseph Pulitzer, Jr., upon reaching the age of twenty-one; Herbert, upon reaching twenty-one; Dumont Clarke, New York banker, and J. Frederick Kernochan, lawyer and jurist. Alfred Butes, a secretary, was to act as trustee during Herbert's minority. All actions of the trustees were to be by majority vote.

The income from the newspaper trust was to be distributed as follows: three-fifths to Joseph, one-fifth to Ralph, and one-fifth to Herbert.

Those arrangements were completely upset by the codicil, the mysterious and secretly incubated document which JP executed aboard the *Liberty* in Long Island Sound, off Greenwich, on March 23, 1909, at the time when his yacht was supposed to be somewhere out on the bounding main en route for Lisbon.

Under the codicil, the income from the newspaper trust was to be distributed three-fifths to Herbert, one-fifth to Ralph, one-tenth to Joseph, and the remaining one-tenth to such of the principal editors and managers of *The World* and the *Post-Dispatch* as the trustees considered most deserving and valuable. The term of the trust was the lifetime of the two youngest sons, Herbert and Joseph, and upon its expiration, one-tenth of the stock of both newspapers was to be sold "to one of the principal editors or managers of each of the said newspapers whom my trustees may consider most deserving in point of ability and integrity."

Equally striking were the changes in the trustees. Instead of J. Frederick Kernochan, Codicil No. 1 appointed George L. Rives, lawyer, who was helpful in bringing about the agreement with Columbia; the others are "My son Joseph when he shall attain the age of thirty years, and my son Herbert when he shall attain the age of twenty-one years." The same trustees were named as executors of the estate, along with the Union Trust Company of New York (later absorbed into the Central Hanover Bank and Trust Company). "My son Ralph," who at the time of the birth of Codicil No. 1 was nearly thirty years of age, was conspicuously omitted, both as trustee and executor. And that was the way it stayed, unchanged by later codicils.

The later testimony is that Codicil No. 1 was conceived in haste and brought forth in a hurry. William B. Hornblower, who drafted the will of 1904 and this first codicil, registered great surprise when they were published, after JP's death. Hornblower said he was sure it was all a mistake; that the dropping of Ralph's name as executor-trustee was an oversight; that JP had not intended to imply lack of confidence in his oldest son.

"I recall the circumstances," Hornblower said in a letter to Ralph, published simultaneously with the filing of the will. "Your father was far from well and was desirous of starting at the earliest practicable moment for Europe on his yacht.

"My best recollection is that your father instructed me to insert your name as one of the executors who were also to be trustees under the will and the codicil. I certainly have no recollection to the contrary." Hornblower's theory was that because of the haste in preparing the codicil, Ralph's name fell out through carelessness in copying from the draft. Unfortunately, he said, the original draft of the will and the codicil had somehow got lost. "Of course," he said, "the unfortunate omission cannot be changed by explanation, but I think it is due you that an explanation be made."

There was never any explanation as to the change in the allotment of income from the newspaper trust, and why Herbert was raised from a fifth to three-fifths, and Joseph was dropped from three-fifths to a mere one-tenth. Nor was it made clear why Herbert was chosen to become a trustee at the age of twenty-one, whereas Joseph had to wait until he was thirty.

Herbert's income from the newspaper trust was to be paid to his guardians until he should reach twenty-one, and thereafter to him personally. However, the incomes of Joseph and Herbert were limited to $20,000 a year from each newspaper until they should reach the age of twenty-five; between twenty-five and thirty they were to get $30,000 from each newspaper, and double that amount if they married with their father's approval.

The unpaid portion of Herbert's and Joseph's incomes (that is, until they should be thirty years old) was to be divided thus: one-third to the Metropolitan Museum of Art, one-third to the Philharmonic Society of New York, and one-third to the School of Journalism (to be deducted from the two-million-dollar endowment).

One thing that stands out in this No. 1 Codicil is the ascendancy of Herbert. He received the better treatment all along the line. As to the other descendants, JP registered much uncertainty. In the main will he set up a trust fund of $2,000,000, the income of which was for the use of his widow during her lifetime, and upon her death it was to be divided among the grandchildren, per stirpes, and not per capita; but Codicil No. 1 changed all that. Upon the death of the widow, the two millions were to be divided as follows: Half a million to the New York Association for the Blind, and the rest "to my son Herbert and his issue." (This was changed in the later codicils.)

Noteworthy also was the ascendancy of Dunningham. Whereas originally he was to receive $25,000, Codicil No. 1 bequeathed $100,000 "to my faithful valet, Jabez E. Dunningham" (provided, of course, that he was still in JP's employ at the time of the testator's death, which he was).

At the time of JP's death, Jabez had been in the Pulitzer service about twenty years. Although described in the will merely as "my faithful valet" he was more major domo than valet. Wherever JP was in residence, whether on the yacht, or in any of the homes and villas, or even on a transatlantic liner, Dunningham ruled the menage with steel hand encased in glove of softest kid. New secretaries quickly discovered that the most effective approach to JP—if they wanted a day off or a leave of absence—was through Jabez. Barnes found to his chagrin that any attempts at direct correspondence with JP were discouraged. "Mr. Pulitzer asks that you kindly address your letters to myself personally," Dunningham informed Barnes when the latter communicated his willingness to rejoin the staff aboard the *Liberty*.

This thickset, heavy-mustached Englishman, Dunningham—so Barnes noted—was the one and only person who had JP's complete confidence and any accurate knowledge of JP's plans and intentions. Dunningham knew the destination of the yacht when even the captain could not state precisely where he was bound. "Don't ask me—ask Dunningham," Dixon would answer when the secretaries cautiously tried to elicit information.

While other men of university education and extensive culture were kept at respectful distances, Dunningham, who dropped his h's without bothering to inquire what became of them, wrote JP's most intimate letters, made out his personal checks and showed him where to sign, and was always the one to go ashore with JP's letters, telegrams, and cablegrams whenever the *Liberty* put into a port.

Dunningham could open up telegraph and cable offices in remote ports of Europe at hours when even royalty could not gain access. He could commandeer anything the Chief wanted, from the latest model hot-water bag to an entire hotel or the best suite of an ocean liner. He could produce apples out of season from remote parts of the globe and the choicest of foods and the finest vintages; he could charter special trains or parts of trains; nothing seemed impossible; all JP had to do was to signify his wish and *presto!* Aladdin Dunningham rubbed the magic lamp, and all was in readiness. And with equal speed he could rub out all the arrangements, like Prospero with a wave of the wand, and the whole carefully built structure of plans and orders would vanish and "leave not a wrack behind." Jabez was the first to answer when JP started his morning and the one to put him to bed at night.

Sharply in contrast to JP's confidence in Dunningham and his increasing favor toward Herbert are the indications of mistrust toward other heirs and his anxiety about the preservation of *The World*. In the will, he made it plain enough that he wanted *The World* perpetuated. But in the five years between the will and the first codicil he seemed to feel that he hadn't made his position strong enough.

In the original will he had said:

"I further authorize and empower my said trustees at any time to sell and dispose of said stock, or any part thereof at public or private sale at such prices and on such terms as they may think best. . . . This power of sale however is limited to the stock of the Pulitzer Publishing Company, and nothing shall be taken to authorize or empower the sale of any stock of the Press Publishing Company, publisher of *The World* newspaper. I particularly enjoin upon my sons and my descendants the duty of preserving, perfecting, and perpetuating *The World* newspaper in the same spirit in which I have striven to create and conduct it, as a public institution from motives higher than mere gain."

In the first codicil, on the same subject, he said:

"This power of sale is limited to the stock of the Pulitzer Publishing Company of St. Louis and shall not be taken to authorize or empower the sale or disposition under any circumstances whatsoever, by the trustees, of any stock of the Press Publishing Company, publisher of *The World* newspaper. I particularly enjoin upon my sons and my descendants the duty of preserving, perfecting, and perpetuating *The World* newspaper (to the maintenance and upbuilding of which I have sacrificed my health and my strength) in the same spirit in which I have striven to create and conduct it as a public institution from motives higher than mere gain, it having been my desire that it should be at all times conducted in a spirit of independence and with a view to inculcating high standards and public spirit among the people and their official representatives and it is my earnest wish that said newspapers shall hereafter be conducted upon the same principles."

In addition to the excess income from Joseph and Herbert's shares in the newspaper trust, the codicil gave half a million dollars to the Metropolitan Museum of Art for "a Joseph Pulitzer bequest to purchase works of art" and half a million to the Philharmonic Society "for a Joseph Pulitzer bequest, the income to be applied and used to perfect the present orchestra and place it on a more independent basis, and to increase the number of concerts given in New York City, which additional concerts I hope will not have too severely classical programs, and to be open to the public at reduced rates, and to recognize my favorite composers, Beethoven, Wagner, and Liszt." (This bequest in a later codicil was so bound up with restrictions on the Philharmonic Society that it was never fulfilled.)

Other evidence of hasty drafting appears in the first codicil bequest of $100,000 to be distributed among secretaries, readers, companions, and editorial writers of *The World* "with a preference given to my personal secretaries and readers," but also including "John M. Touhy," *The World's* London correspondent. Accuracy! Accuracy! The correct name was *James* M. Touhy.

The first codicil was executed aboard the yacht in the presence of Frank I. Cobb, hastily summoned from New York and evidently enjoined to secrecy, Randall Davies, and Morgan M. Mann of Pelham, New York (no further identification).

This important piece of business once disposed of (to the temporary easing of JP's mind, let us hope), the *Liberty* proceeded eastward. It seems to have been a rough crossing. According to various memories, most of the staff spent most of the time in the throes of *mal de mer*. JP bore up well for a few days, and then succumbed to his old enemy, the common cold, which this time developed into a violent cough. Dr. Wrench failed to recognize the symptoms of whooping cough, and could only administer sedatives.

The yacht Liberty

When the *Liberty* finally reached Lisbon, a specialist summoned from Pau imparted the unpleasing news. JP had never been through whooping cough. It might sound amusing, but for the fact that the affliction may be very serious in adults. In JP's case it appears to have affected the heart. Anyway, it added no strength to a constitution already depleted.

But the book of troubles was by no means finished. At Lisbon, a new secretary came aboard, William Romaine Paterson, a young Englishman of many promising qualities, but at the moment, as it turned out, infected with smallpox. Paterson was bowled over almost as soon as he reached his cabin, and when the *Liberty* reached Gibraltar, the trouble was apparent. British authorities put Paterson in the detention hospital and ordered the entire yacht and its occupants, including JP, fumigated and vaccinated. Weeks elapsed before he could proceed to Marseilles, and thence to Aix-les-Bains where, for the time being, he got rid of his cough.

As soon as JP was able to attend to *World* affairs, he found the office in a frightful tangle. Just before his departure, he had made Charles E. Chapin city editor of *The* (Morning) *World,* and had appointed Horatio W. Seymour as editorial supervisor—a new title, never worn by any other *World* man before or since. Van Hamm was continued as managing editor, but with clipped wings. JP believed that this was going to be a perfect plan; instead, it proved to be a perfect nuisance.

Chapin had been making a wonderful success as city editor of *The Evening World.* JP saw no reason why those remarkable talents should not be just as effective on the morning paper, not knowing that city editors cannot be transplanted—at least not as a rule. City editors generally develop their own peculiar genius, if any, in one environment, and do not feel at home elsewhere. In Chapin's case, he was a "natural" for *The Evening World,* but out of place on the other side of the partition.

Seymour and Chapin both came from Chicago by way of the *St. Louis Post-Dispatch.* Chapin had been city editor on the *Chicago Herald,* had held the same position in St. Louis, and was brought to New York in one of the general shifts of Pulitzer forces. He took to *The Evening World* like a duck to water. Seymour was more of the statesman-editor type. He had been editor of the *Chicago Tribune,* and joined the Pulitzer organization in 1907.

JP's idea was to give Chapin plenary authority over the staff and full powers to get the news, no matter if he had to invade the territories of the telegraph-cable news editor and the managing editor; Van Hamm's job was to see that the news was developed in the most effective way for publication; above him, architecturally as well as in theory, JP installed Seymour to occupy JP's own office in the Dome, using the big desk and the highback chair (furniture now in possession of the School of Journalism at Columbia). Seymour's commission was to "STOP MISTAKES!"

Curtailment of Van Hamm's authority was no doubt the result of his bungling on the Panama stóry. The colonel took it all in good part. The complaints that assailed JP's unwilling ears when he reached Europe came chiefly from Seymour. The new editorial supervisor was grieved because his authority was not respected. Pulitzer flew into a terrible rage and shot burning messages to New York. He ordered Seitz to straighten out the tangle. Tell Seymour, he said, that Mr. Pulitzer is much upset by his report. It was an exceedingly bad report. Tell him I won't have it. I want peace. Everybody's duty has been clearly defined. Chapin is to be a great city editor. Van Hamm is responsible for what goes into the paper. Seymour is the final critic and censor. But peace I must have. If Seitz can't straighten out the mess, then drastic measures must follow.

Seitz tried valiantly to restore harmony among the Battling Three, but it was no go. JP threw up his hands. Chapin went back to *The Evening World.* Seymour continued as "editorial supervisor" until his death in 1920, but with powers limited to the final approval of copy for the editorial page. His authority dwindled under the ascendancy of the robust Frank Cobb. Seymour was distinctly an office genius, and always observed the clause in his contract which barred *World* editors from writing for outside publications. He belonged to the old-fashioned school of newspaper men who were content, even glad, to submerge their own personalities and ambitions in the welfare of their newspaper. He was shop-conscious.

Back on *The Evening World* Chapin got free rein to develop the genius for news getting which made him almost a legendary figure in New York's journalism, as well as the model for the hard-boiled city editor types of screen, radio, stage, and fiction. He ruled *The Evening World* staff with a rod of iron. Many are the stories about his office tyranny. One is that Irvin S. Cobb, the humorist, who was a rewrite man on *The Evening World,* hearing one day that Chapin was ill, remarked:

"I hope it is nothing trivial."

Another one was about the late Shep Friedman. Shep was tardy in coming to work one day and, knowing that Chapin would penetrate any subterfuges like "a tieup in the subway," decided to make it a good one.

"Boss," he said, "you won't believe this, but just as I was leaving the apartment house, a fellow came out and said a man died next door and asked me please to help carry out the corpse."

"Good," said Chapin, "write a story about it. We'll put it on page one."

The story, of course, did not appear, but Friedman never forgot the worry of it.

Another Chapin legend was that the Criminal Courts reporter, late one day in arriving from New Jersey, called up Chapin from the ferry terminal and reported himself on duty.

"Cover the flood," Chapin ordered.

"What flood?" the reporter asked.

"The one you're in," Chapin replied. "It must be terrible. I can hear the boats whistling."

The oldest legend of all, attributed to Chapin and, it must be admitted, to other city editors, concerns the reporter who called up on a story and said the man he tried to interview threatened to break his neck. The answer was, "Go back and tell him he can't intimidate me."

None of the legends measured up to the final tragedy of Chapin's career. Whatever misery he had caused to others was abundantly atoned for. He to whom life was harsh found sweetness in the approach of death. In September, 1918, Chapin and his wife had become badly involved in debt. Mrs. Chapin was a grand-niece of Russell Sage. At one time she was heiress to fifty thousand dollars, but the Chapins, in rather typical newspaper-folk manner, had not only dissipated her fortune but much more. Mrs. Chapin became obsessed with a fear of poverty in old age. Chapin shot and killed his wife as she slept. His story was that he intended to shoot himself next, but lost his nerve.

A medical commission found that Chapin was sane, but things were made very easy for him at the Criminal Courts Building. The District Attorney consented to a plea of guilty to murder in the second degree, and Chapin was sentenced to Sing Sing prison for twenty years. He became a prison favorite. At first his duty was to edit the prison's weekly newspaper, the *Sing Sing Bulletin*. Chapin made it much too lively, and even in prison managed to score beats on the New York papers. In one issue a convicted bigamist wrote:

"A good wife is a jewel. I have been a gem-collector."

Wrathfully, the Superintendent of Prisons demanded that henceforth the superintendent must censor all the news copy. Warden Lawes refused to yield that prerogative. Governor Alfred E. Smith ended the controversy by abolishing the paper.

After that Chapin was assigned to cultivate the Sing Sing gardens and look after the birds. He loved the work, and dreaded the day when the expiration of his sentence would set him free. Friends visited him in prison, but he refused to see any relatives. He rejected all suggestions for a plea for pardon and said he would refuse a pardon if it were offered. On the morning *World* during the night club era we heard from time to time that Chapin was permitted to come down to the city on week-ends and visit certain resorts, but we could never prove the story. Under the new rule, we should have printed it anyway.

Finally, in December, 1930, having served more than half his term, Chapin was overtaken by pneumonia. He was moved into the death house, where things are always made more comfortable for those who are about to die. Warden Lawes took his favorite prisoner gently by the hand.

"Charley," he said, "is there anything you want?"

"Yes," replied the famous ex-city editor. "I want to die and get it over with." He chatted pleasantly with the Catholic, Jewish, and Protestant chaplains, being friendly with all three faiths, but a member of none. Just before he died he said, "Don't forget to feed the birds."

Chapin was seventy-two years old when he passed away. His body was sent to Washington to be laid beside the wife whom he had freed from the fear of poverty in old age.

But at the time of JP's European trip in 1909, Chapin was going like a house afire. However, he could not work in harness with Van Hamm and Seymour, and that was that. What might have been a restful spring season at Carlsbad was ruined by this office furor, which for a time threatened to blow the dome off the Pulitzer Building. JP scuttled the Ideal Editorship plan and proceeded with his Odyssey.

For the first time in several years, JP did not go to Bar Harbor for the summer. He may have had some lingering apprehension about the Panama prosecution, but what seems more likely is that of all the modes of living he had tried since the beginning of his affliction, life aboard the *Liberty* appealed to him most of all.

He loved the boat. For the first time in his life, something had measured up to hope and expectation. Everything had been planned for his convenience and carried out under the watchful eye of Secretary Arthur Billing. In his other living quarters, he was in constant dread of falling downstairs or stumbling over furniture or bumping his nose into a door. But aboard the yacht he could roam about unaided, feeling his way by familiar objects and going up or down the narrow companionways without fear. "Nothing in my life," he said, "has ever given me so much pleasure."

The summer's cruise took him to the Far North. Barnes was picked up at some English port, along with Touhy's latest list of possibly eligible candidates. The *Liberty* touched at Oslo for exchange of messages with the home office and then, proceeding slowly along the coast of Norway, went on to North Cape. Here the company caught a brief glimpse of Kaiser Wilhelm's great yacht *Hohenzollern*. The German sailors painted the name of the yacht on a high cliff overlooking a fjord. Not to be outdone, the *Liberty's* crew climbed still higher and painted "Liberty" above the German.

JP was inexorable in his demands for descriptions. More than ever, it seemed, he wanted every detail that might enable him to re-produce a panorama in his mind's eye. Often he grew impatient with the best word-painting efforts of the secretaries and would break into a fit of scolding, followed by an outburst of tears.

"Pity a poor old blind man," he would cry. "It's no use, I can't see a thing—not even a glimmer, and you fellows don't help much. Take me to my cabin."

Ten minutes later he would be completely absorbed in the news, dictating messages to the office and hearing long reports on the progress of things at home. He was especially interested in the mayoralty campaign of 1909. From the outset, *The World* had urged the nomination of Judge William J. Gaynor, either as a Republican-Fusion candidate or on the Democratic ticket. Tammany Boss Charles F. Murphy, a much better chooser of candidates than some of his predecessors—or his successors—picked Gaynor, although the Judge was anything but "regular" in regard to Tammany. This was the famous campaign in which Gaynor went to Democratic headquarters to make his acceptance speech and said: "So this is Tammany Hall!" He had never been inside the place before.

On the southward cruise, the *Liberty* put in again at Oslo and JP's party went ashore for a brief rest. By exhaustive search, Pollard managed to find a small hotel on the outskirts of the Norwegian capital and practically bought the place to insure privacy. Mr. Pulitzer also had to have his daily drive; and the natives were amazed to see the tall American with the flowing beard and the brigand-type hat driving through their streets in the royal carriage with the royal horses. It seems that Norway's king owned no equipage of his own but hired the best the livery stables could produce. JP was entitled to the same privilege.

One afternoon they drove past a sign marked "Private" and were well inside the grounds of Dr. Sundstrom's sanitarium for lunatics before the mistake was discovered. The secretaries were afraid to tell JP about it, but Barnes let the cat out of the bag after lunch. Unexpectedly, Mr. Pulitzer was uproariously amused.

"My God," he laughed. "Why didn't you leave me there?"

The *Liberty* also visited North Germany and Denmark and then sped across to Leith, Scotland, for another checkup with *The World*. There was some talk about going on to Reykjavik, Iceland, but north of the Orkneys, JP suddenly changed his mind and ordered the next stop to be Dunkerque. After pauses at Gibraltar and Cartagena, there was a full stop at Cannes, and a good-bye to Barnes, who had been invited home to participate in the Hudson-Fulton Celebration.

"I am King Lear, deprived of my children!" JP exclaimed with mock tragedy. He was a good actor when he chose to be. The Barnes experiment was not entirely happy. Barnes's account of the trip is that he had reached a few conclusions which he thought JP ought to know about. One of them concerned Master Herbert, who had come aboard with his English tutor, Milligan, for the last part of the trip. Barnes reported that Master Herbert, then aged fourteen, was too much for Milligan, and ought to be in a military school. JP didn't like Milligan and berated him without mercy. Milligan afterward went to live in Nairobi. British East Africa probably seemed like Paradise after hunting adjectives with Pulitzers.

In these last three years of his life, JP was frequently at his worst. Annoyances of any kind sent him into tantrums that were sure to be followed by long spells of intense self-pity. He was starving for companionship and yet always appeared to be building walls against anyone who might prove to be the needed friend.

For the early fall, he returned to Aix-les-Bains; and from there, much refreshed by the summer's expedition, he directed *The World's* campaign on behalf of Gaynor. *The World* recognized Gaynor's many weaknesses, chiefly his capriciousness of temper, but set off against them his unquestioned fearlessness as a judge and his knowledge of municipal affairs. Also, *The World* did not hide the fact that Gaynor was Tammany's choice, but stoutly maintained that he would never be Tammany's creature.

One strange development of the campaign was that *The Evening World*, with JP's knowledge and consent, ran a daily column by Arthur Brisbane, in sponsorship of William Randolph Hearst, the Independent candidate. *The World* widely advertised and promoted the Brisbane articles. The Hearst editor's attacks on Gaynor were so sharp that Gaynor sued the Press Publishing Company, publisher of both *The Evening World* and *The World,* for libel.

Cobb handled the incident with good nature. The fact that Gaynor, *The World's* own candidate, was suing *The World,* he argued, showed how independent Gaynor was. He was nobody's pocket judge. The libel suit was dropped after the campaign ended with victory for Gaynor. Hearst always maintained that he was counted out, and that the ballot boxes in the districts favorable to him were thrown into the East River.

JP, meanwhile, had moved his quarters to Berlin, taking a specially prepared residence at No. 23 In den Zelten, just back of the Tiergarten. For weeks ahead of the guest's arrival the house had been overhauled and equipped with every available device for greater silence and greater comfort, although JP intended to make only a short visit. Short though the Berlin stay was, it was comparatively happy. He refused to worry about office affairs.

JP had greatly benefited by the northern cruise, and was prepared to have a good time in Berlin and forget all about the office. But right at the outset, there was another emotional upset.

From the *New York Herald,* October 5, 1909:

"ALBERT PULITZER SUICIDE IN VIENNA."

"Well-known Journalist Took Poison and Then Shot Himself Before Mirror." Special Dispatch to the *Herald* via the Commercial Cable Company's system:

Vienna, Monday—Mr. Albert Pulitzer committed suicide yesterday at the *Grand Hotel* where he had lived for several years. Mr. Pulitzer was known in the fashionable hotels and streets because of his original eccentric character.

"Mr. Pulitzer's suicide was due to a distressing nervous illness. Yesterday he remained at the hotel, and was seen alive for the last time at three o'clock in the afternoon. He passed a bad day and was much depressed owing to his illness which had reached an acute stage and caused him much torture. Mr. Pulitzer had his servants execute several orders which would keep them away for some time. Then he retired to his bedroom.

"His physician called and found the door locked. As nobody opened when he knocked, the physician summoned a hotel clerk, who burst open the door. Mr. Pulitzer was found on the floor. A revolver in his right hand and a wound in the right temple removed all doubt as to the cause of his death. Also, it seems, he had taken a dose of poison, as a partly emptied bottle was found near him.

"Mr. Pulitzer made a will in 1903, leaving all his fortune to the Societe Voluntaire Viennoise de Sauvetage, but the Society will not inherit much, as his fortune had considerably dwindled, due to the fact that he had transferred most of it into an annuity."

"WELL KNOWN IN JOURNALISM HERE" [Here follows a brief review of Albert's life, mentioning that he followed "his brother" to the United States, but does not give the brother's name. Also fixes the date of Albert's marriage to Miss Fanny Bannard, "a noted English society woman," as 1877 and states that "his only son, Walter, was born a few years later." (Contradicted by Albert's will.)]

"Mr. Walter Pulitzer, sole heir to the estate, is an author and has also composed several songs which have been heard at the theaters here. He is leaving for Vienna, where he will close up the affairs of the father's estate. According to him, the value of the fortune will exceed $6,000,000."

From *The World:* "Albert Pulitzer, founder of the *New York Morning Journal*, committed suicide last night in this city [Vienna] where he had made his home for years. . . . His attendants were dismissed early last evening on the pretext that he wished to be left alone."

"Mr. Pulitzer spent most of his time in Europe from 1895 (when he sold the *Journal*) to 1907, when he came to New York and announced his intention of starting a newspaper here. The project was not put into effect and he returned to his home in Vienna."

Nowhere is there any reference to Joseph Pulitzer or any mention of Walter, only son of the deceased.

From that time on, *The World* and its editors took the attitude that for news purposes, Albert Pulitzer had never existed. When Walter finally managed to crash into *The World's* columns in connection with his bankruptcy in 1913, he was not connected either with Albert or with Joseph.

Addenda on Walter Pulitzer:

Oct. 27, 1917. Wife's separation suit dismissed.

Nov. 14, 1917. Found guilty of having indecent pictures in his possession.

Feb. 20, 1918. Wife gets divorce . . .

Sept. 6, 1926. Walter Pulitzer dies.

There was a sequel to Albert's suicide, but it was not recorded until many years later. The memoirs of Lieutenant-Colonel Norman G. Thwaites revealed that the invalid in Berlin was not indifferent to the fate of his brother. JP sent Thwaites to Vienna with fifteen thousand dollars, to see that Albert received "a decent burial." The secretary did not arrive in the Austrian capital until several days after the tragedy and found everything in a mess. The Viennese Salvation Army chiefs could find no trace of the estate they were supposed to inherit, and lost all interest in the matter. Albert had some friends who thought he should be buried in the Catholic faith, but they had neither funds nor authority to arrange a requiem mass; by diligent searching, Thwaites finally found Albert's body, "lying in an open box of the cheapest kind" in a mortuary in the Jewish section of a cemetery, "covered with a cheap white cloth." The supposed millionaire was about to be buried as a pauper.

The face was unmarred, Thwaites reported. The bullet had ranged upward through the temple, making its exit at the back of the head on the left side—a terrible wound. He arranged at once for "a better-class burial" with Jewish rites. In a severe snowstorm, the casket, covered with flowers, was laid in the ground while a male choir sang the Hebrew chant for the dead "beautifully," Thwaites commented. "It was a long walk to the place of interment, and the exquisite service moved me deeply."

He was the chief mourner, but at the moment of casting earth to earth, a young, red-bearded man pushed forward to the graveside and cast a handful of soil on the coffin, declaring that he was "next of kin." The young man's identity was not disclosed.

Further inquiry by Thwaites produced no trace of the supposed fortune. He did, however, learn that Albert had put a large part of his estate into the purchase of an annuity which gave him enough to live on in luxury, but not enough to enable him to go back into the newspaper business. Apparently he was afraid that he might be tempted to return. (If certain other publishers might only follow his example.)

It appeared that Albert, after selling the *Journal,* and having then arrived at the climacteric middle age for males, went abroad and began to do strange things. He roved for a while from capital to capital, but finally settled in Vienna, living at once the life of an invalid and a sybarite. He never lost his appetite for news, and, like JP, insisted on having the newspapers read to him. Albert, however, preferred female readers.

He cursed the doctors for their inability to cure his malady, a psychotic neurosis, of which we do not know the nature. The mild-mannered woman who took care of him at the last said he spent day after day in a chair moaning to himself:

"Wenn ich nur Mut dazu haette!" (If I only had the guts to do it!)

On Decision Day, he sent to a Viennese apothecary and asked for prussic acid, with a vague explanation of wanting it for "experiments." The druggist, suspecting the truth, sent him a harmless fluid savoring of almonds. After Albert discovered the deception, he got out an old army revolver and completed the experiment with himself as witness before the mirror.

"Look here, upon this picture, and on this;
  The counterfeit presentment of two brothers . . ." (HAMLET)

one brother desiring the courage to die; the other calling upon the remnant of his strength for courage to keep on living . . .

For once, JP refused to submit to depression. He felt a resurgence of gaiety in the strange return of almost normal health that marked his October in Berlin. "Mr. Pulitzer, the distinguished American journalist, and gentlemen of his staff" were frequently noted at the art galleries or at symphony concerts in the brown autumn afternoons, at the opera in the evenings, and dining in Berlin's most favored hotels and restaurants. JP reveled in the music of Wagner, Beethoven, and Liszt, and was even patient with the descriptions of art works given by the secretarial staff.

At the end of October he boarded the *Liberty* and went on a leisurely voyage through the Mediterranean. The early winter found him comfortably ensconced at the Villa Arethusa among the pines on the rocky crest of Cap Martin, on the Mediterranean coast, just inside the French border, a neighbor of Eugénie, ex-empress of France.

No other residence in Europe afforded him such solid satisfaction. He had experimented at living in most of the better-known spas and the gay resorts of the Mediterranean. *The World's* bureaus in London and Paris had searched the continent for pleasant dwelling places, but none suited him half so well as this quiet peninsula jutting out into the Bay of Monaco, between Monaco and Mentone, more Italian than French in its native character.

The Pulitzer villa, leased for a long term, lay apart from the quaint little village, sheltered from public view on one side, but commanding a fine view of the bay on the other. From the broad veranda, a series of terraces, embellished with palms, flowers, fountains, and rococo statuary, led gently to a sharp, cliff-like slope, falling away abruptly to the deep blue waters of the bay.

JP never tired of hearing descriptions of the landscape. In the twilight, or in bright moonlight, he would try hard to obtain just a glimpse, but it was no use. By this time eyesight was little more than a memory. Imagination, aided and abetted by the descriptive powers of Pollard, Seitz, and the others, had to be the Baedeker. Pulitzer had first come upon the villa back in 1896, but did not engage it until much later, staying meanwhile at a fairly quiet hotel. Here it was that he underwent the strenuous treatments of Dr. Ernst Schweninger, personal physician to the great Bismarck—the doctor whose chief method was to place the patient on the floor, front side up, and jump upon him, the theory being apparently that if the man could stand the jumps he could recover from anything.

It was also at Cap Martin, although the exact date seems to be in dispute, that JP had his quarrel with Auguste Rodin, the great French sculptor. This happened either in the season of 1909-1910 or the one following. By some arrangement or other, never very clear, Rodin had been commissioned to do a bust of Mr. Pulitzer. The sculptor moved into the villa with his assistants and much equipment—also much noise—and prepared to go to work.

This ought to have been a historic occasion, a grand meeting of great minds—Pulitzer, the liberator of journalism, exchanging animadversions with Rodin, the liberator of sculpture; both of them smashers of traditions; Pulitzer, the devastator of stupidities in print; Rodin, the breaker of conventions in art; Rodin, the enemy of frozen traditions, the rebel against rules which had insisted that heroes must always be Men on Horseback, and statesmen always carved with noble poses and frock coats; Pulitzer, the demander of truth, the whole truth, and nothing but the truth in public affairs.

Strangely, the great men did not kindle at each other's spark; in fact, they disagreed as only great men can who think alike on different subjects. In short, they quarreled. The trouble was evident at the outset. Mr. Rodin's medium was the human form, whereas to JP the torso was distasteful if not tabu. Not that he objected especially to nude figures of bronze or stone; he admired good craftsmanship in all media; but his personal preference was for portraits of famous persons, always fully clad with the costumes of their period. Such portraits, he thought, were very useful and informative addenda to history and the biographies. Depersonalized art—types rather than actual persons—had no appeal, and he froze instantly toward anything of the strip-tease genre. No doubt he knew all about Rodin's great interpretations in stone—*The Burghers of Calais; Adam; The Thinker; The Kiss*—but when it came to being Exhibit A in a Rodin masterpiece, he objected right away.

The great men communicated through intermediaries. Monsieur Rodin desired that Monsieur Pulitzer should take off his coat, vest, shirt, and what he had underneath and pose in the half-shell.

The explosion that greeted this announcement reverberated through the quiet countryside. True, it was not investigated by the local authorities; the Cap Martin Prefect of Police did not have a report on it; nor was it recorded in *The World,* but it would serve. JP was outraged. If Rodin had dropped a hammer and a chisel on the floor just above JP's bedroom, he could not have committed a greater offense or upset more gravely his patron's equilibrium. Any degree of bodily exposure except that which is permitted to gentlemen in evening dress was, to Mr. Pulitzer's mind, abhorrent.

With burning wrath and lightning speed, a secretary was dispatched upstairs to the Rodin atelier.

Abso . . . lutely nothing undoing!

Great Master Rodin was temperamental, too. He was seventy years old at this time, and his naturally indulgent nature had been thrown out of gear by the persistent interferences of that expatriated

American lady of advancing years, the Duchesse de Choiseul, who had completely dominated the life of this great artist for several years, in art, in business, and in domestic affairs. Her fantastic whims had become Rodin's rule of life. She washed his face, combed and brushed his hair, put on his boots, and dressed him up à la mode in a way that fretted his normally easy-going disposition. She called herself his Muse, his Influence—"the fool, he called her his lady fair"—but Rodin's colleagues and assistants named her "The Influenza." So in l'Affaire Pulitzer, perhaps, the supreme artist, poet-in-stone, and creator of a new school was not entirely to blame. He had his afflictions, too.

There was much arguing about this matter of the neck and shoulders that Rodin wished to see in order to interpret Pulitzer to the world. Rodin threatened to pack up his traps and go back to Paris. Finally compromise lifted her unlovely head—it was arranged that Mr. Pulitzer would take off his collar and undo one button (only one, mind you) on condition that but one secretary and one sculptor's assistant be present in the atelier during the sittings.

Thus it was arranged, but JP lost all interest in the project. He went through the sittings in sullen silence, and refused to converse. The bronze version of the bust now stands within the main hallway of the Columbia School of Journalism. Rodin's biographers listed it as a "remarkable portrait . . . capturing all the intensity, *yet serenity*, of the blind man."

Much more pleasant was JP's experience with John Singer Sargent, when the famous portrait was to be made. There was, according to report, a misunderstanding in the preliminaries to the sittings. The story is that when Sargent was first approached about a commission to paint the portrait, he refused. "No more mugs!" Sargent exclaimed, meaning nothing offensive—merely that he was tired of doing portraits on order. Later, the tale goes, the great painter encountered the great journalist aboard a transatlantic liner and was so much impressed with the majesty and tragedy of the face that he asked permission to paint it. The story is apocryphal, but apocrypha are always interesting.

The sittings were arranged, and took place in Sargent's London studio in Tite Street, for six days in June, 1905, while Mr. Pulitzer was spending the early summer in London, as he liked to do. JP was in an unusually vivacious mood and chatted unrestrainedly with Sargent while the painter worked and consumed fine Turkish cigarettes. Even the cigarette smoke did not seem to bother the sitter. Things went along rosily for three days, and then a British peer, of bounding proclivities, crashed into the studio and tried to interest JP in some fantastic project. Sargent saw his subject change swiftly from serenity to rage, and at once got a new idea of the portrait. "Tell him to go away!" Pulitzer shouted, while Thwaites deftly propelled the intruder out of the studio. The incident helped the finished product, because both rage and serenity are in the face. "I want you to paint me just as I am," JP had instructed Sargent, "with all my suffering there."

The orders were obeyed. The portrait is one of Sargent's masterpieces. The left side of the face expresses tenderness, the right side, with the totally blind eye, is full of anger, and a touch of cruelty. If you put a piece of paper over one side and then the other, you can easily see the contrast.

Mr. Pulitzer's preferences for conventional portraits of famous persons were in keeping with his general inclination toward the classic in all branches of art. In his codicils, however, he stressed a caution against "too severely classical programs" by the Philharmonic; Beethoven, Liszt and Wagner he considered not too severely classical. Still, he did not mind taking an occasional flier into the realm of the exotic and the Oriental. For years he cherished a desire to possess a fine statue of Buddha, but found none that pleased his fancy. In 1894, when he enticed James Creelman, the famous reporter of great news events, away from the *New York Herald*, and sent him to the Far East to cover the Sino-Japanese War, he also commissioned the distinguished correspondent to find him a Buddha. He was willing to pay up to ten thousand dollars.

This was the time when the *Herald* executed one of its acts of professional gallantry toward its Pulitzer rival. Announcing Creelman's departure, the *Herald* ran a picture of *The World's* new correspondent, with a big caption reading: "Great Reporter!" Beside Creelman's picture, the *Herald* carried one of Joseph Pulitzer, entitled: "Great Editor!" (Private inquiry by James Gordon Bennett, II. "When is this man Pulitzer really going to retire?")

Creelman's coverage of the Asiatic conflict attracted world-wide attention. One of his dispatches told of the capture of Port Arthur by Japanese troops. Creelman declared that the Japanese had "massacred" large numbers of Chinese. Tokyo angrily denied the story, but Creelman stuck to his guns. After peace had broken out, as it occasionally does in the Orient, Creelman went hunting for Buddhas. He searched far and wide, and finally somewhere in China he found a beautiful statue with an enormous jewel in the forehead. According to the charming Mrs. Creelman, who has survived her distinguished husband, the Buddha was a wonderful specimen, fit for the finest temple.

Creelman, she recalled, entrusted the statue to the American consul-general at Hong Kong, Rounsevelle Wildman, who was preparing to leave for the United States with his wife, their two children and a nurse. The Buddha was carefully packed among the Wildman baggage.

Saturday, February 23, 1901. From the *New York Herald:*
San Francisco—The Pacific Mail steamer *City of Rio de Janeiro* struck a submerged rock about five o'clock yesterday morning just outside the Golden Gate and sank in about twenty minutes with a loss of 128 lives.

The *Rio de Janeiro* had just completed a voyage from Oriental ports, and her passenger list included many Americans from the Philippines and China, among them the United States Consul-General at Hong Kong, Mr. Rounsevelle Wildman, his wife and two children. . . .

The vessel had reached the approach to the Golden Gate on Thursday night but had been prevented from entering by an unusually heavy fog, and had anchored for the night. About five o'clock yesterday morning (Washington's Birthday) the fog lifted slightly. Captain Ward weighed anchor and the boat headed toward San Francisco in charge of Pilot Frank Jordan, who had been ordered to go ahead by Captain Ward in spite of his protest. The pilot, who was rescued, said later that Captain Ward was anxious to reach port as the liner was overdue, and that he the pilot had no choice but to follow the captain's orders.

Of the two hundred and seven souls aboard the sunken ship, seventy-nine were rescued, including twelve white passengers; eleven officers; fifteen Asiatic steerage passengers and forty-one Chinese of the crew. Most of the passengers were asleep when the vessel crashed against the hidden rock.

At the point where the steamer sank, the water is exceedingly deep and nothing was ever salvaged, of ship or cargo or bodies. The Pulitzer Buddha rests there to this day, as far as we know. Both Pulitzer and Creelman were greatly upset by the incident, and JP never attempted to replace the cherished idol. He is reported to have paid about ten thousand dollars for it.

In spite of the death-premonitions, JP did not give up trying to find both the ideal doctor and the ideal companion. The search for distinguished medicos of great reputation was always going on, with the assistance of *The World's* European bureaus. During the winter and early spring of 1910, JP invited several specialists to Cap Martin, but always insisted upon privacy. He dreaded consultations. By-and-by, he put aside the search for specialists, and ordered his head-hunters to find him a good, all-around medical man to replace Hosmer. He wanted a serious-minded practitioner, a man who was at once seasick-proof and capable of inspiring confidence. The "author-physician," Wrench, failed to inspire that feeling. JP had again developed a bronchial cough. The symptoms of whooping cough returned, with attendant strain upon the heart. "Do, for God's sake," JP implored the London and Paris correspondents, "find some first-rate man. He may even be a hunchback or stutter, as long as he is reliable." At the same time, he instructed Hereford of the Paris office to keep a sharp lookout for William B. Hornblower, the will-drafting lawyer from New York, in case he should happen to visit Paris; JP must see him right away. Meanwhile, he told Hereford, find some other lawyer, expert in the drawing up of wills. The reason is to be found in the Surrogate's Records:

January 17, 1910: "I, Joseph Pulitzer, of the City of New York, being of sound mind . . . do make, publish, and declare this as a *Second Codicil* to my will. . . ."

There are no really drastic changes this time. In place of Dumont

Clarke, "lately deceased," Codicil No. 2 appoints Charles E. Hughes, "now or lately Governor of New York," as executor-trustee with a fee of $100,000 in lieu of commissions; Frederick N. Judson, president of the Pulitzer Publishing Company, is named as executor-trustee "until my son Joseph reaches the age of thirty"; and J. Angus Shaw, president of the Press Publishing Company, is to act in the same capacity "until my son Herbert reaches the age of twenty-one." (It turns out that Herbert has the longer wait, because he was sixteen when JP died, whereas brother Joseph was twenty-six and needed only four years to become executor-trustee.) Judson and Shaw are awarded $50,000 each, in lieu of commissions.

This codicil was executed aboard the yacht *Liberty* in the Mediterranean, exact spot not specified, on Benjamin Franklin's Birthday (National Thrift Day) in the presence of Louis Thomas Campion, of the Pulitzer household staff; Randall Davies, of 106 Oakley Street, London, S.W., the secretary-solicitor; and Ship's Master, Hiram Dixon, of 186 Hancock Street, Brooklyn.

The will now gets a four-month respite while JP devotes himself to more public matters. Much inspirited by the success of *The World's* campaign on behalf of Gaynor for Mayor and Charles S. Whitman for District Attorney, JP is maneuvering for a chance to have *The World* take the lead on some great national issue. The cables again begin to hum and the letters grow longer. Between the lines of extended "suggestions" to Seymour, which in reality are instructions for Cobb and the entire staff of editorial writers, one may suspect the jealous thought that those editors are getting along better and better in JP's absence.

The World by this time has a mind of its own. The Chief's orders are given respectful attention; but, because of the delays caused by distance and invalidism, they often arrive too late—the decision has already been made. Furthermore, JP's ideas are becoming more and more abstract, dealing with general principles and not with specific news events. Some of the orders cannot be taken seriously. "Do not write one line about tariff," may seem sagacious to the man in the Mediterranean, but to the men on Park Row, following developments in the Payne-Aldrich tariff controversy, it sounds like non-sense.

Still, it must be admitted that JP has a genius for picking the spots where Taft is going to be weakest—first, his inconsistency on the tariff question, in signing the Payne-Aldrich Bill in spite of its excessive "protection" schedules, then vetoing the bills designed to remove the inequalities of the Act and give some relief to the Farm Belt; second, "Taft's itch for travel," as JP put it. "He never opens his mouth without putting his foot in it, and he never opens the door of a Pullman without wanting to put his foot inside." Taft's Pullman meanderings, JP thinks, lower the dignity of the Presidency, cheapen his personality, and lessen his influence with Congress.

Little did he foresee the day when the special train and the radio would be a Chief Executive's chief mechanisms to bring issues home to the people and weaken the resistance of Congressional minorities.

In spite of Taft's weaknesses, JP wants *The World* to emphasize Taft's moves for economy and retrenchment, making this *The World's* "paramount, conspicuous, continuing, and cumulative" feature. But don't, begs JP, yield an inch in opposing Taft on preparedness for war! Sheer jingoism, he calls it, by which Taft shows his ignorance of European conditions. JP recognizes no compulsion for the United States to take part in European politics. If the editors don't agree with the policy of his paper, he orders, in a sudden burst of irritation, the least they can do is to remain silent.

Back in his mind, there is a dread of the return of the Rough Rider. T.R. has been hunting big game in Africa and is now preparing for the triumphant return. JP fears that Taft's weakness will prove a stepping stone for a Roosevelt third term. In this connection, JP, after combing history and constitutional law, finds no objection to a third term, providing that the right man is in the White House. But he wants no more of the Big Stick. Gratification comes in here, because of *The World's* big victory in the Panama case and the quashing of the indictments in the Southern District of New York on January 25, 1910. As for T.R.'s personal return from Africa, the orders are to treat it with dignity and as far as possible with silence, reminding us of T.R.'s own favorite story of the school teacher who said to the pupil, all I want from you is silence and damn little of that!

Throughout the winter and spring season at Cap Martin, the *Liberty* is keeping ready at all times for sudden jaunts into the Mediterranean. The skipper never knows what the orders will be. There are several such trips to historic places: Corsica, Naples, Monte Cristo, Elba. And one to the Piraeus. JP thinks everybody ought to take a fresh look at the Acropolis. The secretaries are thoroughly coached on what to describe to him. But at the last minute, when all the staff have gone ashore, JP has an emotional attack and refuses to leave the yacht. Alone with the faithful Dunningham, he bursts into a fit of tears and sobbing.

It is becoming more and more obvious that Jabez is to Pulitzer what Oliver Dain was to Louis XI of France. Beginning as a barber, Oliver became personal valet, personal advisor, and finally the chief privy counselor. King Louis, incidentally, was a favorite character in JP's cycle of fiction. He read and reread Scott's *Quentin Durward,* and also various biographies of Louis in French and German.

On these excursions, JP has been revolving in his mind plans for combating the wave of anti-Japanese agitation in the United States. He wants Cobb to go to Japan for a series of articles on what Nippon's Elder Statesmen really think of America. Cobb is unreceptive to the idea and Seitz is chosen instead. The articles appear toward the close of 1910. JP also wanted a man to go to the Philippines, "to learn what a mess we have made there," but he never found the right man.

At various stops in the Mediterranean he receives piles of *Worlds;* he rages because the editors have not been keeping up with Taft's policies closely enough. Possibly they have been taking too literally his injunction to be silent if they don't agree with JP. Whatever the reason, they have aroused fierce displeasure. Never, never, JP fumes, has he known *World* editors to become so near to being muzzled as they are about Taft. "If there is anything I hate," he says, "it is for *The World* to sit on the fence and fail to do its duty about men in high places."

Back once more in Cap Martin's balmy seclusion, he still is unsatisfied about the will, and returns to the tinkering. This time the thing that seems to bother him is the family problem. Has he been too generous? Has he been liberal enough? Will they criticize him after death for his public benefactions? Out of this whirlwind of uncertainties emerges Codicil No. 3.

"In witness whereof (this instrument being written upon nine sheets, each being authenticated with my signature and written only on one side) I have hereto set my hand and seal at Cap Martin in the Republic of France on this eleventh day of May in the year one thousand nine hundred and ten."

Striking provisions in the third codicil:

The trust funds for his daughters, Edith and Constance, are increased from $250,000 each to twice that amount.

The trust fund for his wife, Mrs. Kate Pulitzer, is increased from two million to two and one-quarter million, the extra quarter million, upon her death, to be divided equally between Edith and Constance. If either of them dies before the other, the survivor gets the extra share.

Special attention is paid to the provisions for Herbert. JP seems to fear that his youngest child may be reckless with money. Advised now that he cannot legally restrict the amount that Herbert may spend over his allotted $30,000 between the ages of twenty-five and thirty, JP invokes wisdom and discretion.

"I solemnly entreat Herbert," he says, "that voluntarily, with the portion of this money in excess of the annual payments, although such excess be absolutely his own, he shall do therewith what I should myself do: accumulate and invest the remainder and expend no part of the same until he reaches the age of thirty years."

The income of one-tenth of the newspaper trust is made available to editors and managers of *The World* and the *Post-Dispatch*, instead of "an editor or a manager."

Reviewing his benefactions to "public and humanitarian causes" both in his lifetime and now by his will, the testator says:

"If any of my children think excessive such gifts of mine outside of my family, I ask them to remember not only the merit of the causes and the corresponding usefulness of the gifts but also the dominating ideals of my life.

"They should never forget the dangers which unfortunately attend the inheritance of large fortunes, even though the money come from the painstaking affections of a father. I beg of them to remember that such danger lies not only in the obvious temptation to enervating luxury, but in the inducement . . . to withdraw from the wholesome duty of vigorous, serious, useful work. In my opinion a life not largely dedicated to such work cannot be happy and honorable. And to such it is my earnest hope—and will be to my death—that my children shall, so far as their strength permits, be steadfastly devoted."

With the approach of summer, the *Liberty* was dispatched across the Atlantic, and JP followed on the *S.S. Cedric*. He had no mind for another trip like the last one, but preferred the greater security of the Cunard liner. The *Liberty* took him off at Quarantine, and thence to Bar Harbor. The summer was reasonably pleasant, the usual residence at Chatwold being varied by short cruises up and down the coast.

Meanwhile, *The World* had scored new triumphs both in progress and reform. In connection with the Hudson-Fulton Celebration of the previous year, the newspaper offered a prize of ten thousand dollars for the first airplane flight between Albany and New York, covering roughly the same course as Mr. Fulton's justly famous steamboat in 1809. The offer was held open up to October, 1910.

On May 29, while JP was busy with his plans for the summer, Glenn Curtiss made the prize-winning flight.

"At times," *The World* chronicled, "Mr. Curtiss's machine sped sixty miles an hour. All records in aviation were broken by this flight. Records for speed, for distance, and for both combined, went down before the steady wings of the *Curtiss Aeroplane*. Exact figures for the flight were: Start, Albany, 7.03 A.M.; landed at Gill's Farm, Camelot, near Poughkeepsie, 75 miles from the starting point, 8.26 A.M.; left Gill's Farm, 9.26 A.M.; landed at Inwood, 62 miles from Gill's Farm, 10.35 A.M.; left Inwood, 11.42 A.M.; arrived at Governor's Island, Noon."

Mr. Curtiss made 137 miles in 152 minutes. Congratulations poured in upon *The World*.

President Taft: "It seems that the wonders of aviation will never cease. I hesitate to say that the performance of Mr. Curtiss makes an epoch, because tomorrow we may hear that some man has flown from New York to St. Louis."

The World and the *Post-Dispatch* promptly offered a prize of thirty thousand dollars for the first flight from New York to St. Louis, or the other way round.

Among its civic achievements this year, *The World* brought about reform in the machinery of admitting immigrants to citizenship. As a result of Federal legislation sponsored by *The World*, the number of first and second naturalization papers issued in one year was quintupled.

The World also campaigned successfully for the Dual Subway system.

Meanwhile, Theodore Roosevelt had grabbed the Republican leadership in New York State with devastating results. With an eye toward 1912, and the hoped-for elimination of Taft, his "ungrateful friend," the Rough Rider bludgeoned the Republican Convention into nominating his friend, Henry L. Stimson, for Governor. But he dared not, at this moment, make an open break with Taft. Out in Kansas, T.R. had roared for "New Nationalism" and against "political corruption"; but in New York, he put a soft-pedal on Progressivism. The platform followed the path of reaction; Taft's administration was enthusiastically endorsed and the Payne-Aldrich Tariff praised for the protection from which all blessings were supposed to flow. Nothing was said about income tax, popular election of United States senators, workmen's compensation, or Initiative and Referendum.

Hearst, who had been flirting with the Roosevelt forces, nominated for the governorship, an independent candidate, John J. Hopper. The Democrats named John A. Dix, a "regular," acceptable to Tammany. *The World* supported Dix solely for the purpose of stopping T.R.'s third term drive. For the first time in sixteen years, the Republicans lost the governorship. Dix won.

In New Jersey, the Democrats, with hearty support from *The*

World, nominated for governor Woodrow Wilson, president of Princeton University.

JP devoted much of the summer to an intensive study of Wilson's record and his possibilities as a Democratic candidate for president in 1912. As far back as 1907, he had been causing *The World* to keep Wilson in the forefront of public attention. In 1908 he urged Wilson as a presidential candidate to head off Bryan, for Wilson was not only a candidate acceptable to the solid South but, "a statesman, a scholar, and a man of very extraordinary ability."

He was disappointed in Gaynor, but did not fail to send a message of sympathy when the mayor was shot by a crank. Gaynor was aboard a ship at Hoboken about to sail for Europe when the attempted assassination took place. A *World* photographer was lucky enough to get a picture of Gaynor just after the assailant fired. Gaynor recovered from the wound, but never regained *The World's* confidence.

Meanwhile, JP sailed for Europe, once again aboard the *Liberty,* much too impatient to await the outcome of the fall elections. He spent the early fall at Wiesbaden, and then moved to Cap Martin for the winter and spring, keeping the *Liberty* under steam at Mentone for cruises in the Mediterranean.

The search for another secretary-companion continued without abatement. A discreet notice in the London *Times* brought another host of applicants, most of them unfit. However, JP did find one acceptable candidate. Alleyne Ireland joined the household at Cap Martin after a long and rigid series of tests and cross-examinations at the hands of James M. Touhy, Ralph Pulitzer, and several others.

Ireland—a native of Manchester, England; educated in British schools and the University of Berlin; certified able seaman; globe-trotter; newspaper correspondent; lecturer; adventurer; Philippine campaigner under General Leonard Wood—was about forty years old when attracted by the "ad" in the London *Times,* which chanced to catch his eye in the city of Hamburg in the fall of 1910. Out of thousands of answers, his was the only one that produced any memorable results. Admitted to the staff on what JP termed "probation," but actually regarded with favor, he was of the secretarial force from the late fall of 1910 to the end of JP's life.

Ireland's *Adventures with a Genius,* recording his one year with JP, is without doubt a Pulitzer classic.

That Ireland did not become the ideal companion is merely another evidence of human limitations. To pass the intelligence tests was difficult enough; to pass the good manners, good taste, good nature, and goodfellowship requirements, was even more difficult. Ireland's only drawback was a harsh voice, and he took lessons for that. But how to gain the final admission into JP's complete confidence and share the burden of his soul was something that no man ever understood.

The faithful valet Jabez did well enough for practical purposes.

Remarkable that JP, who specified "no entrance diploma" for his School of Journalism, could be so super-exacting in the matter of admissions to his friendship. To the last, he kept on searching, but never found the Horatio to whom he could be Hamlet, the Jonathan who could be permitted to hail him as a David. There was a gate through which one could not pass; yet inside the wall was a hungry soul, yearning for human sympathy and understanding, eager to recognize the face of the friend whom he could grapple to him with hooks of steel.

What he wanted was comradeship; but, with the possible exception of Davidson, who shared lodgings and all his knowledge with JP in St. Louis, he had never in all his life been able to say:

> *"Ich hatt' einen Kameraden*
> *Einen besser'n findst du nicht."*

Every so often he would rail against it; compensating for emotional starvation with his talent for emotional self-dramatization. "What I need," he cried, "is rest, understanding, sympathy—friendship—yes, my God!—friendship!" What enraged him most of all was that so many men should prize his friendship so lightly—he, who could do so much for a friend, in the way of wealth or reputation. Why were they not willing to pay the little sacrifice? He had tested scores, perhaps hundreds of men in one way or another, university men, self-made men, young men, old men, men of different nationalities, races, creeds, and professions. And how had they turned out! No sympathy, no understanding, no tact, no forbearance—not even any manners in some cases (he was rather tolerant toward moral frailties of the individual but not of government); no accurate knowledge of any subject; no memory to speak of; but a vast amount of arrogance, self-esteem, stupidity, ingratitude, and general incompatibility. Whenever he reviewed the procession, he never failed to register amazement. Being frail himself in health, he had no understanding of the other deficiencies.

One might well ask, since mankind proved so great a disappointment to JP, why did he not turn to God in search of peace and find comfort in the Everlasting Arms?

One might also wonder why, since physicians were unable to save him, he turned not to one or more of the so-called healing cults.

To raise these questions indicates a misunderstanding of the man's essential nature. Though he often despaired, JP never gave up. Faith-healing requires resignation, and resignation was not within the capabilities of JP's being. Though he never found the physician who could restore even a measure of health, he never gave up trying; and the fact that life was painful did not induce him to accept the universe without putting up a fight.

The only public prayer JP ever uttered was for *The World,* that God might grant it to be a continuing institution forever unsatisfied with merely printing news. Whatever private prayers he made were most likely prayers for continuing courage and the stout heart to keep on living—unsatisfied.

Besides, it would have been embarrassing for JP to become a faith-cult disciple, even if he had been so inclined, because *The World* had established a reputation for publicizing all such movements in a very frank manner. *The World* reported in vigorous fashion all the news developments in connection with the growth and spread of Christian Science, particularly the Mrs. Eddy-Mrs. Stetson controversy; getting off notably on the wrong foot on one celebrated occasion by reporting Mrs. Eddy dying from cancer, years before her death, and instigating a "next of kin" suit by her son, George Glover, to gain possession of her vast properties. Glover made a private settlement and left *The World* holding the bag.

Since a one and only companion was out of the question, JP followed the method of variety. He handled the corps of secretaries as a city editor does a staff of reporters, assigning each one a separate function, and finding a mischievous pleasure in switching the assignments without notice. A secretary delegated to recite the news to JP at breakfast would have to work far into the night, preparing the grist for the morning's conversation; and sometimes in vain, because at the last minute JP might call for another man.

The only safe rule was for everybody to know everything.

News for the breakfast table had to be carefully chosen. JP wanted nothing exciting at that time. What he desired in the morning were crisp, bright condensations concerning the latest books, the latest plays, music, amusing incidents; light controversies in the various fields of art and culture. No crimes, no scandals.

After breakfast and a cigar, he would take a drive in an automobile or go for a horseback ride, accompanied by a groom or a secretary. After that he would be ready for more serious work, going over the news in detail, this time including the important events, and then dictating letters or cables to *The World*.

Luncheon depended largely on his mood. If he felt like discussion, most of the staff would be present, and the talk would touch on public events; but if he was not in the humor, only one or two secretaries would be present, and the instructions from Dunningham would be:

"Mr. Pulitzer wishes the conversation at lunch to be light and non-controversial."

After luncheon, JP would retire to his bedroom and lie down while Friedrich Mann, the German secretary, read a German play, carefully arranged and condensed. As the secretary read he would gradually lower his voice. When JP began to feel sleepy, he would say *"Leise"* (softly), and the reader would subdue his voice to a low murmur. As the listener became still more sleepy, he would say, *"Ganz leise"* (very softly), and the reading would drop to a mere whisper, continuing until JP was fast asleep. Mann had to be very careful not to stop murmuring before Morpheus was actually in control of the situation, otherwise JP would be awakened by the cessation of the soothing sound.

About four o'clock, JP would dress and go out for a walk or another drive or a ride in the saddle. If he walked, it was usually along the winding road near the top of the crest overlooking the Bay of Monaco. Sometimes he would stroll into the village. Either way, it was a perilous journey. JP depended implicitly on his escorts to keep him out of harm's way. If an automobile suddenly swerved toward their side of the road, the secretary had to shove the Chief dexterously to one side. JP never seemed to mind these little escapes, and kept right on talking. What annoyed him and completely upset him was to be spoken to by strangers. "Tell him to go away," he would shout. "I won't have it. Tell him I'll have him arrested!"

For an hour before dinner he would listen to the reading of a novel, a biography, a work on history, or something else of a serious nature. Selection of the reading depended entirely on his mood. Several biographies, like Monypenny's *Life of Disraeli,* would be read to him many times.

Dinner at Cap Martin was semi-formal. Dinner jackets were the rule unless full dress was specified. Food for conversation was "topics in the news," but the tenor must be amusing and not exciting. JP craved a good laugh, but care had to be exercised not to cause him to laugh too heartily, because that was painful.

"Stop! Stop! For God's sake," he would cry, whenever a secretary or a guest proved too humorous. "You're hurting me!"

He found pleasant amusement in after-dinner games of questions and answers, especially if he could uncover a large area of insufficient knowledge on the part of one of the participants. The dinner talk sometimes lasted until nine o'clock or later, again depending upon the mood. After giving the good-night signal, he would retire with a secretary for some light reading in the library while Mann played the piano, selecting whatever of Beethoven, or Liszt, or Wagner, or even Bach might seem to be in harmony with the evening's mood, or with the reading, concluding always with the "Liebestod" from *Tristan and Isolde.*

On the cruises aboard the *Liberty,* the foregoing routine was necessarily adapted to life at sea. Walks around the wide decks took the place of rides and drives ashore.

While at Cap Martin, JP would usually drive to Monte Carlo or to

Nice once or twice a week to attend a concert, preferably in the afternoon. If no box was available, he would engage enough seats to be sure of protection on both sides. His favorite seats were on the aisle. During the concerts he would listen attentively, often beating time with his hand or moving his head. In characteristic fashion, his mind moved on several tracks at once, and even while listening to music and beating time, he would say to Thwaites or Pollard or Ireland: "Beautiful passage there, but I think the pianissimo was overdone did you send those cables to Seymour ouch the violins came in too harshly remind me to give a memorandum for Cobb on Taft remind him of what Bismarck said revenge is a delicacy which ought to be taken cold."

Pulitzer took several cruises through the Mediterranean with the secretarial staff that last season at Cap Martin, but many more were planned and never taken at all. After elaborate preparations for departure and much moving of baggage from villa to yacht, just as often as not the orders would be changed, and everything would have to be moved back to the house.

There was another trip to Athens, but without tears this time. Some weeping occurred during a visit to Corsica, but JP was not the mourner. His yacht guest on this occasion was the famous Colonel Henry Watterson, owner-editor of the *Louisville Courier-Journal*. JP did not go ashore, but "Marse Henry" felt obligated not only to inspect all of the local sights connected with Napoleon's birthplace, but a considerable number of local bars.

On returning to the yacht, the great Kentuckian, so the story goes, was so overcome with tragic emotion and other stimuli that he cast himself into JP's arms and sobbed over Napoleon's misfortunes, until gently disentangled by Jabez and led to his cabin. JP was, like Mark Twain on his first meeting with Grant, embarrassed.

Later in the spring, the little household moved to Wiesbaden where JP took more treatments. One night, JP and a few of the staff motored to Frankfurt to attend the new opera, Strauss's *Rosenkavalier*. The road was rough and so was the performance. JP got up in the middle of the second act and said, "My God, I can't stand any more of this. Go get the car!"

Throughout this last Odyssey (1910-1911) JP followed closely, but rather despairingly, new changes in *The World*. Luckless Colonel Van Hamm had been succeeded as managing editor by Charles M. Lincoln, brought down from Herald Square. Chapin, who had returned to *The Evening World,* had been replaced by Arthur Clarke. About the same time, another *Herald* luminary came under the aegis of the Dome, ace reporter Herbert Bayard Swope, the dynamic go-getter from St. Louis, protégé of F. D. White, who was a sort of general manager for both the *Post-Dispatch* and *The World,* with his office in New York.

Lincoln introduced a new emphasis on serious, important news, and Seymour, who continued to act as "censor-critic," without much authority any longer to stop mistakes but with power to complain about them, was quick to comment to JP about a new dullness in *The World.*

JP agreed. He complained bitterly. This, he wailed, is the last straw that breaks the poor blind camel's back. The paper, he thought, was getting worse—lacking in fresh ideas—overloaded with politics. It is verbose, he insisted, and calls to heaven for intelligent condensation. "Do, do," he implored, "take all the heavy stuff and boil it down. Look out for the things that are distinctive, original, dramatic, romantic, thrilling. Also whatever is curious, unique, odd, and humorous, but without offending good taste."

Let *The World,* he also begged, always have an original striking news feature, a campaign, or a crusade, something commanding public attention and respect. No paper can be great if it merely follows the hand-to-mouth policy of taking whatever news comes in and handling it in routine fashion.

Make *The World,* he pleaded, a paper for the masses, and by that he meant for everybody, from the highest officials in Washington down to the people in the streets and the factories—a paper that everybody can understand and enjoy!

Beware of stupidities! That was his continual exhortation in cables and letters. Also, watch out for careless editing. He was greatly incensed over *The World's* attempted word-portrait of Henry L. Stimson, the Republican nominee for governor (at this writing, Secretary of War). What is "ordinary height"? he demanded to know. And what is "a sizable nose"? That story about Stimson ought to be hung up on the bulletin board as a warning and a horrible example. (It was. The unfortunate author was William Preston Beazell, a first-line reporter, but a fact-hunter, not a word-painter, now Secretary of the New York State Spa Commission and of the Citizens' Crime Commission.)

Style, diction, care! Those he stressed, again and again. Those he wanted, instead of loose reporting and routine editing. And—oh! What about news judgment? Who in God's name put the story of the *Los Angeles Times* explosion on page thirteen? Wonder they didn't put it on page eighty-seven! One of the biggest stories in years! The *Times* building was dynamited on October 1, 1910, with a loss of twenty-one lives. This was the crime for which William J. Burns obtained the confessions of the McNamara brothers, who were defended by Clarence Darrow.

Most wretched of all, he complained, is *The World's* handling of public dinners and meetings. What people want to know about such affairs, he said, is, first, who was there; second, who spoke; third, who else was present. There ought to be descriptions, little word-pictures of speakers and notable guests. As it is, he wailed, every time I read one of those accounts in *The World,* I am sure to become sick. But, he cautioned, don't let the writers become too clever.

Mrs. Pulitzer joined JP in London and they returned to America once more aboard the *Cedric.* In spite of the usual preparations and precautions, there was a slip-up. The Pulitzer suite was too close to a family with two children. One child cried all night and the other one all day. Curiously, JP was interested, rather than annoyed. He wanted word-pictures of the wailers, and identifications, as to which one cried at night, and which during the day.

The *Liberty* took him aboard again at Quarantine. Established once more in Chatwold's tower of silence at Bar Harbor, he held conferences all summer with Hornblower about the new will, the one to end all wills and codicils. Meanwhile, he threw an anchor to windward and executed Codicil No. 4, this time on board the *Liberty* off Kennebunkport, Maine, on July 12, 1911. The provisions for Constance and Edith are changed into a joint trust fund of

$1,500,000. The million-dollar bequest to the Philharmonic is made conditional upon the Society's becoming a membership corporation with one thousand paid-up subscribers, a condition never fulfilled.

The temptation to take a hand in politics was too strong. He kept calling up the office by long-distance telephone, a new plaything for him, but the results were always bad. Too much excitement, followed by nervous reaction and marked depression. He obtained more satisfactory results by slipping away in the *Liberty* and anchoring off Greenwich for direct conferences with Cobb and some of the other executives. His chief concern in political affairs was in fostering the candidacy of Woodrow Wilson, a policy to which *The World* was firmly, though not publicly and irrevocably, committed, before JP went away.

October brought the Pulitzers back to their town house on East Seventy-third Street. During the summer season at Chatwold JP had spent much of his time with his sons, Ralph and Joseph, while the secretaries took turns at leaves of absence. The daily staff gatherings and the discussion-dinners were replaced by question-answer sessions with the sons. But with the removal to New York, his emotional excitement also returned, and it became clear to everybody that he ought to go far away from *The World* as soon as this could be arranged. Amid the bustle of preparations for departure, he could not forget business, and gave personal attention to the purchase of the paper mills at Pyrites, New York, a white elephant, as it turned out, which the heirs unloaded years later at considerable loss.

His plan was to go to Jekyl Island for the early winter and then take the *Liberty* for a leisurely cruise through the Caribbean. Meanwhile, he had kept in touch with Barnes and decided to give him another trial as a companion, inviting him to go along for the winter at Jekyl Island, at any rate. Barnes accepted with alacrity and without salary.

The *Liberty* left New York on October 18. At the outset it was plain that JP's health was precarious. One day he would seem amazingly strong and in fine humor; the next day he would be utterly worn out, unable to take his walks on deck.

The dinner sessions were not resumed. Instead of discussing poli-

JOSEPH PULITZER
This photograph was taken on the Riviera

tics, he gave most of his time to plays and novels of the lighter sort. Although never passionately fond of American humorists, he turned now to "Artemus Ward," "Mr. Dooley," and George Ade. Macaulay's essays remained in favor, but of the new books he risked only George Horace Lorimer's *Letters of a Self-Made Merchant to His Son.*

Aboard the *Liberty* this time were Herbert, just approaching his sixteenth birthday, and accompanied by the tutor-governess, Elizabeth Keelan; Alleyne Ireland; Barnes; Norman Thwaites; Pollard; Mann; a new ship's surgeon, Dr. Guthman, and, of course, Dunningham.

Opportunities for conversation were not many, but Barnes recalled one in which JP expressed a fear of social changes to come. What he dreaded most, according to the naval writer, was the muzzling of the press through political manipulation or through governmental action.

In some ways, Barnes thought, JP seemed to believe that the Constitution was outgrown, although he had never publicly admitted such a view; and he prophesied that the Democratic party would be the one to break away from the basic laws which had insured thus far the country's progress and safety.

On the third day out, JP did not appear on deck at all, and report quickly spread that he was quite ill. The *Liberty* put into Charleston, and Dr. Robert Wilson was called into consultation. He found the patient suffering from an acute attack of indigestion. Under sedatives the pain gradually disappeared, and JP was able to lunch on deck. At one of his last luncheons with the staff he seemed almost well, in high good humor and inclined to lively conversation. He predicted a Democratic victory in 1912.

Barnes found it advisable to return to New York, and JP asked him to get in touch with Hornblower's office and request that a member of the firm come down to Jekyl Island to complete the will.

Friday, October 27. JP is out of sorts and does not appear on deck. Saturday, October 28, he remains in his own quarters.

Sunday, October 29. At 3 A.M. Ireland is awakened by Dunningham. JP wants some reading. Ireland goes with an armful of books and finds him in considerable pain. Selecting Macaulay's essay on Hallam, the secretary reads, interrupted occasionally with a request from JP to repeat certain passages.

At 5.30 A.M., JP is suffering acutely and Dunningham summons Dr. Guthman. After half an hour the reading is resumed, but only for a few moments. Ireland is told to get some sleep. "We'll finish that this afternoon. Good-bye, I'm very much obliged."

Somehow JP manages to drop off to sleep. Meanwhile, Mrs. Pulitzer has been summoned from New York.

Charleston, South Carolina, October 29, 1911.

Life aboard the *Liberty* follows the ordinary schedule. Ireland is asleep, exhausted by the long reading in the early morning. The others pursue the regular duties. JP wakes up shortly before noon and summons Mann to read the *Life of Louis XI*. JP soon becomes drowsy. Mann lowers his voice, and continues reading.

"Softly now"—the JP signal for diminuendo.

Mann's voice drops to a whisper, but the reading goes on, becomes barely audible.

JP murmurs: *"Leise, ganz leise."*

He is asleep now. Mrs. Pulitzer enters and takes Mann's place at the bedside.

"Mild und leise" . . . (these are from the "Liebestod." Does he hear music?)

> *"Mild and gently*
> *See him smiling*
> *See his eyelids*
> *Open softly.*
> *Look you, friends—*
> *See how radiant*
> *See how lovely*
> *Always kingly*
> [Aye, every inch a king!]
> *Ever gracious*
> *Haloed in star-dust*
> *Rising higher. . . ."*

It is 1.40 P.M. Eastern Standard Time. The *Liberty* is as quiet as a painted ship on a painted ocean. Death is here and JP is leaving now. . . . What are those last lines from the "Liebestod"?

> *"In dem wogenden Schwall*
> *In dem toenenden Schall. . . ."*

> *"In the billowing wave*
> *In the thunder's roar*
> *Into the World-Spirit,*
> *Sink,*
> *Be swallowed up*
> *Into Perfect Peace."*

He goes out so quietly that it seems now as if he had never closed the door.

New York, November 2, 1911.
From *The World*, page one:

JOSEPH PULITZER'S BURIAL

Simple but Impressive Services Are Held in St. Thomas's Church, Attended by Men Representative of Every Walk in Life, Before His Body is Committed to the Grave in Woodlawn Cemetery.

A TRIBUTE OF SILENCE IN
TWO NEWSPAPER PLANTS

Wheels Stop and All Work Ceases for Five Minutes in Offices of The World *Here and* The Post-Dispatch *in St. Louis During Last Rites—Grand Army Commander Places Flag on Coffin.*

At the close of an ideal Autumn Day
the body of Joseph Pulitzer was buried
in Woodlawn Cemetery yesterday. Engraved on a silver plate on the coffin was
this inscription:

> JOSEPH PULITZER
> *April 10, 1847*
> *October 29, 1911*

The World reporter goes on to state that there were more than six
hundred persons inside St. Thomas's Protestant Episcopal Church,
then still under construction, and more than two thousand gathered
outside in Fifth Avenue. A jam of people and automobiles extends
from the church down to Forty-second Street and east to the Grand
Central Station (also under construction), where a special train
waits to take JP's body to the cemetery. One of the three coaches is
entirely filled with "floral tributes."

The pallbearers are Nicholas Murray Butler, president of Columbia University; Lewis Latham Clarke, banker; Colonel George B.
McClellan Harvey, whose friendship with JP survives the many
office disputes; Frederick N. Judson, president of the Pulitzer Publishing Company (publishers of the *St. Louis Post-Dispatch*); Seth
Low, former Mayor of New York; St. Clair McKelway, editor of the
Brooklyn Eagle; General John B. Henderson; Dr. James W. McLane
(personal physician); George L. Rives, banker; J. Angus Shaw,
president of the Press Publishing Company, publishers of *The
World*.

The body reaches New York, aboard a special train, at 2.05 P.M.
October 31, and lies in state in the library of the home at Nos. 7-15
East Seventy-third Street.

Between eleven and twelve o'clock on the morning of the funeral,
members of *The World* organization pay their last respects. Also,
General George B. Loud, Commander of the Grand Army of the
Republic, Department of New York, places on the casket a small
silk American flag, saying:

"On behalf of fifty thousand Civil War veterans (of the North), in tribute to his memory for the nation he loved for which he pledged his life, I reverently place this flag upon the casket of Joseph Pulitzer."

Relatives present at the funeral services, beginning at 2.45 P.M., include Mrs. Pulitzer, the widow, heavily clothed in black; Mr. and Mrs. Ralph Pulitzer, the latter the former Frederica Vanderbilt Webb; Mr. and Mrs. Joseph Pulitzer, Jr.; Herbert Pulitzer, aged sixteen; Mrs. Worthington C. Davis, sister-in-law of the widow, and her son, Master Worthington Davis. With the family are Miss Maude Macarow, Mrs. Pulitzer's private secretary; Miss Ruth Lawrence, and Dr. Hosmer.

Two daughters, Constance and Edith, arrive too late for the services; Miss Edith is enroute from Paris; Miss Constance, coming from Colorado Springs, arrives the morning after the funeral.

The Order of Services:

1. "Largo"—Handel (William Macfarlane, organist, and Miss Loretta De Lone, harpist)
2. Processional Hymn—"Abide with Me" (Monk)
    (Surpliced choir of 45 male voices)
3. The Order for the Burial of the Dead
    (Dr. Ernest M. Stires, rector)
4. Burial Chant (Felton)
5. Hymn—"Lead, Kindly Light" (Dykes)
6. Responses (Macfarlane)
7. Recessional Hymn—"Hark! Hark, My Soul!" (First Tune. Smart)

From *The World:*

"There was no eulogy.

"During the reading [by Dr. Stires] the noise by the workmen rebuilding the church . . . came through the open doors, and the tumult of traffic on Fifth Avenue blended with the music of the choir."

(It makes no difference now.)

"As a fragrant background of color for the coffin at the foot of the chancel were arranged the floral tributes, lilies of the valley, Mr.

Pulitzer's favorite flower [that and wild olive] supplying the dominant note.

"There were 116 floral pieces, varied in design, though of a generally simple character. Completely covering the coffin was a blanket of lilies of the valley and orchids. From the employees of *The World* and the *St. Louis Post-Dispatch* came more than forty of the floral pieces. The New York Association for the Blind sent a blanket of violets. . . .

"From the editors and staff of *The World* was a large wreath of orchids and oak leaves . . . 'In affectionate remembrance.' *The Evening World* and its staff sent a wreath of roses and lilies of the valley; from the *Post-Dispatch,* a high circular easel of orchids."

Captain Dixon and the crew of the yacht *Liberty* sent white carnations fashioned into the form of a lifebuoy.

Almost overlooked, and only casually mentioned in *The World's* report, is a stately wreath of roses, with a card:

REPUBLIC OF COLOMBIA
To Her Friend.

Colombia remembers the Panama Canal even if *The World* forgets.

Other floral pieces are:

Orchids from Mr. and Mrs. Joseph Pulitzer, Jr.; lilies of the valley from Miss Edith Pulitzer; orchids, lilies, and President Taft (!) roses from Miss Constance; chrysanthemums from *The World's* mailing room; violets and lilies of the valley from Adolph S. Ochs, principal owner of the *New York Times* [twenty years later Mr. Ochs tried in vain to purchase *The World,* under a plan to permit the workers forty-nine per cent ownership]; and a similar wreath from Melville E. Stone, general manager of the Associated Press.

Of JP's personal staff are present George Ledlie, Arthur Billing, Norman G. Thwaites, Harold Stanley Pollard, and Friedrich Mann, secretary-pianist—he who played the "Liebestod" at signing-off time; the secretaries have sent lilies of the valley.

From *The World:* "One of the striking features of the morning assemblage was the 'old guard' of former editors and reporters" . . . among them:

Civil Service Commissioner James Creelman (of the Sino-Japanese War and the $10,000 Buddha); Supervisor of the New York City Record David Ferguson (anonymous reporter of Equitable scandals); Robert Adamson, secretary to Mayor Gaynor; Frank Perley, former secretary to Governor Higgins; Walter (Walt) McDougall (cartoonist); Winfield R. Sheehan, secretary to Police Commissioner Waldo (later famous as a Hollywood producer and as husband of Mme. Jeritza); Hugh J. Beirne, secretary to District Attorney Whitman; Frederick A. Duneka of *Harper's,* former London correspondent of *The World.*

Also William O. Inglis; Frederick F. Burgin; Joseph N. Quail; Samuel W. Taylor; Jonas Whitley (of Sullivan & Cromwell fame); Edward Fales Coward; former Congressman Frank E. Shober; George H. Dickinson; Hugh Hastings (the Blizzard reporter); Arthur Greaves, city editor of the *Times;* James B. Townsend; Fire Commissioner Joseph Johnson, fiery of title, of hair, and of temper—later of Hollywood—author of "Look around you now and choose the nearest exit—in case of fire, walk, do not run, toward that exit."

Charles W. Fisk; Mrs. Elizabeth C. Seaman (the Nellie Bly who went around the world in seventy-two days); George F. Spinney; "Cabel" [Oh! Oh! Accuracy, accuracy, accuracy! *The World* slipped up here and made it "Cabel" instead of "Caleb"] M. Van Hamm, former managing editor, he of the Panama Canal series; Bradford Merrill, former managing editor; John Norris, former business manager; George W. Olney. . . .

"Close to the flower-wreathed chancel"—returning to the flower-wreathed account in *The World*—"sat three blind men representing the Blind Men's Club, an adjunct of the New York Association for the Blind. This little delegation was headed by William H. Patrick, the club's president, and its presence at the service bore eloquent testimony to the Association's grateful affection for Mr. Pulitzer."

Prominent personages at the funeral also include Alton B. Parker (former candidate for president of the United States); Supreme Court Justices Gerard and Giegerich (*The World* that morning reprinted the fact that Giegerich had paid nine thousand dollars for his nomination); District Attorney Whitman; Congressman William Sulzer, later the ill-fated Tammany candidate for governor, impeached and removed from office by reason of a Tammany "squeal" about unrecorded campaign gifts; Borough President George McAneny (later President of the Board of Aldermen and still later associated with the *Times*); Justice Newberger; Howard Taylor; William Leary; and John D. Crimmins.

Of the New York Publishers' Association: William C. Reick (*New York Sun*); Carr V. Van Anda (managing editor of the *Times*); Charles R. Miller, editor of the *Times;* Herman Ridder, *New Yorker Staats-Zeitung;* John A. Hennessy, managing editor of the *Press;* J. F. Foster; and William Payson Call.

The funeral procession enters the church to the "Largo." As the casket is born up the middle aisle, the choir begins "Abide with Me," as at the same time Dr. Stires begins the Order for the Burial of the Dead.

> *"Abide with me—fast falls the eventide*
> *The darkness deepens. . . ."*
> (Or does it?)

From the Order for the Burial of the Dead:

". . . God is our Refuge and Strength, a very present help in trouble . . . and though my body be destroyed yet shall I see God, whom I shall see for myself and mine eyes shall behold. . . . We brought nothing into this world and it is certain we can carry nothing out. . . ."

(The question is, What is it that we leave behind, and how long will it last?)

"The Lord is my light and my salvation. . . .

"I will lift up mine eyes unto the hills, from whence cometh my help. . . .

". . . Thou foolish one! That which thou sowest is not quickened, except it die! . . ." (This also includes *The World.*)

Burial chant—"Lord, let me know mine end, and the number of my days; that I may be certified how long I have to live. . . .

"For man walketh in a vain shadow and disquieteth himself in vain: he heapeth up riches, and cannot tell who shall gather them. . . ."

> *"Lead, Kindly Light—amid th' encircling gloom.*
> *Lead Thou me on!*
> *The night is dark, and I am far from home. . . .*
> (Not any more!)

> *"Keep Thou my feet—I do not ask to see*
> *The distant scene. . . ."*
> *". . . I loved the garish day. . . .*
> *"So long Thy power hath blest me, sure it still*
> *Will lead me on*
> *O'er moor and fen, o'er crag and torrent, till*
> *The night is gone.*
> *And with the morn, those angel faces smile. . . .*
> (Katherine Ethel. . . . Lucille Irma!)
> *Which I have loved long since and lost awhile."*

The World: "For five minutes at the beginning of the services, not a wheel turned nor was a word spoken in the offices of *The World* and of the *Post-Dispatch* in St. Louis. The presses were brought to a standstill, the electric lights extinguished, the power controlling the elevators, air compressors, ventilating apparatus, and the heating systems, cut off. More than 400 motors controlling the machinery in *The World* building and one third as many in the St. Louis offices were brought to a standstill. The telephone and telegraph systems were disconnected, so that during the period of mourning the two offices were cut off from the outside world.

"In the business offices of the two newspapers the clerks paused in their duties and outside persons having business there paused until the 'silent period' had ended and *The World* went on once more on its course."

[For about twenty years more. A good idea of how *The World* looked and felt during the period of silence may be obtained by visiting the Pulitzer Building today.]

Recessional:

"Hark! Hark, my soul! Angelic songs are swelling
O'er earth's green fields and ocean's wave-beat shore. . . .

"Angels of Jesus, Angels of Light
Singing to welcome the pilgrims of the night."

The World: "When Dr. Stires came down into the chancel from the pulpit at the close of the service, he brought from the altar a bunch of chrysanthemums and placed them on the coffin as he stood in silent prayer."

The body is borne from the church . . . again, the "Largo."

Only the family and a few friends witness the final chapter at the crest of the hill on which Woodlawn Cemetery stands.

At the Graveside:

"I heard a voice from Heaven saying unto me—Write, from henceforth blessed are the dead which die in the Lord; even so, saith the Spirit, for they rest from their labors. . . ."

As the casket is lowered into the grave close beside that of the beloved Lucille Irma, to whom the School of Journalism is dedicated, a terrific reverberation shakes the whole metropolitan area.

The Atlantic fleet is visiting New York. The line of battleships, cruisers, destroyers, torpedo boats, and other naval craft stretches for six miles up the Hudson. The big guns are saluting Secretary of the Navy George von L. Meyer. Tomorrow President Taft is to review the fleet, and there will be more cannonading. But Joseph Pulitzer will not mind the noise.

This year's review of the fleet is part of the new preparedness program and Taft tells the press next day that the United States is ready for any emergency.

A New Era has begun.

10. New Freedom

A SILURIAN REMEMBERS

To BECOME a Silurian, one is supposed to have been a newspaperman in New York thirty years ago. Under the old rules, I
should not become eligible until January, 1942; but the Silurian
Society, two years ago, in connection with the annual dinner, soft-
ened the entrance requirements in favor of youth and let me in.

*"I am a Silurian—
I'm proud of my Memory!"*

The winter of 1912, when I arrived in New York, was one of the
coldest on record; and my own prospects were somewhat chilly. Like
many another western reporter of the early nineteen hundreds, I had
always been led to believe that New York was the one and only place
for successful journalism. Decision in my case was superinduced by

317

the fact that the *Denver Times* had been sold and my position as star reporter, editorial writer, dramatic-and-music critic, and book reviewer was in apparent jeopardy.

Denver was in a ferment at that time. The Wild West journalism, the blood-and-thunder age when blackmail was in flower, when Bonfils and Tammen shook the local sugarplum trees for the benefit of their *Post*—"the paper with a heart and soul"—this age was passing. Hell-roaring adventure was going out of Denver's journalism; hardier souls were moving away—some to San Francisco, which was also rated a "good newspaper town"; some to Honolulu (including Peggy Goodenough Hull, thereby taking all the charm out of Denver); others to New York.

Even Hugh O'Neill, who had been editor of the *Denver Times* and partly responsible for a monthly loss of $28,000, had decided to pull up stakes and move to the Big City.

"Look," he said, "at the Denver people who have made good in New York!" Alfred Damon Runyon, former top writer for the *Rocky Mountain News;* Nell Brinkley, the artist; Bide Dudley; Martin Dunn; Arthur La Hines. "Why," O'Neill said, "they must be getting at least seventy-five dollars a week!" (Anybody in Denver who drew down more than fifty a week was in the managing editor class.)

"Furthermore," O'Neill remarked, "the New York papers are great institutions. You don't hear of *them* being bought and sold. They are too big, too important."

During the week of doubt, I had occasion to interview Mme. Ernestine Schumann-Heink, the famous opera singer, who was giving a recital in Denver. Arrangements were made on the telephone with her manager, but there was a mixup. Madame was becoming near-sighted; when I approached her on the mezzanine of the Brown Palace Hotel, she threw her arms around me and exclaimed, "My son! My son!"

Not until I was disentangled from her capacious embrace did she discover that I wasn't even a relative. "You look like my boy," she explained. After which, the interview prospered. I confided my aspiration to get out of Denver. "Fine," she said; "all good writers go to New York. I will give you a letter of introduction to my dear friend, Ralph Pulitzer."

She dashed off a note. Neither of us noticed, until too late, that she spelled Pulitzer with two *l*'s.

Alfred Patek, who had succeeded O'Neill at the *Denver Times*, gave me a note to A. E. Woods, telegraph-cable news editor of *The World;* I also knew Patek's daughter Florence, a former sob-sister of Denver who had joined the staff of *The World*.

Among other introductions, I had one from O'Neill to former President Theodore Roosevelt (whom he did not know), then contributing editor of the *Outlook,* with offices in the Metropolitan Life Building.

So I came to New York. On the same train was Alfred J. Mc-Cosker, who had just been graduated with honors from the *Denver Times* advertising-promotion department. McCosker, the same who is now one of radio's most successful moguls (and certainly one of the most human), was the man who first wrote a daily column of automobile news for Denver. He stopped off at Chicago, but not for long.

When I disembarked from the D. L. & W. train at Hoboken, I thought there must be a terrible accident in New Jersey. Everybody was running toward the terminal.

"Where's the fire?" I asked a guard whom I took for a policeman.

He said, "Aw, those are commuters. They are always running to or from ferryboats."

"Thank goodness," I thought, "a newspaper man doesn't have to be a commuter."

The Hudson River was almost choked with ice and the ferryboat had to crash its way across to Manhattan. Standing out on the deck, looking at the skyline, I experienced a great thrill, but nobody else appeared to care about it. The commuters took a rest until the boat reached the other side and the race started all over again.

At Chambers Street, I checked my suitcase and wandered up to Park Row. I had heard something about that. After locating *The World*, the *Sun*, the *Tribune*, the *Press*, the *Journal*, the *American*, the *Staats-Zeitung,* and the *Mail* in the City Hall area; ascertaining at the same time the general whereabouts downtown of the *Globe* and the *Post,* the *Wall Street Journal,* and the *Journal of Commerce;* and obtaining a rough idea as to the location of Herald Square, Times Square, and the *Morning Telegraph* uptown, I took a walk down to the Battery to inhale some courage before attacking the bulwarks of New York's journalism.

First, I tried *The World.* The uniformed attendant in the reception room on the twelfth floor took the Schumann-Heink note inside, reappearing presently to direct me to Mr. Pulitzer's office. You had to go through a long narrow passage filled with lockers, at the peril of your overcoat, then into an elevator barely big enough for three people, and up to the sixteenth floor in the Dome.

A secretary greeted me without emotion.

"Mr. Pulitzer," he said, "has nothing to do with appointments to the staff. You had better see the city editor, Mr. Clarke."

Exploring my way back to the reception room, I explained to Jimmy, the guard, that it wasn't Mr. Pulitzer I wished to see—it was Mr. Wood. He took another note inside.

Wood came out, a lovable old chap with white hair.

"I just stopped by the city desk," he said, "and told him about you. He says he hasn't got room for another cockroach."

Miss Patek was sympathetic, but it did not take long to establish that so far as I was concerned, New York's golden opportunity was with the *Morning Telegraph,* through the good offices of Bide Dudley, who had been my city editor for a time in Denver.

The *Morning Telegraph* was then owned or controlled by the Lewis Brothers, in co-operation with William "Bat" (two-gun or three-gun) Masterson, expert practitioners of predatory journalism. William E. Lewis was president and publisher; Irving Lewis was (in name only) managing editor, a Johnny-could-play-only-one-note in newspaperdom, his one and only admonition to the staff being— "Don't editorialithe!" Shep Friedman was nominally night city editor, but really boss of the staff; and poor Jack Blauvelt, city editor. I was added to the payroll at twenty dollars per week. (Alfred Henry Lewis, the third brother, was not actively associated with the paper. He was the author of *Wolfville Stories,* and contributed also to New York lore by nightly drinking coffee out of a soup-bowl at Rector's.) Another Lewis, Charley, was make-up man, a philosopher who daily thanked the proper authorities for providing enough liquor and enough women to please everybody. Bide Dudley covered the news of the theaters. Everybody on the staff who felt like it contributed to the "Beau Broadway" double-column feature on page one, forerunner of the gossip columns of today.

One of my first assignments on the *Telegraph* was to cover a bomb explosion in West Seventy-fourth Street. A profoundly dissatisfied suitor had sent a lady an infernal machine done up in a candy box which, when opened, emitted a quick passport to oblivion —what a wreck!

Arriving at the scene of the crime, my first impression was reporters, reporters, reporters. It seemed as if I had never seen so many journalists in one place since Magistrate Brown's famous breakfast to the press in Denver. Each newspaper (except the *Telegraph*) had at least two men on the job, a district man and a staff reporter. It was easy to tell them apart. The district men wore derby hats, white collars and surtout overcoats; whereas the staff writers wore turn-down hats (Richard Harding Davis style), long, loose raglan coats, and soft collars, and carried Malacca canes. They would hook the canes on their left arms while holding their copy paper or notebooks in the left hand and taking notes with the right. It was quite an art.

There were photographers on the scene as well, but not so many as nowadays; and of course the news-reel men did not come along until ten years later, at which time they asked to have the whole crime re-enacted.

In Denver, on occasions like this, no two reporters would speak to each other and each one tried to "scoop" the others; but in New York, to my surprise (and pleasure), the reporters were as clubby as pigeons—freely exchanging information and telephone numbers. Certain men, I remember, stood out in that first group: Robert O. Scallon (*The World*); Edwin C. Hill (the *Sun*); Parke "Jeff" Handley (the *Press*); Severance Johnson (*New York American*); Dennis Tilden Lynch (the *Tribune*); Alva Johnston (the *Times*). Some of these men did not ordinarily cover crimes, but this was a Saturday night, when anybody was likely to be stuck with a late trick.

After obtaining all the available details about the bomb-in-the-box, most of us adjourned over to Healey's place at Sixty-sixth Street and Columbus Avenue to get a drink and reconstruct the plot for the benefit of metropolitan readers. In the ensuing days I followed the bomb story, at the same time studying the *modus operandi* of the press. One thing that struck me forcibly was the sagacity and thoroughness of *The World's* reporter, Scallon. He would spend hours at a time running down some piece of evidence which other reporters and even the police considered unimportant, developing surprising results.

Scallon's method was: "Keep pecking at the story; by-and-by you will crack it!" He would work all day, collecting a vast amount of notes, pausing now and then to collect a drink. By eight o'clock in the evening, he would have quite an accumulation of both. He would then go back to *The World,* fall asleep on his typewriter for half an hour, wake up just as the night city editor was getting worried, spend another half hour straightening out his notes; and from then on would type without a pause, unfolding his news with amazing clarity, putting in each detail at just the right place with faultless accuracy, at the same time keeping the high-lights well stressed—altogether, turning out a typical *World* story.

Looking back after nearly thirty years, one can see how *The World* set the pace and dominated the metropolitan press; and how on every story, it was usually *The World* man who commanded greatest attention and respect. Every *World* man that one encountered seemed to be a superb artist in his particular field, whether of crime, politics, or general human interest.

One feels now that this period, beginning about 1912 and continuing up to America's entrance into the First World War, was the golden age of New York newspaper work, especially for the reporters on the morning newspapers. Press time of first editions was much later than today (except on the *American*); a reporter had time to develop his story and to write it the way he wanted; space rates were liberal and most of the reporters were on space, at $7.50 per column for regular news and double for exclusive stories. Interesting assignments were both plentiful and remunerative. Good reporters could make as much as two hundred and fifty dollars a week, and seldom less than seventy-five dollars.

The life was very pleasant; the little indulgences were inexpensive

Herbert Bayard Swope

Frank I. Cobb

Walter Lippmann

Heywood Broun

—ridiculously cheap in comparison with the scale of today. Hard liquor was two drinks for a quarter in good saloons and not over fifteen or twenty cents at the better bars; free lunch was plentiful and very good. In connection with the police vice and graft investigations of 1912 and 1913 and the mayoralty campaign of 1913, delightful rendezvous for the press were afforded along "politics row" by the McAlpin, Martinique, Knickerbocker, Imperial, Breslin, Victoria, Prince George, Hoffman House, and Albemarle—clear down to the Broadway Central, where Governor William E. Sulzer made his headquarters.

The restaurants, cafés, and "cabarets" were nicely managed and reasonably priced—no cover charges, no hat-grabbing; no gouging, clipping, high-pressuring, high-hatting, photographing, or any of the modern annoyances of the so-called night clubs. No gossip columnists lay in wait; excellent cuisines, with or without entertainment according to your taste, were to be found at Rector's and also George Rector's, Café de Paris, Louis Martin's, Beaux Arts, Bustanoby's, Shanley's, Churchill's, and Maxim's. For heartier amusement one could go to the German Village across from the Metropolitan Opera House, or to Billy Gallagher's at Forty-seventh Street and Seventh Avenue. And for occasional splurging one could go to the old Waldorf, or Delmonico's, or Sherry's, without too great a strain upon the exchequer. There was no "café society."

While there was delightful camaraderie among the reporters, barring certain exceptions to be noted presently, the newspaper competition was keen. The leaders in the field—*The World, Sun, Times, Herald,* and *Tribune*—strove to excel in news gathering and news presentation, in writing, and in typographical display. Curiously, very few stories were signed. By-lines were the exception, even for distinguished writers like Frank Ward O'Malley of the *Sun* and Joseph Jefferson O'Neill of *The World.* Yet whenever an outstanding story appeared, everybody knew immediately who wrote it.

In all this competition *The World* was a leader, but there was one respect in which *The World* excelled them all: that was in the field of public service. When it came to starting and to carrying out campaigns and crusades in the people's behalf, *The World* was without a peer. *The World* was always in a fight and enjoying it.

Even as early as the winter of 1912, the one following his death, Joseph Pulitzer had become merely a legend and a tradition in New York journalism. Few of *The World's* own staff had ever met him or even seen him, except in connection with the funeral. Although the Pulitzer watchwords, "Accuracy, Terseness, Accuracy," were blazoned on the bulletin boards in the newsrooms of *The World,* JP did not figure at all in the sentiments of the staff. Their devotion was to the newspaper, not to the founder. They identified themselves as *World* men, and not as Pulitzer disciples.

Everybody in the newspaper field seemed to recognize and acknowledge that *The World* was different from the other papers. *The World* was an institution which could never be bought, sold, or abandoned. Hadn't JP so provided in his will? Why, they said, even JP's death and funeral provided just another news story for *The World,* and one that was not specially well handled, certainly not executed in typical *World* fashion. During the moment of silence, on the day of the funeral, the great machine stopped, but right afterward went clattering on, picking up the thread of public affairs and resuming the quarrels and the fights just as if nothing had happened.

Meanwhile, new figures and new forces were emerging in *The World's* organization. When I was walking down Broadway one evening with the late Spencer Bull, also of the *Telegraph,* we observed a tall, hero-sized man turning into Churchill's. He was wearing a long raglan big enough for his entire family, and carrying as a walking stick the largest piece of bamboo ever seen outside of a jungle. He had a large, Grecian head with Roman nose, topped with waving reddish hair, which at this moment was covered with a greenish fedora. The face, though handsome, was intelligent.

The man fascinated me, although it would be difficult to say why. This was no strange phenomenon; he fascinates everybody—one way or another.

"Ah-a-a-a," quoth Spencer Bull, who knew everybody on Broadway, "methinks Achilles dineth with Lucullus. Behold!"

"Who is that—the owner?" I asked.

"Better still," replied Spencer, "he owns the owner."

I still registered unenlightenment. A hurdy-gurdy down the block on Forty-seventh Street played everybody was doing something, doing it, doing it. This was New York life, I thought, music on every block and Apollo going into Churchill's.

"Who is the guy?" I begged Spencer to unfold.

"Hasn't anybody ever told you the right time of day?" he asked.

"I know," I said, "that's Richard Mansfield, the actor!"

"Mansfield's been dead five years—you dope!"

"James J. Corbett?"

"Pooh!"

"Kyrle Bellew?"

"Not handsome enough!"

"Edouard de Reszke, or his brother Jean? Louis Eugene O'Brien?" (He came also from Colorado.)

"Hah-hah!"

"James K. Hackett?"

He groaned.

"Dustin Farnum? Brandon Tynan? Arnold Daly? William Goadby Loew?" (I had been reading *Town and Country*.)

"No! No!"

I tried Christy Mathewson, John J. McGraw, Wilton Lackaye, John Jacob Astor, Alfred G. Vanderbilt, William Travers Jerome, Henry Miller, Clifford Hartridge, Delphin K. Delmas, everybody I could think of.

"Wrong—all wrong—you're a way, way off . . . you poodlehead," said Bull.

"That man is Herbert, by-the Bayard, grace-of-God, Swope! Lit'rally," he said, *"The World's* greatest reporter—New York *World* or whole wide world. Either way it makes no difference, he's the greatest that ever came down the pike.

"When you saw him just now," Spencer Bull continued, "he was no doubt starting to work on the assignment which he received on the telephone at two o'clock this afternoon. If it were later in the season, he would just be coming in from the races at Belmont, or Aqueduct, or Jamaica, having won, or lost, a considerable amount of money; if he had lost, he would recoup handsomely before the end of the evening. Meanwhile, he is going to talk to his useful friend, Jim Churchill [former police captain], and find out what is what.

"The reporters on the other papers," added Mr. Bull, "who have been working hard all afternoon on the same assignment, by this time are back in their offices writing very good but probably incomplete stories. Before *The World* goes to press, Swope will have not only all the information the others have dug up, but much more besides. *The World* will tell not only everything that has happened on the story today, but everything that is going to happen tomorrow, the next day, and the day after. All the other papers have to do is to follow Swope's leads."

"How does he do it?"

"By the method of personal fascination. He finds out who is the principal source of information and proceeds to fascinate that person. He will not let the victim go until he has coughed up all he knows. In the Charles B. Hyde story, he got hold of Hyde and charmed him so thoroughly that Hyde practically admitted everything and returned to New York to face trial."

"Is he a fascinating writer also?"

"Only in the sense that he always tries to put in some little touches that will please and flatter his informants, even if they are on the wrong side of the story. In general style, he is a master of turgidity. He writes by ear. But as a story-getter—irresistible, unsurpassable!

"Swope," my informant continued, "is a Harvard man without benefit of sheepskin, I believe. He comes from St. Louis. The family are German-Jewish. Three brothers came to St. Louis from Germany and went into business and all did very well. Of the present generation, H.B.S. is the only one addicted to literary pursuits. He started on the *St. Louis Post-Dispatch*. After a brief career on the banks of the Mississippi, he deliberately chose to come to New York. Had he elected otherwise, I am sure New York would have been glad to come to him—but let us pause for some refreshment. . . ."

It required the rest of the evening for Bull to orient me in Swope-lore. By the time we had inspected the last available Broadway landmark to make sure that everything was battened down for the night, I was convinced that H.B.S. was the colossus of journalism.

And at that time, he was. Of all the now famous, outstanding, remarkable, talented, and conspicuously able reporters of the era, many of whom were on *The World*, H.B.S. towered above the rest like a Paul Bunyan.

My friend did not exaggerate. The newspaper history of New York in the twenty years that followed JP's death cannot be understood unless one thinks largely in terms of Swope.

He was the first to win the Pulitzer Prize for the best example of a reporter's work. This was for his articles in 1916 about conditions in Germany.

He was executive editor when *The World* won the Pulitzer Medal for distinguished public service. This was for the Ku Klux Klan series of 1921.

It was during Swope's regime that *The World* became chiefly instrumental in bringing the National Democratic Convention to New York—something which had not happened since 1868.

The tide of destiny turned against *The World* at the time when H.B.S. decided that the fate of the newspaper no longer coincided with his personal ambition. He it was who put the handwriting on the wall in 1928 by resigning from *The World*. After that, it soon became evident that the ship was going to sink.

And here is a revelation. Swope was the man behind the scenes at the time of the sale of *The World*, in February, 1931. He was chiefly responsible for the stirring up of the workers and the organization of their fight to set aside the sale and to preserve the newspaper with its Pulitzer tradition under a plan of co-operative employee ownership. If that is news, make the most of it.

H.B.S.'s newspaper career was so outstanding, so dynamic, so brilliant, in some respects so disastrous, at any rate, so memorable, that even today he is introduced on public occasions, and referred to in the press, not so often as chairman of the New York State Racing Commission, but as the former executive editor of *The World*. He is today's most distinguished ex-journalist.

At the "Information, Please" radio program last year when H.B.S. was guest of honor along with Deems Taylor, another distinguished *World* alumnus, he was introduced by Master of Ceremonies Clifton Fadiman as the famous newspaperman, "two-time winner of the Pulitzer Prize." Slightly inaccurate. H.B.S. was a winner, but not a two-timer.

During the "battle of the experts," Fadiman asked for the names of five famous women in history or fiction who had disobeyed orders and thereby met a tragic fate. Swope mentioned Lot's wife. Had he, too, looked back at devastation?

As the record stands today, there is praise for his excellent reporting; laurel for his public service; condemnation for his personal ambition (coupled to some extent with neglect of duty); and tears for his failure to save *The World*.

The other great personality who must be reckoned with in the history of *The World* after JP died is Frank I. Cobb, chief editorial writer, who became the editor upon the demise of the founder, and was the most powerful single force in carrying on *The World's* tradition up to the time of his death in December, 1923. Had Cobb lived only ten years longer, the story might have been different. Cobb was a fighter and had no personal ambitions other than to keep *The World* going.

Here ends for a time the narrative of the Silurian.

ARMAGEDDON

"And he gathered them together into a place called in the Hebrew tongue, Armageddon."—Revelation 16:16.

The World went forward with JP's plan to nominate Woodrow Wilson for President of the United States. As the nation swung into the preliminaries of the 1912 campaign, popular favor was coming strongly toward the scholar-historian whom *The World* had urged for governor of New Jersey in 1910; the same Wilson of whom JP had said to his editors five years before: "This is the type of man the Democrats ought to nominate for president, ridiculous though the suggestion may appear at this time."

Wall Street did not share this opinion. Mr. Wilson was against the trusts, and as governor of New Jersey he had declared war on monopolies operating within the state. The financial interests were uneasy; and Tammany, under the leadership of Charles F. Murphy, who always kept one foot in Wall Street, also feared the ascendancy of Wilson.

Conservative Democratic opinion, as represented by Alton B. Parker and Thomas F. Ryan, swung toward Governor Harmon of

Ohio, or Oscar W. Underwood of Alabama, then chairman of the House Ways and Means Committee. (This was the same Underwood for whom Alabama persistently cast twenty-four votes in the Democratic Convention of 1924.)

Early in the political season, Colonel George B. McClellan Harvey, former managing editor of *The World,* then editor of *Harper's Weekly,* started beating the tom-toms for Wilson in the columns of the magazine. This unexpected support did not sit well either with *The World* or Mr. Wilson's other liberal friends, because Harper and Brothers were commonly understood to have Morgan backing (or Wall Street backing, anyway).

Colonel Harvey was given to understand, in no indirect manner, that his championship of Governor Wilson was embarrassing to the candidate. Harvey ceased his efforts; later, when the New Freedom was in the saddle of government, he repudiated Wilsonism and all its works. Before that, however, he had an interview with J. P. Morgan I, who had frankly opposed Wilson's election.

"If you see Mr. Wilson again," Morgan said, "tell him for me that if there should ever come a time when he thinks any influences or resources that I have can be used for the country, they are wholly at his disposal." *

The World preserved a careful impartiality toward all the Democratic candidates, until the choosing of convention delegates proved that no candidate had the necessary two-thirds majority; after that *The World* was unreservedly for Wilson.

Meanwhile, Theodore Roosevelt's third-term campaign started with a rush that threatened to sweep the Taft supporters off their feet.

As early as February, seven governors of seven states sent a round robin to T.R. "A large number of Republican voters favor your nomination," the manifesto declared, "and a large majority of the people favor your election. . . ." Signed: Stubbs of Kansas; Carey, Wyoming; Glasscock of West Virginia; Bass of New Hampshire; Aldrich of Nebraska; Osborn of Michigan; and Hadley of Missouri.

---

* *J. Pierpont Morgan: An Intimate Portrait,* by Herbert L. Satterlee. The Macmillan Company, 1939.

A few days later, T.R. announced: "I will accept the nomination if it is tendered to me."

In March, *The World* says, editorially: "American politics has produced nothing more extraordinary than Mr. Roosevelt's loss of strength since the announcement of his candidacy. Up to that time he was a formidable figure. . . . He was professedly fighting for a principle. . . . Mr. Taft was growing steadily weaker. He himself admitted the possibility of his defeat. The turn came when Mr. Roosevelt announced his candidacy. He was no longer disinterested. The mask had been removed."

Hope was father to that analysis. The Rough Rider was not exactly weak. Colonel Roosevelt went to Chicago with 450 delegates and seventy-eight contests involving 254 other votes.

May. From *The World:*

"FOR PRESIDENT—WOODROW WILSON.

"The Democratic party must not only rise to its opportunity but to its responsibility.

"How can it do its duty better than to match sanity against lunacy; the historian against the Rough Rider; the education of public opinion against the debauchery of public opinion; the first term against the third term; the tariff reformer against the standpatter; the man who would prosecute trust magnates against the man who protects trust magnates; the man with clean hands against the man who draws his campaign funds from Wall Street; the supporter of constitutional government against the champion of personal government; law against lawlessness; Americanism against Mexicanism; the Republic against the Dictatorship?

"Who represents these issues better than Woodrow Wilson?"

Even before that, T.R. had begun enriching political vocabulary by announcing: "My hat is in the ring!" He also issued this ringing declaration:

"If they ask for the sword, they shall have it. We stand at Armageddon and we battle for the Lord!"

On the first test of strength—the question of admitting the contested delegations, the Roosevelt forces came short of a majority. They were strong, but not quite strong enough.

Arriving in Chicago for the convention, T.R. was interviewed by the press while admirers almost mobbed him at the railroad station.

Q. How do you feel, Colonel?

A. (With powerful click of big teeth.) I feel like a bull moose!

That's how the Bull Moose Progressive Party got its name.

Shortly before the call to order, T.R. reiterated:

"If they ask for the sword, they shall have it. We stand at Armageddon and we battle for the Lord."

The first test of strength came on the motion to admit the contested delegations. The Bull Moose Progressives were powerful, but not strong enough. Roosevelt was a few votes short of the necessary majority.

The Progressives withdrew and held their own meeting in another hall—one of the wildest meetings ever witnessed. That was the beginning. In August the Progressives held a full-fledged convention and nominated T.R. The Republicans met next day and nominated Taft for a second term.

The Democrats met in Baltimore on June 25. Conservatives won the first bout by choosing Alton B. Parker for temporary chairman, eliminating William Jennings Bryan by 69 votes. Wall Street sentiment now favored Champ Clark, Speaker of the House of Representatives. Murphy swung New York's ninety votes to Clark.

On the eleventh ballot, Clark had 556 votes; Woodrow Wilson only 354½. Only the two-thirds rule (now abandoned) saved *The World's* candidate from defeat.

After that, Wilson gained on each ballot. After the forty-third vote, the convention adjourned over Sunday, with Wilson leading.

Monday, July 1, *The World* goes all-out for Wilson. In the biggest typographical display ever given to a *World* editorial, Cobb declares:

"NO COMPROMISE WITH RYAN AND MURPHY!"

"Compromise," the editor says, "was possible until it became apparent to every intelligent man that the Ryan-Murphy-Belmont-Hearst coalition had set out to strangle progressive Democracy.

"Compromise is no longer possible. There can be no Democratic harmony . . . no Democratic unity . . . no Democratic integrity until the Convention overwhelms this shameful alliance between corrupt finance and corrupt politics . . . As Stephen A. Douglas once said, 'There can be no neutrals in this war—only patriots or traitors.' "

Woodrow Wilson is nominated on the forty-sixth ballot. *The World* predicts his election. The rest of the campaign is easily remembered.

The *New York Herald* tries to boycott Theodore Roosevelt. Bennett will not permit the Rough Rider to be mentioned by name, only as "the third-term candidate" or "the third-termer." The plan does not work. It never does. In October, T.R. is shot but not seriously wounded by a crank in Milwaukee. The *Herald* has to print the news, including Roosevelt's name. Wilson, out of courtesy, cancels the rest of his speeches and the campaign ends one month before election. The result: Electoral vote—Wilson, 435; Roosevelt, 88; Taft, 8 (Utah and Vermont). Popular vote: Wilson, 6,293,454; Roosevelt, 4,119,538; Taft, 3,484,980. Wilson has 1,311,064 fewer votes than the combined Roosevelt-Taft strength—showing how badly "the third-termer" split the normal Republican majority.

The World takes victory in a solemn spirit. The work that confronts Wilson, Cobb's editorial stresses, is "to restore popular confidence in the institutions of the Republic and re-establish a government of the people, by the people, and for the people."

"If he should fail," Cobb says, "the consequences will be doubly disastrous. If he succeeds, as *The World* believes he will . . . this nation will indeed have a new birth of freedom."

In the New York State campaign, *The World* throws down the gauntlet to Murphy, announcing that under no circumstances will the paper support John A. Dix for re-election. The Tammany boss, uncannily astute in some ways, goes through the motions of keeping hands off. The Democrats nominate Congressman William L. Sulzer, idol of an East Side district, who has been showing independence of Murphy.

The boss smiles. What *The World* and the party do not know is that Murphy's watchdog, Matt Horgan, is being assigned to Sulzer's headquarters to look after campaign contributions. Horgan initiates Mr. Sulzer in the art of concealing money. Sulzer takes a large portion of the contributions and invests the money in Wall Street. Horgan knows all about it. He is destined to be chief witness for the prosecution in 1913 in the impeachment proceedings that follow Sulzer's break with Tammany.

WORLD AGAINST BECKER

Long before the November Battle of Ballots, New York is thrown into a turmoil that excites the entire country.

Friday, July 12. In the West Side Court, Herman Rosenthal, gambler and prominent unsophisticate, charges Police Inspector Hayes and Captain Day with oppression in keeping a policeman on the Rosenthal premises, No. 104 West Forty-fifth Street. Rosenthal relates that his place has been raided by Police Lieutenant Charles Becker and the Strong-Arm Squad on April 15, since when he has been unable to do business. Magistrate Butts refuses to issue a warrant, holding the evidence to be insufficient. Reporters interview Rosenthal. He says a certain police lieutenant was his partner for twenty per cent of the profits, having put up a fifteen hundred dollar mortgage. But they quarreled, and then came the raid.

Rosenthal says he knows all about the system—who gets the graft and who pays for protection. It seems that he has been to Mayor Gaynor and to District Attorney Whitman with his tale of woe, but has received no sympathy.

Saturday, July 13. The newspapers give prominent space to the Rosenthal story, *The World* most of all. *The World* sends H.B.S. to Newport, to interview District Attorney Charles Seymour Whitman at his summer home.

MR. WHITMAN: "I have had Rosenthal's charges under investigation for some time. I have no sympathy for Rosenthal the gambler; but I have real use for Rosenthal, who, abused by the police, proposes to aid decency and lawfulness by revealing conditions that are startling. The trail leads to high places . . . this man will have a chance to tell his story to the Grand Jury."

Rosenthal, meanwhile, keeps open house for the press. He talks freely, revealing, incidentally, that he has been down to *The World* and made an affidavit naming the police lieutenant who was his partner. The *Morning Telegraph* reporter so informs his office—after which other things happen. Lieutenant Becker and his attorney, John W. Hart, go to *The World* and ask to see the Rosenthal affidavit. After studying the charges, they say Becker has no statement, being under Department rules, but that Rosenthal is a damned liar.

Sunday, July 14. *The World* publishes Rosenthal's affidavit, revealing Lieutenant Becker's 'share in his [Rosenthal's] gambling establishment. Police Commissioner Rhinelander Waldo, on vacation, returns from Toronto. His secretary, Winfield R. Sheehan, has nothing to say. Gamblers are in a panic. Rosenthal, meanwhile, gives more interviews. It seems he knows a lot about the Tenderloin, but has forgotten that the First Commandment is: "Thou shalt not squeal!"

Mayor Gaynor, sought for comment at his home in St. James, Long Island, asks the reporter, "Who sent you here?"

"My city editor," the reporter answers.

GAYNOR: "You're lying. A damn fool sent you here."

Monday, July 15. *The World* publishes more about the Rosenthal case, including the statement that he will make more charges in the West Side Court. District Attorney Whitman makes an appointment for Rosenthal to see him the next morning, after which he will be presented to the Grand Jury.

The *Morning Telegraph* reporter, mentioned above, returns to covering the Harry K. Thaw sanity hearings at White Plains. After finishing the story that evening, the reporter is introduced to Jack Rose, a pale, nattily dressed, harmless-looking individual, hairless as a Mexican pup—hasn't even an eyelash.

"Mr. Barrett," says Shep Friedman, night city editor, "I want you to go with Mr. Rose. He's getting an affidavit about Rosenthal. He has a car outside."

We drive downtown, Rose talking very quietly, the theme of the conversation being that Rosenthal is a scoundrel. It is a balmy summer's evening and the ride down Broadway very pleasant in the open touring car, a red one, not the gray car that Rose used later that evening.

Arriving at an old-fashioned brownstone house in East Seventeenth Street, Jack leads the way swiftly into the downstairs dining room. A plump, rather pretty, middle-aged matron and several nicely

dressed gentlemen are seated around the table. The lady is introduced as Mrs. Dora Gilbert, Herman Rosenthal's first wife. The
gentlemen smile, but there are no other introductions. Later, from
photographs, I seem to identify Bridgie Webber, Harry Vallon, Sam
Schepps, all gamblers involved in the case. There may have been
others. No gunmen, however.

Dora breaks out a bottle of champagne, and conversation pro-
gresses easily. It seems that the *Morning Telegraph* is about to get an
exclusive story for once in its life. A lawyer is coming up with an
affidavit which Dora is going to sign, telling what an awful time she
had with Rosenthal and how he tried to force her into a life of shame.

"What a story!" everybody says, and it seems advisable to agree.

Dora introduces another specimen of the Mumm group, and adds
more comment, but not many details. After a while more men come
in, and one produces the affidavit, which is several pages thick.

They show Dora where to sign. She does not take the time to read
it. The others are positive that this will show Rosenthal up.

Dora says she wouldn't do anything to hurt Herman, but she is
not going to stand for his attacks on a fine man like Becker. Everybody says that's the spirit.

On the way uptown again in the red car, Rose finds that this is
indeed a great story and what a fine thing for the *Morning Telegraph* to be getting it all by itself. He waves a cheerful good-bye in
front of the old car barn which is the *Morning Telegraph's* office,
and the red car heads down Eighth Avenue.

Shep Friedman says to write just a brief introduction to the Dora
Gilbert affidavit, and never mind about the circumstances under
which it was given out, and about the champagne.

"For tomorrow," he says, "you go back to the Thaw story."

This was about eleven o'clock.

Tuesday, July 16. "Extra! Extra! Herman Rosenthal murdered!"
by four gunmen in front of the Hotel Metropole just off Broadway
on Forty-third Street.

At 1.56 o'clock that morning, the gambler, who has been sitting
with friends in the restaurant, is called outside. Four assassins jump
out of a gray touring car across from the hotel, close in on Rosenthal,
and fire several shots at close range.

The gray car gets away.

There is no pursuit. All cabs in the block have been sent away on long errands. Although several policemen are on duty within a stone's throw of the hotel, they do practically nothing. The license numbers which they turn in, for identification of the murder car, are all wrong. Charles Gallagher, a singer, turns in the correct number, NY 41313, at the West Forty-seventh Street station and is locked up as a material witness.

The night clerk at the Elks Club, across from the hotel, also has the right number, but he decides this is a good time to take a long trip out of town.

H.B.S. calls District Attorney Whitman at his town residence, the Hotel Madison Square at East Twenty-sixth Street. Whitman reaches the station house at 3.25 A.M., takes charge of the investigation, and orders Gallagher's release.

One hour later, Lieutenant Becker came in and took a look at the body of Rosenthal. According to Rose's testimony at Becker's trial for murder, the lieutenant said to him later: "It was a pleasant sight to me to look and see that squealing Jew there, and if it hadn't been for Whitman, I would have reached down and cut his tongue out and hung it up somewheres as a warning to future squealers."

Statement by Whitman: "I accuse the Police Department of New York, through certain members of it, with having murdered Herman Rosenthal. Either directly or indirectly it was because of them that he was slain in cold blood with never a chance for his life."

The *Morning Telegraph's* "exclusive story" about Dora Gilbert looked unimportant beside the headlines of the murder.

The Harry K. Thaw hearing that day was brief, and I returned to the *Telegraph* unexpectedly early in the afternoon. When I walked up to the city desk, who should be standing there but Jack Rose, freshly dressed—looking as free from care as from hair. He smiled pleasantly. Some story, he said. Some story, I agreed, not knowing which one he meant. I walked to the outer door with him to inquire whether he had any ideas about the murder. He said he hadn't one in the world.

City editor Jack Blauvelt didn't seem to know anything about the

Dora Gilbert expedition of the night before, so I gave him the details. He looked dubious.

"Perhaps you'd better work up a story about it," he said.

But for the moment, he gave me some rewrite. After a while Irving Lewis came out.

"About latht night," he said, "the betht thing ith to jutht forget it." Later, Shep Friedman reinforced the suggestion. I spoke about it to Ashby Deering, the *Telegraph's* top reporter, who was covering the murder story . . . asked whether he thought I should tell the District Attorney? He strongly advised against it.

A wise newspaperman, he remarked, keeps his eyes and his ears open and his mouth shut. If you can't print your story, don't talk about it.

July 18, Jack Rose, Bridgie Webber, and Harry Vallon, sensing Whitman's net closing about them, stood on the corner opposite police headquarters and debated whether to give themselves up. The affirmative won. They went into headquarters and asked to see Police Commissioner Waldo. Their names didn't mean a thing to the lieutenant in the commissioner's reception room. He told them the commissioner was too busy. They went away. Jack came back later and persuaded the police to arrest him. Webber and Vallon followed. Whitman had them put in the Tombs and by July 29 had obtained their confessions.

In substance, they charged that Becker had forced them to bring about the murder; at Becker's instigation Rose had hired the four gunmen to do the shooting for a thousand dollars, promising them immunity and an easy getaway.

New York well remembers the rest. Becker was tried, convicted, and electrocuted. The four gunmen—picturesquely termed "Gyp the Blood," "Lefty Louie," "Dago Frank," and "Whitey Lewis"— were convicted and put to death. All through the investigation and the trials, *The World* led the field with many exclusive stories by Swope and others. *The World's* editorials aroused public opinion.

Gaynor took the wrong side of the controversy and stayed there. The only thing he blamed Becker for was for sitting down at table with a man like Rosenthal.

Whitman wanted to be the Fusion candidate for mayor in 1913.

William A. Orr, now of Metro-Goldwyn-Mayer, then first-rank reporter for the *Tribune,* was Whitman's chief worker among the
Republican-Fusion leaders. But they chose the late John Purroy
Mitchel, then Collector of the Port of New York. I well remember
how Orr cursed for a whole afternoon when the decision was announced.

The following year Whitman was elected governor. The story
went around town that this was *The World's* reward to the district
attorney for all those exclusive stories by Swope.

H.B.S. was known for a time as "the reporter who made Whitman
governor."

Whitman was governor at the time of Becker's execution. Mrs.
Becker, an expectant mother, pleaded for mercy up to the last mo-
ment. At the funeral there was a plate on Becker's coffin reading
"Murdered by Governor Whitman," but the police had it removed.

Though relentless in its demands for the punishment of Rosenthal's killers, *The World,* in its more philosophic editorials, expressed a doubt as to any permanent benefits. After the conviction
of Becker, *The World* said:

"For a little while a purified city; and then a new Becker, new gunmen, a new gang rule, a new system, a resurrection of all the evils
which we think we are burying, unless there is also passed a death
sentence on the conditions which directly created those evils.

"So long as an Anglo-Saxon hypocrisy persists in making felonious
everything that it considers shocking, so long as it brands as crimes
those practices which other broad-minded and equally civilized nations handle as public nuisances, so long as an Albany legislature
. . . strives to create fiat chastity, fiat sobriety, and fiat frugality
in conformity with its own professed ideals, just so long will human
nature, following the dictates of its foibles, evade such laws by
subterfuge and by corruption and as soon as corruption is employed
. . . just so soon shall we again have a debauched police force, a
system, a Becker, gangs, gunmen—a city shamed before the world."

Investigations of police corruption followed the Becker case with
important results. A committee of the legislature, headed by Senator
Robert F. Wagner, conducted one inquiry, while a committee of the
Board of Aldermen, with Henry Curran as chairman, dug up the

more sensational evidence. Counsel to the Curran committee was a young Assistant District Attorney, Emory R. Buckner, who became United States Attorney in the night club era, later joined Elihu Root's law firm, and died only recently.

Buckner uncovered an amazing trail of graft and corruption, leading to the conviction and imprisonment of four police inspectors, Sweeney, Murtha, Hussey, and Thompson. A police captain named Walsh, brought into court practically on his deathbed, revealed the system of paid protection for vice and gambling. The inspectors' own bank accounts supplied the missing links in the evidence. They had top-notch counsel—among them Francis Wellman, the great authority on cross-examination, and John B. Stanchfield.

Decorating the press table were Swope; Alexander Woollcott (*New York Times*); Bill Orr; William A. Willis (*Herald*); George Morris (*Telegram*); and "Jeff" Handley (*Press*).

Right in the middle of the trial, Woollcott leaned across the press table and whispered, excitedly:

"What do you think? I've just found the loveliest *pension* in Greenwich Village that you can possibly imagine!"

If it were possible for a newspaper to blush, *The World* did so in connection with the Sulzer impeachment in 1913. As a member of the House of Representatives, Sulzer was chairman of the House committee which investigated the Panama Canal scandal in 1912, and *The World* gratefully supported his ambition to become governor, believing Sulzer to be independent of Tammany.

And, indeed, he seemed to be. Once installed in Albany, Sulzer caused a widespread investigation of graft in the state highways. He struck right into the roots of the Tammany bagman system.

Boss Murphy immediately stirred up his friends in the legislature, with the result that a committee was authorized to investigate Sulzer's campaign contributions. Matt Horgan supplied the backbone of the evidence.

The World at first was incredulous. Sulzer had sworn that his election fund was only $5,460. Tammany, said *The World*, must have expended the remainder without Sulzer's knowledge. It seemed inconceivable that a governor would deliberately falsify.

But as the Frawley committee uncovered the evidence, *The World* became alarmed and urged Sulzer to answer the accusations. The governor talked but evaded the issues.

"The whole truth, Governor," *The World* implored. "Nobody can destroy Governor Sulzer except Governor Sulzer. Murphy cannot do it. Tammany cannot do it. No conspiracy can do it."

Sulzer declined to appear before the committee. Frawley's investigators produced the record of his dealings in Wall Street. *The World* declared:

"The honor of the state is involved and the governor must answer!"

Still no reply from Albany, other than vague counter-charges about a Tammany conspiracy.

The World: "Explain or resign!"

The committee completed its probe and recommended impeachment. *The World* commented sadly:

"The best thing the governor can do is to resign and spare the state further humiliation. His case now is beyond explanation. Possibly William Sulzer can live down these revelations, but Governor Sulzer cannot live them down. The painful process of rehabilitation belongs to private life."

The Assembly, with Alfred E. Smith as majority leader, impeached Sulzer by a vote of 79 to 45. The Senate, sitting as a Court of Impeachment, removed him from office. William Sulzer became the forgotten man.

Much more glory-getting was *The World's* fight in the same year on behalf of the Fusion ticket: For Mayor, John Purroy Mitchel; for Comptroller, William A. Prendergast; for president of the Board of Aldermen, George McAneny.

Tammany's candidate was Edward E. McCall, chairman of the Public Service Commission. Murphy had turned thumbs down on a renomination for Gaynor, in spite of Gaynor's co-operation with the Police Department during the Becker affair and the vice and graft investigations.

Gaynor announced that he would run independently. A crowd gathered at City Hall and begged him to accept "a people's nomination."

Gaynor's campaign slogan, emblazoned on banners, was proclaimed in his speech of acceptance:

"I have been mayor."

He spoke the truth. The day after his "nomination" he sailed for Europe. One week later, his body lay in state in City Hall. Gaynor had died at sea.

Mr. McCall preferred to fight with knives and clubs. Resenting *The World's* description of him as Murphy's candidate, McCall directed personal attacks against Ralph Pulitzer, declaring that if elected he would put Mr. Pulitzer and *The World* out of business. *The World* made answer:

"Tammany bosses and Tammany officeholders have been trying to put *The World* out of business for the last thirty years. We wear their hatred as a badge of journalistic honor."

The enjoyable feature of that campaign, so far as the press was concerned, was the daily encounter between McCall and a *World* reporter, Harold Vivian. The scene of battle was McCall's head quarters in the Hotel Breslin. McCall was continually in a fury because Rollin Kirby, *The World's* cartoonist, pictured the Tammany Tiger with one arm around McCall saying: "He's good enough for me!"

To make things worse, somebody kept delivering *The World* every morning to McCall's apartment. He called it an outrageous attempt to invade the sanctity of his home. Most of the New York papers were supporting Mitchel, a notable exception being the *Morning Telegraph*. But McCall seemed to regard *The World* as a personal enemy. The result: Mitchel—358,181; McCall—233,919. Those figures appear small in comparison with 1937 figures: LaGuardia (Fusion, Republican, American Labor)—1,344,630; Mahoney (Democrat)—890,756.

Naturally *The World* was elated at the 1913 results, hailing the election as "a day of retribution for the shameless system that organized corruption has entrenched in Tammany Hall."

From the standpoint of reportorial excellence, 1914 started out as a Louis Seibold year, rather than one of the Herbert Bayard Swope vintage. In that year *The World,* following the JP maxim, "Turn on the light," published the results of its investigation into the financial and legislative affairs of the New York, New Haven, and Hartford Railroad, a story of the kind that was Seibold's meat.

Considerable zest was added to *The World's* campaign for a reorganization of the New Haven road by a series of disastrous wrecks in 1912 and 1913. In most cases, responsibility was concealed by the coroner, who, under the Connecticut system, was a little czar, and conducted investigations in private.

In one of the worst of the wrecks, near Stamford, Connecticut, *The World* lost a faithful reporter, Gregory T. Humes, who was a passenger on one of the trains which collided. The story was told on a bronze plaque back of the city editor's desk:

IN MEMORY OF
GREGORY T. HUMES
Reporter on *The World*
Mortally injured in the Stamford Railroad Wreck
He thought first of his paper and with indomitable
courage sent the news of the disaster.
Born April 12, 1878
Died June 13, 1913

The World started off the new year with a powerful series on the financial structure of the New Haven, giving a history of the intricate operations by which the road obtained control of some 336 railway, steamship, and trolley lines:

$204,000,000 of the New Haven's resources invested in outside ventures.

$12,000,000 of New Haven stockholders' money gone "into thin air" in the purchase of the New York, Westchester and Boston Railroad.

New Haven stock, under management of Charles S. Mellen, president, dropped from 225¼ to 65⅜.

Huge amounts expended by the New Haven for political aid and intensive legislative lobbies, described later by Mellen as "music by the whole band."

Purchase by the New Haven of the Metropolitan Steamship Company, a competing line, in defiance of the anti-trust law.

In Washington, the new Democratic regime was electrified by *The World's* disclosures. Adopting a resolution by the independent George W. Norris of Nebraska, the Senate requested the Interstate Commerce Commission to investigate. Hearings began in April. Star witness, Charles S. Mellen, marvelously informed on operating details, was unenlightening on financial deals, and attributed to J. Pierpont Morgan sole responsibility.

"Mr. Morgan," said Mellen, "treated me like an office boy!"

J. P. Morgan the Second denied Mellen's charges, blaming Mellen for deterioration of the railroad. (Morgan had caused Mellen's removal and the appointment of Howard Elliott as president.)

The I.C.C. report blasted the entire management of the New Haven, past and present directors alike, including the Morgans and Mellen as well. *The World,* in a Cobb editorial, demanded action against the financial higher-ups. Cobb wrote:

"The New Haven was looted under the personal auspices of men who posed as great captains of American finance. . . .

"The trouble with this country today is not in the policies of the Administration. It is in the policies of men of wealth, education, and understanding who hesitate at nothing to gain power and profit.

"Prosperity is excellent in itself, but there are better things than prosperity. Honesty is better. Justice is better. Liberty is better."

By direction of President Wilson, the Department of Justice brought civil action also against the New Haven directors, which was settled by a "consent decree" under which the road divested itself of collateral properties listed at $74,000,000.

A Federal Grand Jury in New York indicted twenty-three directors and former directors. Mellen was given immunity as a star witness. Only eleven of the group were put on trial: William Rockefeller, Robert W. Taft, Lewis Cass Ledyard, Charles M. Pratt, D. Newton Barney, Frederick F. Brewster, Henry K. McHarg, James S. Hemmingway, A. Heath Robertson, Edward D. Robbins, and George MacCulloch Miller. Six were acquitted. The jury disagreed on the others, and prosecution was finally dropped.

Rodman Wanamaker, son of the famous Philadelphia merchant, was very much aviation-minded. In 1914 he caused a flying boat to be built and named *America*. Wanamaker planned a transatlantic flight, and engaged Commander J. C. Porte, British Royal Navy, to make the historic venture.

During the summer, Porte had the *America* up at Hammondsport, New York, for trial flights on Lake Keuka. Reporters assigned to cover the preparations found the British flier singularly unco-operative. They considered Porte high-hat.

As time for the major flight approached, *The World* sent H.B.S. to Hammondsport to cover the plans for the final takeoff. The other newspapermen warned him that Porte was stiff-necked and uncommunicative.

The next morning, Porte came down to breakfast and said to the maître d'hôtel:

"Mr. Swope says he will be down right away. He wants you to have his breakfast ready—orange juice, two poached eggs with crisp toast, a rasher of bacon, and piping-hot coffee. See to it, please."

After extracting all the news out of Hammondsport, H.B.S. proceeded to the Azores, to await Porte's arrival on the first leg of the contemplated flight. Thwaites, late of JP's personal staff, was assigned to take over at Hammondsport. Then came the assassination at Sarajevo. Porte and Thwaites immediately reported to the British consul in New York and the flight was off.

Swope went on to Germany. He obtained several exclusive stories out of Berlin, including the narrative of Captain-Lieutenant Otto Weddingen, commander of the German submarine *U-9,* which sank three British cruisers.

Shortly after his return to New York, he was appointed city editor, by personal direction of Ralph Pulitzer.

Other achievements by *The World* in that first year of war included exclusive reports from Arno Dosch, the only correspondent with the German army invading Belgium. Later in the conflict Dosch went to Paris and joined *The World's* staff there as Arno Dosch-Fleurot.

Captain Thwaites, having gone to the Western Front with the Fourth (Royal Irish) Dragoon Guards, wrote a diary of war published by *The World* as "Life in the Trenches."

E. Alexander Powell, *The World* correspondent in Antwerp, remained on duty while the city was being shelled by the Germans; after the capture, as "Herr Powell," he interviewed the German commander, Von Boehm, and related to him the stories he had obtained of German atrocities. "Lies—all lies!" Von Boehm exclaimed. Powell, by using the interview as a disguise, got the atrocity stories into his dispatches, adding in a footnote: "My American readers may judge for themselves the accuracy of these charges."

The World gave hearty co-operation to the Santa Claus ship which carried Christmas gifts to children of the warring countries whose fathers were killed in battle. The idea originated with James Keeley, publisher of the *Chicago Herald*.

Most of the American newspapers and newspapermen considered the European war a colossal bore. In New York it played havoc with the lucrative "space" system—except for the lads who covered the Liberty Loan Drives, in which three and four columns or more per day were "must." They used such large quantities of the material given out by Liberty Loan Headquarters, that they were called "paperhangers—not reporters."

Probably most of us did not realize that the golden era, which reached its climax in 1912, was going forever. The war brought the handout system, organized publicity, government press releases, long speeches and statements to fill up columns. Formerly the newspapers had to send out their men to hustle for news, but after the war it poured in upon them in floods and the big problem was what to do with it all.

The war took the edge off accuracy. It introduced propaganda. It established the "reported on high authority" system, leading to the "informed circles," "administration spokesmen," "sources close to such and such," and all the other depression journalese mechanisms of today.

The First World War blazed the way for the Second World War to produce the present complicated cross-crediting of news sources. Recent example:

"Two proclamations by King Peter [of Yugoslavia, upon assuming the throne] were broadcast in English by the British Broadcasting Corporation and transcribed here by the Columbia Broadcasting System, the Associated Press reported."

The city editorship of Swope, like most of his undertakings, was dramatic and dynamic at the outset. He attacked the news with such zest that the staff was galvanized—also partly paralyzed and somewhat amused. Swope exercised a proprietary interest in the news. "Who is covering my Republican committee?" or "Who's covering my subway accident?" or "Who's covering my murder trial?" he would ask the assistant city editor, John H. Gavin. Coming in late one day, during a heavy winter, he demanded to know: "Who is covering my snowstorm?"

Right at the beginning of his term on the city desk, H.B.S. had a severe illness which kept him away several weeks, and Arthur Clarke, his predecessor, who had been assigned to other duties, had to return to the post, without the title.

In that year, 1915, *The World's* list of outstanding beats was topped by a major sensation of the war—the exposé of the German espionage and sabotage plots in this country. *The World* obtained the series exclusively because of Louis Seibold's excellent connections in Washington. Seibold was one of the few newsmen able to get along well with President Wilson; he and Cobb were about the only two in whom the wartime president had complete confidence.

Public opinion was ripe for indignant response to *The World's* exposé. The sinking of the *Lusitania* in May, coupled with the mild remonstrances of the Administration in Washington, built up a fire of anti-German resentment. Ex-President Roosevelt fanned the flames.

The *Lusitania* tragedy news came right in the midst of the Barnes-Roosevelt libel suit trial in Syracuse, New York. (William Barnes of Albany and New York was the Republican State Boss. T.R. had charged in *The Outlook* that Barnes and Murphy had a corrupt bargain to divide political patronage and power in the Empire State. Barnes sued T.R. for $6,000,000 but got nothing.) T.R. was on the stand at the time. Edwin C. Hill managed to pass him a telegram from the *New York Sun*: "*Lusitania* sunk by German submarine. Get comment from Roosevelt."

T.R. whispered: "See me at recess time!"

During the next intermission in the trial, the reporters gathered round the Rough Rider. What a galaxy of journalists was there:

Louis Seibold and Charles S. Hand of *The World;* Samuel M. Williams, *Evening World;* James Montague, *New York American;* William A. Willis, *Herald;* Charles Hambidge and Rodney Bean of the *Times;* Stuart Crawford and Robert B. Peck of the *Tribune;* and your humble servant from the *New York Press.*

T.R. absorbed all the details of the *Lusitania* sinking but offered no comment. Next day, when it became evident that Secretary of State Bryan was merely going to write another note, the Colonel could not restrain his temper. Collecting the press around him at recess time, and snapping his teeth like an indignant turtle, he fairly hissed:

"This is off the record. But I would just like to say to you fellows that I would rather have Barnes and Murphy in Washington today than Wilson and Bryan, because Barnes and Murphy, by Godfrey, have at least GOT GUTS!"

Wilson refused to be stampeded on the *Lusitania* crisis. Privately he told Cobb: "I intend to handle the situation in such a manner that every American citizen will know that the United States has done everything to prevent war. Then if war comes we shall have a united country, and there need be no fear about the result."

After the trial, T.R. went back to Oyster Bay and conducted a one-man, front-porch campaign for American intervention against Germany.

The World's revelations began in August. Day after day the newspaper published full texts and facsimiles of letters, telegrams, and other messages, proving beyond all question that the Kaiser's Government was engaged in a far-reaching plot to stop the flow of munitions to the Allies. The documents were obtained by a United States Secret Service man, who seated himself next to Dr. Heinrich F. Albert on the Third Avenue "El" in New York and, by a remarkable sleight-of-hand, exchanged his own briefcase for the one carried by Albert.

Dr. Albert, who had come to this country in the official guise of a "financial agent" of the German Government, was one of the higher-ups among the conspirators. Others involved by *The World* were:

Von Bethmann-Hollweg, the German Chancellor and foreign minister.

The German Ambassador in Washington, Count Johann von Bernstorff.

Captain Franz von Papen, German military attaché in Washington, at the moment Nazi Ambassador to Turkey—a good man to watch at all times.

Hugo Schmidt, representative of the Deutsches Bank of Berlin.

Hugo Schweitzer, a German-American chemist.

S. Sulzberger, banker, of Frankfort, Germany.

The program for the conspiracy embraced the following objectives, all of which seem to have a familiar ring in terms of World War Number Two:

To control or influence the American press; to establish "news services," and, if possible, to purchase newspapers, including the *New York Evening Mail*.

To support the German propaganda weekly magazine, *The Fatherland,* edited by George Sylvester Viereck.

To publish books; to put propagandists on the Chautauqua circuit, an institution greatly favored by Secretary of State Bryan.

To organize strikes and walkouts in munitions plants.

To corner the American market in war chemicals . . . chlorine, picric acid, etc.

To cut off the supply of cotton to England; to acquire airplane plants and patents; to purchase munitions plants secretly. (One was built and operated at Bridgeport, Connecticut, obtaining large contracts to supply Great Britain and Russia but never delivering the goods.)

To promote anti-British legislation in Washington; chiefly, an attempted embargo on arms. Several Senators, Representatives, and other prominent personages were listed as friendly to the enterprise. Correspondence between William Travers Jerome and Arthur von Briesen, mentioning a possible fee of $10,000 and $10,000 expenses for handling "a delicate matter" also emerged from the Albert portfolio.

Germany issued sweeping denials. Von Bernstorff, in a three-thousand-word statement to Secretary of State Lansing (Bryan

having resigned with a God Bless You to and from Wilson) called*
The World articles "inspired and romantic tales." Foolish man!
Little did he reckon that the British Secret Service was watching a
certain newspaperman, James Francis Jewell Archibald, bound for
Vienna on a mysterious errand. When Archibald got to Falmouth,
the British seized his papers—everything in *The World* was confirmed, with additional revelations even more sensational. Archibald was carrying secret messages from Dr. Konstantin Theodor
Dumba, the Austro-Hungarian Ambassador in Washington, to his
home government, and also messages from Von Bernstorff. Dumba
was asking for big sums of money to cripple munitions plants. Von
Bernstorff, in a letter to his wife, related the sad tale of the theft
of Albert's papers. *The World* obtained the entire new series of
documents for exclusive publication in America.

Dumba was a naïve soul; even his name seemed to be spelled
wrong. Interviewed by *The World* in Lenox, Massachusetts, about
the Archibald papers, he said: "Yes. That is true. Von Bernstorff
and I dined with Archibald before he sailed and entrusted him with
some secret and valuable papers. I cannot understand why he was
so careless."

Wilson demanded the recall of Dumba. The dismissals of Von
Papen and Captain Karl Boy-Ed, German naval attaché, followed
soon afterward. Why Wilson did not at that time also ask the recall
of Von Bernstorff is still a question for argument.

Other news beats by *The World* in 1915:

Efforts by German agents to cause an Atlantic coast shipping strike
through the attempted payment of one million dollars to union
leaders.

Exclusive statement from Kaiser Wilhelm, obtained by *World*
reporter Gus C. Roeder. The Kaiser said: "I did not want to have
this awful war . . . it was brought on by other nations . . . but it
will end well for Germany . . . I am in the field with my brave
soldiers. Victory will be ours!"

Exclusive statement to the American people from King Albert of
the Belgians.

Exclusive interview by Karl H. von Wiegand with Pope Benedict
XV, expressing the hope that America would avoid anything tend-

ing to prevent an early peace. The interview was hotly disputed. The Vatican settled the matter by stating officially that every word was correctly reported.

Somewhat discouraged by the unstimulating environment of Frank A. Munsey's *New York Press* in the spring of 1916, I knocked once more at the portals of *The World*. H.B.S. was encouraging. "I think you have real possibilities as a *World* man," he said. Shortly thereafter he put me on the staff. Surprising, the difference it made in one's feeling toward life! Just to be able to say, "I am Barrett of *The World*," was inspiring.

The day I went to work for *The World* was the happiest and at the same time the most anxious of my life. *The World* was right in the midst of the Arthur Warren Waite crime—the story of the dentist who poisoned his wife's mother and father. Waite had been arrested the night before, but *The World* was looking for "the other woman," with whom Waite had shared a "studio apartment" in the Hotel Plaza.

H.B.S. came in fairly early that day, dispatched the staff on various angles of the story, and then hauled me along while he rode uptown in the subway, bringing me up to date on *The World's* coverage. Substance of instructions: *"Cherchez la femme*—and, goddamit, find her!"

World beginner's luck and a certain portion of hard work enabled us to land the lady exclusively in our net by the following evening. As she afterward, through much tribulation, became a church soloist, there is no occasion to revive unpleasing memories. Nobody could ever forget the thrill of seeing one's own exclusive story in *The World,* effectively illustrated by an exclusive photograph, even though it did not carry one's by-line. Very few stories in *The World* at that time were signed. It was *The World*'s glory, not the individual's, as far as the public was concerned—but, of course, in the newspaper field, everybody knew who wrote practically every story. My all-sufficient reward was a cash bonus and the privilege of covering Waite's trial and subsequent execution.

Swope went back to Germany that summer and remained until late in the year, returning with Ambassador James W. Gerard and the warning that Germany was about to resume unrestricted submarine warfare. Gerard denied the submarine story, for diplomatic reasons, but it was one hundred per cent correct.

Swope's investigations in Germany were published in a series by *The World,* the pick and shovel work of sorting the material and typing the manuscript being executed by Lewis Gannett. The same material was later published in Swope's book, *Inside the German Empire.* This was the series for which H.B.S. won the Pulitzer Prize, the first ever to be awarded for an outstanding example of a reporter's work. Meanwhile, Ralph Pulitzer had also done some reporting based upon his airplane flights over the Western front.

By 1917 everybody on *The World* knew that the United States was going to war against Germany. From then on, *The World* was on a war basis. H.B.S. went to Washington and became a dollar-a-year man as special assistant to Bernard M. Baruch, chairman of the War Industries Board.

From the beginning of the war in Europe, the dominating force in *The World's* policy was Cobb. The man from Michigan was intensely pro-Ally, not merely for reasons of natural sympathy for Britain and France, but because, like Wilson, he believed that German imperialism was the chief barrier to the advance of peace and civilization. Like Wilson, Cobb wanted "peace without victory," but only in the sense that victory should not bring a train of reprisals and counter-oppressions leading to new wars in the future. More definite in his objectives than Wilson, he wanted the Allies to win the war, but not to sow the seeds of revolution and fresh conflicts.

Believing, naturally, that the safety of the nation depended to a large extent upon Wilson's re-election in 1916, he was sagacious enough not to disturb the rather popular impression that it was Wilson who was keeping us out of war. *The World,* during the 1916 campaign, centered its fire to a large degree upon the pro-German or anti-British elements that were supporting Charles Evans Hughes. *The World's* exposures of German propaganda in 1915 ran logically into election year, with further disclosures proving Germany's interest in the defeat of Wilson.

The President himself did not pull his punches on the issue of pro-German support. In an open letter to Jeremiah O'Leary, head of one of the Irish anti-British groups, Mr. Wilson said:

"I would feel deeply mortified to have you or anyone like you vote for me. And since you have access to so many disloyal Americans and I have not, I will ask you to convey this message to them."

Every newspaperman realized, however, that for the average man in the street the determining issue was whether it was true what they said about Wilson, that "he kep' us outta war."

When the ballots were being counted that November, *The World* pulled one of its historic boners. Before the results had come in from the West Coast, including California's then thirteen electoral votes, the newsboys were shouting:

"*World* concedes Hughes' election!"

Even the stalwart Republican organ, the *New York Tribune,* had not gone that far. But since *The World* was supposed to be the voice of the White House, Mr. Hughes went to bed believing he was the next president of the United States.

About three o'clock in the morning, a reporter sought admittance to the Hughes apartment in the Hotel Astor. A secretary said:

"The President cannot be disturbed!"

"When he wakes up," replied the reporter, "just tell him that he is no longer president. Wilson is re-elected."

It was a narrow squeak for Wilson's New Freedom. Wilson had a margin of only twenty-three votes in the Electoral College.

Before Wilson's second inauguration, it was abundantly clear that the United States would soon be at war with Germany. From then until after the Armistice, there was active co-operation between the Administration and the Golden Dome. *The World,* quite generally, was regarded as "Wilson's mouthpiece"—an inaccurate designation, because the paper criticized Wilson quite severely on some of his actions, notably his reappointment of Albert S. Burleson as Postmaster General.

Cobb also found fault with Wilson for not opposing Prohibition vigorously enough. Cobb called the war-born Eighteenth Amendment "a legislative lie—the most shamelessly mendacious piece of legislation that any Congress ever enacted."

When Wilson vetoed the Joint Resolution to submit the Prohibi-

tion Amendment to the states, Cobb called it "not only a highly courageous act, but a highly moral and patriotic act." Congress, of
course, overrode the veto, and the rest of the story everybody knows.

Cobb and Wilson disagreed on the Woman Suffrage Amendment.
The World's policy, up to the final enactment, was against Votes for
Women. JP had set the pattern on that issue. But with the Wilsonian
principle that the president ought to be the party leader, in Congress
as well as in the executive branch, *The World,* including Cobb, was
in sympathy.

"Mr. Wilson," wrote Cobb,. "established something that more
nearly resembled responsible government than anything that had
gone before."

One can only speculate as to how Cobb would have regarded the
New Deal, but it seems a fair assumption that he would have broken
with F.D.R. on the "rejuvenation" of the Supreme Court.

On the supreme issue—war against Germany, with the hope of a
new international order—Cobb and Wilson saw eye to eye. Early in
the morning of April 2 when Wilson had decided to ask Congress
for a declaration of war, he called Cobb, then in Washington, to the
White House. The die was cast, but he wanted Cobb to know the
reasons. Both knew what war meant to democracy, but agreed on
the impossibility of avoiding the conflict.

The World's activities during the war were tremendous. Both at
home and abroad, the newspaper followed the highest Joseph
Pulitzer tradition. John Wanamaker wrote: "It seems as if Joseph
Pulitzer were living his life all over again!" Although the *New
York Times* won the Pulitzer award for public service during 1917
because of its publishing in full so many reports, documents, and
speeches relating to the war, *The World* excelled both in journalism
and in patriotism. Right after the declaration of war, *The World,*
seeking to stimulate recruiting, which was at a low ebb, set the
example by offering all eligible employees the difference between
army pay and their *World* salaries if they would enlist in the Army,
the Navy, or the National Guard. (This did not apply to draftees
later.) The story goes that one reporter enlisted the week after he
had been hired by *The Evening World,* but Ralph Pulitzer made no
exception in his case.

Woodrow Wilson wrote the latter: "I have heard with the greatest pleasure of *The World's* action regarding war service . . . you cannot know what genuine and deep satisfaction such evidences of patriotism excite in me."

Ralph Pulitzer himself enlisted as a lieutenant in the Naval Reserve, being assigned to coast patrol duty aboard a submarine chaser. He had the chaser built at his own expense and gave it to the Navy.

At *The World's* suggestion, American and Allied aviators flew over the German lines, dropping hundreds of thousands of copies of President Wilson's address to Congress, printed in German and bearing the American flag. This was the first instance of pamphlet bombing, so far as the United States is concerned.

The World raised the funds for a gift to "Papa" Joffre, hero of the Marne, when he came to America with René Viviani in 1917. The memorial was a gold replica of the Statue of Liberty. Sixty thousand persons witnessed the presentation in Central Park—the only time managing editor Charles M. Lincoln ever got stage fright.

World employees subscribed to $130,000 worth of First Liberty Loan bonds. Out of 150 *World* men at the war front, five were killed and six wounded.

The World fought against fraudulent and wasteful war charities. Beginning with an exposé of an "Army and Navy Bazaar" which took in $72,000 and netted only $754 to buy comfort kits for soldiers and sailors, the crusade, conducted by the writer under Swope's direction, resulted in widespread investigation and corrective legislation; war grafters were convicted and wasteful "committees" abolished. Out of 534 war charities investigated, 384 were put out of business.

In connection with the big "Hero Land" bazaar at the Grand Central Palace, *The World* published an approved list of war charities which did not include many of the high-sounding "committees" with prominent names. Several of the latter were British. There was a terrific uproar. Major (former Captain) Norman G. Thwaites, the former *World* man, who was then attached to the British Intelligence office in New York, went around telling his friends that H.B.S. was "pro-German" and would be "presently attended to." He had to make a meal of those words.

The World campaigned successfully for Daylight Saving as a war measure and also for War Food Gardens. People were encouraged to "Save for Hoover."

On the political front, *The World* campaigned unsuccessfully against John F. Hylan, the Tammany-Hearst candidate for mayor. W. P. Beazell's admirable series entitled "Who is John F. Hylan?" —exposing the candidate's adventures in Black Diamond Coal and the Lawrence School of Public Speaking—failed to turn public opinion in favor of re-electing John Purroy Mitchel. Hylan sued *The World* for $1,000,000, but dropped the action right after election, since it became obvious that neither Tammany nor Hearst would foot the legal expenses. Mitchel, during the campaign, was lampooned by the Hearst papers as being petted by William K. Vanderbilt, and exclaiming to his wife with delight: "My dear, Mr. Vanderbilt called me Jack!" After election the retiring mayor enlisted in the Army Air Corps and was killed in a practice flight. *The World* tried to raise funds for a Mitchel Memorial, but without much luck.

"NEVER LACK SYMPATHY WITH THE POOR."

Even in the stresses of war, *The World* did not forget JP's injunction to fight for the underdog.

Emil Monjelard, a middle-aged French army volunteer, upon returning to America from the Western front in 1918, found that the lots which he had purchased for a modest home on Long Island, had been sold for unpaid taxes in the trifling sum of $8.50. A tax-lien shark, who had bought title at public sale, demanded $650 to return Monjelard's property.

Monjelard had paid his taxes regularly. What he did not know was that when he bought the lots there was a concealed delinquency of back taxes. Bewildered, he did what thousands of New Yorkers had fallen into the habit of doing—he wrote to *The World*. The late Van Ness Harwood, a top-notch investigator-reporter, was assigned to the case. Harwood discovered that Sergeant Monjelard was only one of many thousands who had lost property through the operations of a Long Island tax-shark ring. At the same time he found that many other thousands of the thrifty poor class had been defrauded by land companies which had bought large tracts, under blanket mortgage, and then split them up into building lots to be sold on the installment plan. The buyers never obtained title.

The World's exposé induced Mayor Hylan to appoint an investigating committee, headed by Nathan Hirsch, wealthy cotton merchant and philanthropist. At Hirsch's request, Harwood was assigned to work with the committee, with his salary paid by *The World*. The campaign had far-reaching consequences: through the committee's efforts, and the attendant publicity, 9,500 parcels of land, valued at $5,000,000 and lost to purchasers through the tax-lien system, were restored to the owners. Many other buyers, defrauded by land companies, obtained title to their lots. The legislature passed corrective legislation. One of the new statutes made it a felony to sell lots on the installment plan without putting the buyer's money into a trust fund, to insure final delivery.

At Mr. Hirsch's request, the late Samuel Untermyer, distinguished New York lawyer, undertook a collateral investigation, establishing that the building business in New York was controlled by a corrupt ring. This led to the Lockwood Inquiry, of which more anon.

Nathan Hirsch in a report to Mayor Hylan:

"Harwood's remarkable ability and untiring efforts have done much toward the success of the Committee."

The World also pioneered in the encouragement of aviation during the war period. In 1919, the three Pulitzer brothers established the five-thousand-dollar Pulitzer trophy for the longest single flight. The winner for three successive years could keep the trophy. Winner for the first year was Captain Mansell R. James, Canadian war ace, who flew from Atlantic City, New Jersey, to Boston. On his return flight, James was lost, and no trace was ever found of his Sopwith-Camel plane. The Aero Club of America had failed to provide adequate maps for the contestants.

Billy Sunday, the evangelist, was big news for *The World* in wartime. After sensational success at saving souls throughout the nation, Billy, in 1917, decided to storm the Capital of Sin, the Metropolis of Iniquity, the Swamp of Perdition, the Gateway to Hell, the Sodom and Gomorrah of the Modern World (these are Revivalist terms), Babylon-on-the-Subway, New York City!

He did pretty well at that. Some 98,000 sinners hit the sawdust trail, and Billy donated $120,000 to the Red Cross and the Y.M.C.A. for war work.

The World's revival staff was headed by the late Joseph Jefferson O'Neill, who was friendly to Billy and at the same time not unfriendly to John Barleycorn. O'Neill's graphic, human accounts of the revival sessions pleased the evangelist and his friends immensely. At the end of at least one prayer a day, Billy would say:

"And, oh, yes, Lord, don't forget to bless Joe O'Neill—he's a good scout, Lord."

Exclusive to The World, from the Eastern front: January 19, 1918 (by Arno Dosch-Fleurot)—Kerensky is accused by the Bolsheviki of having betrayed the Revolution.

January 20 (from Petrograd)—The Russian Constitutional Assembly dies at birth.

February 19 (by Arno Dosch-Fleurot)—"The Bolshevist revolution would not have taken place, a separate armistice would not have been signed with Germany, but for a whole series of mistakes toward Russia by the Allied Governments."

March 3, to *The World* (confidential)—"No A.P. man in Petrograd so I am filing full and urgent morning and evening stories and intend to stick to end." (Signed) Dosch-Fleurot.

The treaty between Germany and Russia was signed at Brest-Litovsk, Poland, on July 14. *The World* editorial used this as an object lesson to the Allied powers to urge a clearer definition of war aims.

August 18—Dosch-Fleurot begins a series of articles describing the red terror in Russia. Washington gets more information from *The World* than from diplomatic sources.

November 24—Dosch-Fleurot reaches Berlin, an exile, so far as Communist Russia is concerned.

FLASHES FROM THE WESTERN FRONT.

By Lincoln Eyre.

January 27, 1918—"Pershing's force is a real army now . . . fit for battle."

February 4—German-American artillery duel.

March 11—Germans bombard U.S. positions in Lorraine sector. "Our boys bear up well."

March 12—"We have taken our revenge."

The World ran a series of articles on alien prison camps in this country, proving that Germany had no excuse for mistreating American prisoners of war.

After prolonged digging for evidence, and many hearings, *The World* obtained freedom for Charles Stielow, an upstate New York farmer, sentenced to die for the murder of Charles B. Phelps and a housekeeper. In this investigation, the new science of "finger-printing of bullets" first appeared. Governor Whitman, pardoning Stielow, gave full credit to *The World*. The investigation was by Isaac D. White, head of *The World's* Bureau of Accuracy and Fair Play.

Charles S. Hand of *The World* campaigned for lower telephone rates, maintaining that the New York Telephone Company, then under government control, was earning millions more than the eight per cent "fair return." The company reduced its rates.

As the war tide rounded the corner in 1918 and it became apparent that Germany and Austria would accept Wilson's fourteen points, the President turned once more to Frank I. Cobb. Dropping his editorial duties for the time, Cobb became a member of Colonel E. M. House's mission which went abroad to prepare the ground for the Armistice.

Before Cobb sailed, Wilson had already made up his mind to attend the coming Peace Conference in person; to this plan Cobb gave a preliminary assent, but on reaching London, the editor was amazed and shocked at the attitude of British and French leaders. He feared that the Allies were going to impose ruinous terms upon Germany and that Wilson's dream of international peace would crash. Under the circumstances, he felt deeply that it would be a mistake for Wilson to attend the Peace Conference. In his diary, Cobb noted "general comment" in Paris that since Wilson had maneuvered the Central Powers into surrender, the President could now be pushed aside while the Allies dictated their own terms. "There is a certainty," he wrote, "that the chauvinistic elements will try to wreck the President's program."

Colonel House appeared to feel the same way about it, but neither of them could persuade Wilson to give up his dream of coming to Europe in the role of world peacemaker. The late Edward R. Stettinius, Sr., in charge of co-ordination and purchase of supplies for the Allied forces, also shared Cobb's misgivings about the results of a dictated peace.

(E. R. Stettinius, Jr., is co-ordinator of American defense materials in the "all-out aid to Britain" program of today. Another curious parallel between 1918 and 1941 is that Congressman Charles A. Lindbergh, Sr., defeated on the war issue in 1916, got out a booklet entitled "Why Your Country Is at War." It was suppressed by the Federal Government.)

After the Armistice, Cobb felt that his mission had been a complete failure. He recorded that Herbert Hoover and General Pershing agreed with him that it was a mistake for President Wilson to come to Europe. When the members of the American Peace Commission were announced—Wilson, Secretary of State Robert Lansing, Colonel House, General Tasker A. Bliss, and Henry White—Cobb called it "a purely personal commission of excellent gentlemen, who, apart from the President, have no political standing."

"The President," he added, "has increased his troubles at home and abroad. Root should have been a member, also Knox [Philander C. Knox, former secretary of state] or Borah."

Cobb felt that Colonel House was not representing the truth about Europe strongly enough, and he therefore decided to make a last desperate appeal to Wilson in person. He sailed for the United States—too late! The President had already left. The ships passed in midocean.

Mr. and Mrs. Wilson were aboard the *S.S. George Washington,* bound for Europe and disaster. Preceding them across the Atlantic, the *S.S. Orizaba* carried the greatest collection of newspapermen ever assembled on one ocean. The ship was filled with editors, correspondents, experts, and run-of-the-mill reporters, all bound for the Versailles Peace Conference. *The World* delegation on the *Orizaba* included Ralph Pulitzer, editor, president of the Press Publishing

Company; Charles M. Lincoln, managing editor; Louis Seibold, chief political writer; and Herbert Bayard Swope, city editor, on special duty.

Cable from Paris, December 18, 1918:

"FLORENCE D. WHITE,

"THE WORLD, NEW YORK.

"TELL COBB AND SEYMOUR FOR EDITORIAL GUIDANCE I HAVE RE-VERSED VIEWS ORIGINALLY OPPOSED TO PRESIDENT'S COMING. POSSIBLY NEEDLESS TO EMPHASIZE BUT DON'T LET FALSE CONSIS-TENCY CONTINUE REPETITION OF OPPOSITION. . . ."

(Signed) "RALPH PULITZER."

The *Orizaba* had been scheduled to leave at noon, December 1, 1918, from Hoboken. Newspapermen were requested to be on board not later than 10.30 A.M. An hour later all of the press were accounted for except H.B.S. As noon approached, Mr. Pulitzer and the others became anxious. Telephone calls to the Swope residence and *The World* office produced only the word that so far as anybody knew, Mr. Swope was en route to the ship.

The noon deadline found *The World* men imploring the captain to hold the ship. He agreed to wait one-half hour, after which, he said, H.B.S. would either have to swim, fly the ocean, or crash the *George Washington*. However, nothing really drastic resulted. Just as the second time limit was expiring an electric truck sped along the pier, and sitting atop the pile of baggage was journalism's Paul Bunyan. After getting aboard he kept shouting last minute instructions to Alex Schlosser until the ship pulled out.

[H.B.S. always liked to dramatize his arrivals and departures on occasions like this. When Ralph Pulitzer came back from Europe one time in the late twenties, H.B.S. arranged to go down the Bay on the Government cutter to meet the Pulitzer ship at quarantine. But when the cutter left the Battery, there was no sign of Swope. Just as the cutter came alongside the steamship, a small motorboat dashed out from Staten Island, bringing the belated editor. Ship newsman reporter Johnny Parker greeted him with delight.

["I knew you'd make it, Boss," Parker exclaimed, "but I really thought you'd come down the Bay on a battleship!"]

In addition to those coming over on the *Orizaba, The World's* staff at Versailles also included James M. Touhy, head of the London Bureau; Lincoln Eyre, brilliant young member of the Paris Bureau who had turned in an impressive list of scoops from the Western front; Arno Dosch-Fleurot, previously noted; Cyril Brown, from the Berlin Bureau; and William Cook.

Louis Seibold accompanied President Wilson to London, Rome, and other cities, obtained an interview with Pope Benedict XV, and described the American base at Brest. Lincoln Eyre penetrated into Germany and gave a first-hand description of conditions under the spread of Bolshevism and civil strife.

The European plenipotentiaries who met at Versailles were for the most part unfamiliar with American newspaper methods. They were amazed to find that the journalists from the United States took seriously Wilson's dictum, "open covenants openly arrived at." European diplomatic tradition was all to the contrary. Overriding Wilson's preferences in the matter, the Council, representing the principal Allied and Associated powers, voted to exclude the press from all the sessions at Versailles.

American journalists protested strongly, and the rest of the press joined in. Swope was chosen chairman of the entire Fourth Estate to lead the fight for publicity. The battle was not wholly successful. The Council decided to admit a few chosen press representatives at the opening plenary session. As a token of appreciation, the press failed to elect Swope among the few to be admitted. It made no difference; he got in anyway. He dressed in the formal diplomatic manner, with high hat, cutaway coat, wing collar, spats, and all the rest of it, and passed through the outer guard in a military car.

The World's representatives at Versailles covered the peace conference in the same fashion as they would have covered a national political convention in Chicago, Cleveland, or Philadelphia. Among the outstanding beats by *The World* at Versailles were:

By Swope: Exclusive verbatim report of the second plenary session at which the Covenant of the League of Nations was first introduced.

By Swope: Exclusive summary of the Reparations Clauses of the Treaty.

By Swope: Exclusive summary of proposed amendments to the

Covenant. With these changes, the document became practically what it was on final adoption. The New York *Herald* described this as "the greatest journalistic beat of the Conference."

By Swope: First news of Italy's withdrawal from the Conference, in the argument over Fiume. First authentic figures on the cost of the War.

The Versailles Treaty was signed on June 28. Mr. Wilson submitted it to the Senate on July 10. It was rejected. The War was over, and the foundation laid for the next one.

By the time *The World's* special group had returned to New York, it was plain to everybody in the office that Swope was much too important a personage ever to be city editor again.

It was also apparent that Charles M. Lincoln, who had acted as office manager and co-ordinator of *World* activities during the peace conference, was thinking over the advice formulated by another *World* man, Joseph Johnson, who was Fire Commissioner of New York under Gaynor. The advice was: "Look around you now and choose the nearest exit. In case of fire, walk . . ."

After Swope had been installed in a special office with the designation "advisory editor," and the pleasant duty of finding fault with the paper, managing editor Lincoln remembered the Johnson slogan. He took a walk.

11. Postwar Fever

"What cause can be given for the gigantic collapse of the rule of intelligence, or morals and of law. . . . What has happened to the great democracies of the world. . . . Have they failed to give this modern world that leadership which it had to have if it was to move forward on a high plane of liberal and increasingly competent democracy?"—NICHOLAS MURRAY BUTLER (January 1, 1941)

IN THE stressful period immediately following the Treaty of Versailles, *The World* teetered uncertainly on its political axis. Cobb startled the country one day by proposing: "FOR PRESIDENT— HERBERT HOOVER!"

The editorial stated that *The World* did not know, nor care, about Mr. Hoover's political affiliations, that his record as Chairman for the Relief Commission in Belgium and as United States Food Administrator was sufficient to command the confidence of the nation.

Neither the Democratic party nor the Republicans responded to the suggestion with any great alacrity. Some people were saying that Mr. Hoover was not even a citizen.

Many Democrats were hoping that Woodrow Wilson would run again. Many others were praying that he would not be a candidate. The draft-Wilson movement died aborning when Cobb in *The World,* on the basis of authentic personal knowledge (always a dangerous thing for an editor to rely upon), declared flatly: "No Third Term!"

"The World," he wrote, "does not believe that President Wilson under any circumstances will consider a renomination; nor could any sincere friend of the President desire that his splendid career should end in such an anticlimax."

Valiantly, but with no more success than King Canute achieved,

363

when he tried to stop the tides of the sea, *The World* struggled
against the wave of "return to normalcy." In vain *The World*
argued, reasoned, pleaded for the United States to adhere to the
League of Nations. Wilson's time had passed. The long day was
over. His work was done, undone, as it turned out.

Cobb, too, was dying. He did not know it, or if he did, kept it
to himself. He knew that Wilson was dying, but he never mentioned the coincidence. "Old W.W.," he said during his last illness,
"wants me to take up golf." There was only a month and a half between their deaths—Cobb's on December 21, 1923, and Wilson's
on February 3, 1924. The statement made by Wilson on the occasion of Cobb's death was the last one ever signed by the retired
President.

New times, new trends, new tunes, new faces. Calvin Coolidge
had emerged as the "strong, silent man"; he had remained silent as
governor of Massachusetts while the Boston police were clamoring
for better wages and better working conditions (the station houses
were deplorable); he remained grimly mum while Police Commissioner Curtis gave his ultimatum; he did nothing for several days
after the strike was called and mobs raged through Boston, smash-
ing windows. Only after Mayor Peters, acting under an old and forgotten statute, had called out the militia in Boston, did the governor
act. He called out more troops and superseded the mayor. After that
the police were beaten, and Coolidge refused to let them return to
their jobs. "Deserters, not strikers," he called them, and the nation
seemed to applaud. Coolidge was the logical Republican choice for
vice-president in 1920, a trifle too wiry to head a "normalcy" ticket.

The new era was pushing aside the old one as ruthlessly and relentlessly as jazz replaced ragtime, and swing later supplanted jazz.

The Hearst newspapers, riding the wave of the new isolationism,
clamored for the end of "Wilsonian Internationalism." The Senate
put the sign of death on the League of Nations. The Republicans,
recognizing the strength of Hughes, threw a sop to the Geneva ad-
herents, by a mild endorsement of the World Court.

In *The World* organization, a new era also arrived. H.B.S. became executive editor. "Managing Editor," the title usually bestowed
upon the man chiefly responsible for news, was not dramatic enough,

not comprehensive enough, to fit the new protagonist. Swope's functions, we learned, extended not only to the news, but to the "features," and came dangerously near treading on the editorial-writing department headed by Cobb.

The earlier fascination which H.B.S. exercised upon Ralph Pulitzer at the outbreak of the war, leading to his appointment as city editor, was doubled, tripled, and quadrupled by Swope's mastery at Versailles. R.P. was completely hypnotized by the magnetic charm of the more dominant personality. The only chance for any independent Pulitzer judgment was during the periods of the day when Swope was absent from the office or not on the telephone. During the racing season, R.P. had a reasonable opportunity to think things out for himself.

JP's eldest son must not be underestimated. He liked to work. He liked to write editorials. He enjoyed the grind of following the news and analyzing it. He accepted gladly the task of planning for *The World* while Joseph the Second conducted the successful *St. Louis Post-Dispatch*. (The younger brother, Herbert, did not become a power to be reckoned with until much later in the twenties.)

As far as JP's commandments for *The World* were concerned— to fight for progress and reform—and his admonition to the sons to devote themselves to useful work, Ralph Pulitzer could truthfully have said, in Franklin Delano Roosevelt phraseology, "I accept the platform one hundred per cent." His weakness was not in the direction of that "enervating luxury" which JP so greatly deplored; he did not care much for "society"; he had no political ambitions. His aspirations were all for the continued growth, influence, and success of *The World*.

Weakness lay in the fact that he leaned toward intellectualism rather than toward the everyday thoughts and feelings of the man in the street; he was, in the political sense, a liberal; but in all things not sufficiently fundamental; perhaps because he had not come to his position in life via the rough route, but rather by the smooth, paved highway on which there were no struggles for existence.

Ralph Pulitzer, in brief, was a thinker, not a fighter. He committed the mistake of believing that idealism would prevail somehow, but somehow without dust and heat. He was not forceful.

Swope, on the other hand, was in all respects emphatic. He was by instinct, experience, and long practice, a gate crasher; a beater-down of obstacles and opposition; a dominator; a skillful opportunist; a showman and a salesman; a quick, sharp thinker, but not a logician; an eager grasper of high-lights and display points, but not a searcher for the deep things. He thought in terms of places, dates, people, actions, fights, contests, races, bright sayings, clever phrases, smart behavior.

Mrs. Ogden Reid, guiding spirit of the New York *Herald Tribune,* furnished an excellent keynote to H.B.S.'s internal cosmos when she introduced him at the *Herald Tribune* Forum in 1940, as honor guest on the "Information, Please" radio program. She said: "So far as I know, Herbert Bayard Swope has never, up to the present, been asked a question that he could not answer." This was correct. Swope always had an answer, but not always the right one.

Swope was sufficiently happy when going places and doing things in a manner that would command attention. He liked to be admired, preferably by people whose opinions were important; he did not mind being belittled (behind his back, of course) by persons of no consequence; he enjoyed being surrounded by people who were smart, or wealthy (preferably both), or fashionable, or popular, or important. His technique of compelling attention covered a wide range of mechanisms, ranging all the way from superior knowledge of something to the familiar device of always coming late on all occasions.

The other principal characters in the last decade of *The World* were:

Walter Lippmann, editorial writer, coming first as an assistant to Cobb; succeeding as chief editorial writer after Cobb's death. Beginning his brilliant career as editor, essayist, commentator, analyst and student of public affairs on the staff of the *New Republic,* Lippmann went to Paris as an advisor to the American Delegation at the Versailles Conference, after which he joined *The World.*

Florence D. White, general manager. For years—beginning long before JP's death—four men had been striving for supremacy in the business office downstairs: White, Don C. Seitz, Bradford Merrill, and John Norris. And for a long time each of these executives had an office exactly like the others; their functions were confused and overlapping—the logical result of JP's theory that two or more men on every job will insure efficiency. It did nothing of the kind. The Big Four watched each other, and the best watcher won. Norris went to the *Times* and died; Bradford Merrill went to the *American*. Don Seitz went to the business management of *The Evening World* and was finally forced out. Only White remained.

Arthur Krock, personal advisor to R.P. on matters of general news and politics, now Washington columnist for the *Times*.

Claude G. Bowers, editorial writer for *The Evening World*, historian, politician, author of *Hamilton and Jefferson*, Jackson Day dinner speaker, Democratic keynoter of the 1928 Convention, became U. S. Ambassador to Spain, but stayed mostly in France.

Harold Stanley Pollard (JP's former secretary), who bore the title of "editor" on *The Evening World;* quiet, forceful writer; not afraid of judges, as we shall see.

Others taking part in the drama included Eugene J. Young, foreign editor, who later occupied the same position on the *Times;* J. Earl Clauson and William Preston Beazell, assistant managing editors under Swope (note that they were assistant managing editors and not assistant executive editors. There was only one executive editor and they were his prophets). James S. Griffith, cable and telegraph news editor; Herbert Gaston, who had the night shift on the same job, now Under-secretary of the Treasury in Washington; myself as city editor, succeeding John H. Gavin, who became sports editor, and later was Surrogate of Hudson County, New Jersey; James Robbins, sports editor, now yachting editor of the *Times;* Isaac D. White, director of the Bureau of Accuracy and Fair Play; Louis Weitzenkorn, Sunday news editor; Paul Palmer, Sunday magazine editor, succeeding John O'Hara Cosgrave.

Upon becoming chief of the news realm, H.B.S. required a little time to blow the men down whom he either did not like or who did not like him. His first task, naturally, was to provide a suitable office for himself. The old managing editor's cubby-hole was knocked out and a new partition extended far out into the city room. The interior of the Swope quarters was fitted up with something old and something new,—a couple of high-backed chairs from the Joseph Pulitzer days and two enormous early Baumann desks. He had some rugs, too, the first ever seen on the twelfth floor.

Before the New Order was firmly in the saddle, however, there were a few odds and ends from the War era to be cleaned up. In Washington, the Harding administration had inherited the problem of disposing of surplus army supplies: canned foods; boots and shoes; olive-drab shirts; undershirts, socks; saddles and bridles (the War Department in 1917-1918 still thought cavalry would be useful in France).

The goods were disposed of, for the most part, by private sale to speculators who in turn unloaded them wherever they could. A large quantity of the foodstuffs was taken by the Department of Markets in New York.

Some members of Congress suspected either graft or favoritism and demanded an investigation by the Department of Justice, then under Attorney General Harry M. Daugherty, the man who brought about the nomination of Warren Gamaliel Harding for President by the Republicans in 1920. Head of the "G-men" in the Federal Bureau of Investigation at that time was William J. Burns, internationally famous detective.

Being assigned to the story (this was before I took the city desk), I went to Washington and conferred with Charles Michelson, then chief of *The World's* Bureau, now Director of Publicity for the Democratic National Committee. Michelson pooh-poohed the story. However, by poking around the national capital, I did discover something mighty queer about the Department of Justice. One of Burns's confidential investigators, on the "private payroll," was none other than the notorious Gaston B. Means, fake sleuth, confidence man, swindler, and manufacturer of fraudulent evidence.

Means had come into front-page publicity in 1917 in connection with the murder of Mrs. Maude A. King, a Chicago heiress whom Means had swindled out of large sums of money. Mrs. King was killed under mysterious circumstances at Concord, South Carolina, Means's home town. Harry M. Friend, a reporter for the *Chicago*

NORTH

Tribune, later for *The World,* first broke the story. Means was tried, but acquitted by the home-folks jury.

During the war, Means did undercover work for the German government, while his friend Burns looked out for British interests. Means is reported to have cleaned up handsomely. During the Harding regime, he gained the confidence of Evalyn Walsh McLean, Washington society leader, and when the Lindbergh baby was kidnaped Means managed to swindle Mrs. McLean out of $150,000 on the pretense that he could ransom the child, already murdered. For that crime he went to prison, where he died.

The appointment of this unsavory person to the Department of Justice looked strange indeed; but—embarrassing moment—I learned that our Washington Bureau knew all about the Means matter, as Means was an old acquaintance of "Buck" Bryant, one of the Washington staff. *The World* published the story on page one, but the rest of the inquiry was dropped, under orders. Too bad we did not follow the trail at that time, leading to the little green house in K Street, and the other scandals of the Harding administration.

The Department of Justice kept Mr. Means out of sight for a while until people forgot. He reappeared in connection with the Teapot Dome scandals. He was assisting McLean in trying to block the Senate investigation. A series of mysterious telegrams were introduced in evidence, but they meant nothing until *The World,* through a fortunate stroke, obtained the key, which proved to be an old code of the Department of Justice, undoubtedly furnished by Means.

JP's policy was never to drop a story involving the public interest until you have gone clear to the bottom of it. Looking back now, we can see how *The World* in its last ten years was too easily satisfied with routine coverage when it should have been leading the hunt. Right at the outset of his executive editorship, H.B.S. threw cold water on the Lockwood investigation.

This was an inquiry by a committee of the New York Legislature, with Senator Charles C. Lockwood as chairman. The inquiry was a direct result of *The World's* own exposé of the tax-lien evil and the land frauds. Samuel Untermyer, working with the Hirsch committee, had found evidence of a corrupt monopoly in the building industry. He turned his minutes over to Tammany's District Attorney, Edward Swann, and nothing happened. Under prodding from *The World*, and from Governor Alfred E. Smith, the legislature ordered the probe which Swann had avoided.

Untermyer was aided by Deputy Attorney General Berger, Emory R. Buckner, William A. De Ford (out of deference to Hearst), Stanley Richter, and Van Ness Harwood of *The World*. The other papers also furnished reporters who acted as investigators. The opportunity for public service was golden. The economic backlash of the war had left a national shortage in housing, a wave of rent profiteering, and a general paralysis of building. This was the beginning of the Dry Era, national prohibition having just become the law of the land.

Revelations by the Lockwood inquiry were (1) A carnival of graft and price fixing; widespread extortion from building contractors by business agents of the Building Trades Council of the American Federation of Labor; (2) Prices of building materials boosted as high as 300 per cent—prices and supplies both being controlled by the ring; (3) Collusive bidding on public contracts (Exhibit A, the new $20,000,000 courthouse in New York)—all bids controlled by "The Code of Practice" administered by the building czar, John T. Hetrick. (He later went to prison.)

Three grand juries went into action. Indictments were returned against contractors, officials of the Building Trades Council, and dealers. The city canceled the courthouse contract and ordered a rebidding. But for some reason or other, H.B.S. did not like the story. To make things worse, Untermyer kept telling *The World* how he thought the matter should be handled. Finally Swope shouted to Harwood:

"Tell Mr. Untermyer that I will not permit *The World* to become his personal organ!"

Harwood resigned from the staff, and the Lockwood investigation eventually evaporated in "remedial legislation." But there was one little flare-up. Bob Scallon, who was "pecking around" on the investigation, made a slip. Untermyer, who had gone South for a rest, sent word to Beazell that "a deal" had been made with the District

Attorney's office by which "Fishhooks" McCarthy, a building contractor with high connections at Tammany Hall, was to plead guilty to conspiracy and get a suspended sentence. Beazell turned the tip over to the city desk and I gave it to Scallon.

Bob reported that he had verified the story. He said he had learned that McCarthy had been given a private hearing in Justice McAvoy's chambers. McAvoy was not a friend of *The World*. Scallon wrote the story that night and it came out on page one. Next day, Justice McAvoy cited Beazell, Scallon, and Ruel P. Smith (night city editor) for criminal contempt of court. At the preliminary hearing, H.B.S. was able to prove that he knew nothing about the story (although he was executive editor), having been absent from the office all evening. Justice McAvoy took a strong dislike to the city editor, calling me "the most evasive witness I have ever heard" and adding me to the list of defendants. At the subsequent trial, we were defended by John B. Stanchfield's office. Stanchfield's recommendation was: "Put Scallon on the stand before McAvoy and let those two Irishmen fight it out." Much more effective was the quiet assistance of Louis Seibold, who discussed the matter with McAvoy privately at the Manhattan Club.

Ruel Smith and I were acquitted; Beazell and Scallon given suspended sentences. "Fishhooks" McCarthy went on trial and got off with a fine. The Lockwood investigation became a legend and the chairman became a Supreme Court Justice. The matter did not acutely interest *The World*, which by this time was well started on its dizzy career through the social and political currents of the twenties.

The World goes haywire in quest of talent. "We must be intelligent," is the word that flashes through the shop. We realize it when we see H. G. Wells covering the Arms Limitation Conferences in Washington and reporting political conventions, along with the famous Spanish novelist, Blasco Ibañez, author of *The Four Horsemen of the Apocalypse*.

The fifteen-thousand-dollar holdup and murder of Frederick Parmenter, paymaster's guard at South Braintree, Massachusetts, gets only passing notice. The arrest of Nicola Sacco and Bartolomeo

Vanzetti, anarchists accused of the crime, evokes no editorial display. How are we to know history in the making? Besides, everything else is thrown aside to make room for the Wall Street bomb explosion . . . thirty killed, one hundred injured, $2,000,000 in property damage.

In its leisure moments, *The World* is experimenting with the Belin process for the transmission of photographs by wire. Photographs are exchanged between *The World* and the *St. Louis Post-Dispatch*. It is a highly interesting process, but Belin and *The World* make the mistake of showing it to too many experts. Other processes for photograph transmission leap ahead of M. Belin's, and *The World* loses the leadership.

The new intellectual regime is earmarked by the appearance of the "Op Ed" page—the one opposite the editorial page. *The World* goes into rhapsodies announcing the arrival from the *Tribune* of Heywood Broun, and his column, "It Seems to Me." H.B.S. makes a further raid on Mrs. Reid's menagerie of genius and extracts Franklin Pierce Adams, native son of Chicago, with his "Conning Tower." The new salaries, whispered around the city room, cause the staff to gasp—$350 per week is the word. Swope's own salary is $52,000 plus bonuses from the one-tenth interest in the newspaper trust.

The ascendancy of Lippmann in the Dome is attested by editorial emphasis on disarmament, disarmament! Battleships breed wars, *The World* contends, and pours its approval on the Hughes program for the Washington Conference. How can *The World* suspect that history will write the sardonic footnote to this unpreparedness crusade? We know now that military weakness on the part of the democracies only invites aggression on the part of the dictator nations. . . .

Cobb was a favorite in the city rooms of both *Worlds,* morning and evening. He liked to talk with the reporters who were working on any story in which he was interested. He always wanted the "lowdown" on a situation, even though he could not print it.

Lippmann is the opposite type. He likes to think things out for himself. He is a keen analyst, but facts are sometimes annoying—they have a way of upsetting theories.

Lippmann's arrival was so unostentatious that few in the city room knew him by sight. Charge up Bad Break No. 1 to city editor Barrett. The first time Lippmann came to my desk, I had just telephoned to the editorial auditor, E. E. Bowns, to send up a messenger. (Mr. Bowns had installed the messenger system to save Western Union and Postal charges. His messengers were a remarkable collection of scholarly-looking gentlemen who took longer to get to a given point than it once required to get from the Nile to the Jordan.) Consequently, when the quiet, well-dressed, scholarly-looking man came to my desk and started to address me, I was annoyed.

"Sit down and wait," I told him. "We'll have the package ready for you in just a moment!"

"Excuse me," he said. "I am Walter Lippmann. I wanted to ask you about the housing story."

Seibold and John J. Leary, Jr., the labor reporter, did much to maintain the old *World* tradition, in the early twenties. Leary was awarded the 1920 Pulitzer Prize for good reporting on the national coal strike. Seibold won the 1922 prize for his interview with President Wilson in 1921, the first ever granted by a chief executive while in office. Seibold also did a remarkable series on the spread of profiteering. It was Seibold who exposed the huge fund raised for the attempted nomination of General Leonard A. Wood for President in 1920. William P. Beazell and Russell B. Porter campaigned for better subway service, and Beazell did a series on the spread of the luxury craze throughout the nation.

The World took only casual notice of the fact that the results of the 1920 presidential election were broadcast for the first time. Station KDKA in Pittsburgh gave bulletins on the returns, thereby foreshadowing the end of the day when "Extra! Extra!" gave first word of election results.

So far as radio is concerned, *The World* has a blind spot. The revival of the Ku Klux Klan in the South is treated at first as a distressing but not transcendent social phenomenon. The Klan grows and grows; adopting the new high pressure sales technique, agents of the hooded order appear in all sections, getting a nice rakeoff on all the ten-dollar memberships (including hood and gown); house-to-house coffee salesmen become Klan propagandists.

The World wakes up with a jolt in the summer of 1921 when a former official of the order comes to the office with a complete file on the Klan: the ritual, the roster of national and state officers, and an impressive dossier of incidents and outrages. A sale is arranged; *The World* pays ten thousand dollars and starts the series in the early fall. The effect in Metropolitan New York, with its large Catholic and Jewish population, is tremendous. Great crowds gather outside the Pulitzer Building every night to grab the papers as they come off the press. Out of town, copies of *The World* with the Klan articles begin to sell for fifty cents and a dollar. Washington takes alarm and Congress orders an investigation.

The Pulitzer Prize for Public Service (awarded in 1922), the $500 gold medal, with appropriate flowers, goes to *The World!* The Advisory Committee evidently likes Klan exposés, because the same award for the following year goes to the *Memphis Commercial Appeal*, "for its courageous attitude in the publication of cartoons and the handling of news in reference to the operations of the K.K.K."

Rum Row now makes its appearance outside the twelve-mile limit, but *The World* handles all news about it gingerly. Things everywhere are changing, changing; the cavalcade of news pushes the old traditions into the ragbag. Youth becomes hot, frank, and flamboyant. Freud and psychoanalysis become the badges of well-informed conversation. Atlantic City inaugurates the bathing-beauty contests. Ziegfeld's Follies dominate Broadway along with various "Revues." Messrs. Gallagher and Shean put their trademark on popular conversation.

This is a mad era, no mistake. People react quickly and violently to everything, it seems—ideas, styles, new ways of making or obtaining liquor, new hunches in the stock market—everybody is keeping cool with Coolidge but keeping hot on individual manias.

Samuel Spewack throws a flood of light on certain outbreaks of violence in various countries, including the United States. Spewack traces them to the dingy headquarters of the Sacco-Vanzetti Defense Committee in a small office up a rickety flight of stairs in Boston. There are three typewriters, plenty of paper and stamps. "Click, click, click, went the typewriters and bombs exploded all over the earth," Spewack reports. Workers go on strike at home and abroad. Capitalism, it seems, is about to murder the innocent anarchists from Italy—that's what the typewriters are saying.

(About this time, Boy Sam Spewack meets Girl Bella Cohen in *The World* office and a famous partnership is formed, beginning with the words, "I do.")

Deems Taylor brings a most welcome new era in music criticism and reporting. Deems takes the hocus-pocus aura away from music and brings it inside the door of the average reader. *World* subscribers eagerly grab for his daily and weekly reviews. These they think are even better than Huneker's, whose copy is said to have been read with interest even in the composing room. Furthermore, Deems Taylor breaks down the idea that New York is the hub of the musical world. He goes roaming through the country, writing up the orchestras and other activities in Cleveland, Chicago, Cincinnati, St. Louis.

Jack Dempsey, meanwhile, has become the nation's idol by knocking out France's war-veteran champion, Georges Carpentier. The famous heavyweight bout before a record crowd at Boyle's Thirty Acres, Jersey City, gives Swope an opportunity to go to town. For him this is "My prizefight" indeed. He handles all the assignments, and on the day of the big battle is all over the place—here, there, and everywhere except inside the ring; he is a riot and *The World's* photographic and reportorial display is a knockout. Jack Price, ace photographer, scores the best shot of Carpentier taking the count. This is Swope's diet. *The World* mentions casually that for the first time a championship bout was radiocast from the ringside.

In connection with the Dempsey-Carpentier affair, H.B.S. tried a new experiment. He assigned a girl reporter, Isabel Boyd, to watch the crowd and give a word picture of the reactions on the "sea of faces" in front of her. "Keep your eye," he said, "exclusively on the crowd. Don't, under any circumstances, look at the ring." Lot's wife had an easier assignment. Miss Boyd watched the crowd, all right, up to the moment when Carpentier began to cave. She looked back and turned into a pillar of salt so far as reporting was concerned.

This is the age of mah jongg, bootleg whiskey, bathtub gin, baseball scandal, and Fatty Arbuckle. The Protestant Episcopal bishops take the word "obey" out of the Book of Marriage—or at least make it optional. *World* staff members are getting rich, for the time being, by the purchase of stocks on margin. The Pulitzer Advisory Committee has balanced the equation somewhat by bestowing a prize on Edith Wharton for *The Age of Innocence.*

Louis V. De Foe, *The World's* veteran dramatic critic, dies brokenhearted over the passing of old *World* ways. Heywood Broun takes over the drama critic job for a while, and a high-pressure drive starts to replace Quinn Martin as movie critic. The late Ruth Hale (the first Mrs. Heywood Broun) is highly recommended by certain groups as the ideal one for the job, but Swope resists; by-and-by Alexander Woollcott comes from the *Times* to handle theater criticism and Quinn Martin remains in charge of the movies. H.B.S. leaves no doubt that he is deeply concerned in every department of the paper.

The World began to fly the distress signal in financial matters as early as 1922. In that year, prosperity having taken a temporary slump, it ran a campaign to stimulate general employment. The slogan was "Give jobs for Christmas!" The campaign was reasonably successful, but right after Christmas, the iron ball rolled in the office and there was a sharp reduction in *The World's* own payroll (except at the top).

Christmas bonuses, which had been fairly regular in the past, became highly irregular. One year when we got a bonus, we were "invited" by Ralph Pulitzer to give ten per cent of it to the building fund of the Cathedral of St. John the Divine. We gave.

Old tradition does not die at once. To *The World's* credit must be checked up a masterly story by Charles S. Hand on the defeat of William R. Hearst as candidate for the Democratic gubernatorial nomination. Sometime thereafter Hand and H.B.S. come to the parting of the ways—a natural conflict of temperament.

(Charley Hand went to the *American,* but when the Mayor James J. Walker regime took over in City Hall, Mr. Walker invited Hand to become his secretary. Charley refused. "I'd rather clean streets," he said. Walker balanced the score later on by making Hand Street Cleaning Commissioner.)

The World acquires "Kudos"—a favorite word with Swope. Clare Sheridan, the sculptress, does a series on life in Europe, beginning with a Rudyard Kipling interview. "The United States," he declares, "has garnered the gold of the world and lost its soul!" Mrs. Sheridan is in Turkey when the new nationalist party revolts and Mustapha Kemal Pasha abolishes the harems and substitutes votes for veils.

The *New Statesman* (London) : "First place for vigor and intelligence belongs unmistakably to *The New York World*. Its staff includes a group of clever writers unequaled in America. Its tone is courageously liberal."

Spewack goes to Russia and records the disillusionment of Emma Goldman, the anarchist.

The World wins another Pulitzer Prize with the Martin Tabert case, the lad from North Dakota who was beaten to death in a Florida lumber camp. Samuel D. McCoy writes the series. The Whipping Boss is convicted of murder in the second degree and sent to prison. The lumber company pays twenty thousand dollars to the Tabert family. The credit goes to Eugene J. Young for first "spotting" the possibilities of the story, which came in a letter from North Dakota.

The World goes slightly wacky over Emil Coué, the French doctor-without-diploma. It is Coué who devised the method of getting well through persistent repetition of the magic phrase, "Every day in every way I am getting better and better." We did not try it on *The World,* but through *The World's* efforts Coué came to America and instituted clinics which quickly went out of existence.

Charles Merz looms up as a forceful writer on India and conditions in the Far East. Later he joins the editorial writing staff under Lippmann and ultimately becomes editor of the *Times*. Laurence Stallings graduates from the copy desk after winning numerous prizes for the best headlines, begins a feature entitled "The First Reader," dealing with new books. Later, enriched with the royalties from *What Price Glory?*, which he has written with Maxwell Anderson, also of *The World,* he leaves, and "The First Reader" is taken over by Harry Hansen, who comes from Chicago to inject a refresh-

ingly new style into the book department. Forbes Watson becomes
art critic.

Tower of strength to *The World's* prestige throughout the final
decade is Rollin Kirby the cartoonist, winner of two Pulitzer Prizes,
1922 and 1925.

Comic strips undergo a sharp metamorphosis. H. T. Webster introduces new methods in how to torture your wife and also maintain a poker face in difficult circumstances. Denys Wortman introduces "Metropolitan Movies."

Frank Sullivan begins his climb toward the celebrity class. Coming to *The World* from the *Evening Sun,* Sullivan is successively
rewrite man, reporter, feature-writer, and columnist. His beginning
on *The World* is marred by an unfortunate accident. Frank is on rewrite. Late one afternoon, Svetozar Tonjoroff, formerly of the old
Press, calls up with a tip that Mrs. Charles Carey Rumsey has just
died. I give the information to Sullivan to work on. H.B.S., having
just come in, hears about the story, expresses great personal sorrow,
and gives Frank many details about the lady's career in sculpture.
Frank is so impressed with H.B.S.'s knowledge of the Social Register
that he completely forgets to verify the tip. The story goes into the
first edition. Much excitement, as usual. Fortunately, Mrs. Rumsey's
butler is in Times Square that night and happens to pick up a copy
of *The World.* Knowing that his employer is very much alive, he
calls *The World* and after fighting through the telephone answering
service, manages to inform the city desk. Stop press! Recall editions
if possible! Get out a correction! H.B.S. burns up the telephones.
The World publishes retractions for two days. The lady who has
died is not Mrs. Charles Carey Rumsey, but the first Mrs. David Rumsey of Washington Square. No wonder Sullivan became a humorist!

Old *World* readers deplored the disappearance of the old-style
reporting and campaigning. They shook their heads even more sadly
when the paper began to go in for the occult. We gave generous
amounts of space to Sir Arthur Conan Doyle and his spiritualist
experiences—also to those of Sir Oliver Lodge. This might be considered legitimate, but when *The World* ran a daily series entitled

"Life Beyond the Grave," purporting to be a factual account of somebody's adventures on the other side of Jordan, there was a severe strain on journalistic tradition. No doubt the story was a beat, but was it news? None of the other papers gave us any competition in that field.

ALABAMA CASTS 24 VOTES

All other enterprises were overshadowed by *The World's* campaign to bring the Democratic National Convention to New York in 1924. The suggestion originated outside the office. H.B.S. was not enthusiastic about it at first. "But," he said to me, "we will try." Fred Pasley, Chicago alumnus, was assigned to whip up sentiment and prod organizations like the Merchants' Association and the hotel men into feverish activity. He did a magnificent job. A citizens' committee was quickly formed under the added inspiration of Joseph P. Day, the real-estate auctioneer. New York raised the necessary money, which is always the closing argument with the National Committee.

The convention brought headaches as well as triumphs for *The World*. This was the year when the K.K.K. got back of William Gibbs McAdoo, although he was not a Klan supporter. William Jennings Bryan threw his powerful eloquence to McAdoo, fighting tooth and nail against the growing strength of Alfred E. Smith, who in Bryan's eyes represented Rum, Romanism, and all the rest of it. Bryan was determined not to permit a Repeal plank to get into the platform, or to permit a "wet" to head the ticket.

In the ensuing deadlock between Smith and McAdoo the balloting ran on for sixteen days. Delegates went broke. The hotels were alarmed. Day after day, hour after hour, radio listeners heard the stentorian voice of Governor Brandon proclaiming: "Alabama casts twenty-four votes for Oscar—Double You—UNDERWOOD!" Neither Smith nor McAdoo would yield an inch and Bryan was adamant.

After the one hundredth ballot, it became certain that neither faction could carry the nomination (the two-thirds rule being then in effect) and so there was a compromise in favor of temporary political suicide. The leaders agreed on John W. Davis, the Wall Street lawyer, presented as "Davis of West Virginia," and Governor Charles Bryan of Nebraska (brother of William Jennings) was named as candidate for vice-president.

That clinched the election for Coolidge and Curtis. *The World* went through the motions of supporting Davis, well knowing that defeat was just around the corner.

As far as *The World* was concerned, the convention coverage was brilliant and complete. H.B.S. directed the operation in person, at the same time giving sage advice and comfort to the Smith forces. The problem of supplying Mr. Swope with enough boxes and ring-side seats to accommodate his friends was something to worry the city desk. We ran out of general admissions and press badges until we discovered a way of manufacturing them at low cost. Mazie Clemens did a marvelous job in reporting the women's activities.

A glorious three weeks for H.B.S. On all sides he was pointed out as "the man who brought the convention to New York!" ("Kill him," some of the delegates whispered after the 88th ballot.) At the night sessions, the Swope boxes were always filled with distinguished personages. On one of these occasions, as the convention drew near the close, Mrs. Graham Fair Vanderbilt, sitting just back of H.B.S., leaned over and patted his radiant head.

"You handsome boy!" she murmured, loud enough for the press to hear.

The World's original plan was also to bring the Republican Convention to New York in 1928. But after the Democratic fiasco in 1924, the G.O.P. leaders fervently discouraged the idea and the project was quietly dropped.

William Jennings Bryan's next great emergence onto the front page was in 1925 at the Scopes trial in Dayton, Tennessee. This was where the reportorial genius of *The World's* Dudley Nichols (now one of the best-known writers in Hollywood) came into full play. A grand assignment! Who can ever forget the merciless cross-examination of Bryan by Clarence Darrow, counsel for Scopes? At the conclusion of the trial, Scopes, the high-school teacher, was convicted of violating the Anti-evolution Law and fined one hundred dollars. Bryan died of acute indigestion two days later. But why does *The World Almanac,* in its current 1941 issue, refer to Bryan as "counsel for the defense"?

On with the dance! The New Era marches ahead, strewing the bones of puritanism in its wake. *The World* suddenly discovers one of its intangible assets. The thing that sells the Sunday *World* is the weekly cross-word puzzle. It now becomes a daily feature. The nation becomes cross-word puzzle mad. Margaret Petherbridge, F. G. Hartswick, and Prosper Buranelli publish a cross-word puzzle book.

The World loses Russell Porter because he does not see eye to eye with Swope on the treatment of news. The trouble starts in connection with the "Sonny" Whitney story. Mr. Whitney has been sued by Evan Burroughs Fontaine, chorus girl, for a large amount of money. *The World* has the inside tip on this story; Porter and Joe Butler work it up for publication, but at the last moment, when the interests of accuracy and fair play call for a statement from the Whitney side, Mrs. Harry Payne (Gertrude Vanderbilt) Whitney, sculptress, and mother of the defendant, comes to the office accompanied by eminent counsel. There is a long conference in the executive editor's office, after which H.B.S. announces:

"I shall probably be criticized for this, but I accept the responsibility. I am not going to permit *The World* to be used in this manner."

The relatives of Sterling Adair (Miss Fontaine's ex-husband), who had brought the story to *The World* in the first place, took the information over to the *Daily News,* which was glad enough to publish the story, *The World* having done all the pick and shovel work. Russell Porter took a walk and joined the staff of the *New York Times,* followed some time afterward by Hugh O'Connor. *The World,* during this period, ran a fine school of journalism for other papers. Edwin S. McIntosh, now chief political writer for the *Herald Tribune,* was one of our distinguished graduates from the Swope regime, as was also Charles R. McLendon, who became, for a time, night city editor, also city editor, of the *Herald Tribune.* While McLendon was city editor, one of his younger reporters was Herbert Bayard Swope, Jr. It seems that Swope the Second inherited a preference for coming in late, and after numerous remonstrances, McLendon was obliged to sever the relationship. On his way out, H.B.S., Jr., encountered Stanley Walker, former city editor.

"What's wrong?" asked Walker.

"Oh, nothing," said young Swope. "McLendon let me out for being late."

"That makes everything even," said Walker. "Your father fired him ten years ago."

Other *World* alumni from this period include Dan Williams, editorial writer for the *World-Telegram;* William A. Laurence, science reporter for the *Times* (he left voluntarily to accept a much better salary from the latter paper). As we neared the end of the twenties, there was quite an exodus of staff writers headed for Hollywood—Dudley Nichols, Oliver H. P. Garrett, Herman Mankiewicz. Morrie Ryskind made a brief appearance on our staff as a prelude to a successful career in the dramatic field. He and George S. Kaufman wrote *Of Thee I Sing,* which won the Pulitzer Prize for drama in 1932.

The World, it might be added, had no cast-iron prejudices in favor of Pulitzer prize winners. William Burke Miller of the *Louisville Courier-Journal* won the award for good reporting in 1925 by his excellent coverage of the Mammoth Cave tragedy, in which Floyd Collins was trapped and lost his life. Modestly bearing his Pulitzer laurels, "Skeets," as Mr. Miller is quaintly known, came to *The World.* Before he had much opportunity to shine, however, he was caught in the next rolling of the iron ball.

(J.W.B. to M. H. Aylesworth, president of the National Broadcasting Company, fellow University-of-Coloradoan: "Mr. Miller is a good reporter. He is also a much better singer than you ever were . . . NBC needs him.")

(M.H.A. to J.W.B.—"I resent your aspersion. As a U. of C. glee club tenor I excelled you as a pseudo-baritone. Mr. Miller is added to our news department, with the privilege of singing and announcing on the side.")

(Mammoth Cave impulse finally conquers musical urge and Skeets becomes NBC's ace reporter-from-the-spot, and through successive promotions has now become night manager.)

One of our impromptu reporters in the hectic early twenties was Theodore Dreiser. While writing *An American Tragedy* Mr. Dreiser sought atmosphere and color; he requested *The World* to procure for him access to the death house in Sing Sing prison, with permission to interview the next man in line for the electric chair. A tough problem for the city desk. We had to do a little fiction-writing ourselves. We fixed up our plot so as to make Mr. Dreiser a close blood relative of a condemned gangster; and with that bill of particulars, our Brooklyn court reporter, William A. Lowe, obtained an order from Mr. Justice Mitchell May for Dreiser to confer in the death house with his unfortunate next of kin. Luckily Dreiser lived in Brooklyn, which added verisimilitude to our representations.

Before sending him the pass, I telephoned Dreiser and asked if he wouldn't like to write a story for *The World* about the trip to the death house, and his talk with the man who was about to die.

"I'll tell you, old man," said Dreiser, "I'll write it, but you'll have to pay me five hundred dollars." He finally agreed to give the material after the interview to Dudley Nichols. As for Mr. Justice May, in a Kipling manner of speaking, 'e didn't tell nor make a fuss but winked at Dreiser in his mind's eye when he read *The World* next day. . . .

FOOTNOTES ON TIME AND CHANGE (1920-1925)

In this period, *The World* institutes its "Biggest News of the Week" contests, awarding twelve thousand dollars annually in prizes. Essays by high-school students total more than thirty-two thousand a year. "Greatest extra-mural aid to education I know of"—Dr. Frederick Houk, English department, Stuyvesant High School. In the old days, no contest was required to determine that the biggest news was *The World's* exclusive story.

Outstanding articles include a series by Catharine Brody on job hunting in the West and South; Will Irwin's exposé of the Veterans' Bureau in Washington; Frank L. Hopkins's series on growth of receiverships in the Federal Courts (more coming on that in 1929); a series by staff reporter Henry F. Pringle on child labor conditions in the United States. (This is Professor Pringle of the School of Journalism today; author of biographies of Theodore Roosevelt and William Howard Taft.) *The World* also builds up its religious news department under Mary Spencer.

Last of the A.E.F. troops return from France, marching up Fifth Avenue while bands play, "Yes, we have no bananas."

Will Rogers becomes America's poet-lariat-philosopher, Rudolph Valentino in *The Four Horsemen* makes this country sex-appeal conscious; Will Hays becomes czar of movies; Judge Landis, Czar of Baseball; John L. Balderston becomes head of *The World's* London Bureau; Helen Mallory loses to Helen Wills; the Gershwins color American music ultramarine.

The World becomes a "newspaper of selection"; fine writing begins to take the place of news.

Net profits from *The World* newspapers (three-fifths to Herbert; one-fifth to Ralph; one-tenth to Joseph; one-tenth to "principal editors and managers," chiefly F. D. White and Swope) :

1920, $375,000; 1922, $500,000; 1923, $250,000; 1924, not given; 1925, $250,000.

The year 1925 was the one in which *The World* dropped heavily in circulation after raising its price from two cents to three cents. In 1927 the price went back to two cents, but without much effect. Other economic factors had come into play.

It was during this period that the policy of taking everything out of the enterprise, in the way of profit, and putting nothing aside for the rainy day, nor putting anything back into the business to stimulate growth and expansion, came to be the controlling motive of the management.

At the same time, much effort was being expended on experimentation and exploitation. Every new idea that occurred to the executor-trustees or to the council, attended by the paper's chief executives, meeting three times a week in the Dome, was hailed as the stroke of genius that would put *The World* once more in the forefront of the American press.

The News Syndicate worked valiantly to build up a market for "World Features" including Broun and Adams. Clarence Snyder of the syndicate devised some remarkable sales literature, such as: "Read Heywood Broun—His pen jabs you into clear thinking." "Read F.P.A.—His conning tower looms against the horizon."

The campaigns and crusades began to grow sour, while in the political field, *The World* took a position of secondary importance. In 1925, the paper supported State Senator James J. Walker in the Democratic mayoralty primaries against the renomination of Mayor Hylan. It made little difference, because Tammany had already put the finger on Hylan. Walker easily defeated the straight Republican candidate Waterman. In Washington, *The World's* Bureau poked ironies at the Harding and Coolidge administrations, but failed to expose the iniquities of the Harding ring. (As a matter of fact, the *Denver Post* first revealed the Teapot Dome scandal, but dropped the campaign suddenly after Harry F. Sinclair had paid $350,000 to the late Fred G. Bonfils.) After 1924, *The World* and its writers were conspicuously missing from the Pulitzer Awards for good reporting and for public service. Rollin Kirby, however, won the cartoon prize in 1925 and *The Evening World* took the prize for public service in 1929 for a campaign for the improvement of the administration of justice.

The World started a crusade to stop the sale of ethyl gasoline, contending that its manufacture and distribution was dangerous to health. The campaign, as may be seen from the widespread sale of the product today, was a complete dud.

And in the matter of news exploits, the paper was unlucky. *The World* and the North American Newspaper Alliance obtained exclusive rights to the Amundsen flight to the North Pole, but it turned out to be only "a thrilling effort." However, *The World* did the best on Gunnar Kasson's great trip through the wilds of Alaska by sledge and dog team, bringing serum to the victims of the diphtheria epidemic at Nome. The dog Balto got a statue in Central Park for that heroic feat.

All was not loss of prestige in this period, however. *The World* exposed the bonding business of Sinnott and Canty—Sinnott being Mayor Hylan's son-in-law. *The Sunday World* introduced Milt Gross in "Gross Exaggerations" and "Nize Baby" became a favorite character with Justice Oliver Wendell Holmes. Will B. Johnstone struck a happy cartoon note with his "In the Wake of the News."

Other experiments in *The Sunday World* brought both smiles and distress to friends of the paper. The magazine section gave one page a week, edited by Karen Adams, to "Numerology, or the mysterious influence of personal names upon our lives." "This," said *The World's* promotion department, "is in line with *The Sunday World's* already well-known essays in modern occultism, including the once-a-month astrology column by Kevah Deo Griffis and the sometimes startlingly fulfilled yearly horoscopes and predictions of Marion Mayer Drew and Professor Raymond of Paris." *The Sunday World* also had a Red Magic section conducted by Harry Houdini, the magician, but it did not solve the mysterious disappearance of *World* circulation and *World* advertising.

BROUN STRIKES OUT

"The World *enriched public knowledge and quickened public opinion regarding the Sacco-Vanzetti case in Massachusetts. The long growing doubt . . . was strengthened. A marked change has come into public opinion and there is a confident expectation that a new trial is possible."* (*From* The World Almanac *of 1927, reviewing the year 1926.*)

"*Holding the issue of Justice to be paramount in the Republic,* The World *devoted much attention (during 1927) to the effort to save Sacco and Vanzetti. In this, it was unsuccessful."* (*From* The World Almanac *of 1928.*)

Heywood Campbell Broun was born in Brooklyn, on December 7, 1888. He attended public schools, went through the "progressive" Horace Mann High School in Manhattan and spent four years at Harvard (1906-1910), departing without diploma. He wrote one or two fanciful pieces for the *Crimson,* Harvard undergraduate publication, and made his first excursion into metropolitan journalism during a summer vacation, as reporter at space rates on the *Morning Telegraph.* After leaving Cambridge, he became a regular staff writer for the *Telegraph* at twenty dollars a week.

On the *Telegraph,* Broun covered sports, theaters, and other doings of the Great White Way, also contributing to the "Beau Broadway" column. His chief diversion was poker, at which he was never a master; but he also consumed much time at various midtown hangouts, including the Eldorado, a Negro cabaret in the

West Fifties. Other Broadway reporters considered Heywood singularly maladjusted to the tempo of the Tenderloin.

Broun was over six feet tall and heavily upholstered. One might suspect a touch of elephantiasis or pituitary trouble. He was notoriously lazy, but amazingly active in whatever he could do without effort. He loved to talk and he talked continuously; but whenever he was obliged to stop talking and sit down to write, he wrote fluently, turning out exceedingly good newspaper copy in large volume, unhampered by the fussing, fuming, and wasting of time and paper that many reporters and columnists display.

In his early career on Broadway, he was careless about clothes; later, when fame rather suddenly caught him, the sloppy appearance became part of his window dressing—shall we say bay-window dressing?—part of his stock-in-trade. The early Heywood was not nearly so negligent as the famous Broun. Really, he overdid it. It is one thing to be charmingly forgetful of one's hair, face, collar, tie; or careless about the creasing of one's pants; but to come into an office with everything thing unbuttoned, from the collar down to the point of embarrassment, seemed like a deliberate affront to fellow workers.

Although huge of body and bold in ideas, he was constitutionally timid, in war as in love. But every so often, about once in five years, he would over-react to some trivial situation, get into a fight, and take a terrible beating. There is no record of his ever winning these impromptu battles.

The *Morning Telegraph* discharged Broun. He said it was because he was getting only twenty-eight dollars a week and he had demanded thirty dollars. After that, he free-lanced for a while on the *Sun,* and about 1912 went to the *Tribune,* starting as a general news reporter, but gravitating naturally into the sports department. This was lucky for him, because it was in sports that the New York papers first broke away from the old tradition of unsigned articles. Sports writers, under their own names and frequently using first person singular, were the first to build up personal followings. Heywood had a gift for pungent phrases, apt comparisons, and pithy, understandable metaphors—also the art of personalizing his reports. In a short time, "Heywood Broun Says" became a popular quotation.

In 1916, Broun persuaded the *Tribune* to accept a thrice-a-week column on books, also under his signature. It soon became apparent that the reading of books required effort, and having not enough literary material, Broun filled the column occasionally with animadversions about himself, later about his infant son, or anything that came to mind. One day the managing editor said, "Those off-hand pieces of yours are better than the ones about books." The column was therefore changed to "Books and Things." It became more popular than the previous one, but not nearly so good as Broun's baseball reports, which have rarely been surpassed.

In the First World War, after America got in, the *Tribune* sent Broun to France with the A.E.F., as a special correspondent, but he did not get along well with General Pershing, and he was soon recalled, returning to his "Books and Things" and sports writing. In 1921, under the seductive persuasions of H.B.S. and the added lure of much larger salary (about $350 a week) Heywood came to *The World,* along with F.P.A., and established his column, "It Seems to Me," on the page opposite the editorials.

It was evident by then that Mr. Broun had risen far above his old associates and had arrived at a plane of distinguished journalism. He became a central figure in the "Algonquin Circle," a notable conglomeration of famous and not so famous writers, actors, and talkers who lunch at the Hotel Algonquin for the purpose of seeing and being seen. Wherever Broun went, he talked as long as anybody would listen, and it was all good stuff. Arthur Garfield Hays esti mated that only ten per cent of Broun's best ideas ever found their way into print. In or out of the column, he was always manufacturing observations, some to be printed, others merely to be heard, admired, or gasped at. Broun seldom stepped out of character. He was always Broun the columnist, Broun the liberal, Broun the intellectual. This lasted until 1934 when he became head of the American Newspaper Guild. After that he divided his time between the role of Broun the columnist and Broun the labor leader.

(Broun was married twice. First to Ruth Hale, newspaperwoman and organizer of the Lucy Stone League, on June 6, 1917. Their only

child, Heywood Hale Broun, was born March 10, 1918. The purpose of the Lucy Stone League was to encourage married women,
especially professional women, to use their maiden names.)

Once firmly established on *The World,* Heywood was careful to
cultivate the Broun legend. The lateness of his copy was traditional,
so he made it as late as possible without missing the edition; this was
as much a part of the Broun lore as the disorderly attire. In addition
to "It Seems to Me," he reviewed plays and contributed a weekly
feature for the drama page entitled, "Seeing Things at Night."
One time he forgot that he already had one such column in type and
turned in another. Both appeared in the same section of *The Sunday World.* Henry Jenkins, foreman of the composing room, said,
"I guess Heywood is seeing double this week."

The World gave Broun practically carte blanche to write as he
pleased and what he pleased. The theory was that he had an
enormous following. Actually, the circle of admirers among *World*
readers was not over twenty-five thousand—at least that was the
drop in circulation that coincided with Broun's departure from the
paper. The Broun articles were for Broun fans, just as the F.P.A.
columns were for Adams fans; whereas Frank Cobb wrote for the
entire circulation.

Broun's writings were distinguished by charm and a certain tolerance and breadth of viewpoint, but they had neither a wide range of
knowledge nor depth of culture nor spiritual insight. They were
good copy, not great literature. They represented a curious case of
arrested mental and emotional development. "The Boy Grew
Older," up to a certain stage, but never attained full maturity. The
Broun cosmos revolved around a central ego, which never became
attuned to the real universe. All of his writings, whether in or out of
the column; whether of the theater, of books, or his own doings,
were projections of Broun. They might wear various dresses, but
there was no successful disguise.

Back of this continuous, but somewhat restricted outflowing of the
ego, there was a reservoir of unsatisfied emotion, or ambition, which
would occasionally erupt in violent exhibitions, either an unsuccessful brawl or a fierce attack upon some supposed case of wrong. In
either case, the outburst was rarely justified by circumstances; it was

merely the result of overemotionalized ideas. Broun worshiped notions; he had less respect for facts; if they got in his way he kicked
them aside or ignored them.

These accumulated frustrations, relieved by eruptions, account
for his exaggerated reaction to the Sacco-Vanzetti case. He had not
personally investigated the matter as a fact-gathering reporter; he
had merely followed the hue and cry of the radicals and the
"liberals." His one-man revolt was based on emotion and not on
evidence.

Nicola Sacco and Bartolomeo Vanzetti, Italian immigrants,
were arrested in Massachusetts on May 5, 1920, on suspicion
of having taken part in an attempted holdup in Bridgewater, Massachusetts, on December 24, 1919; but after a preliminary investigation both were charged with participation in the holdup murder of
a paymaster and his assistant at South Braintree on April 15, 1920.
Sacco established an alibi as far as Bridgewater was concerned, but
Vanzetti was tried and convicted on that charge before both of them
were found guilty of the South Braintree crime. The second trial did
not take place until May 31, 1921, and lasted until July 14. Nearly
six years elapsed before they were sentenced to death. The delay
was due to a long series of appeals and motions for a new trial.

In 1926, the defense attorneys produced their most sensational
new evidence in support of a motion for new trial. This was a statement by Celestino F. Madeiros, convicted murderer, to the effect
that he took part in the South Braintree crime and that Sacco and
Vanzetti were not involved. Madeiros refused to name the other
participants, but the defense lawyers produced a mass of affidavits
and exhibits purporting to show that the crime was the work of the
Morelli gang of Providence, Rhode Island, a band of freight-yard
robbers. Judge Thayer rejected the evidence, and on this issue the
Supreme Judicial Court refused to reverse him.

This decision, handed down on April 5, 1927, practically ended
all hope of the defense for a new trial. Their next move was to petition Governor Alvan T. Fuller for clemency. Sacco refused to sign
the appeal, saying that it would compromise his principles. Sacco's
contention was that a capitalist society had determined to kill two

of its anarchist enemies, and that petitions were useless. His theory was probably wrong, but his forecast was correct.

Both sides, however, urged the governor to appoint an impartial commission to assist in determining the facts. He named an Advisory Committee, consisting of Abbott Lawrence Lowell, president of Harvard; Samuel W. Stratton, president of the Massachusetts Institute of Technology, and Robert Grant, former probate judge. Defense counsel had no confidence in the commission; and when they learned that the hearings were to be secret, and that certain witnesses were not to be cross-examined, they were about to withdraw entirely, but Frankfurter and others, confident of Lowell's fairness, dissuaded them.

The committee held its private hearings, independently of the governor, between July 11 and 21. The governor pursued his own inquiry, aided only by his counsel, Joseph W. Higgins.

On August 3, Governor Fuller denied the petition for mercy, announcing that he, as well as the Advisory Committee, believed that Sacco and Vanzetti were guilty.

Up to this point, Heywood Broun had taken no specially fervent interest in Sacco and Vanzetti; but the decision of the governor and his committee brought forth a torrent of rage in "It Seems to Me" on August 5.

"What more can the immigrants from Italy expect?" he demanded. "It is not every person who has a president of Harvard University throw the switch for him. If this is lynching, at least the fish-peddler and his friend, the factory hand, may take unction to their souls that they will die at the hands of men in dinner jackets or academic gowns, according to the conventionalities required by the hour of execution."

World readers were electrified by this flaming transfiguration of the normally easygoing, sometimes apathetic Broun. Many were shocked at the attack on Harvard; others delighted. All were struck by its ferocity. Words of caution from R.P. and Lippmann produced no assuagement of the tempest. In the next day's *World*, Heywood followed up the attack with a still deadlier thrust at his Alma Mater.

"Shall the institution of learning at Cambridge," he asked, "which we once called Harvard, be known as HANGMAN'S HOUSE?"

This was too much. *The World's* Council-in-Dome was profoundly shaken. The business office demanded the suppression of Broun. Large advertisers were threatening to cancel contracts. "The big department stores," it was reported, "do not desire the patronage of bomb-throwers." Harvard alumni indignantly protested. Other readers telephoned, telegraphed, wrote letters. The uproar was terrific.

Ralph Pulitzer was not a reactionary, nor was he red-radical. In his undynamic way he had sympathized with the Sacco-Vanzetti defenders; unrealistically, he believed that *The World* was helping their cause by its liberal attitude. In that respect, he was wrong and Broun was right. Causes are not won through intelligent editorialization alone if the power-house is weak. Facts are the greatest weapons in the world, but they are no good in feeble hands. Broun had the power and the fury, but he was weak on facts.

R.P. directed Lippmann to turn Broun's talent into other channels. Any further thoughts on Sacco-Vanzetti were "out." The columnist ignored the diplomatically worded hint. He continued to pour out fire and brimstone against Lowell. But the articles never reached the composing room. On the same day, August 6, Governor Fuller gave out the full report of the Advisory Committee. Two days later, Lippmann, apparently impressed, commended the committee, but added:

"The possibility of error is not wholly disposed of, particularly in the case of Vanzetti. Therefore it seems to us the course of wisdom to show mercy by commuting the sentence to life imprisonment."

Straddle magnificent! But it pleases nobody. Broun now goes on strike. He will not—says he cannot—write about anything but "the legalized murder conducted under academic auspices and prestige." Execution cum laude! That was about the way he confided it to his typewriter. The keys responded but the pages did not go to press. "It Seems to Me" did not appear. Nevertheless, he refused to change the aria. It was murder, murder, nothing but legitimatized murder.

Frankfurter and other distinguished liberals came rushing to New York and went into prolonged session with Lippmann. With good effect. On August 10, *The World's* entire editorial page was given over to the Sacco-Vanzetti affair—an exhaustive analysis by Lippmann and a forceful cartoon by Kirby. This had the effect of consuming at least one reader with resentment—his name was Broun. To think that Lippmann, after disciplining a fellow liberal, should suddenly go "all-out" for the aid of Sacco and his partner! He turned in another column on the same subject.

Meanwhile, readers demanded to know what had become of Broun. In response to many inquiries, R.P. published an explanation in place of "It Seems to Me." The title might have been "It Seems to Be Missing," but R.P. preferred the conventional. The article read:

"REGARDING MR. BROUN.
"The World has always believed in allowing the fullest possible expression of individual opinion to those of its special writers who write under their own names. Straining its interpretation of this privilege, *The World* allowed Mr. Heywood Broun to write two articles on the Sacco-Vanzetti case in which he expressed his personal opinions with the utmost extravagance.

"The World then instructed him, now that he had made his own point clear, to select other subjects for his next articles. Mr. Broun, however, continued to write on the Sacco-Vanzetti case. *The World,* therefore, exercising its right of final decision as to what it will publish in its columns, has omitted all articles submitted by Mr. Broun."

Heywood Broun made no reply immediately, but continued the silent rebellion. It was a sort of sit-down-on-the-column strike, since he would not give up writing for "It Seems to Me," and would not write on anything except the magnificent obsession. Nothing else is worth writing about, he insisted to friends, nothing else worth even thinking about, if in this nation it is possible for innocent men legally to be put to death, or if a state like Massachusetts can refuse to insure a fair trial.

Broun's opinions, of course, were based upon second-hand information. It would have been much better for all concerned if *The World* had undertaken its own independent investigation, as it did in the Stielow case. But we were in a new era, one where facts counted for much less than Mr. Somebody's opinion or Mr. So-and-So's comment. To Heywood Broun's credit, it must be recorded that he did not blame capitalism for the execution of two anarchists. His attack was directed entirely at Governor Fuller and the Advisory Committee, particularly the Harvard member of it.

Followed a five-day deadlock. On August 17, *The World* published Broun's farewell. In a letter to R.P., he wrote:

"By now I am willing to admit that I am too violent, too ill-disciplined, too indiscreet to fit pleasantly into *The World's* philosophy of journalism. And since I cannot hit it off with *The World,* I would be wise to look for work more alluring. . . . In farewell to the paper, I can only say that in its relations to me it was fair, generous, and gallant. But that doesn't go for the Sacco-Vanzetti case." ·

To which R.P. replied in Broun's own column:

"I am sure Mr. Broun will be the first to admit that he has never been directed to write a word against his conscience. The issue is simply whether or not he may direct *The World* to publish his column against its conscience. *The World* still considers Mr. Broun a brilliant member of its staff, albeit taking a witch's sabbatical. It will regard it as a pleasure to print further contributions from him, but it will never abdicate its right to edit them."

Broun moved out of *The World* and began writing for the *Nation,* the *New Republic,* and other publications. Coincidentally, it was just about this time that a new book appeared, entitled *Anthony Comstock, Roundsman of the Lord.* Its co-authors were Heywood Broun and Margaret Leech. A year later she became the second Mrs. Ralph Pulitzer.

Heywood stretched his witch's sabbatical to five months. It produced no happiness, nor any great financial reward. Through the kindly intervention of H.B.S. and others, the quarrel was adjusted and Heywood returned, but without fanfare—no apologies being given or asked.

Five months later came the permanent break. In May, an article which Heywood had dashed off for want of other material appeared in the *Nation.* For some reason never explained, it enraged R.P. and the council far more than the previous rebellion. Although not flattering to *The World,* the contents of the article failed to justify the

extreme penalty imposed—instant dismissal without notice or hearing. No appeal, either. R.P., it seemed, had not studied Massachusetts justice in vain.

Broun catalogued the fatal article as "The Piece That Got Me
Fired." There ought to be a place in New York, he wrote, for a
liberal newspaper. *The World* comes closest to being a *Manchester
Guardian* but falls short of being "liberal" because it changes opinions so rapidly. During the Sacco-Vanzetti affair, he said, *The World*
shifted so frequently that it seemed like an old car going up-grade.

In the same article he declared that New York editors live in
mortal terror of the Roman Catholic Church, and that the metropolis
will never know a truly liberal newspaper until one is found that
has no affiliation with, or timidity about, any religious, racial, or
political group. (This comment contrasts strangely now with
Broun's subsequent conversion to Catholicism.)

On the morning after the *Nation* article appeared, R.P. announced that Mr. Broun had been dismissed for insubordination.

"I don't understand what he means," Heywood replied. "Insubordination might cover anything from taking money out of the
cash-drawer to sitting on Ralph Pulitzer's hat."

After another strange interlude of free-lancing, Broun joined the
Scripps-Howard organization, with carte blanche to write as he
pleased on any subject. The new liberty seemed to cramp his style.
He continued to revolve in the Swope orbit with F.P.A. and other
old cronies. In 1930, against Roy Howard's wishes, he ran for Congress but was defeated by Mrs. Ruth Pratt. Three years later he
organized the American Newspaper Guild and became its perennial
president until 1938.

In his Scripps-Howard column of September 19, 1933, he wrote:
"My best friend died yesterday." He went on to say that Ruth Hale
was the real author of his best pieces. "I feel that she is still looking
over my shoulder." Six months later he married Connie Madison,
the former Mrs. Johnny Dooley.

By the spring of 1938, it was current rumor that Heywood was
on the way out with the Howard group. Aylesworth, then an unhappy member of the same organization, explained it to me one
day at lunch.

"Roy Howard would have let Heywood out at the end of his first contract," said M.H.A., "but he was afraid Heywood couldn't get another job."

The separation came in 1939. Heywood's own version, given in his *Connecticut Nutmeg,* was that Howard had to reduce salaries and felt it wasn't fair to the younger writers to retain such an expensive man as Broun. "I can't possibly find fault with that," Broun replied. "It is the same thing I have been saying in the Guild for the last five years." So, he said, they had a drink and parted as friends.

The same year witnessed Heywood's conversion. He wrote only one or two articles about that, promising a more complete thesis at some later day.

He was engaged as columnist for the *New York Evening Post,* but his first and only article appeared on December 14, 1939—a veiled prediction of a third term for F.D.R. Four days later he died of pneumonia and was buried with an impressive requiem mass in St. Patrick's Cathedral. Mgr. Fulton J. Sheen, professor of philosophy in Catholic University, Washington, told how Heywood, the former idol-smasher, humbly bent the knee and asked a blessing . . . how he had also declared: "The Church is the only moral authority remaining in the world."

Remarkable, too, was the fact that Heywood was so quiet in such a distinguished gathering of writers, public officials, and other admirers, high and low, all come to pay him tribute.

His face was in repose, and for once his clothes were neatly pressed and properly buttoned, and that was something.

Sacco and Vanzetti, meanwhile, had gone to their death on August 23, 1927, three weeks after Heywood's last protest on their behalf. The execution took place in the State Prison at Charlestown, Massachusetts, amid a wave of public hysteria never precisely duplicated. The year 1927 seems to have been a harvest time for strange outbreaks of mass-psychology. This was the year when Lindbergh made the famous flight to Paris and became the national idol. Radio broadcasting, which was then becoming universal, was showing its effect on public opinion, and the national election returns of 1928 were to break all previously imagined records.

Sacco and Vanzetti's last hours produced more excitement than the execution of Lieutenant Becker and the gunmen. The prison was guarded by militia, with machine guns and searchlights mounted on the walls. The crowds were kept far away; newspaper writers were herded into one room.

For this assignment I had selected Arthur Chamberlain, a cold fact-getter, not a color-artist—neither radical nor reactionary. But he fared no better than the rest. The warden ruled that only one reporter was to be admitted to the death chamber. Election fell on the Associated Press representative.

Madeiros was first to die, silent to the last, rejecting religious ministrations, and refusing to recant his confession of guilt in the South Braintree affair.

Sacco was next. As he entered the room he shouted in Italian, "Long live anarchy!" As the guards strapped him in the chair, he said, "Farewell, my wife and child and all my friends," and as the black hood went over his head, he said: "Farewell, mother!"

Vanzetti was last, and the most composed of the three. He shook hands with the warden and the guards and thanked them and protested his innocence. Turning to the invited witnesses of the execution, he said, "I wish to forgive some people for what they are now doing to me." But he did not specify which ones.

The press room surged with tense anxiety. This was just past midnight and there were editions to be caught . . . as the A.P. man came in after the final act, the reporters clamored for details. The A.P. man begged for time and air. Seating himself in the center of the crowded room, he unfolded his notes.

"Well, gentlemen," he announced, "the execution went off without incident."

The World's crusading power in these latter days appears to shift over to the evening side. John H. Tennant, who has been with the Pulitzer organization since the nineties, fights heroically to preserve the old tradition against the inroads of economy and intellectualism. Another stalwart upholder of JP methods is Harold

Stanley Pollard, JP's former secretary. *The Evening World* takes for its province the administration of justice and runs a series of news articles and editorials by Pollard regarding the bail-bond racket. Tennant's investigators prove that habitual criminals with long records easily get bail. Judges of the (criminal) Court of General Sessions begin to tighten up, with the result that underworld lawyers go into the supreme court and obtain reductions in bail. *The Evening World* calls attention to several instances where General Sessions fixed the bail at $25,000 and substantial reduction was obtained from Supreme Court Justice Aaron J. Levy in the higher tribunal. Interviews with prominent members of the bar evoke the opinion that "there is no constitutional right to bail in the cases of confirmed law-breakers."

Justice Levy objects. He does not like the tone of Mr. Pollard's articles. A court functionary brings word to Pollard that Levy would like to see him in chambers right away. Pollard is not impressed.

"Please inform Mr. Justice Levy," he says, "that my office is on the eleventh floor of the Pulitzer Building, and I shall be pleased to see him here at any time during the day. In the late afternoons, I am generally to be found at the Harvard Club, and after that at my residence, if he finds other hours more convenient."

Not much time elapses before a deputy sheriff arrives with a warrant, summoning Pollard into court on charges of criminal contempt. The editor pleads not guilty and obtains an adjournment. When he next appears, Pollard is accompanied by Charles Evans Hughes as counsel. Justice Levy agrees with Mr. Hughes that there was no intent to wrong the court. He praises *The Evening World's* public-spirited interest in the administration of justice. An eloquent decision, but not so illuminating as a later one in the matter of the Long Island Lighting Company. In brief, he pronounces Mr. Pollard blameless.

The Evening World, incidentally, specializes in radio and automobile news, productive of enough advertising to help keep the business office quiet.

Nineteen twenty-eight is the year of changes in the Pulitzer Prizes. The terms of the award for the best editorial, instead of specifying, as JP did, "clearness of style, moral purpose, sound reasoning, and power to influence public opinion in the right direction," now make it read, "power to influence public opinion *in what the writer conceives to be* the right direction."

Change in the terms of the award for the best novel: The way JP wrote it was, "the American novel which shall best present the wholesome atmosphere of American life and the highest standard of American manners and manhood." The Advisory Board changes it to read, "*preferably* one which shall best present the *whole* atmosphere of American life."

The prize for the best history of the services rendered by the American press during the preceding year is discontinued, for lack of competition. (The prize established by JP for the best essay or the best idea on how to improve the School of Journalism was discontinued back in 1921, also for lack of competition, and the cartoon prize substituted.)

With regard to the prize for good reporting, the Advisory Board felt it necessary to be more explicit. Whereas JP specified "strict accuracy, terseness, and the accomplishment of some public good," the new wording is "strict accuracy, terseness, *the preference being given to articles that achieve the accomplishment* of some public good." (There was no award of the reporting prize in 1928.)

After *The World* had gone, the terms of all the awards were modified still further.

GOOD-BYE, MR. SWOPE

Nineteen twenty-eight was also the year of the Brown Derby.

The World committed itself hook, line, and sinker to the nomination and election campaign of Alfred E. Smith as Democratic candidate for President, and to the adoption of a "wet" platform. No fault could be found with a newspaper for taking sides on a national issue; the trouble was that *The World* also became a part of the political machinery. It is difficult for a newspaper to cover the news and at the same time be a part of the show.

(You might just as well expect an impartial criticism by Alexander Woollcott of *The Man Who Came to Dinner* with himself in the wheel-chair part.)

In the 1928 campaign, Swope, Ralph Pulitzer, Walter Lippmann, and Claude G. Bowers were all part of the brain trust affiliated with the Smith campaign. Joe Canavan was borrowed from
his post as night city editor to act as publicity advisor in the New
York headquarters in co-operation with Mrs. Belle Moskowitz, the
governor's political mentor. Joe did not return, because he became
secretary to Lieutenant-Governor Lehman.

Preparations for covering the national conventions kept *The
World* office in a turmoil—tickets, tickets, tickets, reservations,
changes. *The World* staff which was to handle the Republican affair
at Kansas City and the Democratic gathering at Houston, Texas, included Ralph Pulitzer; Ralph Pulitzer, Jr.; Swope, Michelson, and
two reporters from the Washington office; and Dudley Nichols. But
just before the departure there was an added starter. I was instructed
to make reservations for Miss Margaret Kernochan Leech, who was
to do some special features on the conventions, including the so-
called "woman's angle."

Miss Leech had already made a dent in American literature. Born
in Newburgh, New York, graduate of Vassar, 1915, she had written
extensively for magazines. Her books included *The Back of the
Book* and *Tin Wedding,* and she had collaborated with Heywood
Broun on *Anthony Comstock, Roundsman of the Lord*—that is,
Miss Leech wrote some of the chapters and signed them; Broun
wrote others and signed them. The combined product appeared in
1927 before the Sacco-Vanzetti upset.

In the same year, she wrote *The Feathered Nest.*

And so—on to the conventions! Between the Republican nomination of Hoover at Kansas City and the start of the Democratic
struggle at Houston, *The World* delegation had time for a side
trip into Mexico.

At Houston, H.B.S. exerted powerful efforts on behalf of Smith,
at the same time directing *The World* staff. He collaborated with
Mrs. Moskowitz in suppressing the telegram Smith sent from New
York right after the platform was adopted. Smith did not like the
Prohibition plank, and did not propose to pussyfoot on Repeal. The
message was not read to the convention until after Smith had been
safely nominated and it was then too late for the Dry South dele-

gates to do anything about it. They compensated by bolting the ticket and voting for Hoover in the fall election. The dry Democrats contended that they had been sold down the river. It made no difference; Hoover was as good as elected when nominated. You can't beat two chickens in every pot and two cars in every garage, backed up by religious and sectional prejudice; not on a Prohibition issue in a time when everybody knows where to get all the liquor he wants.

Returning to New York, Swope sat with the inner council of the Democrats, but it seemed to us in the office that his heart was not in the work. The Smith campaign got off to a flying wrong-way start with the acceptance speech, broadcast from Albany to a waiting nation. Owen D. Young, a Smith supporter, listening in his home, with Merlin H. Aylesworth at his elbow, shook his head.

AYLESWORTH: What do you think?

YOUNG: I think the election is all over except the counting of the Hoover vote.

Smith's "raddio" voice was no match for Mr. Hoover's well-placed microphony. The Republican standard-bearer's voice carried conviction, even when he declared at Newark, "We have abolished poverty!"

Lippmann's editorial arguments for Smith were unanswerable from the standpoint of logic, but voters are not logicians. *The World* was fighting its last political fight and at the same time heading for the last roundup. Swope let himself slip into the depths of gloom and did not even go to Saratoga for the racing season.

Meanwhile, there was another job for the city desk. Swope called up on August first and gave orders for us to arrange certain details for the marriage of Miss Leech and Ralph Pulitzer. There must be no advance publicity. A dignified announcement would be given out for the morning papers. Well, Harry Friend was accustomed to these difficult missions. He arranged everything. This was in the reign of City Clerk Michael Cruise, afterward indicted for income tax evasion. A deputy clerk went to the house and made out the license just before the wedding.

Mr. and Mrs. Pulitzer went abroad on their honeymoon, returning in time for the closing weeks of the election campaign. On the ship coming back, R.P. encountered Roy W. Howard. They had a drink together. Conversation drifted around to the possibility of Mr. Howard's buying *The Evening World.*

The answer was the one already familiar to *World* readers. The Pulitzers had repeatedly stated: "Under our father's will, we cannot sell *The World.* We could not if we would and we would not if we could." Attorney Hornblower had backed up this declaration with a $10,000 opinion to the effect that JP's newspaper trust, so far as *The World* was concerned, was irrevocable and perpetual. They could not sell *The World.* As to the *Post-Dispatch,* that was different. (There was a time back in 1915 when the executor trustees announced that they were going to sell the *Post-Dispatch* to raise money to pay off the taxes on the Pulitzer estate.)

Howard replied: "Suppose we leave it this way . . . if you ever do decide to sell *The Evening World,* let me have the first offer."

Ralph Pulitzer agreed, stipulating in return that if Mr. Howard decided to sell the *New York Telegram,* the Pulitzers were to have the first bid. The bargain rested that way until late in 1930.

During Ralph Pulitzer's absence, H.B.S. had been in a melancholy state. He had experienced premonitions of death. He had even gone to a psychoanalyst. The medical consultation was not a happy one. The interview with the doctor was repeatedly interrupted by telephone calls for Swope. Mr. Morgan wanted to speak to him, Mr. Thomas Lamont, Mr. Owen D. Young, Mr. Bernard M. Baruch, Governor Smith, Franklin D. Roosevelt—they all had to speak to Swope.

The psychiatrist concluded that Swope was a paranoiac, suffering from delusions of grandeur, and that he had hired somebody to pretend that these important people were on the telephone.

On his return to New York Ralph Pulitzer began by congratulating Swope on the success of *The World's* campaign against radium dials for watches. Several persons in New Jersey had been poisoned, some had died. Walter Lippmann started the crusade— one of the few times Lippmann ever became red-hot in print.

Without premeditation, Swope said to R.P., "Yes, that was rather a nice bit of work." (Suddenly) : "Ralph, suppose you let that be my exit line!"

The rumor about Swope's leaving *The World* flew all over town. Winchell carried it in his column.

"*The World,* October 22, 1928. From the Executive Editor.
"Dear Jim:
"I want you to know, at first hand, that I have resigned to take effect January first. I told R.P. just after he got back from Europe that I wanted to be freed from the daily grind and that I'd like to have him get a new boy. He said he could understand my effort to escape the pressure of detail now that I had become 'very wealthy'— the phrase is his, I don't know how much money that implies—but that he wanted me to stay on in a sort of all-around consultative capacity. I may do this, but I am determined not to be tied down and worn out. I saw——[a high executive on another New York newspaper] not long ago, and it frightened me. He's a death's head; not permitted to work. It is unnecessary to add that Ralph and I continue warm friends.

"With this note goes my very real affection, in which I know you believe.

"Faithfully, H.B.S.
"Mr. J. W. Barrett
"City Editor."

But in the meantime—the election. Swope had no illusions about Smith's chances.

"The campaign was pitched wrong from the beginning," he said. "It was conducted altogether on too low a plane."

The World men did a workmanlike job on election night. Everything went off according to our plans right up to the final concession of Democratic defeat. (No danger of a mistake this time. Electoral vote: Hoover, 444; Smith, 87. G.O.P. campaign expenses, $9,433,604; Democratic, $7,122,511.)

For the first time on record, H.B.S. took a drink of hard liquor in the office. He invited the news editors to come in and share the bottle of Scotch, at the same time confirming the word about his successor—Ralph E. Renaud, managing editor of the *New York Evening Post.* A further topic of conversation in the gray morning hours was: How long is *The World* going to last? But on that question, nobody had any definite knowledge. The impression was that it was not going to last very long.

The World's 1928 election returns were widely broadcast. N.B.C. had the Associated Press service and refused to use *World* figures; however, resourceful reporter Charles Sloan, under H.B.S.'s direction, went out and lined up other stations with the aid of Major Andrew White of the Atlantic Broadcasting Company; thereby helping to form the chain later known as Columbia Broadcasting System, Inc., of which H.B.S. is now a director.

The confusion that prevails among *The World* staff is the kind familiar to newspapermen—at least to those who have continued to work in a shop after getting pretty definite word that the enterprise is about to fold up. Is the handwriting really on the wall? Can it be that Joseph Pulitzer's newspaper is no more permanent than Frank Munsey's various experiments? Staff morale hits a new low, on both the morning and evening sides, but the old spirit refuses to die. It flares out again and again, in old-*World* style stories, in news beats, and little campaigns.

Ave atque Vale . . . this is for Swope. R.P. gives him a farewell dinner at the Players' Club in Gramercy Park, a small, "sweetly solemn" affair. H.B.S. has recovered from his melancholia—no more death forebodings. He is as gay as anybody around the table, which isn't saying much. There is an overtone of death, but not of an individual, only of an institution, and a chapter that is about to close. Even Swope's new double-breasted dinner jacket seems to herald a coming era. Others present are Griffith, Tennant, Beazell, Weitzenkorn, F. D. White, John F. Bresnahan (business manager), Pollard, Paul Palmer, Walter Lippmann, Ralph Pulitzer, Jr., and myself.

After appropriate (and occasionally unfortunate) remarks by the little circle, each man taking turn in paying tribute, R.P. presents the gold watch. There is not much Swope can say, and he might say too much. "We live a little," he says, "and we die a little, each day." (The dies have it!)

Before the end of that December, Mr. Pulitzer gives another dinner, this one to F. D. White, general manager, in appreciation of his fifty years of service to the *Post-Dispatch* and *The World*. White is leaving also, and about the same time, *The World* editorial staff gives H.B.S. a good-bye dinner at the Machinery Club. Woollcott, returning as a *World* alumnus now, makes everybody laugh by telling how he and Swope covered the steamship *Empress of Ireland* disaster in 1915; Walter Lippmann delivers the memorial: a book of letters and tributes from the staff, not a watch this time. Lippmann seems to be having hard work to keep from saying we who are about to die salute you who got out just in time, but his closing is impeccable:

"Herbert—you are a lucky, fascinating devil!"

He *was* lucky, at that.

12. Last Round-up

"Unarm, Eros; the long day's task is done
And we must sleep . . ."
—ANTONY AND CLEOPATRA, Act. IV, Scene 12

RALPH E. RENAUD was a playwright and water colorist as well as a newspaperman. Before coming to New York, much of his experience had been in Philadelphia. Why he had been chosen to succeed Swope was never fully stated, but it was a symptom of economy. Swope was a high-priced man. Renaud was a good managing editor, not an executive editor.

Why the Pulitzer executors did not appoint either James Earl Clauson or William P. Beazell, who had been to H.B.S. like two shards to a beetle, was not discussed, either. To have promoted either of these assisting managing editors to fill the higher post would have been more in keeping with JP tradition—that of encouraging *World* men to rise to the top. But perhaps the executors felt that Clauson and Beazell were so equally matched in ability that a choice would be unfair—they could be happy with either, were t'other dear editor away. Renaud's appointment was attributed partly to the influence of Julian Mason, editor of the *Post,* who later went out to St. Louis and joined Joseph Pulitzer on the *Post-Dispatch.*

Renaud's arrival, on January 1, 1929, was like a fresh breeze in a smoky room after a hard wake. He was enthusiastic. He was hot after news. *World* traditions, it was evident, were not going to bother him. From all he could learn, everything under the previous regime was all wrong.

"God Almighty!" he ejaculated, after a few days of looking around. "This place is full of old men. Everywhere I look, I see another bald head or another white beard. Even you, mister," he said to me, "don't look so damned young."

Renaud himself was about fifty-three. He called everybody "mister," without the first or last name. Our first acquaintance was not conducive to harmony. Just before coming to *The World* he had taken a boat trip to the West Indies, and had brought back a large collection of water colors he had painted. One day soon after his entrance upon our scene, he laid one of these sketches on my desk. I glanced up from a pile of copy.

"My goodness," I said, "you've cut your hand!"

"Are you blind?" he retorted. "That's a sunset over Miami, from a Grace Line steamer, by yours truly! How do you like it?"

I said, "The picture is lovely."

Beazell took farewell soon after Renaud's arrival; Clauson remained for the finish. Renaud moved Clauson over to the day side and brought in a new night managing editor who had one question for all situations, which was: "Why wasn't I told about it?"

Renaud was full of ideas for campaigns and crusades.

"First of all," he said, "we ought to investigate prescription liquor. I just know that it's bad!"

Through the co-operation of the Health Department, we obtained prescriptions for liquor in large lots. These were augmented by individual physicians friendly to members of the staff. Everybody got sick and had to have a prescription for bourbon, rye, or Scotch. We had the prescriptions filled by druggists in various parts of the city, enough to give a cross-section. The Pease-Lederle Laboratories made the analyses at wholesale rates.

As the laboratories required only one or two ounces from each pint bottle, the rest was ours. We soon accumulated enough hard liquor to fill an entire storage cabinet, but we prudently waited for the chemist's report. Except for two samples of Scotch showing "traces of lead" every bit of our prescription whiskey was one hundred per cent pure. So ended the first crusade. We were glad to assure New Yorkers that they might safely enjoy whiskey as a medicine.

But what to do with our very large residue, not used in the laboratory tests, was a problem. Renaud said, let's sell it to the staff at cost and pay for the experiment. The city desk did a brisk business for a few hours at three dollars a pint (dirt cheap at any bootlegger's counter). Jim Clauson objected. He was afraid Winchell would hear about it. We canceled the sale and recalled the liquor. Some of it had been consumed upon purchase. But still the problem remained: what to do with the liquor?

The matter was put up to the council up in the Dome. The word came down, "Give the whiskey to the Old Men's Home."

A few days later, Renaud asked what became of the liquor.

"I gave it to the old men, as directed," I said. "Your own share, you will find in the storage cabinet."

"You see," I explained, "almost everybody around here is an old man, as you recently remarked, and each old man has a home."

"Well," he said, "I don't feel right about it, but I will swallow my feelings."

After that we got along better. Anybody who felt sick could always obtain a shot of Father Jim's medicine. The prescription seemed to improve *The World* as well; the paper began to hit on all cylinders. David Steinhardt, receiver in many bankruptcy cases, disappeared. *The World* disclosed that Federal Judge Winslow had been appointing Steinhardt in case after case without any tangible reason. Representative Fiorello H. LaGuardia introduced a resolution demanding a sweeping investigation of the bankruptcy-receivership-refereeship-trusteeship system in New York, rightly charging that there was a "bankruptcy ring," and asking for Winslow's impeachment. The House Judiciary Committee referred the matter to the Attorney General; a Federal Grand Jury in New York got busy.

The World was right on top of that story. Our reporter, George Hall, obtained beat after beat. Max D. Pinner, a Federal court attaché, who had looked out for Steinhardt's interests, tried to commit suicide. Pinner gave *The World* a full account of the workings of the "system." Steinhardt killed himself, Winslow resigned—"not because I have done anything wrong," he said, "but because my usefulness has been impaired."

The trail shifts over to Brooklyn. *The World* reveals that Federal Judge Grover A. Moscowitz has been feeding receiverships, trusteeships, attorneyships, and refereeships to his "former" law partners who have an office in Montague Street with the judge's name still on the door. Congressman Arthur W. Somers moves for impeachment, but a subcommittee, after long hearings, reports that Moscowitz is censurable, not impeachable. The minority report is disregarded. Moscowitz remains on the bench. LaGuardia has backed *The World's* efforts one hundred per cent, but when city election time rolls around, *The World* turns a cold shoulder to LaGuardia as the Republican candidate for mayor. *The World* states, editorially, that it prefers a second term of Tammany's James J. Walker to Major LaGuardia, but at the same time suggests a "protest vote" in favor of Norman Thomas, the hardy perennial of the Socialist Party, running at this time for Mayor.

(Thomas polled 175,697 votes, the highest ever given to a Socialist candidate in New York City; Walker's vote was 867,522; LaGuardia's 367,675. As *The World* remarked, "A very large number of men and women voted for Thomas who have no sympathy for the Socialist program.")

Meanwhile, following the trail of corruption, *The World* exposes the inside iniquities of the defunct City Trust Company and its connections with the State Banking Department. Superintendent Frank Warder resigns and is indicted. Mr. Hall, prowling around in the investigation of bucketshops, discovers that Bishop James Cannon, Jr., arch-foe of liquor, advisory member of the Methodist Board of Temperance, Prohibition, and Public Morals, has lost large sums of money in wildcat speculation. The committee of bishops hear Cannon's confession of weakness (the money tempted him and he did bite). He is a repentant sinner, not a culprit; they forgive him. He remains in his post.

The World in this year 1929 also has a series on rackets and racketeers, indicating that New York loses $200,000,000 a year through industrial and commercial piracy. Not much is done about it. The District Attorney's office says it does not know of the existence of a single racket. Courtenay Terrett, the author of the series, later did it into a book entitled *Only Saps Work*.

Interesting newspaper work, all this, but sounding curiously superficial now, in the light of hindsight. Why did the newspapers, including *The World,* fail to follow the main current of national history? Coolidge's "prosperity" was crumbling under everybody's eyes, and we refused to perceive it. As early as March 26 there was an earthquake in the stock market. The margin-buying "lambs" were shorn, but the professionals got in on the upswing. The New York banks, encouraged by the Federal Reserve Board, rushed in with money to steady the brokers. Charles E. Mitchell, as president of the National City Bank and director of the Federal Reserve Bank, led the chorus of "all is well."

President Hoover will not be shaken out of his confidence in double-portions of chickens and two-car garages. The dominant national issue, he tells the Associated Press at its annual convention, is obedience to law and law enforcement. Life and property are more unsafe today, he asserts, than in any other civilized nation in the world. Mr. Hoover is just as deeply interested in peace and disarmament. This is the year when the Kellogg-Briand Treaties go into effect, under which forty-five nations pledge themselves to renounce war as an instrument of national policy. The United States at the same time suspends construction of three cruisers.

As for the general public, people refuse to be frightened. They are still painting the clouds with sunshine, listening on the radio to Rudy Vallee crooning "Deep Night" and praising the importance of getting a little kiss each A.M. and the same each night. The nation eats, drinks bootleg liquor, and makes merry on the rim of an economic volcano. And *The World* is waiting for the sunset.

When the Wall Street crash finally comes in October, *The World* cheerfully enters the conspiracy of hope. "No panic!" is the instruction in the office. The Rockefellers are praised for announcing that they are buying heavily in standard securities, such is their faith in the fundamental soundness of the nation.

As 1929 closes, there is a spontaneous blowing off of steam. At Christmas and New Year's it seems as if all downtown is drunk. Even the trainmen on the suburban lines join the commuters in downing the contents of bottles that pop out of every other pocket.

The whole world seems cockeyed and pie-eyed. Damn everything! So this is prosperity!

Rumors meanwhile are again going around that *The World* is for sale. James M. Cain, one of the new editorial writers, who manages to preserve a gorgeous irony, is walking along Park Row one day in front of the Pulitzer Building.

His companion remarks: "This place is for sale."

Cain says, "That story is ridiculous—everybody has denied it."

"I know," says the friend, "but just the same, it is for sale. You can tell it, just by looking at it. Everything about the place says, 'For Sale.' "

Mr. Cain later wrote *The Postman Always Rings Twice*.

Generoso Pope, the sand and gravel magnate who also owns two Italian-language newspapers, is anxious to get *The World*. He has long been ambitious to own an English-language newspaper in New York. He has approached the Pulitzer situation through several channels, but always gets the same answer: they cannot sell. However, Mr. Pope keeps on trying right up to the last. Adolph S. Ochs, principal owner of the *New York Times,* has also discussed a plan for purchasing *The World* and permitting the workers to own 49 per cent of the stock. The Pulitzers give no indication of interest. Swope has also talked with friends about the possibility of taking *The World*. Bernard M. Baruch is interested. Baruch says, "If Swope would be the editor of *The World* and really work at the job, I would buy the paper gladly. It is a perfectly bankable proposition."

However, we make the turn of the year without a sale.

New York, February 10, 1930. AN ANNOUNCEMENT:

"Ill health compels me to obey the orders of my doctor and go abroad for several months' complete rest and detachment from all office responsibilities. I have asked my brother, Herbert Pulitzer, to take over my duties; and in order that he shall have the proper corporate authority to execute these duties, I and my fellow directors, at my request, have unanimously elected him president of the Press Publishing Company.

"I feel that on my return after convalescence, I shall find that the men of *The World* organization have given him the same fine loyalty that they have always given me, and for which I now thank them. [Signed] RALPH PULITZER."

A statement:

"In taking over the responsibilities which my brother and co-directors have placed upon me, I should like now to say just one thing to the staff of the two papers:

"*The World* and *The Evening World* have an unbroken record of independence, of courage, and of devotion to the public welfare. In that tradition, I intend to the best of my ability to carry on. [Signed] HERBERT PULITZER."

The Nation: IT SEEMS TO HEYWOOD BROUN: "On the face of things, the sort of journalism which Ralph Pulitzer had to offer seems not at the moment successful. I think I am well aware of the many imperfections in the man and in the method. And yet in all sincerity I cannot say other than . . . 'Good try!' "

At the time of becoming president of the Press Publishing Company, Herbert Pulitzer was thirty-five years old. The supplemental statement given out in connection with Ralph's retirement emphasized Herbert's newspaper training. He had, the statement said, "come up through the ranks." Educated at St. Mark's Preparatory School in Southborough, Massachusetts, with two years at Harvard, Herbert enlisted in the World War as a Navy air pilot and saw some service both at home and abroad. On returning from the war, he became a reporter on *The Evening World,* covering the run-of-the-mine assignments, City Hall, ship news; the state legislature in Albany. He also went to Russia as a special correspondent for *The Evening World.*

From the beginning of his active journalistic work, Herbert seems to have had a strong preference for *The Evening World.* This was natural. His oldest brother, Ralph, was editor of *The World,* and the other and older brother, Joseph, was running the *St. Louis Post-Dispatch.*

In accordance with the terms of the Pulitzer will, Herbert had become an executor-trustee when he reached the age of twenty-one, in 1917. The other executor-trustees were Ralph and Joseph. A fourth executor was the old Union Trust Company which later was absorbed into the Central Hanover Bank and Trust Company, but this executor was not a trustee. The three brothers, after 1917, had exclusive control of the newspaper trust, subject of course to the terms of the will as interpreted by the Surrogate's Court.

Herbert was not hurried in his march to power. After the preliminary newspaper training period, he went abroad much of the time and established a "shoot" in Scotland. In August, 1926, he married Mrs. Gladys Mildred Munn Amory. On their honeymoon they went abroad and joined Ralph, who had been spending several months hunting big game in Africa. This was the expedition on which Ralph was narrowly saved from a charging lioness and a rhinoceros by quick action on the part of a guide.

The Herbert Pulitzer's first child, a daughter, was born in June, 1928; their second child, in 1930. Ralph's second marriage, as previously noted, took place in August, 1928. His oldest son, Ralph, Jr., was married the following summer to Miss Bessie Catherine Aspinwall. Things were moving rapidly in the Pulitzer family during this last quarter of the twenties. Meanwhile, Mrs. Kate Davis Pulitzer, mother of the three brothers, died in France on July 29, 1927, leaving an estate of about $2,700,000, the bulk of which went to the sons. Herbert, the favorite and youngest, was with her at the time of her last illness. Ralph and Joseph inherited the big mansion at No. 7-15 East Seventy-third Street. They had it remodeled into an apartment dwelling, but preserved the outside architecture, Italian Renaissance by McKim, Mead, and White, in its original beauty.

Returning from Europe toward the end of 1927, Herbert Pulitzer, for the first time, established offices for himself. The old suite on the eleventh floor, once occupied by the *San Francisco Examiner,* where Hearst conducted his negotiations and successfully took away the entire staff of *The Sunday World,* was remodeled and redecorated. Herbert was a cosmopolitan by this time; in accent, manner of speech, dress, and general demeanor he might easily have been taken for a British earl. The nickname for Herbert, bestowed by various employees, was "The Young Marster." His was the most impressive suite of offices in the building. He far outshone Swope in this respect. The old tradition was against all such "dog." The offices and desks of previous managing editors were merely so much space in which to work.

From then on, until his accession to the presidency, Herbert Pulitzer spent several hours each day in the newsrooms of *The Evening World,* sitting alongside of Managing Editor John H. Tennant and City Editor John T. Rainey, following the ebb and flow of the news and the details of the make-up. The three frequently lunched together at Racky's, the little green-front restaurant back of the Pulitzer Building, where prohibition was more honored in the breach than in the observance.

No such interest was displayed by H.P. with regard to the morning paper. Few of the staff knew him even by sight. Bill Laurence, who had tutored him in Harvard, went unrecognized by his former pupil. But men of the evening staff, like the late George Buchanan Fife, assured us that Herbert was not a bad fellow at all, and as a cocktail mixer—perfect!

The task which confronted Herbert in February, 1930, was enough to stagger the stoutest-hearted newspaperman. *The World* was being talked of as "on the way out." Although circulation in all three branches, morning, evening, and Sunday, was improving, advertising, due to a number of reasons, among them the belief of businessmen that *The World's* primary appeal was to low-income families, was falling off, especially for the morning and Sunday papers. *The Evening World* was carrying the financial burden for all three, which did not improve the internal morale.

Certain rugged newspapermen with imagination and ability have taken over a situation like this and turned poverty into profit. Others, under like circumstances, have failed utterly. Revival of *The World* called for tremendous enthusiasm, tremendous endurance, and an extra portion of hard work, plus ability and the will to compete. To put your paper ahead, you have to be thoroughly wild about it.

Notwithstanding his commendable qualities, one of which was to be a gentleman under all circumstances, Herbert Pulitzer lacked this flaming spirit, for which he is not blamable; his upbringing was not of the fire-producing kind. As Barnes had once remarked, Herbert was going around on his father's yacht and bullying his tutor when he should have been in a military school.

Now that the opportunity, which to other men would have been the chance of a lifetime, was on his doorstep, the youngest Pulitzer did not know what to do with it. Not that he was unwilling, exactly; but he lacked the ability to get down into the grime, the heat, and the toil of a great newspaper, into the ferment of excitement out of which come great news beats and opinion-compelling editorials.

How hard did he try? None but the man himself can answer that question. As to how long he tried, the answer is plain. The record is that within one year, *The World* enterprises were sold to Roy Howard. Active negotiations on the part of the Pulitzer executors began in April, 1930, two months after Herbert's coming into power.

There is no convincing evidence that *The World* situation was either helpless or hopeless in 1930. There was competition, to be sure, but not unfair, and not one-sided. Ever since the sharp drop which followed the temporary experiment of a three-cent morning *World,* the circulation had not done badly; at least the bottom had not dropped out of the enterprise, and *The World's* position in the field may be seen from the following comparison:

NEWSPAPER	1927 CIRCULATION MORNING	CIRCULATION EVENING	CIRCULATION SUNDAY
The World	287,970	290,106	583,163
Times	356,471		610,041
Herald Tribune	285,800		345,484
American-Journal	225,081	696,447	1,083,911
Sun		257,057	
Telegram		181,937	
	1928		
The World	302,199	305,746	593,746
Times	392,800		656,338
Herald Tribune	289,674		366,220
American-Journal	227,969	686,740	1,099,735
Sun		265,440	
Telegram		195,759	
	1929		
The World	336,869	291,792	542,655
Times	418,687		697,337
Herald Tribune	309,959		404,539
American-Journal	210,020	635,401	1,102,230
Sun		283,435	
Telegram		235,576	

NEWSPAPER	1930 CIRCULATION MORNING	CIRCULATION EVENING	CIRCULATION SUNDAY
The World	351,862	304,242	576,660
Times	437,367		752,689
Herald Tribune	312,528		419,488
American-Journal	200,919	634,483	1,121,539
Sun		307,707	
Telegram		219,354	
	1931		
The World	313,011	276,267	491,796
Times	416,995		719,051
Herald Tribune	292,164		430,029
American-Journal	225,004	629,154	1,033,313
Sun		298,791	
Telegram		236,581	

The comparison is among the standard-sized papers. One must also take into consideration the encroachments of the tabloids into the circulation of "popular" papers like *The World* and the *American.* Starting from scratch in 1919, the *Daily News* by 1930 had reached 1,313,000 daily and the then astonishing Sunday figure of 1,616,106. The *News* has since gone well above the two million mark.

The Pulitzer enterprise in New York had a name—not so bright as formerly, but something to work with. And the organization was still sound at heart. On *The Sunday* and *The Evening World* staffs, a certain demoralization had set in by 1930, but nothing irreparable. On the morning staff, there was a sort of devil-may-care spirit of adventure and fraternity. We suspected that disaster lay ahead, but the general reaction was, oh, what the hell, we're going to get out a good paper anyway.

By 1930 many of the men of other years had gone—Nichols, Garrett, Pringle, Quinn Martin—but the ones who remained, while perhaps not so brilliant as writers, were top-notch news-getters: George Hall, Allen Norton, Phil Pearl, Jack Leary, Bill Garrison, Geraldine Sartain—and the enfant terrible of the group—A. A. Schechter, the prodigy from Pawtucket, who is now director of news and special events for the National Broadcasting System—the same Schechter who rode uptown with Thomas Lamont after the Wall Street crash.

Schechter was the reporter who covered the John Coolidge wedding in Connecticut, disguised as a caterer's assistant, wearing a tuxedo. The press had been barred from personal attendance at the reception following the wedding of the ex-president's son, but *The World* correspondent in Hartford arranged matters with the caterer. Obviously, Schechter was the man for the job, but there was one drawback—he did not possess a dinner-jacket. We told him to get a good one and charge it up to expenses.

Quite a few guests at the reception seemed impressed with the good-looking waiter in the new suit, but none suspected the truth. Between trips to the commissary, it was easy for the reporter to jot down a note or two.

After the wedding, Schechter turned in his expense account: item, one dinner-suit with accessories, $50. (He had bought the outfit wholesale.) Editorial Auditor E. E. Bowns, watchdog of the treasury, demanded an explanation. He also desired to have the suit attached to the bill as a voucher. The city desk offered technical objections: the suit was being cleaned of ice cream spots, the tailor had mislaid it, somebody had mislaid the address of the tailor. By such mechanisms we kept the controversy in suspense until Bowns forgot about it. Meanwhile, word had gone through the business office not to be too particular about expenses. The management wanted to show a loss, not a profit.

On *The Sunday World,* the esprit de corps was marred by little incidents that kept the staff in a turmoil. One day the entire staff of the three newspapers was assembled to hear the details of a new group insurance plan. The agent who had arranged the policy explained the procedure. "You see," he said, "on this application blank you state your name, your age, your sex——"

Julia McCarthy of *The Sunday World* interrupted:

"I don't mind telling my name and age," she stage-whispered, "but I refuse to mention my sex in the presence of Weitzenkorn!"

She did not need to worry about the insurance, because Weitzenkorn, her Sunday news editor boss, immediately discharged her.

It was about this time that a young man crashed the city room one day by the easy device of going first to the restaurant in the Dome.

"When do I go to work?" he demanded. "Just name anything that anybody else is doing around here, and I'll prove I can do it better."

Since he refused to consider "no" as a suitable answer, we hired him as office boy. Within a few weeks he was assistant movie and drama critic. After that he went to Hollywood and became one of the foremost writer-producers of the West Coast. His name was Norman Krasna.

In view of the rumors flying around town that *The World* was for sale, the other newspapers were amazed at the beats and exploits chalked up by the staff. It was considered all the more astonishing because the famous news-getter Swope was no longer in our midst.

The World led the field in covering the New York judiciary investigation conducted by Isidore J. Kresel for the Appellate Division of the Supreme Court, exposing the bail-bond racket and the fixing of cases in the magistrates' courts. Magistrate Jean Norris, in charge of the Women's Night Court, was removed. Several others either resigned or were ousted. The star witness was the Chilean stool pigeon, Chile Mapocha Acuna, of whom Stanley Walker, city editor of the *Herald Tribune*, wrote his underworld jingle, beginning:

> *"There once was a human spittoon-ah*
> *Named Chile Mapocha Acuna,"*

The World staff amused itself at odd times by adding verses and setting the entire balled to the tune of "The Gay Caballero." It was the story of an innocent lass ensnared in the toils of the law through Mapocha's machinations.

> *"The next day, in General Sessions,*
> *The girl made some awful confessions,*
> *So they put her away*
> *For a year and a day*
> *To cure her erotic obsessions . . ."*

The tale rambled on and on. "She got out of jail, on fraudulent bail, and went to the Appellate Division," finally appealing to the Governor, who counseled her "to spill the whole story to Kresel."

In the series of scandals growing out of the Cotter-Butte Mining Company bankruptcy, leading to the indictments of Tammany District Leader Martin Healy and Magistrate George F. Ewald, *The World* got the head start and led all through the investigation. George Hall, the wonder-working reporter from Baltimore, pried these exclusive stories out of the Federal Building in spite of other newspapers and the opposition of United States Attorney George Z. Medalie, who tried in vain to find the leak in his own office.

President Hoover found *The World* at once a solace and an annoyance. Although its editorials cordially supported Mr. Hoover's efforts for arms reduction and international arbitration, and cooperated in his policy of "no panic" in business, *The World* challenged his declarations on law enforcement. Washington was blaming the Democrats in New York City for the collapse of prohibition. We sent Schechter upstate and established that there were as many speakeasies per capita in a Republican stronghold like Binghamton as there were in the greater city, and that even in dry Henry Ford's own bailiwick, Dearborn, Michigan, there were fourteen blind pigs on one block.

On top of this, *The World* came out in the early fall of 1930 with a series of articles by Major Maurice Campbell, former Prohibition Administrator for New York, telling of the obstructions and interferences in prohibition enforcement. Washington was upset, but Major Campbell had names, dates, places, and knew what he was writing about.

The biggest scoop of the year, and of many years, was *The World's* exclusive revelation of the disappearance of Justice Joseph Force Crater. We had a clean beat on the first story and led with most of the subsequent revelations. We were still hot on the trail when our own newspaper vanished—under circumstances almost as mysterious as the Crater case.

All the prestige which *The World* was reviving through its old-fashioned news beats was demolished and swept away in one gigantic blunder that carried it right up to the brink of the final disaster.

By way of background, one should remember that at the time Herbert Pulitzer succeeded Ralph as president of the Press Publishing Company, Roy W. Howard had resumed his efforts to acquire *The Evening World*. Although Herbert informed him then that there was nothing doing, the new president renewed the definite promise that if they did decide to sell any of *The World* papers, they would give Mr. Howard first opportunity to make an offer.

Howard rested on the promise and made no further approaches.

At the close of the American Newspaper Publishers annual convention in New York in April, 1930, John F. Bresnahan, business manager, invited Howard to visit the World Building. After a rather perfunctory tour of the plant, Howard was guided to the office of the new president on the eleventh floor. Present were Herbert Pulitzer, and F. D. White, retiring general manager. How did Mr. Howard like our building? Oh, very much. Very kind of them to ask him. They got down to business. What they wanted was to arrange a deal by which Howard would take the morning and *Sunday Worlds* and sell the *Telegram* to be merged with *The Evening World*. Howard was not interested.

The Scripps-Howard chairman, by December 1, had concluded that none of *The Worlds* was for sale, but on that date, Herbert Pulitzer renewed the negotiations, this time backed up with the presence of Joseph, who had come on from St. Louis.

What had occurred to change the Pulitzer attitude?

Whatever may have happened inside the Pulitzer family, the activity of the St. Louis brother is certainly to be noted. But the thing which had happened right in the public eye was that *The World* had lost face—it had been "shown up." It is hard to escape the suspicion that the paper had either been "framed" or had been wilfully encouraged in a disastrous editorial venture.

On July 29, 1930, when midsummer dullness was on the news, and most people's minds were on vacations, Walter Lippmann, ill in bed at home, received a telephone call from Washington. An insistent individual said he had something of the utmost importance. He wanted to see Lippmann, but finally consented to talk to H.E.C. "Buck" Bryant of the Washington Bureau.

The telephone caller was Ralph S. Kelley, a government employee. Beyond learning that Kelley had been in the Department of the Interior for the past twenty-five years and for six years had been a division chief of the General Land Office with headquarters in Denver, Bryant could pry little out of the man except that he had a sensational story and wanted to sell it to *The World*. "Buck" so informed Lippmann.

After talking with Herbert Pulitzer, Lippmann requested Kelley to come to New York at *The World's* expense. Kelley unfolded his

tale to Lippmann and Renaud. He represented that the Interior Department, under Secretary Ray Lyman Wilbur, was giving away millions of acres of oil shale lands in Colorado, Utah, and Wyoming,
having a potential value of forty billions of dollars. After ascertaining that the matter was one of news and not of editorializing, Lippmann withdrew, passing the responsibility to Renaud. The managing editor, after a long long session with Kelley, placed the
proposition before *The World's* Council-in-Dome, including H.P.
The vote was unanimous—to buy the articles from Kelley "if a price
could be arranged, satisfactory to Mr. Pulitzer."

Just before getting in touch with *The World,* Kelley had been
transferred from the Denver office to the main department in Washington, and had been placed in charge of shale oil claims. Being of a
highly sensitive and emotional disposition, although a faithful
worker, Kelley suspected a plot to get him out of the way. He did not
report for duty in Washington immediately but carried on his negotiations with Renaud. Later, he reported at irregular intervals, assert-
ing that he was sick, and obtaining sick-leaves.

August 11. Kelley wired to Renaud: "Anxiously awaiting answer
on matter we discussed." Renaud replied: "Mr. Pulitzer examining
documents. Response favorable."

(These notations are from the record of the hearings before the
Senate Committee on Public Lands, 1931.)

August 20. Renaud saw Kelley in Washington with Elliott Thurs-
ton of *The World's* Bureau and offered $12,000 for the articles, on
condition that Kelley continue in the Department until the articles
were finished and then resign. If he should be discharged before
resigning, the price was cut to $6,000. Accepted.

(Kelley's pay from the Government was $3,600 a year; *The
World* therefore paid him nearly four years' salary. An amazing bargain! Kelley was also promised fifty per cent of the syndication
profits.)

September 11. Kelley signs contract with Press Publishing Company.

September 25. Secretary Ray Lyman Wilbur returns to Washington from vacation.

September 28. Kelley resigns in letter to Wilbur, charging mal-administration in oil shale land patents. Letter published by *The World* and other newspapers.

September 29. *The World* syndicate, under F. B. Knapp, starts big sales drive for Kelley articles. Telegrams, airmail, and special delivery letters play up "amazing oil scandals, revelations that will rival Teapot Dome, will lead to Congressional action and many important resignations. Billions lost in oil land grab." Knapp sends two salesmen, Moyer and Williams, to canvass important newspapers in big cities. Knapp to salesmen: "Renaud expects us to sell these articles!"

September 29. Washington. Secretary Wilbur asks Department of Justice to investigate Kelley's charges. Kelley refuses to co-operate. He is suspended from duty, resignation unaccepted, pending further inquiry.

Also September 29. Knapp to Dwight Perrin, *St. Louis Post-Dispatch:* "Articles will undoubtedly cause a sensation . . . full of dynamite . . . naturally, we had to pay Kelley a big price."

October 1. From Buffalo. Williams to Knapp: "Papers here refuse oil story at any price." (The syndicate was asking anything from $50 to $500, depending on the paper and what the traffic would bear.)

October 2. Knapp to Williams in Chicago: "Hearst not interested in oil story. I am afraid it is going to be a terrible flop." Knapp to Moyer in Pittsburgh: "I am doing my best to hold the bag. Have not as yet passed the bad news around. Papers say the stuff is too deadly dull."

October 3. Knapp to Moyer: "The Kelley series is almost a complete flop. . . . Bovard [managing editor] of the *Post-Dispatch* rang me up and said he would not print the series if he were paid to do so. . . . If he could publish a digest, he would pay $350 to help us out. . . . It was a hopeless story to sell."

October 4 and 5. New York. *The World* advertises "Kelley's own story of oil graft totaling forty billion dollars," etc.

October 6. Kelley articles begin. Only a few other papers carry them. Syndicate sales—$1,250. Knapp to Bovard: "It is a meager

list . . . the results of two weeks' intensive effort. . . . Your opinion is the same as we are getting from other leading papers. . . . I
knew this when we started, but I had nothing to do with preparation
of the copy. . . . It was handed to me."

Although the response among *The World* Syndicate's newspaper
clients was lukewarm, Washington was not apathetic. Hoover was
thoroughly angry. At the outset of his administration, he had announced emphatically that there would be no Teapot Dome scandals
in his time—no further leasing of oil lands of any kind. The trouble
in oil shale was due to the fact that many tracts had been patented
under the old Mineral Lands Act, and could not be set aside by the
new Leasing Act of 1920. For two years, Wilbur had been fighting
to oust the holders of these old claims who had not done the required
one hundred dollars' worth of development work. The United
States Supreme Court (Wilbur *vs.* Krushnic) had decided that the
old patentees could not be ousted merely because their work had
lapsed. The government had to show that the holder intended them
to lapse. Thousands of these cases were under adjudication in the
department.

Investigation by Deputy Attorney General Richardson brought
out the fact that of 40,000 acres of oil shale claims which had been
approved in the Department, Kelley himself had passed favorably
on 20,000 acres. Many others had been decided in the courts under
the Krushnic precedent. Richardson reported that there was not a
shadow of justification for the "graft" and "steal" charges. Kelley's
"bombshell" quickly evaporated.

I warned Renaud at the outset of the Kelley venture that there was
trouble ahead. Being from Colorado, I was familiar with the fable of
"billions in oil shale." There are, as Kelley said, "Millions of acres"
of such lands, but nobody has ever found a practical and economical
way of extracting the oil, and much of the shale lies in remote and
inaccessible sections. As an old settler remarked: "The ile is theer as
riprisinted, but to git it out ye'd have to hire a pack-train of bald
agles." I suggested to Renaud that we consult the Colorado State
Geologist, Dr. Russell George, who knew all about oil shale. After
the series was launched, and *The World's* attorneys became worried,
I sent Dr. George a set of the Kelley articles and asked his opinion.

He reported the whole situation grossly exaggerated by Kelley, who, it appeared, had a complex on the subject. We paid Dr. George $50 for his opinion. Had we consulted him beforehand, we could have saved $10,700.

The World could have avoided the whole fiasco by following its own rule of accuracy and fair play. It did not make any effort to obtain Wilbur's statement until after the series began. The most casual inquiry should have satisfied *The World* that there was nothing to back up Kelley's charges of corrupt intent. The amount of oil shale under patent, in comparison with the vast areas remaining locked up in the public domain, was negligible.

Under the circumstances, *The World* should have apologized. Instead, it took refuge in technicalities. Lippmann editorially contended that oil shales constituted an intricate technical problem which only a Congressional inquiry could settle, and that it was *The World's* duty to bring Kelley's charges out in the open. As to whether it was our duty to pay Kelley three years' salary and then some, the opinion was not so positive.

On October 28, President Hoover publicly spanked *The World*. He called the Kelley articles "infamous, scandalous . . . baseless."

"As a piece of journalism," said President Hoover, "it may well be that the newspaper involved was misled. It certainly does not represent the better practice of American journalism."

The World answered, "Mr. Hoover is much more angry at an official who sought to save the nation's property than he ever was with the rogues who sat in the same cabinet with him while they were selling out the nation's property." (Meaning Daugherty and Fall in the Teapot Dome leases.)

When Congress met in December, 1930, Senator Walsh of Montana called for an investigation. The resolution was referred to the Senate Committee on Public Lands.

December 23. Secretary Wilbur, in a letter to *The World:* "These charges of Mr. Kelley with their irresistible inference reflect seriously upon my good name and I cannot let such an unwarranted attack go unchallenged. . . . I am presenting this matter so that you have opportunity as an act of simple justice to see that amends are made for this serious reflection upon me."

December 25. A statement by *The World:* "In publishing Mr. Kelley's articles, *The World* did not endorse nor guarantee the validity of his criticisms. It merely affirmed its conviction that his charges were made in good faith and with technical competence. As to the question of Secretary Wilbur's personal integrity, *The World* can only say that it has never believed nor implied that in all these complicated transactions, he did any dishonorable thing."

February 27, 1931. Secretary Wilbur, in a letter to the Senate Public Lands committee: "As the newspaper in question has changed hands and stopped publication, I do not know whether anything can be gained by personal examination of the members of the old management, contemptible as their conduct has been."

After hearing Kelley at length, the committee dropped the investigation. The letters and messages from the files of *The World* were read on the floor of the Senate on March 3, and there the matter ended. By that time *The World,* too, was ended.

December 1, 1930. Roy W. Howard, ill at his home in Pelham, New York, receives a telephone call from Herbert Pulitzer. Herbert's brother, Joseph, is here from St. Louis, and they have been talking things over. They would like to confer with Mr. Howard about his recent (not so recent) offer to buy one of *The World* papers. Roy is too ill that day, but on December 3 they meet in Joseph Pulitzer's apartment in the Ritz-Carlton Hotel.

The Pulitzers have a new proposal, which is to let Mr. Howard take the morning *World* (for a suitable price, of course). They will take all the daily features—F.P.A., Frank Sullivan, Elsie McCormick, also cartoonists Wortman and Kirby—thereafter issuing one evening and one Sunday paper. Howard does not like the idea—not with all the window dressing out of the showcase. Well, then—how would he like to buy all three of *The World* papers?

This is a surprising turn. Howard asks them to name their figure. They hem and haw, talk about the "very large profits," etc., and ask him to make the offer. Tentatively, he bids. The conference is adjourned to await the arrival of Ralph, who has been hunting beetles in Africa for the Carnegie Institution in Pittsburgh. Joseph Pulitzer's aide-de-camp, Keller, is coming from St. Louis. Tom Sidlo, the prominent Cleveland lawyer, partner of Newton D. Baker, and counsel for the Scripps-Howard interests, engages a suite at the Savoy-Plaza, right across from the $50,000 Pulitzer Fountain bequeathed by JP to the city.

Conferences are on now in earnest. *The World* is on the market. Rumors float around town. Vincent Leibell and former Senator Thomas Sheridan, Tammany stalwarts, are engaged to represent the grandchildren, "the minor heirs," who are the ultimate beneficiaries of the Pulitzer fortune. Gene Pope, the Italian-American publisher, renews his efforts to get *The World,* appealing to his friend Sheridan, but gets no satisfactory response.

The Christmas holidays cause a postponement. December 24 in *The World* office is intuitively recognized as "our last Christmas eve." The city staff gets commendably drunk. Renaud is taking a day off, still arguing that Kelley was right. There is a holiday gathering in Clauson's office, and enough liquor to go round—a nice affair, no rough stuff. Everybody sings "Noel, Noel, Noel, Noel." The Christmas carols float out into the city room and the copyreaders pause to listen. The tune shifts: "*The World* in solemn stillness lay, to hear the angels sing." Anyway, we feel sure there will never be any other such Christmas—no definite word—Alphonse Tonietti, like a true philosopher, tries to reassure all hands, but everybody knows this is the beginning of the last round-up. "Merry Christmas to all, and to all a good-night." No tears. Save them for the finish. Meanwhile the meeting is adjourned until New Year's afternoon, on which occasion, with the echoes of *The World's* apology to Wilbur still humming about our ears, there is a party in the Yosian Brotherhood rooms. No more carols now—the theme song is "Renaud, you're driving me crazy!" The Yosian suite has a piano to furnish a sort of accompaniment. The Yosian movement, incidentally, has been founded by J. Otis Swift of *The World's* staff.

The World, meanwhile, performs its annual good deed by raising funds to buy coal for poor people who live in cold-water tenements. This was originally an *Evening World* enterprise, but this year, by direction of Herbert Pulitzer, both sides co-operate. NBC gives us time on the air and the results are good. The coal is all delivered during the holidays, but on February 16, donations are still coming in. I go into *The Evening World* to talk to Tennant about holding over the balance of the fund for next year.

Tennant pushes back his horn-rimmed glasses. "There won't be any next year," he says. "Scripps-Howard have bought the whole works."

I report the conversation to Renaud. The word spreads around the office. Staff members huddle in small groups, whispering. Renaud comes back from the president's office and emphatically denies the story. Tennant, for diplomatic reasons, also denies it.

The contract of the sale and purchase of *The World* has been signed at midnight on January 31, 1931, at the Savoy-Plaza. The price is $5,000,000, $500,000 down, $500,000 in ninety days. Thereafter a series of annual payments beginning in 1934 and continuing until 1942. The balance is to be paid out of profits from the combined newspapers. The sale needs only the approval of the Surrogate's Court.

The lawyers have discovered the way to get around that clause of JP's will which enjoined the heirs never to sell the stock of the Press Publishing Company. Number one—the will says, do not sell *stock*. It says nothing about the newspapers which are the assets (or liabilities) of the Press Publishing Company. Number two—courts have held that trustees must exercise judgment to protect an estate. The law cannot compel the Pulitzer brothers to hold a property if its losses imperil the future of the residuary legatees.

February 20, 1931, Saturday. Alexander Konta, old friend of Frank Cobb, also quite friendly with Karl Bickel, president of Mr. Howard's United Press, asks me to lunch at Racky's.

"Everything is settled," he assures me. "Scripps-Howard are going to take all three papers. Foley [the Surrogate] is going to sign the order on Tuesday. Notice will be posted in the *Law Journal*.

"You have nothing to worry about personally," he adds. "Bickel says you are to go with the *World-Telegram*." This is the first time I heard the name of the new paper.

Returning to the office, I communicate my information to Renaud. And again, he brings assurances from the president's office that there

is not a word of truth in the story. Why doesn't he issue a statement?
Renaud says, Mr. Pulitzer feels it is not up to him to deny false
rumors.

Well, the sale of *The World* is news, just like any other important
event. We ought to find out about it, even if we can't print it.
Schechter is assigned to interview Foley, but the Surrogate has gone
out of town for the Washington's Birthday week-end. When he
finally is reached on Monday evening, he sends out word that "the
Pulitzer matter will come up at four o'clock Tuesday."

Tuesday, February 24. The *Law Journal* notes on the Surrogate's
Calendar: "Estate of Joseph Pulitzer." This, then, is the final chapter.

Tuesday, February 24, 1931. Office of the managing editor, *The
World:*

"Gentlemen," said Mr. Renaud, addressing Clauson and myself, "tonight we will get out the last issue of *The World.* There will
be no *Evening World* tomorrow. You may so inform the staff. All
three papers are being merged with the *Telegram,* and the first edition of the *World-Telegram* will be published tomorrow in the
other building, under Scripps-Howard ownership.

"Those of the staff who are to go with the *World-Telegram* are
being privately notified," he added. "If you have not received word
by this time, you are probably not among the elect. . . .

"Needless to say," he added, "I knew nothing about all this until
a few moments ago. The Pulitzer trustees have been lying to me right
straight along, from hell to breakfast . . . They say now they had
to do it."

"What about the announcement of the sale?" I asked. "We are to
cover the windup of *The World,* I assume, just like any other story?"

"I have no word on that," Renaud said. "There is to be a statement
after the hearing before the Surrogate this afternoon. Meanwhile we
will carry on as usual." (Exeunt omnes.)

4 P.M. The Hall of Records. Before Surrogate James A. Foley.
Special Issues—"Estate of Joseph Pulitzer." Hear ye, hear ye.
. . . A distinguished group it is, of lawyers and clients that gather

in the high-ceilinged room. A few reporters whisper: "Is this the sale of *The World?* What'll happen to the staff?"

Your Honor . . . Rogers Bacon, legal front man for three trustees, is about to assail the ears of the court. But what's the matter? An interruption—Abraham L. Bienstock of Max D. Steuer's office wants a five-minute delay. Mr. Steuer is on his way over here. He represents Paul Block, newspaper publisher (affiliated from time to time with William Randolph Hearst). Surrogate Foley says Mr. Steuer will be heard (you can be very sure of that). Meanwhile, proceed. Mr. Bacon conveys the information, which everybody knows by this time, that a sale has been arranged—price, $5,000,000—observes, en passant, that none of the principal editors and managers, who have a sort of one-tenth interest in the newspaper trust, has been served in this proceeding. As to them, Mr. Bacon says the Surrogate will surely find that the trust is invalid. (Cart precedes horse here. If they have any rights at all why were they not notified?) Now John J. Jackson, tall, iron-haired, iron-dispositioned attorney for the Press Publishing Company, explains the need for haste. The papers are losing money (*et comment!*). The morale of the staff is evaporating. The Surrogate's approval most urgently requested.

Steuer enters, out of breath. Mr. Block, he says, has been trying to buy these papers, but has experienced only a runaround. Block was willing to pay as much as $10,000,000 for all three, but was informed *The Evening World* was not for sale. Mr. Block is rushing here from California (has he been a guest at San Simeon—Mr. Hearst's castle-on-the-skyline?). He will certainly pay half a million more than Howard.

Proceed, proceed. Steuer can sit in as a friend of the court. Witness after witness, the three brothers included, testify to the losing power of *The World* papers. Herbert, the president, calm, well-tailored, gives the figures: $1,677,000 for last year; tells of "efforts" to sell the papers, contacts with "everybody I thought would be interested" —Reid of the *Tribune,* Ochs of the *Times,* Bernard M. Baruch, Swope, but no specific offers . . . Mr. Howard's is the only concrete proposition.

MR. STEUER: In all these negotiations, aside from those with Mr.

Howard, you did not at any time state that *The Evening World* was included in your offer—did you?

HERBERT PULITZER: That is correct.

STEUER: And after you decided to sell the evening paper, you did not so inform Paul Block—did you?

HERBERT PULITZER: I believe not.

Ralph, accompanied on this occasion by the very charming new Mrs. Pulitzer, and Joseph, of Clayton, Missouri, swank-suburb of St. Louis (reporters note); both testify to their firm belief that Howard's offer is the best. Frederick J. Fuller, representing the bank which is a co-executor under JP's will, commends the bargain. What are these papers really worth, asks the court. Fuller answers:

"Not exceeding two million dollars!"

Sad news for Brother Howard, who is paying two and one half times that figure, but the snappy little publisher is not worried about that. What he wants is action, action. The assets are evaporating— hints at sabotage on the part of the workers. (How little he knows! If *The World* had been as careful about the oil shale matter and the Bernard Smith case as the employees were about these last issues of Joseph Pulitzer's *World,* all this might not have happened. The "Ben" Smith case, involving a mistaken identity, got us into a libel suit for $1,000,000.)

Mr. Howard feels that he is carrying a bucket of ice cream across the desert. All this legal delay will leave him holding only the bucket. Speed, speed, if Your Honor please. What is the obstacle? Mr. Jackson explains, the clause in JP's will: "I enjoin upon my sons the duty of preserving, perpetuating, etc. *The World* newspapers, to the building up of which I have sacrificed my health, etc."—as for that, says Jackson, it is: "merely the expression of a wish and cannot be taken to enjoin the sale of a property!"

Steuer wants the hearing adjourned to Thursday, to give Block time to arrive and formulate an offer. But Foley marks the case "matter finally submitted and decision reserved." However, he says he will wait until eleven o'clock tomorrow morning, for the trustees to hear the Block proposal. This wrecks the Howard plan for a quick windup of *The World.* Instructions are issued to carry on, carry on. *The Evening World* will come out tomorrow, rain or shine.

Wednesday, February 25. *The World* comes out as usual. Prominent story on page one is about the sale of *The World*. The *Times* gives it a big headline, with much detail and a "sidebar" story about Joseph Pulitzer and his enterprise, starting from Mako, Hungary, and winding up in the Surrogate's Court.

11 A.M. Counsel meet in Surrogate Foley's chambers. Block is here but wants more time. Rumor spreads that Block is acting for Hearst. Reluctantly, Foley adjourns to one-thirty P.M., but makes it clear that Block must deal with trustees, not with the court.

H.B.S. makes a new offer through John N. Wheeler of the Bell Syndicate, now head of North American Newspaper Alliance. Swope's proposal is backed by Owen D. Young, Bernard M. Baruch, Gerard Swope, and W. Averill Harriman. The trustees are not receptive. Gene Pope tries again through Sheridan, but gets nowhere.

In *The World* office, the staff becomes restless. What the hell is this all about, and where do we migrate from here? Bresnahan calls up from the business office to blow off steam about the trustees—he'll show them! *The Evening World* is carrying a front-page box featuring recent circulation increase. (The box disappears in the next edition.)

"Why don't you fellows do something?" Bresnahan asks. Just then Gustavus A. Rogers, former associate-in-law of Franklin D. Roosevelt, calls up about a personal matter and learns of our situation. "As I recall it," he said, "Mr. Pulitzer's will provided that the editors and managers were to have the right to buy the paper on liberal terms . . . are you doing anything about that?"

We have no counsel, I remark. Why not engage one? Would he take the case? Yes, if properly authorized and requested. A petition by the workers will suffice for the present—stating that we would like to buy the paper and run it on a co-operative basis. The counsel fee is not important at the moment, but time is vital.

I call up H.B.S. He says the Rogers program is extraordinarily sound. Adolph Ochs made this very proposal not so long ago, Swope remarks. It was Ochs's desire to have one conservative paper and one liberal paper, *The World*, the latter in one-half ownership with the employees—it was a marvelous plan.

Ask for two weeks' delay in which to organize the co-operative plan, Swope urges. I can get you all the capital you need . . . but obtain a delay! He suggests Louis Levy as counsel, but there is no time now; the clock says one twenty-five.

I manage to get a private word with Foley in chambers. This is off the record, just so that he will know why we are in court. He will recognize Rogers.

The courtroom is full of *World* men and women, signers of the authorization for Rogers to intervene on our behalf. Block is here, whispering with Steuer. The trustees look uneasy. Their counsel ask for a hearing in chambers.

Rogers, interposing, identifies his clients. "These loyal workers who have given of their lives and best efforts to *The World,* would like to carry on the institution in the spirit which the Founder intended." A chorus of objections. Counsel huddle in front of the bench. Foley invites Rogers to participate.

The Surrogate does not recognize the right of the employees, but he says there will be no decision until tomorrow. (Another day, another *World!*) All offers are up to the trustees.

The World offices are in a whirlwind of excitement.—Subscriptions fly around the editorial rooms.—Men and women pledge their life savings.—Others go down for more money than they ever hope to possess.—Now the composing room, the business offices, the press-room, the mailing room—thousands and thousands of dollars.

Renaud says: "The trustees ask me to say that the first half-million from Mr. Howard will be used for the benefit of the workers. Meantime, there will be no reprisals!" For which relief, much thanks, but we are busy now.—A mass meeting of *World* people is called for nine-thirty in the grand ballroom of the Hotel Astor.

Swope is burning up the telephones. "Great work, great work.— We'll get you all the money you need." I heard him the first time, but where is it coming from and how soon? We need some definite pledges, not general promises. "Don't worry about that!"

Pledges are coming in from *World* bureaus all over the globe. John L. Balderston in London, Beatrice Baskerville in Rome; Ernest K. Lindley wires pledges from Albany. Many friends of *The World* there, including the legislative correspondents. Lieutenant-Governor Lehman commits himself for $150,000 (but this must be kept secret!).—Cables, telegrams, letters, and telephone calls convey promises of money. There is at least half a million in sight. Now the Hollywood group, Nichols, Garrett, Joe Johnson, Quinn Martin —what about Winfield R. Sheehan? Rogers gets him on the telephone, but obtains only an I-will-let-you-know.

Where is Mr. Ochs? Unfortunately, in Honolulu. "Had I been in New York," he said later, "I am sure I could have saved *The World.*"

The mass meeting overflows the ballroom and out into the corridors. We organize the Joseph Pulitzer Employees' Association: Barrett, president; Phil Pearl, secretary; Rogers, counsel. James M. Cain casts the one dissenting vote. "Otherwise," he explained later, "it would have looked too much like a steam-roller."

The executive committee telephones all over the United States that night from Rogers's home. Efforts to reach John D. Rockefeller, Jr., are futile. He is taking a rest in Arizona and cannot attend to any business matters for several weeks.

Thursday, February 26.

This is the big day. Now or never, if *The World* is to be preserved and perpetuated. The central committee awakes to fame but not to fortune. One million dollars on paper is not better than five million dollars in cash and commitments.

At eleven o'clock, Paul Block withdraws his offer. Privately, he implores Howard to let him have at least one of the three *Worlds,* but there is nothing doing. Why did you want to spoil my party, Howard demands.

"Honestly, Roy, I didn't know it was you. I thought it was Herbert Swope."

"Well, you got yourself into it—get yourself out!"

The Surrogate gives out word that his decision will not be ready for several hours. Instructions in *The World* office are to carry on. *The Evening World* makes its last appearance.

Hearst has been calling Swope. There was talk of a possible merger of *World* and *American,* with H.B.S. at the helm, but Swope wants too much authority to please the Lord of San Simeon. The plan is dropped, hot-potato-fashion. Where are Swope and his group? They are not going to do anything until the Surrogate decides. It is up to the employees to obtain a further postponement.

J. David Stern of Philadelphia, after telephoning all over town, locates me in the Forty Winks Club. He has been trying to buy these papers for many months, but never was permitted to arrive at first base. He formulates a new offer, taking the employees in for a forty-nine per cent interest, and sends it to Rogers, who sends it to the trustees, but there is no response.

Rogers, meanwhile, has repaired the gaps in his legal fence and files a new petition on behalf of principal editors and managers, to wit, Foster Gilroy, promotion manager, and Barrett, city editor. This is under the one-tenth interest clause, a shrewd move suggested by Abraham Benedict, associated with Rogers. The petition is to set aside the sale on the ground that principal editors and managers were not made parties to the action. The new papers are filed with Foley and served on Jackson. *The World* attorney returns the copy, informing Rogers that the editors and managers have no standing.

"I am now addressing Surrogate Jackson," Rogers gibes on the telephone. "Why not write Foley's entire opinion?"

It gives one a curious feeling—this business of working for a newspaper about to die. One keeps saying, This is my last assignment schedule, these are the last stories, be sure to cover the Surrogate's Court, meanwhile, the run of the day's news." Alex Schlosser, the faithful, the uncomplaining, the friend of all the staff—Alex is running the city desk today. Alphonse Tonietti, who has been everything from special European correspondent to assistant city editor, is on the other side of the desk, reading papers, taking telephone calls. The city editor, it appears, is out on an important story, personally covering the fight to save *The World*. Tom Hanly, the regular first assistant, is taking his normal day off.

The pending sale of *The World* is an important story, to be sure, but there are others. Vivian Gordon, prospective witness against the vice ring, has been murdered in Van Cortlandt Park. (When will ladies learn that the wages of squealing is death?) The Vivian Gordon story leads the schedule. Memorandum for Albany man: The Joseph Pulitzer Employees' Association is filing incorporation papers today with the Secretary of State.

Where is the money to buy *The World*? The pledges are enormous—nobody can figure out the precise total, there are many duplications—but the gross amount is short of one million dollars. Newspaper work goes on. Night side follows day side, but nobody goes home. Everybody waits for Foley's decision—hours and hours go by. The first edition comes out—all about Vivian Gordon, but not so much about *The World*. We meekly wait and murmur not; perhaps this is not the end.

The trustees have arranged to meet in Jackson's office down on Nassau Street. Everything is ready.—The $500,000 check, duly certified.—Notices to the workers: "Dear Sir or Madam—You are hereby notified that your employment by the Press Publishing Company is terminated as of February 28, 1931." How do they feel so positive about that? Bill Garrison and Emily Genauer are keeping the telephone open from the Hall of Records to the city desk. Ben Franklin, night city editor, is ready to shoot the decision into type as soon as it comes over. Wait, wait, wait.

Swope keeps calling. "Send another letter," he insists. "Put it up to Herbert Pulitzer good and hard. Tell him you have the plan and the money in sight. What you want is ten days' delay.—The money is assured. I have definite commitments up to $20,000,000. I can't appear in the matter, but you can bank on it." (He was talking then in the presence of Owen D. Young.)

The point which H.B.S. avoids is that the trustees have already sold their papers to Howard, subject only to the Surrogate's O.K. No other offers were either invited or considered.

However, the letter is written. Jack Leary takes it down to Jackson's office and delivers it to Herbert Pulitzer, who reads it without comment, except to say: "Thank Mr. Barrett for me. Assure him that the employees will be taken care of."

I also receive a nice note from Ralph Pulitzer. "Dear Mr. Barrett: I want to tell you how much I regret the termination of our long association on *The World*. It has been a deep satisfaction to work with the men and women of the staff who have done so much to make it a great newspaper. You may be assured of my grateful appreciation of your own services and my thanks for your past loyalty."

Friday, February 27, early A.M., the City News Association tele-type flashes: "Foley approves *World* sale!" Emily Genauer tele-phones at the same moment. Garrison is marathoning to the office. Victory is not ours! The headline is already written. Franklin takes the copy, slugs it "World-Foley." Lindesay Parrott, a new member of the staff, lights a cigarette and typewrites the last story that will ever appear in *The World*. Tap, tap, tap . . . copy boy! . . . tap, tap . . . tap . . . tapatapatap . . . copy! Elenore Kellogg, Pa-tricia McKeefe, and Geraldine Sartain are crying. The notices of *The World's* end are now going up on the board . . . tap-tap-tap tptptptptptptptptptp . . . COPY! . . .

The presses roar. A crowd outside grabs for papers . . . the last copy of *The World* (soon to be worth fifty dollars apiece). Who cares? Damdamdam! Never mind, the paper is out. Good work, everybody! Not even one typographical error. Who said "sabotage"?

Swope on the city desk wire again . . . Too bad! How did the staff take it? On the chin! What does he suppose? Poor children, he says, have you any liquor? Heywood Broun and Ruth Hale are coming down with bottles of Scotch.

Renaud puts up a notice of his own: "I want to say that never in all my life have I ever seen or heard of a finer spirit or of better work on a newspaper, under the most difficult of circumstances. I had always thought that *The World* was a great paper . . . now I know. By God! There are MEN on *The World!*"

The Brouns arrive and move into Renaud's office. The staff gathers around the city desk. A song! A song! "JP's body lies a-mould'ring in the grave, but the staff goes marching on . . . Glory, Glory, Hallelujah!" Have a drink, everybody! Song! Song! "There once was a human do-do-do . . ." (the song is modulated out of respect for ladies). Another drink, another song. Everybody must give us a li'l song! Parrott offers to fight any gentleman in the shop. Now come *The World* alumni from the other papers: Great work, boys! You put out a wonderful paper . . . More songs . . . more praise. The office looks like election night . . . people going and coming . . . three o'clock in the mo-o-o-rning!

This is too tame! Motion is made, duly seconded, and carried that we do now adjourn to Daly's, the official speakeasy around the cor-

The last issue of a great newspaper

ner, where there is lots of room, a piano, and what not. We march
down Park Row, singing a thunderous l'envoi . . . Daly embraces
us. The place is yours and the drinks are on the house. No, no, no!
Somebody suddenly protests . . . we must go back to the office and
get out an extra announcing that. We are going to start a newspaper
of our own and that we shall not go home until morning (meaning
Saturday, February 28). The idea dies.

Renaud comes in, and the Brouns . . . More friends arrive . . .
the party goes on and on . . . Renaud is one of us! Hooray! He
makes another speech . . . Broun speaks . . . Ruth Hale speaks
. . . all speak . . . Barrett falls asleep. . . . The celebration
continues until emotion runs out and the families begin to call
up. . . .

The staff met in the old city room every day until Monday, when
word came from downstairs that our show was over. The Joseph
Pulitzer employees assembled from time to time in Rogers's office
until realism set in and the necessity for getting a job became paramount. New York began to forget. The story of Joseph Pulitzer
and his *World* faded away into legend and the rest was silence. I
still have the watch—engraved on the back: "To James W. Barrett,
From the staff of *The World*, February 27, 1931."

What else? We carried the legal fight all the way up to the Court
of Appeals, on the issue of the rights of the principal editors and
managers. Curiously, Surrogate Foley had not covered this in his
decision of February 27. He said it was a matter to be decided after
the sale.

"The Surrogate," Rogers argued in the Appellate Division,
"wrote a new will for Joseph Pulitzer." The highest court in the
state denied the appeal, but without opinion. At any rate, we had
paid our little tribute to JP . . . Rest! Rest! Perturbed spirit. . . .

*"He that goeth forth and weepeth, bearing precious seed, shall
doubtless come again with rejoicing, bringing his sheaves with him."*
. . . there are no recriminations.

Index

439